MACMILLAN **EXAMS**

Ready for
CAE
coursebook

Roy Norris

With Amanda French

Suitable for
the updated
CAE exam

Contents Map

Introduction

Welcome to *Ready for CAE*, a course which is designed to help you prepare for the Cambridge Certificate in Advanced English examination.

This book contains a wide range of activities aimed at improving your English and developing the language and skills which you will need to pass the examination. As well as providing relevant practice in reading, writing, listening and speaking, each unit of *Ready for CAE* includes one or more *Language focus* sections, which analyse the main grammar areas at advanced level, together with *Vocabulary* slots, which give particular emphasis to collocation.

The course also includes a systematic approach to word formation, which appears as a task type in the *Use of English* paper. At regular intervals you will find special sections which focus on the most important aspects of this task, ensuring that you are properly prepared to deal with it in the examination.

Throughout the book you will find the following boxes, which are designed to help you when performing the different tasks:
- **What to expect in the exam**: these contain useful information on what you should be prepared to see, hear or do in a particular task in the examination.
- **How to go about it**: these give advice and guidelines on how to deal with different task types and specific questions.
- **Don't forget!**: these provide a reminder of important points to bear in mind when answering a particular question.
- **Self help**: these contain a number of supplementary activities and study tips, many of which are aimed at helping you increase your vocabulary store.

Further information and advice is included in the five supplementary '*Ready for ...*' units, one for each of the five papers in the examination. These are situated at regular intervals in the book and can be used at appropriate moments during the course. The *Ready for Writing* unit contains model answers for each of the main task types, together with advice, useful language and further writing tasks for you to complete.

At the end of the book in the *Grammar reference* you will find detailed explanations of the grammar areas seen in the units. There is also an extensive *Wordlist*, which builds on the vocabulary areas seen in the units. At appropriate points in the book you are encouraged to refer to the *Wordlist* to help you perform specific speaking and writing tasks.

Overview of the Examination

The Cambridge Certificate in Advanced English examination consists of five papers, each of which carries 20% of the total marks. A low mark in one paper does not necessarily mean a candidate will fail the examination; it is the overall mark which counts. A, B and C are pass grades; D and E are fail grades.

For more information and advice on each paper, see the appropriate '*Ready for ...*' unit, as well as the relevant sections in the main units of the book.

Paper 1 Reading 1 hour 15 minutes

There are four parts to this paper, with a total of 34 questions. Each question in Parts 1, 2 and 3 carries 2 marks, and each question in Part 4 carries 1 mark. Texts are taken from a variety of sources including newspaper and magazine articles, fiction and non-fiction books, leaflets and brochures.

Part	Task Type	Number of Questions	Task Format
1	Multiple choice	6	Three short texts on the same theme followed by two multiple-choice questions on each text. There are four options for each question.
2	Gapped text	6	A text from which paragraphs have been removed. Candidates replace each of these in the appropriate part of the text.
3	Multiple choice	7	A text followed by multiple-choice questions, each with four options.
4	Multiple matching	15	A text or texts preceded by multiple-matching questions which require candidates to find specific information.

Paper 2 Writing 1 hour 30 minutes

There are two parts to this paper, each of which carries the same number of marks. Part 1 is compulsory, so must be answered by all candidates, whereas in Part 2 candidates choose one from five tasks. Candidates are required to write 180–220 words for Part 1 and 220–260 words for Part 2.

Part	Task type and format
1	Candidates read input material from a variety of sources, for example, advertisements, diaries, emails, letters, newspaper articles and survey results. They must use this information to write one of the following in an appropriate register: • an article • a proposal • a letter • a report
2	Candidates choose one question from a choice of five. Tasks may include any of the following: • an article • a letter • a character reference • a proposal • a competition entry • a report • an essay • a review • an information sheet • a contribution to a longer piece such as a brochure or a guidebook

The last question offers you the chance to write either an article, an essay, a report or a review on one of the two set reading texts. There are two options for this question, one for each set text.

Paper 3 Use of English   1 hour
This paper consists of five parts with a total of 50 questions, which test understanding and control of language in context. Each correct answer in Parts 1, 2 and 3 receives 1 mark; each correct answer in Part 4 receives 2 marks and each answer in Part 5 receives either 0, 1 or 2 marks.

Part	Task Type	Number of Questions	Task Format
1	Multiple-choice cloze (Emphasis on lexis)	12	A text with 12 gaps; there is a choice of four answers for each gap.
2	Open cloze (Emphasis on grammar)	15	A text with 15 gaps, each of which must be completed with one word.
3	Word formation (Emphasis on lexis)	10	A text with 10 gaps. Each gap must be completed with the correct form of a given word.
4	Gapped sentences (Lexis)	5	Five questions, each with a set of three gapped sentences. The gaps in each set must be completed with one word which is appropriate in all three sentences.
6	Key word transformations (Lexis and grammar)	8	Gapped sentences which must be completed in three to six words, one of which is given.

Paper 4 Listening   about 40 minutes
This paper consists of four parts with a total of 30 questions, each of which carries one mark. Each part contains one or more recorded texts, and all recordings are heard twice. Candidates are tested on their ability to understand gist, main points, specific information, attitudes and opinions.

Part	Task Type	Number of Questions	Task Format
1	Multiple choice	6	Three short unrelated extracts from exchanges between interacting speakers. For each extract there are two multiple-choice questions, each with three options.
2	Sentence completion	8	A monologue lasting approximately 3 minutes. Candidates write a word or short phrase to complete sentences.
3	Multiple choice	6	A conversation between two or more speakers, lasting approximately 4 minutes. Multiple-choice questions have four options.
4	Multiple matching	10	Five short monologues on the same theme, each lasting approximately 30 seconds. There are two separate tasks. For each task you are required to select the correct option from a choice of eight.

Paper 5 Speaking   15 minutes
There are four parts to this paper. There are usually two candidates and two examiners. Candidates are required to demonstrate their spoken language skills in a range of contexts.

Part	Task Type	Time	Task Format
1	Social interaction	3 minutes	Candidates give personal information in response to questions from the interviewer.
2	Long turn	4 minutes	Each candidate talks about a set of pictures for about 1 minute, and comments on the other candidate's pictures for about 30 seconds.
3	Collaborative task	4 minutes	Candidates are given visual and/or written material and then speak to each other about it for about 3 minutes in order to complete a problem-solving task.
4	Further discussion	4 minutes	The interviewer leads a discussion which is related to the topic of Part 3.

Roy Norris

Long turn

Look at these photos. They show people facing different challenges.

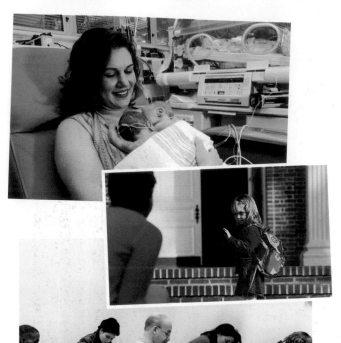

Student A:
Compare two of the pictures and say
- what challenges the people face
- the kind of problems they might encounter
- how they might be feeling

Student B:
When your partner has finished talking about the two pictures, say which of them represents the more difficult challenge.

How to go about it

- When comparing your pictures, talk about the similarities and differences between them.
  eg *Both pictures show..., but this one..., whereas the other one ...*
- Speculate about the pictures as indicated in the instructions. You are not asked simply to describe what is happening.
  eg *They might (well) have problems finishing.*
  She's likely to/She'll probably find it quite tough to begin with.
  I expect/imagine she's feeling a little lonely at the moment.
- Use a wide range of vocabulary. For example, when speculating about people's feelings, go beyond the use of simple words such as *happy, sad* or *nervous*.

Before you do the task, complete the following exercise.

Useful language

Arrange the words and phrases in the box into three groups according to whether they can be used instead of:

very happy	**sad or wanting to cry**	**nervous or worried**
	tearful	

~~tearful~~	anxious	delighted	apprehensive	miserable	elated
close to tears	thrilled	tense	weepy	on edge	overjoyed

Now change roles. Follow the instructions again using the remaining pictures.

Reading:
CAE Part 3

Multiple choice

1 ⬤ You are going to read an article about Ellen MacArthur, a young woman who sailed single-handed round the world. With your partner discuss your ideas on the following:

- the type of person who would take up such a challenge
- their reasons for doing so
- the preparation required
- their feelings during and after the event
- the conditions they experience at sea

2 Now read the article. For questions **1–7**, choose the correct answer **A**, **B**, **C** or **D**.

How to go about it

- Before you look at the questions, quickly read through the whole text to get an idea of the content.
  Give yourself three minutes to read the text on page 8. Look for information on Ellen MacArthur which is relevant to the points in exercise 1. Compare your answers with a partner.

- During both your quick read and your more detailed read, you will need to use context to help you guess the meaning of unknown vocabulary, as you may not take a dictionary into the exam.
  Discuss with your partner the possible meanings of the words in bold in the first two paragraphs.

- Read each question carefully and find the parts of the text which relate to each one. In Part 3 of the Reading paper, the questions follow the same order as the information in the text.
  Don't choose your answers yet. In the margin, mark the general area of the text which is relevant to each question.

- For each question, eliminate the options which are clearly wrong and choose the best answer.
  Underline key phrases or sentences in the text which help you make your choice.

- Re-read the questions. Do the options you have chosen accurately reflect the information you have underlined in the text?
  Justify your answers to your partner, explaining why other options are incorrect.

AROUND THE WORLD IN 94 DAYS

In February 2001, at the age of 24, Ellen MacArthur became the youngest and fastest ever woman to sail round the world. After 94 days alone on board her yacht Kingfisher, she finished second to Michel Desjoyaux of France in the single-handed Vendée Globe event.

In sport, like life, the winner is usually **fêted**, and **runners-up** quickly forgotten. This time the roles were reversed and it was Ellen, weighing just 50 kilos and barely 1m 60 tall, that really captured people's imaginations and emotions. One newspaper in France, where she was and is a real heroine, summed up the national mood there with the headline 'Well done, Michel, bravo Ellen'.

As with many spectacular achievers, the signs were there from an early age, even in the unpromising nautical terrain of **landlocked** Derbyshire. Her great-grandparents were sailing people and a great-uncle was a merchant seaman, but any real link with the sea is **tenuous**. There was, however, an Auntie Thea who lived on the east coast of England and had a 26-foot sailing boat called *Cabaret*. It took just one trip on the open sea with her aunt to **spark off** Ellen's lifelong passion. She was eight years old. After that she began saving her pocket money and spent all her spare time reading sailing books in the library, absorbing information like a sponge. With her savings and the help of her grandmother she bought an 8-foot fibreglass dinghy, and from that moment on there was no keeping her away from the water.

Sailing round Britain single-handed at the age of 18 was just the start; Ellen had long since set her sights on the Vendée. But finding the money to undertake round-the-world voyages is no easy feat. She wrote 2,000 letters requesting sponsorship and received just two replies, one, happily, from the Kingfisher company who were looking to expand into France. And in terms of race preparation, if thoroughness was the key to success, Ellen could certainly be considered one of the favourites. In the eight months leading up to the start of the race, she sailed no fewer than 60,000 miles at the helm of her 60-foot *Kingfisher*, far more than the rest of the fleet put together in the same period.

During her three months at sea MacArthur negotiated deadly icebergs, gigantic waves and gale-force winds. She endured the freezing cold of the Antarctic and suffered the blistering heat of the windless doldrums. Racing conditions meant sleeping in 10-minute bursts, a survival suit that stayed on for weeks at a time and hands and wrists covered in sores and cuts. Food was dried or frozen. Water came from a desalinator, which passes sea water through a membrane. 'You don't really wash in the icy waters of the southern ocean,' she laughs. 'Anyway, there's no one to tell you that you smell.'

As *Kingfisher* crossed the finishing line Ellen was surrounded by hundreds of spectator boats and a cheering crowd of 200,000 lined the shore. Stepping off her yacht she looked remarkably composed and seemed to take the change from solitude to public adulation very much in her stride. Her thoughts, she later confessed, were on the realization that she had fulfilled the ambition that had dominated her life for the previous four or five years. 'Throughout that time my sole focus had been crossing the finishing line, and in the fastest possible time.' Now she could savour that moment.

But despite MacArthur's belief that everyone who finishes the Vendée is a winner, she still feels a sense of disappointment that, having taken the lead from the eventual winner Michel Desjoyaux 10 days from the finish, she did not quite have the energy or good fortune to turn her advantage into victory. 'You have to believe you can win from the start,' she asserts. 'Deep down you're a competitor, you don't climb the mast and come back black and blue just for a cruise. You do it because it's a race.'

The public will now be hoping to see a suitable encore, some new feat of endurance to justify her celebrity status. For Ellen can no longer claim, as she did in her post-race press conference, to be the simple Derbyshire girl with 'no mobile, no credit cards, no money, no nothing'; she is a heroine and an inspiration to others of her generation. As if to reinforce this, and despite her reluctance to take on this role, she later commented: 'If there's one thing I've learned in this past year, it's that deep down in your heart, if you have a dream, then you can and must make it happen.'

1   At the time of her achievement we learn that Ellen

    A   enjoyed only short-lived success.

    B   was more famous in France than anywhere else.

    C   attracted more attention than Michel Desjoyaux.

    D   became popular because of her size.

2   Where did Ellen's initial interest in sailing come from?

    A   She came from a family of sailing enthusiasts.

    B   She went to see one of her relatives.

    C   She read widely on the subject.

    D   She lived near the sea.

3   What do we learn about Ellen at the start of the race?

    A   People thought she had a very good chance of winning.

    B   She was a more experienced sailor than the other racers.

    C   She had been waiting for this moment since she was 18.

    D   She had gone to great lengths to achieve her ambition.

4   The writer suggests that one cause of discomfort for Ellen at sea was

    A   the shortage of water.

    B   her failure to sleep.

    C   extremes of temperature.

    D   a lack of cooking facilities.

5   According to the writer, when Ellen finished the race, she was

    A   overwhelmed by her new-found fame.

    B   surprised by the number of people who came to greet her.

    C   able to reflect on her achievement.

    D   delighted to be amongst people again.

6   According to the writer, Ellen

    A   thinks she deserved to win the race.

    B   has mixed feelings about the outcome of the race.

    C   knew she would win the race.

    D   thinks Michel Desjoyaux was lucky to beat her.

7   Which of the following views does the writer express in the last paragraph?

    A   She has the power to motivate.

    B   She has no right to fame yet.

    C   Her comments lack depth.

    D   She needs to change her lifestyle.

◯ Reacting to the text

Talk about one of your own personal achievements. If possible, comment on what motivated you, your preparations and the feelings you experienced.

Language focus 1: Modal verbs 1

Might, could, may, can

1   Sentences **1–7** all contain the modal verb *might*. Match each of the sentences to the idea they express.

> present possibility   future possibility   past possibility
> past possibility which did not happen   annoyance
> concession   lack of enthusiasm

1. You might at least help me!
2. I wish you'd drive more carefully. You might have had an accident back there.
3. I do hope they're OK. They might have had an accident or something.
4. I might be home a bit later tonight. I've got a meeting at five.
5. Put the telly on – there might be something good on.
6. There's nothing on telly, so we might as well go to bed.
7. He might be good-looking, but he can't sing very well.

With no change in meaning, *might* can be substituted by *could* in sentences **1–5** and *may* in sentences **3–7**.

2   ⬭   Complete each of these sentences in an appropriate way. Compare your ideas with those of a partner.

1. I'm so angry with him. I do think he might have…
2. We've missed the beginning, so we may as well…
3. It was rather dangerous. Someone could have…
4. I can't find it anywhere. I think I may have…
5. She might have a university degree, but…
6. Cheer up! It might….

3   The following sentences **1–6** all contain the modal verb *can/can't*. Match each of the sentences to the idea they express.

> request   deduction   criticism   inability
> theoretical possibility   prohibition

1. It can store up to 30,000 separate images.
2. You can be really irritating sometimes, you know.
3. Can you hold this for a second?
4. I can't do it – I'm not tall enough.
5. It can't be very healthy if it's got all that in it.
6. No, you can't! It's far too late.

4   ⬤   With your partner, think of a context for each of the sentences in exercise 3. Use modal verbs to express your ideas.
Example:
1   *This could be somebody talking about a piece of software – a compact disc for example. It might be a shop assistant trying to sell it.*

🅖   Read more about *might, could, may* and *can* on page 216 of the Grammar section.

Extension

1   In addition to using modal verbs, there are several alternative ways of expressing future possibility. In sentences **a** and **b** one of the four possibilities has a different meaning to the other three. Underline the odd one out.

a. There's a *strong/distinct/faint/real* possibility that I could lose my job.
b. There's *an outside/a slight/a fair/a remote* chance that Lara might be at the party tonight.

In sentences **c** and **d** underline the **incorrect** alternative.

c. They have *every/good/little/no* chance of winning.
d. You could *easily/well/conceivably/predictably* get there in under two hours.

What is the difference in meaning between sentences **e** and **f**?

e. She's *highly likely to* pass the exam.
f. She's *hardly likely to* pass the exam.

2   Complete the following sentences so that they express your true feelings about the future.

1. I think I stand a good chance of… (+ gerund).
2. To improve my chances of… (+ gerund), I need to…
3. In the world today we face the very real possibility that… will…
4. There's an outside chance that… will/might/could…
5. It seems highly unlikely that… will…

⬤   Comment on and discuss each other's views.

Vocabulary: Collocations

1 Complete each of the gaps with one of the nouns from the box.

> challenge   success   motivation
> ambition   failure

  a The film 'Star Wars' **was an overnight** _____ .

  b I **have a burning** _____ **to** travel to Australia.

  c When pupils tire of studying, a system of rewards can help **increase student** _____ .

  d Sadly, my attempts to learn Japanese **met with complete** _____ .

  e The government **faces the formidable** _____ **of** reducing unemployment.

2 In exercise 1, the words in **bold** are 'collocates' of the nouns you wrote. This means that they are often used together with those nouns. Write a new sentence for each noun, using the collocates in **bold**. The sentences must be true.

3 ⬤ Compare and discuss your sentences with another student.

4 In sentence **e** in exercise 1, the verb *face* collocates with *challenge*. Which of the five nouns do each of the following pairs of verbs collocate with?

fulfil	a/an _____	end in	_____
realize		result in	
achieve	_____	improve	_____
enjoy		lack	
take up	a/an _____		
rise to			

5 The adjective *formidable* also collocates with *challenge*. All three words in each of the groups below can be used in combination with one of the nouns from exercise 1. Write an appropriate noun in each of the spaces.

  a major/new/daunting _____
  b secret/lifelong/main
  c total/continued/dismal _____
  d huge/great/resounding _____
  e high/strong/poor _____

6 ⬤ Study the collocations in this section for two minutes, then close your book and write down as many as you can remember. Compare your results with your partner's.

Listening:
CAE Part 1

Multiple choice

1 ⊙ What awards, international and national, are well known in your country?

Have you ever won an award, prize or trophy for anything? If so, how did you feel about receiving it?

2 ⊙ 1.1–1.3 You will hear three different extracts. For questions **1–6**, choose the answer (**A**, **B** or **C**) which fits best according to what you hear. There are two questions for each extract.

What to expect in the exam

- There are four parts to the Listening Paper (Paper 4). In Part 1 you will always hear three short extracts from different conversations, usually with two people in each conversation. There are two multiple-choice questions for each extract.
- In the exam, you will hear each extract twice before the next one is played.

Extract one

You hear part of an interview with a musician, explaining why he turned down a prize in a music awards ceremony.

1 Why did Steve's group not go to the ceremony to accept their award?
  A They believed it would be morally wrong.
  B They were busy doing concerts.
  C They did not expect to win.

2 According to Steve, the people who voted for his group
  A have been loyal fans for a long time.
  B will soon lose interest in their music.
  C agree with their ideals and beliefs.

Extract two

You hear part of an interview with Richard Hale, a retired cricket player.

3 What is the main reason for Richard Hale's success?
  A natural talent
  B a lot of practice
  C the ability to concentrate

4 Richard Hale dislikes the way that some current players
  A react to a success.
  B do not learn from their mistakes.
  C believe they are more important than their team.

Extract three

You hear part of an interview on local radio with Lily Simmons, a university student who is taking part in a fund-raising event called *40-hour Famine*.

5 According to Lily, the purpose of *40-hour Famine* is to
  A encourage students to do some charity work abroad.
  B persuade people to give money to charity regularly.
  C help people understand the effects of famine on people's lives.

6 After taking part in last year's *40-hour Famine* event, Lily was
  A proud of what she had achieved.
  B determined to do better in the next event.
  C disappointed she had not fulfilled her aim.

3 ⊙ Do you know of any cases where someone has turned down an award? Why did they reject it?

Talk about something you failed to achieve. How disappointed were you?

Word formation: Nouns

1 Which suffixes are added to the following verbs to create nouns?

> achieve   motivate   fail

2 Complete each gap with an appropriate noun form of the word in capitals at the end of the line. Use each suffix in the box once only and make any further spelling changes necessary. The noun you require may also need a plural ending or a negative prefix (*un-*, *in-*, *im-*, *dis-* etc). There is an example at the beginning (**0**).

> -hood -ship -ure -al -ness -ation
> -ance -ence -iety -ity -ment -age -cy

0	His **latest** _publication_ is **a book** of verse on the theme of relationships.	**PUBLISH**
1	**Light** _____ **will be served** from 3.30pm in the main hall.	**REFRESH**
2	Union members **expressed their** _____ **of** the management's offer by walking out of the meeting.	**APPROVE**
3	**In her** _____ **to** answer the phone, she almost fell down the stairs.	**EAGER**
4	In the interests of safety, a number of **standard** _____ need to be **followed**.	**PROCEED**
5	Her 5,000-metre run **paled into** _____ when compared with the marathon her grandfather completed the following week.	**SIGNIFY**
6	The _____ of the device is what has made it so popular.	**SIMPLE**
7	I cannot comment; I have been **sworn to** _____ on the matter.	**SECRET**
8	**The cost of** _____ has increased by 10% this year.	**MEMBER**
9	Customers will be required to **pay for any** _____ .	**BREAK**
10	**There is every** _____ **that** prices will continue to rise next year.	**LIKELY**
11	He **valued his** _____ too much to ever want to get married.	**DEPEND**
12	It's quite natural to **experience a certain amount of** _____ on your first day at work.	**ANXIOUS**

3 Using the same suffixes as in exercise 2, write noun forms for the following words. The same suffix is needed for all three words. Some words require further spelling changes. The exercise begins with an example (**0**).

0	notorious	_notoriety_	various	_variety_	sober	_sobriety_
1	please	_____	expose	_____	close	_____
2	appear	_____	annoy	_____	rely	_____
3	store	_____	short	_____	pack	_____
4	rehearse	_____	renew	_____	propose	_____
5	efficient	_____	intimate	_____	vacant	_____
6	enjoy	_____	require	_____	commit	_____
7	prosperous	_____	original	_____	familiar	_____
8	leader	_____	companion	_____	partner	_____
9	neighbour	_____	father	_____	adult	_____
10	absent	_____	persistent	_____	evident	_____
11	selfish	_____	tired	_____	careless	_____
12	explain	_____	interpret	_____	apply	_____

4 Look back at the reading text on page 8 and underline those nouns which have been formed by the addition of a suffix to a verb, adjective or another noun. Add them to the list in exercise 3.

Self help

Keep a record in your notebook of noun forms you come across when reading which are new to you, or different from what you expected. Group them according to their suffix endings, as in exercise 3.

Language focus 2: Spelling

1 Look at these two extracts from the reading text on page 8.

> One newspaper in France... **summed** up the national mood there...

> ... she had **fulfilled** the ambition that had dominated her life...

The final consonant of the verbs *fulfil* and *sum* is doubled to form the past tense. Similarly, the consonant is doubled in *occurring* and *beginning*, but not in *happening* or *opening*. Why is this?

2 What is the *-ing* form of the following verbs?

refer	limit	set	upset	target
forbid	write	wait	travel	panic

3 For each of the following groups of four words, find the incorrectly spelt word and correct it. The exercise begins with an example (**0**).

		insistence		
0	importance	~~insistance~~	appearance	tolerance
1	apparent	pleasent	different	independent
2	occasion	accountant	neccessary	accident
3	publically	optimistically	scientifically	dramatically
4	separate	desperate	immediate	definate
5	unreasonable	irresponsable	irritable	indispensable
6	chefs	roofs	safes	leafs
7	exceeding	succeeding	proceeding	preceeding
8	embarrassment	accommodation	bussiness	committee
9	unnatural	unknown	dissappointed	dissatisfied
10	believe	recieve	seize	weird
11	financial	influencial	commercial	beneficial
12	cemetery	factery	bakery	surgery

4 ⬤ Work with a partner. You are going to dictate ten two-word items of vocabulary to each other. Student A should turn to page 207 and Student B to page 208.

Self help

In your notebook, write down at least six of the words from exercises 3 and 4 whose spelling you find unusual and/or difficult to remember. Study the words for one minute. Then close your notebook and write down the words from memory.

Writing:
CAE Part 2

Competition entries

What to expect in the exam

In Part 2 of the Writing paper you might have the opportunity to write a competition entry. You may be asked to propose yourself or nominate somebody else for selection, perhaps for a study grant or a chance to appear on a television programme. Competition entries require you to persuade the judges and give reasons why you or the person you nominate should be accepted.

1 Read the following Part 2 task and the model answer, which is written in the format of an article. Does the answer address all aspects of the task? Would it have a positive effect on the competition judges?

You see the following competition in an international magazine.

Write your **competition entry** in **220–260** words.

> # COMPETITION
> **Secret ambitions**
>
> We are planning a series of six TV programmes called *Masterclass*, in which we offer members of the public with a secret ambition the chance to receive expert tuition from a professional.
>
> What is your secret ambition and why?
>
> Write and tell us about it, explaining what you think it would take to achieve your ambition **and** why you think you've got what it takes.
>
> The ten most convincing entries will be shortlisted to appear on the programme.

Secret ambition? It's a mystery!

Did you know that for every 20,000 novels written, only one gets published? So the likelihood that I'll ever fulfil my ambition of becoming a professional mystery writer doesn't seem very high. But the prospect of turning my lifelong passion into my livelihood and achieving fame and fortune at the same time is just too exciting for me to be put off by dull statistics.

So what does it take to become a writer? Reading is important — all writers need to research their genre thoroughly to familiarize themselves with its codes and conventions. My bookshelves at home are stacked with the novels of all the great mystery writers, which I've read and, in many cases, re-read, despite knowing all the time 'whodunnit'.

Of course, being a writer requires imagination. You have to develop your own personal style rather than simply copy the work of 'the greats'. I've turned out dozens of short crime stories for my university student magazine — some have been published, some not, but I've always aimed to produce original and imaginative material.

Last but not least, successful writers possess enormous self-discipline. I've often sacrificed my social life in order to devote the necessary time and effort to producing a good quality story. And more than once that has meant burning the midnight oil.

We've all got a novel inside us. Getting it out in anywhere near publishable form is no easy task, but with imagination and determination, and the help of an expert on 'Masterclass', who could possibly fail to realize their ambition?

2 Clear organization and appropriate paragraphing are essential features of all CAE writing types. Which of these two possible paragraph plans does the entry follow?

	A	**B**
First paragraph	Introduction: secret ambition and why	Introduction: secret ambition and why
Central paragraphs	**a** Three requirements	**a** First requirement and a quality/reason
	b Three qualities/reasons	**b** Second requirement and a quality/reason
		c Third requirement and a quality/reason
Final paragraph	Conclusion: final comments	Conclusion: final comments

3 To obtain a high mark in the CAE examination you need to use a wide range of relevant vocabulary and structures. Underline examples of more sophisticated language in the model answer.

How does the writer avoid repetition when talking about the requirements?

4 The entry is written in a relatively informal register. Find examples of informal language.

5 To stand a good chance of 'winning', a competition entry should be written in an appealing and engaging style. What techniques are used to get the reader's attention and engage his or her interest?

What is the purpose of the final paragraph?

6 ⬭ Write your own entry for the competition, following the advice in the **How to go about it** and **Don't forget!** boxes.

How to go about it

- Decide what your secret ambition is and why.
- In two columns in your notebook, brainstorm as many ideas as you can for the two remaining parts of the question.
- Discuss what you have written with your partner. Add any more ideas he or she can come up with.
- Select the best ideas. You are asked to write between 220 and 260 words, so two or three requirements and qualities or reasons should be enough.
- Decide which paragraph plan, **A** or **B**, you want to use.
- Write your answer, using the techniques you discovered in the model answer.

Don't forget!

- Give your entry a title. It is best to do this after you have written your answer.
- The register of your answer could be more or less formal than that of the model answer, but it should be consistent.
- Try to use some of the grammar and vocabulary you have seen in the unit.
- Check your spelling.

①Review

Modal verbs

Complete each gap with one word.

1 Sometimes you _____ be so uncaring – I do think you might _____ come to see me in hospital after I'd had my operation!

2 She _____ be just a six-month-old baby, but she's already showing signs of being intelligent.

3 The next bus isn't likely _____ come for an hour or so, so we may as _____ walk.

4 It seems highly _____ that it will rain today, but we _____ well have a few showers tomorrow.

5 You could _____ least have made the effort to do some revision. Now you have absolutely _____ chance of passing the exam.

6 The ruling party succeeded _____ being re-elected, but didn't manage _____ retain their overall majority in parliament.

Spelling

Each numbered line in the following text contains a spelling mistake. Find the mistakes and correct them.

1 Clearly, student motivation is an important influence on learning. It is also believed,

2 though, that students' perceptions of their learning experiences generaly influence

3 their motivation more than the actual, objetive reality of those experiences. The

4 Attribution Theory of motivation identifys two types of student. The first type credit

5 their success to their own ability and effort. If they are successfull in an exam, they

6 attribute their achievement to themselfs, feel proud and are keen to take on further

7 tasks off this nature. They work hard because they see a clear relationship between

8 the effort made and the results obtained. If they fail, they put this failure down too

9 their own lack of effort and are confidant that if they try harder in the future, they

10 will have more success. The second type attribute success to external facters. If they

11 perform well in an exam, they consider that it was easy and they where lucky. They

12 feel little pride in their achievements and show little intrest in taking on further

13 tasks. If they fail, they attribute there poor performance to their own lack of ability

14 and are unlikely to see any reason to hope for an improvment in the future. They do

15 not percieve the link between effort and results, and lack the motivation to keep trying.

Use of English: CAE Part 3

Word formation

For questions **1–10**, use the word given in capitals at the end of some of the lines to form a word that fits in the gap **in the same line**. There is an example at the beginning (**0**).

> **Don't forget!**
>
> You may need to write the negative or plural form of a word.

REWARDING CHILDREN

Cash rewards are a common form of (**0**) _motivation_ used by parents **MOTIVATE**
with high (**1**) _____ to encourage their children to work hard at exam **EXPECT**
time. Some youngsters receive (**2**) _____ of as much as £100 for each **PAY**
A grade they obtain at GCSE. But should such 'bribes' be based on
exam (**3**) _____ or should they, as many parents and teachers feel, **PERFORM**
be offered in (**4**) _____ of a child's effort, regardless of results? The **RECOGNIZE**
latter approach would solve the problem of how parents reward children
with different levels of (**5**) _____ ; imagine, for example, a family with **ABLE**
one child who is (**6**) _____ gifted and another who has learning **ACADEMIC**
(**7**) _____. The dangers of result-related incentives for the second child **DIFFICULT**
are clear; with little hope of obtaining the higher grades, the withholding
of promised (**8**) _____ rewards would only compound the child's feeling **FINANCE**
of (**9**) _____. However, some leading educational psychologists believe **FAIL**
that parents should rely on their own (**10**) _____ in such matters. They **JUDGE**
maintain that if parents know that money will motivate their child, then
they should not be condemned for operating a system of cash payouts.

Word combinations

For sentences **1–10** underline the correct alternative.

1 There's a *heavy/hard/strong/tough* possibility I'll get a pay rise in January.
2 He hasn't got the *fairest/slightest/longest/thinnest* chance of winning the election. He's far too unpopular.
3 There is *every/each/all/very* likelihood that the government will introduce the measures this year.
4 There were far more of them than us. We didn't *stand/face/hold/keep* a chance against them.
5 She was clearly rather worried and seemed close to *edge/nerves/tension/tears*.
6 I'm *elated/delighted/pleasant/anxious* to meet you at last, Mr Wood. Let me take your bag.
7 The young singer *fulfilled/enjoyed/was/became* overnight success last year when her debut single 'Burning Ambition' reached number 1.
8 He had never acted before, but he *rose/arose/aroused/raised* to the challenge and gave a very convincing performance.
9 At 85 she says she's unlikely to realize her *resounding/longing/lifelong/overall* ambition of learning to fly.
10 Snacks and *easy/loose/light/full* refreshments are available in the lounge area.

②Times change

Listening 1:
CAE Part 2

Sentence completion

1 ⚪ These photographs were all taken over 50 years ago.

How has life changed since then? If the same photographs were taken now, which features would be the same and which would be different?

2 ◉ 1.4 You will hear part of a talk on the subject of time capsules. What do you think a time capsule might be?

3 For questions **1–8** complete the sentences.

What to expect in the exam

- There is always a pause before you hear the listening. Use this to read through the questions and predict the type of answer required. eg *Question 1: To fit in grammatically with the beginning of the sentence, we'd probably need to write an adjective to describe time capsules, or a past participle which tells us what is done to them.*
- You can normally write the actual words you hear in the recording.
- Answers can be numbers, single words or short phrases (usually of no more than three words).
- Check your answers; incorrect spelling and grammar may lose marks.
- Part 2 is always a monologue. As with all recordings in Paper 4 Listening, it is played twice.

4 Before you do the task, read all the questions and try to predict the type of information you might hear for each one.

For reasons of security, time capsules are usually [_____ **1**] .

People have been putting things in time capsules for [_____ **2**] .

The main reason for time capsules going missing has been the failure to [_____ **3**] .

The exact location of a capsule containing [_____ *and* _____ **4**] from a popular TV programme is unknown.

The capsule is somewhere in an area that used to be a [_____ **5**] .

Dr Thornwell Jacobs was unable to find sufficient information on [_____ **6**] .

His 'Crypt of Civilization' is situated in the [_____ **7**] of Hearst Hall.

To avoid possible theft Dr Jacobs did not include [_____ **8**] .

What to expect in the exam

The examiner's instructions for Part 3 tasks also appear as written questions above the pictures.

Collaborative task

You belong to a group of friends who have decided to bury a time capsule, to be opened in 100 years' time. The pictures below show some of the aspects of life which can be represented by items in the capsule.

Talk with your partner about the different aspects, saying which items could be included as most representative of our lives today, and then decide which **two** items would be of most interest to future generations.

As with Dr Jacobs and his 'Crypt of Civilization', your time capsule may contain original items and/or models, pictures, films and sound recordings as well as computer software.

- Which items could be included as most representative of our lives today?
- Which two items would be of most interest to future generations?

Entertainment

Technology

House & Home

Travel & Transport

Fashion

Politics

How to go about it

- Evaluate the different items you talk about, giving reasons for your choices.
  eg *An atlas would be an ideal way to illustrate how the world is divided up politically. Maps are constantly being rewritten and people in 100 years' time would be curious to see how international boundaries have shifted since our time.*
- Aim to demonstrate your linguistic ability and use a wide range of vocabulary and structures.
- Address all parts of the instructions, even if you do not reach a final agreement within the four minutes you are allowed for this part.

Useful language

Complete each of the gaps with one of the phrases in the box. There is an example at the beginning (**0**).

are unlikely to be using
be intrigued to see
would not be complete without
~~is a distinct possibility that~~
might conceivably be obsolete
would demonstrate very clearly
is a part of everyday life

0 There _is a distinct possibility that_ people won't ever have seen a pound coin.

1 The time capsule _____ one or two items of fashion clothing.

2 Fast food _____ , so something representing that would be of interest.

3 Future generations would _____ a model of our underground system.

4 The mobile phone _____ how we communicate with each other.

5 DVDs _____ by the time the capsule's opened.

6 People _____ ovens in 100 years' time.

Use of English: CAE Part 2

Open cloze

What to expect in the exam

- The open cloze is a short text with 15 gaps, each of which has to be filled with one word.
- The main focus is on grammatical words, eg prepositions, auxiliary verbs and articles.

1 Read the following text, ignoring the gaps for the moment. Which famous toy is being described?

THE IMPOSSIBLY CURVY DOLL

More than one billion **(0)** _have_ been sold in 150 different countries **(1)** _____ her first appearance at the New York Toy Fair in 1959. Created **(2)** _____ Ruth Handler, the daughter of Polish immigrants, and originally known **(3)** _____ the 'Teenage Fashion Model', she was a perky blue-eyed blonde, with a pony tail and a black-and-white swimsuit.

It was while she was watching her daughter Barbara playing with cut-outs of adult women **(4)** _____ Handler came up **(5)** _____ the idea. **(6)** _____ the time, dolls in America always took the form of babies. When she first proposed a prototype to executives at the toy company, Mattel, she was turned **(7)** _____ . Later, **(8)** _____ , Handler won over the all-male

management, and the first toy doll in the USA with breasts went **(9)** _____ production.

By the late Sixties, she was enjoying the same type of fame **(10)** _____ the *Beatles*. As her world expanded, so **(11)** _____ the profits, and she was making well over $100 million a year for Mattel. She took on numerous different identities, **(12)** _____ as astronaut, vet or surgeon and she acquired many friends, notably Ken, **(13)** _____ name came from Handler's son.

She was **(14)** _____ without her critics. Her shapely figure was essentially unattainable and feminists attacked Handler for presenting young girls with **(15)** _____ image of adult beauty they could never achieve. Handler was not bothered by this. 'My whole philosophy was that through the doll, the little girl could be anything she wanted to become,' she later wrote.

2 Read the text again and think of the word which best fits each space. Make sure you read the example. When you have finished, justify your answers to your partner, with particular reference to words and sentences before and after the gaps.

3 ⬤ Whose opinion do you agree with in the final paragraph? Handler's or the feminists'?

Language focus 1: Talking about the past

A Review

⬤ Complete each of the spaces with an appropriate form of the verb in brackets. Choose from the past, past perfect or present perfect, in either the simple or progressive form. There may be more than one possible answer. If so, explain any differences in meaning.

1 I _____ (never/kiss) anyone until I _____ (meet) you.
2 That's the third time I _____ (have) to tell you to stop shouting!
3 It looks as if he _____ (cry) again. His eyes are all red and puffy.

4 I used to get so annoyed with him. He _____ (always/lose) things.
5 She _____ (eat) a particularly large bar of chocolate and she suddenly started to feel sick.
6 Marjorie _____ (leave) when Paul _____ (arrive).
7 You know that book you _____ (tell) me about last week? Well, I _____ (buy) it. Look.
8 I hated that school. If I _____ (not do) my homework, they used to punish me. If I _____ (do) it, they'd tell me to do it again.

B Further ways of talking about the past

1 Underline the correct alternatives in the following sentences. Either one, two or all three alternatives may be possible.

1 **When I was a teenager I** *used to know/would know/ knew* the words to all the *Beatles* songs.

2 **It's years since** *I've ridden/I haven't ridden/I rode* a bike. **I'm not sure if I could do it now.**

3 **I'd** *like to have travelled/have liked to travel/have liked to have travelled* **more when I was younger.**

4 **I remember** that concert. **It was the first time** *I've seen/ I'd seen/I was seeing* the band play live.

5 **I'd rather my parents** *didn't make/wouldn't have made/hadn't made* me go to piano lessons **when I was little.**

6 She was *going to work/thinking to work/to have worked* in her mother's business, but decided instead to continue her studies.

7 *After he'd done/Having done/Being done* it once, he wanted to do it again.

8 It has not rained since *he's been here/he got here/his arrival*.

🄶 Check your answers by reading the Grammar reference on pages 216 and 217.

2 ⬤ Rewrite sentences **1–5** so that they are true for you. Use the words in **bold** together with an appropriate verb in the correct form. Compare your sentences with those of your partner.

Writing: Formal letter
CAE Part 1

1 Read the following advertisement. Does this type of entertainment appeal to you?

BLACK KNIGHT MEDIEVAL SOCIETY

Our aim is to bring history alive with the very best in open-air medieval entertainment. We offer spectacular jousting tournaments and archery displays, cookery and craft demonstrations, exhibitions of medieval weapons, music and dancing performances and much, much more. A guaranteed fun day out for all the family.

2 Read the following Part 1 task and the sample answer on page 22. Would the letter achieve the desired effect?

You help out on the committee of a Medieval Society which recently organized a Medieval Fair. Read the newspaper report on which you have made some notes and the emails received by the committee, and write a letter to the newspaper, giving the Society's version of events and asking them to print another article.

MIDDLE AGE CRISIS

there was nowhere for people to park

not what our emails say!

Brampton's annual Medieval Fair last Sunday <u>failed to attract the same interest as in previous years</u> and the few people who did turn up were critical of the event. The archery display <u>was rather tedious</u> and visitors were <u>unimpressed by the medieval dancing display</u>. Many also commented on <u>the small number of demonstrations of traditional cookery and craft skills</u>. Given the poor response to the event, it seems unlikely that

kids loved it

not enough space

A great day! Loved the music and dancing – very professional.

The car park was full when we got there so we missed it all – the kids were really upset.

I didn't realize medieval cooking was so good! The clothes making was fascinating.

Write your **letter**. You do not need to include postal addresses.

Sample answer

Dear Sir,

I help out on the committee of a Medieval Society and we're really fed up with the way you reported the annual Medieval Fair last Sunday.

You said that not many people turned up and they were critical of the event. But that's not fair! Many people did turn up, but there was nowhere for them to park when they got there so they missed it all.

Also, you said that visitors were also unimpressed by the medieval dancing display. That's not true! Lots of people said they thought the dancing was good — we've got emails to prove it. One said, 'A great day! Loved the music and dancing — very professional.' And about the archery: how on earth can you say that it was tedious? The kids loved it.

To sum up, it was really successful and we are absolutely disgusted by your report and if you don't print another article we will have no alternative but to resort to further measures, like get in touch with a lawyer.

Yours faithfully

Anna Wojdylo

3 ⊙ Read the letter again and answer the following questions with your partner, giving examples.

Content: Has the writer answered the task fully? Has she expanded on any of the points in the input material?

Organization: Is the letter organized into suitable paragraphs?

Vocabulary/Structures: Is there a wide range of language? Has the writer used her own words? Is the letter accurate?

Register: Is the register consistently appropriate?

4 In **1–4** below, complete the second sentence so that it has a similar meaning to the first sentence, using the noun given in capital letters. In each case, the second sentence is a more formal version of the first.

0 I'm going to write and complain to the council.
COMPLAINT
I intend to make _a written complaint to the council_____.

1 There was nowhere for people to park.
LACK
There was _____.

2 It was really successful.
SUCCESS
It was _____.

3 You said that not many people turned up.
ATTENDANCE
You suggested that _____.

4 Lots of people said they thought the dancing was good.
STANDARD
Many commented on _____.

5 Now write your own answer to the task in **180–220** words. To help you, refer to the Useful language on page 195 as well as the sentences you wrote in exercise 4.

Don't forget!

- Expand on one or two of the points in the input material, adding relevant information of your own.
- Your letter should be consistently formal throughout, with polite but firm language.

Reading:	Multiple matching

CAE Part 4

1 Which walls are shown in the pictures above?
What do you know about any of them?

2   For questions **1–15**, choose from the four texts about walls (**A–D**). The texts may be chosen more than once.

How to go about it

- Skim through all four texts quickly to get an idea of their content.
- Read all the questions to see the kind of information you are looking for.
- Read text A, then look again at the questions, answering any that you can.
- Do the same for the other three texts.
- If there are any questions you have not answered, scan the texts again, looking for the specific information you need.
- To help you, parts of text A have been underlined. Match these parts to the appropriate questions. As you answer the other questions, underline the relevant parts of texts B–D in the same way.

According to the information given in the texts, which wall …

can be seen from a great distance?	1 ____
is susceptible to damage?	2 ____
had additional fortifications running alongside it?	3 ____
was considered a threat to health?	4 ____
quickly fell into disrepair?	5 ____
is no longer very much in evidence?	6 ____
is a series of different walls which were connected?	7 ____
required certain people to pay money when passing through?	8 ____
was built with the help of prisoners?	9 ____
is compared favourably with other ancient monuments?	10 ____
became unnecessary as a result of events elsewhere?	11 ____
was partly demolished by the authorities?	12 ____
proved to be an ideal site for commercial activity?	13 ____
did not always achieve its purpose?	14 ____
offers visitors an insight into the lives of the original guards?	15 ____

A GUIDE TO GREAT WALLS

Whether for keeping people in or keeping people out, all great walls have a story to tell. Trish Walsh investigates.

A

Erected in 1961 to prevent East German citizens crossing to the West, the Berlin Wall initially consisted mainly of barbed wire and armed guards. Within months a concrete wall began to appear, to be replaced on three separate occasions by ever more sophisticated versions, increasingly resistant to breakthroughs. On the east side of the wall, tank traps and ditches were built as protection against attack, and as a further deterrent to would-be escapees.

Although over 170 people lost their lives in Berlin trying to flee to the West, human will and ingenuity often prevailed, with a number of successful escape attempts via tunnels and, on one occasion, in a home-made hot air balloon. The 107-kilometre-long structure lost its relevance in 1989, when Hungary allowed East Germans to pass through their country on their way to Austria and West Germany, and after travel restrictions were lifted, people began to demolish whole sections of the wall. Now very little of it remains and the land has been used for housing and other property development.

B

Stretching for several thousand kilometres from the east coast of the country to the Gobi Desert, the Great Wall of China is said to be the only man-made structure visible from outer space. The oldest section was begun in 221 BC, using soldiers and local people, as well as intellectuals who had been sentenced to forced labour under the repressive Qin dynasty. Not surprisingly, the layers of compacted earth used to construct the wall soon began to crumble, and it was left to the later Han dynasty to restore and add to it.

By now the wall had evolved from a mere defence system for keeping out marauding tribes into a safe haven where trade could flourish, and bustling market towns sprang up at the many busy gates. But the ornate and imposing structure with which we are familiar from photographs was not added until the fourteenth century by Ming, using advanced brick-building technology. It was he who joined the three separate walls to create this truly impressive feat of construction.

C Situated in the north of England at one of the narrowest parts of the country, Hadrian's Wall is arguably the most important monument built by the Romans in Britain. Construction of the wall began in 120 AD on the orders of Emperor Hadrian, who wanted to mark the northernmost boundary of his Empire. The 117-kilometre wall was manned by thousands of troops, who kept watch from numerous turrets and milecastles, and who lived in a series of forts situated at strategic locations.

In the centuries following its abandonment around 400 AD, its stones were used by local people to build houses, walls and even churches. Nevertheless, spectacular stretches of the wall remain and a number of forts and museums along its length can be visited, providing a fascinating glimpse into the lives of the Roman soldiers who patrolled it. Although built of stone, the wall itself is vulnerable to erosion and visitors are discouraged from walking on it. Designated a Unesco World Heritage Site in 1987, Hadrian's Wall ranks alongside some of the more famous architectural treasures in the world.

D Originally known as *Eboracum*, York served as a military base for the Romans, who were the first to build a set of defences on the site. However, most of the 3.5 kilometres of wall – the longest town walls in England – date from the Middle Ages. Throughout their length one can still see a number of medieval gateways, or 'bars', which acted as control points. Non-residents and those who were not members of a guild were charged a toll on items brought into the city.

As York's status as England's second city dwindled in the nineteenth century, York Corporation began dismantling sections of the walls, blaming their decision on the high cost of maintenance. They also argued that the walls were of no historical value and that they caused disease by preventing the free circulation of air. Local people protested vehemently and the York Footpath Association set about restoring parts of the wall, confident that their work would help to attract tourists. The city and its walls now receive a million visitors every year.

◯ Reacting to the text

Tell your partner about a walled city you have visited. Give your impressions of the place, as well as any historical information you know.

Language focus 2: Nouns in formal English

1 ◯ Look at the following pairs of sentences. In each case the first sentence is an alternative way of expressing the second sentence, which appeared in the reading text above. What differences do you notice between each pair of sentences? Comment on the use of nouns and verbs.

1 a The Emperor Hadrian ordered his men to begin building the wall in 120 AD.
  b *Construction of the wall began in 120 AD on the orders of the Emperor Hadrian…*
2 a They built tank traps and ditches in order to stop anyone from attacking the wall.
  b *…tank traps and ditches were built as protection against attack…*
3 a …explaining that they had decided to do so because the walls were very expensive to maintain.
  b *…blaming their decision on the high cost of maintenance.*

2 Nouns help to convey information clearly and concisely, and are far more frequent in formal written English than in conversation. For questions 1–4 below, use the information in **a**, which is more conversational, to complete the gaps in **b**, which is more formal.

Example:
a I thought the painting was very simple and different to anything else I'd seen before. I was very impressed.
b I was most impressed by the simplicity and originality of the painting.

1 a He applied for the job and he was clearly a bit disappointed when he heard they'd turned him down.
  b He was unable to hide his _____ at their rejection of his _____ .

2 a The employees said they thought it would be a good idea if the company reduced the working day by just a little, but management said they didn't approve of the idea at all.
  b Management voiced their strong _____ of the employees' _____ for a slight _____ in the working day.

3 a I have to tell you that I'm not satisfied with the service you offer. I often have to wait a long time for things to get here, even though you say that you send them sooner than 24 hours after you receive an order.
  b I must express my _____ with the standard of your service. Delivery of goods is often subject to _____ , despite your _____ that orders are dispatched within 24 hours.

4 a People fail to understand how important it is to recycle waste, and I think it's because they don't know anything about the environment and they don't get taught enough about it at school.
  b People's _____ to understand the _____ of recycling waste is the _____ of a lack of environmental _____ and insufficient _____ on the subject.

3 In **1–4** above, there are more verbs in **a** than in **b**, and more nouns in **b** than in **a**. What other differences do you notice between the language used in informal and formal registers?

Listening 2:
CAE Part 4

Multiple matching

1   👁 1.5–1.9 You will hear five short extracts in which people are talking about changes in their lives. **While you listen you must complete both tasks.**

2   To make your first Part 4 Listening easier, there are only six options, not eight, to choose from in each task.

What to expect in the exam

- Part 4 consists of a multiple-matching format in which there are five short monologues on the same theme.
- There are two connected tasks. For each task, you must choose five correct answers from a list of eight options.
- In the exam you will have 45 seconds to read through the tasks.
- You hear all the extracts once, then the whole sequence is played again.

TASK ONE

For questions **1–5**, choose from the list **A–F** what led to the change in the life of the speaker.

A   the desire to avoid unwanted attention

B   the desire to travel

C   the desire to maintain a positive relationship

D   the desire to be challenged

E   the desire to show other people were wrong

F   the desire to fulfil an ambition

Speaker 1	1
Speaker 2	2
Speaker 3	3
Speaker 4	4
Speaker 5	5

TASK TWO

For questions **6–10**, choose from the list **A–F** how the speaker feels about this change.

A   excited

B   regretful

C   ashamed

D   scared

E   grateful

F   proud

Speaker 1	6
Speaker 2	7
Speaker 3	8
Speaker 4	9
Speaker 5	10

3   ⬤ Talk to your partner about a time in your life when something changed. Mention the following in relation to the change:
- the reasons for it
- how easy or difficult it was
- your feelings before and afterwards
- other people's attitudes
- the consequences of the change

Vocabulary: Changes

A Verb + noun collocations

○ When or why might you change each of the items in the box?

Example:
You might change your doctor if you moved house or if you weren't happy with the treatment you were receiving.

your doctor	your name	your mind	your tune
gear	the subject	sides	places	a tyre	your ways

B Adjective + noun collocations

1 The following adjectives can all be used with the noun *change*.

Complete each of the sentences **1–4** with a suitable group of adjectives **a–d**. All of the adjectives in each group must be appropriate for the sentence you choose.

a economic/political/social
b dramatic/sudden/considerable
c pleasant/refreshing/welcome
d far-reaching/significant/sweeping

1 It **made a/an** _____ **change to** see Alex in a suit. He looked very smart for once.
2 The Government has announced plans **to make** _____ **changes** to the tax system next year.
3 The **pace of** _____ **change** has been rather slow in this country recently.
4 The lottery win **brought about a/an** _____ **change** in her circumstances, which she is finding it difficult to cope with.

2 ○ Rewrite sentences **1–4** so that they are true for you/your country/the world in general. Use the words in bold, together with an appropriate adjective. Compare your sentences with those of other students in your class.

C Other verbs of change

For questions **1–5** decide which word, **A**, **B**, **C** or **D** best fits each space. The verb you choose must be appropriate for the gaps in both sentences. The words in bold are typical collocates of the verb.

1 a It took him a while to _____ **to being a parent**.
  b You can _____ **the height of the chair** by pulling this lever here.
    A switch   **B** alter   **C** vary   **D** adjust

2 a The old windmill has been _____ **into a small** guest house.
  b Graham Greene _____ **to Catholicism** at the age of 21.
    A transferred   **B** transformed   **C** converted   **D** adapted

3 a **Prices** _____ **according to** the time of year you decide to travel.
  b We were advised to _____ **the children's diet** as much as possible.
    A adapt   **B** shift   **C** vary   **D** modify

4 a Members of the rock group were asked to _____ **their behaviour** or else leave the hotel.
  b We had to _____ **the design** of the car to take account of the rough terrain.
    A modify   **B** amend   **C** transfer   **D** convert

5 a Twelve European countries _____ **over to the euro** on January 1st 2002.
  b I _____ **shifts with** Brian so I could go to my sister's wedding.
    A shifted   **B** switched   **C** transformed   **D** altered

②Review

Language focus: Talking about the past

In **1–8** below, write one of the auxiliary verbs from the box in the first space and an appropriate verb in the correct form in the second space. Use each auxiliary verb once only. There is an example at the beginning (**0**).

have	has	having	had	would
was	~~were~~	been	did	

0 The phone rang just as we ___were___ ___leaving___ the house.

1 It was the first time I _____ _____ abroad.

2 _____ _____ his ambition, he promised to spend more time with his family.

3 Since I've known him he _____ _____ that suit twice.

4 He was to _____ _____ in the final, but he was injured in a league match.

5 It's years since I _____ _____ out to dinner by my partner.

6 When we were little, my dad _____ often _____ us a story at bedtime.

7 I'd have liked to have _____ _____ a second chance, but it wasn't possible.

8 I wasn't allowed to see the film, but they _____ _____ me read the book.

Vocabulary: Changes

1 ◐ For **1–8**, decide whether the meaning of the two items of vocabulary is more or less the same or different. Explain any differences in meaning.

Example:
0 transfer money/convert money
Different. When you transfer money, you move it from one place to another, eg from one account to another. When you convert money, you change it from one currency to another.

1 adjust to university life/adapt to university life
2 adjust a piece of clothing/alter a piece of clothing
3 convert a farm into a hotel/transform a farm into a hotel
4 change your ways/modify your behaviour
5 change your ways/change your tune
6 vary the menu/adapt the menu
7 change sides/switch sides
8 switch to the euro/convert into euros

2 Match each of the verbs in the box with the group of words which collocate with it. The first one has been done for you.

adjust	convert	modify	switch	~~vary~~

1 ___vary___ the menu/your routine/in size
2 _____ to Islam/dollars into euros/the loft into a bedroom
3 _____ your belt/the straps on a bag/the brakes on a car
4 _____ TV channels/university courses/from dictatorship to democracy
5 _____ your language/your views/a piece of equipment

Multiple-choice cloze

1 Read the following text quickly, ignoring the gaps for the moment. Is the writer of the text generally positive or negative about the experience of the first immigrant workers in Britain?

2 For questions **1–12**, read the text again and then decide which answer (**A, B, C** or **D**) best fits each gap. There is an example at the beginning (**0**).

CHANGING COUNTRIES

(**0**) ____ a new life and hoping for a significant (**1**) ____ in their standard of living, foreign workers began flocking into Western Europe during the 1950s. In Britain, some of the first immigrants arriving from the West Indies and the Indian subcontinent were welcomed by brass bands, but the dream of a new life soon (**2**) ____ sour for many.

Attracted by the promise to earn good money and learn new skills, the reality they found was often one of low wages and, in many (**3**) ____ , unemployment. Some did not adapt (**4**) ____ to life in a country of cold weather, cold welcomes and discrimination. The (**5**) ____ of West Indian immigrants (**6**) ____ into the inner cities, areas that were already fraught with social tensions caused by poverty and (**7**) ____ housing. There were cases of open hostility towards the newcomers; in 1958, riots (**8**) ____ out in Notting Hill, West London, when gangs of white youths began taunting immigrants.

Yet despite the (**9**) ____ difficulties they encountered, many foreign workers did manage to (**10**) ____ to their new conditions, settling in their new adopted country and prospering. Their contribution had the effect not only of speeding up the (**11**) ____ of economic change in the postwar period, it also (**12**) ____ Western Europe into a multiracial society.

	A	**B**	**C**	**D**
0	Searching	Wishing	<u>Seeking</u>	Leading
1	switch	change	modification	variation
2	turned	converted	switched	changed
3	occasions	examples	ways	cases
4	closely	greatly	easily	normally
5	most	percentage	majority	number
6	changed	lived	arrived	moved
7	poor	low	few	weak
8	broke	carried	came	started
9	several	high	numerous	heavy
10	amend	adjust	turn	alter
11	growth	motion	pace	step
12	transformed	transferred	modified	shifted

Speaking:
CAE Part 3

Collaborative task

The pictures all show different ways of obtaining information. Talk with your partner about the advantages and disadvantages of each method, and then decide which is the most effective and which the least effective in providing information.

- What are the advantages and disadvantages of each method?
- Which is the most effective method and the least effective method in providing information?

Don't forget!

Aim to use a wide range of vocabulary.

Useful language

In **1** and **2** below, the adjectives and verbs in the boxes can all be used in the corresponding sentence. Mark each adjective **P** or **N**, according to whether it has a positive or negative meaning.

1 This is(n't) a very

Adjective		**Verb**	
efficient		getting	
costly		obtaining	
convenient	method of	accessing	information.
unreliable		finding	
frustrating		gathering	
cost-effective			

2 It/They can

Verb		**Adjective**
provide		biased.
give	information which is	misleading.
broadcast		accurate.
publish		up to date.
		useless.
		comprehensive.
		reliable.
		limited.

Multiple choice

You are going to read three extracts which are all concerned with ways of gathering information. For questions **1–6**, choose the answer (**A**, **B**, **C** or **D**) which you think fits best according to the text.

What to expect in the exam

- In Part 1 of the Reading Paper, there are three short texts, all on the same theme. The texts are taken from a variety of sources including newspapers, magazines, journals, books and leaflets.
- For each text there are two multiple-choice questions, each with four options to choose from. The questions test a number of features including detail (question 2 below), comparison (question 3), reference (question 4), opinion and tone (question 6).

Don't forget!

- Before answering the questions on an individual text, read the whole of it first.
- Eliminate the options which are clearly wrong and choose the best answer.

Smart Shoes decide on television time

Sports shoes that work out whether their owner has done enough exercise to warrant time in front of the television have been devised in the UK. The shoes, dubbed Square Eyes, contain an electronic pressure sensor and a tiny computer chip to record how many steps the wearer has taken in a day. A wireless transmitter passes the information to a receiver connected to a television, and this decides how much evening viewing time the wearer deserves, based on the day's exertions. The design was inspired by a desire to combat the rapidly ballooning waistlines among British teenagers, says Gillian Swan, who developed Square Eyes as a final-year design project at Brunel University in London, UK. 'We looked at current issues and childhood obesity really stood out,' she says. 'And I wanted to tackle that with my design.' Once a child has used up their daily allowance gained through exercise, the television automatically switches off. And further time in front of the TV can only be earned through more steps.

Existing pedometers normally clip onto a belt or slip into a pocket and keep count of steps by measuring sudden movement. Swan says these can easily be tricked into recording steps through shaking. But her shoe has been built to be harder for lazy teenagers to deceive. 'It is possible, but it would be a lot of effort,' she says. 'That was one of my main design considerations.'

1 Gillian Swan's purpose in creating the special shoe was to
   A prove a link between passive entertainment and obesity.
   B help teenagers to lose weight and become fitter.
   C reveal how teenagers prefer to spend their time.
   D find a way of staying in good condition while watching TV.

2 What does Swan say was of particular importance during the development of the shoe?
   A creating a product that would always be in demand
   B designing a shoe that teenagers were willing to wear
   C making sure the technology could not be damaged
   D ensuring that the information the shoe provided was reliable

EXTRACT FROM A NEWSPAPER COLUMN

Now regular readers will know of my antipathy towards anything that invades my privacy, be it subtle or direct, human or electronic. At the same time, I would like to consider myself a man that does not go out of his way to make the lives of others difficult, even if they interrupt the sports event of the season. It is for this reason that I did not hang up as I heard the market researcher announce she was conducting a survey on behalf of my insurance company. Having recently received a settlement for a minor motor vehicle accident, I supposed I was simply somewhere on a list of computer-generated phone calls – and just happened to pick up the receiver before hundreds of other insurance claimants, like a small

21 desert creature being the first of its colony to pop its head above ground, just as an eagle passes overhead.

Despite the distraction of the football, I did my best to provide her with answers that accurately reflected my opinion. These were to be on a scale of 1 (which I was informed meant *extremely dissatisfied*) to 7 (perhaps something approaching *overjoyed*?). This, however, became

31 a rather mechanical process soon after question number ten. By now I no longer had the will to distinguish between 'And how satisfied were you with the time it took to process your claim' and 'And how satisfied were you with the way your claim was processed' and then 'And how satisfied were you with the entire process of processing your claim?'

3 The writer mentions a small desert creature in line 21 in order to emphasize
   A the idea of him becoming a victim by chance.
   B the vast number of people who have car accidents.
   C the distance that existed between him and the researcher.
   D the lack of control that people have over their own lives.

4 *This* in line 31 refers to
   A the scale used to reply to the questions.
   B the type of questions in the survey.
   C the writer's answering of the questions.
   D the attitude of the researcher as she asked the questions.

JUNK

Chrissy tossed the junk mail in the bin, unopened. And in doing so, she unwittingly made a joke and a mockery of the lives, loves and endeavours of countless people whom she would never know. In that casual gesture she trampled upon an awesome human achievement and upon great sacrifices contributed by the natural world. Why didn't she stop to think? Why didn't she dare to care? What a cruel, heartless person.

If only she had seen them, seen their disappointment as she hurled their creation back in their honest faces. The person who cleared the land to plant the fir trees; the people who planted and tore up the fir trees every second or third year; the drivers and the ships' captains who got the trees to the mill; the thousands who work in the mills and in the huge pulping plant and paper factories – if Chrissy had seen them, she would have wept bitter tears of self-reproach to have dismissed their lives so casually.

The copywriter? Did Chrissy not care that he had spent so many lonely hours trying to think of a tempting way to get her to accept ten days' free home perusal of a fifteen-volume history of the Wild West? Was his life to be just a pointless joke because of her actions? The animals and insects that were wiped out when billions of acres of forest and moorland were turned over to single crop, factory, fir tree farming. Did they give their lives in vain?

One can only hope and pray that those involved never discover that after the monumental worldwide effort and the truly awesome consumption of natural resources that went into bringing a piece of junk mail to Chrissy's door, she simply threw it away. Gone, gone, gone; all their hopes and dreams and sacrifices, rejected in that one contemptuous gesture. They must never know, for they would put up their arms in horror (or spindly, leggy things in the case of the insects) and say, 'What *is* the point!?'

5 In the first paragraph we learn that Chrissy
   A gave no thought to global issues.
   B had few friends and acquaintances.
   C rarely considered the consequences of her actions.
   D was not interested in the information she had been sent.

6 The writer's tone throughout the extract suggests that he is
   A critical of Chrissy for her insensitivity.
   B opposed to the production of junk mail.
   C concerned about the workers he mentions.
   D full of admiration for human resourcefulness.

⬤ Reacting to the texts

Do you think Square Eyes would be successful in tackling obesity?

In what ways can market research invade your privacy?

How effective do you think junk mail is?

Language focus 1: Hypothetical past situations

A *Wish/If only* and alternatives

1 ⬭ Look at the following sentence from the third reading text.

If only she had seen them, seen their disappointment as she hurled their creation back in their honest faces. (line 5)

If only is used to add emphasis to hypothetical situations. With past events it can also be used to express regret and/or criticism. Look at the following alternative ways of saying the same thing.

1 If only…
2 I wish…   she hadn't told him.
3 I'd rather/sooner…

In each case:

a Did she tell him?
b How does the speaker feel about this?

2 ⬭ If the subject is the same in both parts of a sentence introduced by *would rather, would sooner, would prefer to* or *would like to*, a perfect infinitive is used when referring to the past, eg:

I'd rather/sooner <u>have seen</u> it with subtitles. Wouldn't you?
She'd prefer to <u>have travelled</u> on her own.
He'd like to <u>have come</u> but he's very busy these days.

How does the meaning change if the present infinitive, *see, travel* and *come*, is used in these sentences?

Practice

For **1–6**, complete the second sentence so that it has a similar meaning to the first sentence.

1 If only I'd gone to France instead.
  I'd sooner _____ .
2 I do think you might have phoned earlier.
  I wish _____ .
3 We don't think you should have done that.
  We'd rather _____ .
4 Don't you regret not going to university?
  Don't you wish _____ ?
5 If only you'd mentioned it before!
  You should _____ !
6 Do you wish you had stayed longer?
  Would you like _____ ?

B Past conditionals

1 Third conditional sentences can be used to talk about imaginary situations in the past, as in this example from the text:

<u>If Chrissy had seen them,</u> *she would have wept bitter tears of self reproach to have dismissed their lives so casually.* (lines 8–9)

Here is a more formal way of expressing the underlined part of the sentence:

<u>Had Chrissy seen them,</u> *she would have wept…*

2 Match each sentence beginning **1–6** with an appropriate ending **a–f**.

Example: 1 c

1 If she hadn't found his name on the Internet,
2 Had I known it was going to rain so heavily,
3 If it hadn't been for her quick thinking,
4 If I didn't have three kids and a mortgage,
5 If they hadn't lost their last three matches,
6 If I got into trouble at school,

a she could have had a serious accident.
b they'd be top of the league now.
c they might never have seen each other again.
d my parents used to stop my pocket money.
e I'd have given up this job a long time ago.
f I would have taken my waterproofs.

3 Look at the sentences in **2** and answer these questions.

1 Which sentences are third conditionals?
2 Which sentences include a combination of past and present time reference (mixed conditionals)?
3 Which sentence uses the past simple to refer to past time?

🄖 Read more about the points in sections **A** and **B** above in Part A of the Grammar reference on pages 217 and 218.

Practice

1 Rewrite the ideas expressed in the following sentences using the structures studied in **A** and **B** above. Write one sentence for each situation, using a different structure each time.

Example:
We didn't get back in time to see him. It was a real shame.
<u>*If only we'd got back in time to see him.*</u>

1 He didn't revise for his exams. He regrets this now.
2 I didn't take any books with me on holiday. I got really bored.
3 It's a good job Steve was there. Thanks to him we were able to get the car started.
4 My parents bought me a video recorder. A DVD player would have been better.
5 I couldn't see the film on telly last night. That was a pity – I really wanted to.
6 My French isn't very good. That's probably why I didn't get the job.
7 They showed us all their holiday snaps. I was hoping to watch the football.

2 ⬭ With a partner write a six-line dialogue. The first or last line of the dialogue must be one of these sentences.

I wish you'd told the truth.
I'd rather you hadn't lent it to him.
If only you'd been there – it was so funny.
I'd love to have seen his face when he found out.
If it hadn't been for your stupidity, we wouldn't be in this mess.

3 ⬭ Read your dialogue to another pair of students, but do not read out the sentence from **2**. Can the other students guess which sentence you chose?

Word formation: Adjectives and adverbs

1 Look back at the second reading text on page 32. Which suffix is added to all of the following nouns to create adjectives?

count _____   heart _____   point _____

2 Using the suffixes in the box, write the corresponding adjective for each of the words below. The same suffix is needed for all three words in each group, though spelling changes may be required in some of them. The exercise begins with an example (**0**).

-ory   -less   -able   -ent   -ative   -ial   -ic   -ous   -y

0 allergy _allergic_   science _scientific_   drama _dramatic_

1	approach	_____	apply	_____	believe	_____
2	argument	_____	administer	_____	provoke	_____
3	introduce	_____	contradict	_____	prepare	_____
4	chat	_____	mud	_____	rock	_____
5	luxury	_____	mystery	_____	monster	_____
6	end	_____	price	_____	sleep	_____
7	persist	_____	appear	_____	obey	_____
8	manager	_____	secretary	_____	territory	_____

3 Complete each gap with the appropriate form of the word in capitals at the end of the line. The word you need may be an adjective or an adverb. A negative affix may also be needed. The exercise begins with an example (**0**).

0 I don't understand how he got the job. He's far too _incompetent_ to be put in charge of a school. **COMPETENCE**

1 Her work has been acclaimed for its sensitivity of style and _____ use of imagery. **IMAGINE**

2 Her performance at work was considered _____ and her contract was not renewed. **SATISFY**

3 It is becoming _____ difficult for artists to obtain public funding for their work. **INCREASE**

4 The assistants in Gamidges are unhelpful and _____. I shall shop elsewhere in future! **COURTESY**

5 My grandfather was extremely _____ about astronomy; the planets were his great passion. **KNOWLEDGE**

6 We strayed from the path at some point and got _____ lost. **HOPE**

7 Although several companies made _____ losses, the market as a whole was buoyant. **SUBSTANCE**

8 The bookcase was placed _____ near the door to hide a huge crack in the wall. **STRATEGY**

Writing: Reports
CAE Part 2

1 Read the following Part 2 task, then look at the two sample answers on page 35 and decide which is better.

You have been asked to **write a report** for an international research company about the nature and quality of advertising in your country.

You should:
- describe some of the positive and negative aspects of **two** different forms of advertising in your country.
- say how effective these advertising methods are.
- suggest one or two changes which could be introduced to counter the negative aspects.

Write your **report** in **220–260** words.

A

Introduction

The aim of this report is to outline the positive and negative features of two different forms of advertising in my country, namely roadside hoardings and banners trailed by light aircraft. It will also consider the effectiveness of these methods and make recommendations for improvements.

Advertising hoardings

These add a touch of colour and sometimes humour to our otherwise drab urban landscapes. Moreover, the size of the posters and the pithiness of the accompanying slogans attract the attention of passers-by and help make the advertisements memorable.

Unfortunately, however, hoardings are also to be found in rural areas, where they appear unsightly and are clearly out of place. In addition, the advertisements can lead drivers to lose their concentration momentarily and are a relatively common cause of accidents.

Aeroplane advertising

Equally distracting are banners attached to light aircraft, which fly for extended periods over our built-up areas and popular coastal resorts. Furthermore, the noise is a considerable source of irritation to local residents and the consumption of large quantities of air fuel can only be harmful to the environment.

On the other hand, aeroplane banners are currently enjoying great success here as an advertising medium. This is largely due to the originality of the approach and its difference from mainstream alternatives.

Recommendations

To discourage noise, air and visual pollution, I would recommend restricting the location of hoardings to towns and cities and limiting the amount of flying time for advertising aircraft. Additionally, smaller hoardings might reduce the risk of accidents caused by distracted drivers.

B

In this report I'm going to describe some of the positive and negative aspects of two different forms of advertising, say how effective these advertising methods are and suggest one or two changes which could be introduced to counter the negative aspects.

Advertising hoardings are very colourful and sometimes very funny, and they look good in our sad, grey cities. And they're very big too, with interesting slogans and that makes people look at them and remember them.

But you get them in the countryside too. They look ugly and I don't think they should be there. They also cause accidents because people look at them when they're driving.

Banners pulled by small aeroplanes also cause accidents. The aeroplanes fly for a long time over the cities and beaches. They're noisy too and that irritates people and they use up a lot of petrol. That's bad for the environment.

But banners like this are very successful here because they're original and different from the typical advertising techniques.

I think they should make it illegal to have hoardings in the countryside and not let aeroplanes with banners fly for very long.

That would stop all the noise, the pollution and the ugly views. And hoardings should be smaller because then they might not distract drivers and cause accidents.

2 ⬭ The content of the two answers is roughly the same, but the type of language used is very different. Work with your partner.

Comment on the following features in each answer:
linking devices
number of nouns
types of adjective

What other differences do you notice?

Find examples in **A** of how the writer makes reference to his/her country.

3 Write your own answer to the task on page 34.

How to go about it

- Decide on the two forms of advertising. Choose from TV, radio, Internet, mailshots, telephone, newspapers and magazines, fliers, transport, sports events or any other medium used in your country.
- For each method, note down your ideas in four separate columns: *Positive aspects, Negative aspects, Effectiveness, Recommendations*.
- Look at the adjectives in section C on page 210 and decide which, if any, will be relevant to your answer.
- Decide how you will organize your ideas into paragraphs. The paragraph structure in the two sample answers is one possibility. How else could you structure your report?
- Write your report using a consistently formal style. Aim to use a wide range of vocabulary and a greater number of nouns than verbs.

Listening:
CAE Part 3

Multiple choice

1 Do you know where the following languages are spoken?

Sami Breton Ladin Provençal Frisian Galego

2 👁 **1.10** You will hear a woman called Helena Drysdale being interviewed about her research for a book on minority languages. For questions **1–6**, choose the answer (**A**, **B**, **C** or **D**) which fits best according to what you hear.

What to expect in the exam

- Part 3 of Paper 4 Listening always contains six multiple-choice questions about a conversation between two or more speakers. The recording lasts approximately four minutes.

1 The main purpose of Helena's journey was to
  A establish precisely where Europe's minority languages are spoken.
  B investigate the effects of climate and location on language.
  C calculate the exact number of minority languages in Europe.
  D assess the current condition of Europe's minority languages.

2 One problem of living in the mobile home was that
  A there wasn't much space.
  B the children had nowhere to play.
  C it became very hot.
  D they all got bored with each other.

3 What does Helena say about the people she met?
  A Not all of them spoke a minority language.
  B Some were more willing than others to express their views.
  C Intellectuals gave more biased information than other people.
  D Older people had a rather unbalanced view of the situation.

4 We learn that people who were punished for speaking Provençal
  A did not take their punishment seriously.
  B felt they were treated unfairly.
  C were made to feel embarrassed.
  D regretted what they had done.

5 What point does Helena make about some local people in a tourist area?
  A They are not interested in preserving their culture.
  B They complain too much about tourists.
  C They sell their land in order to make large profits.
  D Their actions are not consistent with their opinions.

6 According to Helena, language
  A enables people to express their emotions.
  B is an expression of one's identity.
  C is the key to integration.
  D makes everyone different.

3 ⭘ Are any minority languages spoken in your country? Is anything done to ensure their survival? Do you think more could or should be done?

Helena says: *If you spoke a different language, you'd be a different person.* Do you agree with her? Why/Why not?

Language focus 2: Present and future conditionals

1 Match each of the conditional sentences from the listening with one of the explantions **a**–**c**.

Zero conditional: *If you cut a tree back, it grows much stronger.*

First conditional: *If no positive action is taken, they'll simply die out.*

Second conditional: *If you spoke a different language, you'd be a different person.*

a an imaginary situation in the present or future
b a possible future situation and its probable result
c a situation which is always true

2 Look at the following alternative structures to those used in two of the above examples from the listening.

First conditional

If + happen to/should makes an event seem more unlikely, or more of a chance possibility.

If I happen to…   *see anything I think she might like for her birthday, I'll buy it.*
If I should (happen to)…

In more formal contexts, the following inversion is possible:

Should you require any further information, please do not hesitate to contact us.

Second conditional

A *If + were to + verb* also makes an event seem more unlikely.

If I were to tell the boss what you've just said, he'd probably sack you.
Again, an inversion is possible in formal contexts:
Were you to accept our proposal, some funding would be made available to you.

B Compare the following two structures. Which refers to the present and which to the past?

If it weren't for my dog, I'd probably go away more.
If it hadn't been for his time in prison, he might have got the job.

C *Supposing/Suppose/Imagine* can all be used instead of *if*, especially in everyday speech.
Imagine you lost your job. What would you do?

3 For **1–6** below, find one unnecessary word in each sentence or pair of sentences. The word is either grammatically incorrect or does not fit in with the sense of the sentence(s).

Example:
If you ~~would~~ have enough time, will you help me to clean the garage out?

1 If it weren't broken for my leg, I'd definitely run in the London Marathon next month.
2 It's very unlikely you'll see her at the concert, but if you should happen bump into her, give her my regards, won't you?
3 She's always moaning about him – I wouldn't be in the least bit surprised if she would split up with him soon.
4 I know you don't think there's much chance of it happening, but just if suppose you did win first prize. How do you think you'd spend all that money?
5 Imagine that you came face to face with a bull: what might be the sensible thing to do? Would you have run away, for example?
6 We'd have to come to some sort of decision ourselves if the meeting were to put off for any reason.

If + will/would/going to

1 In some situations *if* can be followed by *will*, *would* or *going to* in the same clause. Match each of the functions in the box with one of the sentences **1–6**, according to the idea expressed in the *if* clause. The exercise begins with an example (**0**).

| Willingness | Refusal | ~~Request~~ |
| Intention | Insistence | Result |

0 If you'll come this way, Ms Taylor will see you now.
   Request
1 If you will keep eating chocolate, it's no wonder you're putting on weight.
2 If you won't turn your music down, we'll just have to call the police.
3 If it'll help you relax, I'll get you a drink or something.
4 If we're going to go for a walk, I think we should leave now.
5 If you would just let me explain, I'm sure you'd change your mind.

2 ⬤ Choose three of the sentences in exercise 1 and for each one rewrite the second clause (the part after the comma). Ask your partner to match each of the new sentence halves to an appropriate *if* clause in exercise 1.

Example:
0 *…I'll show you where the lift is.*

🔊 Read more about present and future conditionals in Part B of the Grammar reference on page 218.

Gapped text

1 In what ways is smell an important source of information?

Think of three smells which are in some way important to you, and tell your partner about them. Do you like the smells? Do they bring back any memories?

What precautions would you need to take if you had no sense of smell?

You are going to read an extract from a newspaper article. Six paragraphs have been removed from the extract. Choose from the paragraphs **A–G** the one which fits each gap (**1–6**). There is one extra paragraph that you do not need to use.

How to go about it

- Before you start to make any choices, read through the base text (the main text with the gaps) and answer the following question:
  How can people's lives be affected by having no sense of smell?
- Read all the missing paragraphs and then try to decide where each one should go. (Remember, there is one extra paragraph.) Some parts of the article have been underlined to help you.
  When making your choices, be sure to look at the information both before and after the gap. Underline those parts of the missing paragraphs which help you reach your decision.
- Finally, check your answers by reading the whole article again to ensure that it makes sense. Check that the extra paragraph does not fit into any of the gaps.

SCENTS AND SENSITIVITY

She has never known the fragrance of a beautiful flower – or been able to tell by sniffing whether food is safe to eat. Lucy Mangan on being born with no sense of smell

I am not a fully sentient being. I am referring to the fact that I am congenitally anosmic; or, as I more helpfully put it when people thrust perfumed articles under my nose and invite an opinion on the aroma, I was born without a sense of smell.

1 _____

That experience, however, does not compare to the time I was persuaded by schoolfriends that as I couldn't smell Emma Webster's perfume, I should drink it. This was, I recall, on the grounds that taste and smell are so closely linked that it would give me at least some idea of the delicious scent I was missing. Alas, all it taught me was that perfume is not a beverage, and I was left feeling sick for days.

2 _____

I had enough sense to buy a smoke alarm, but it wasn't until my sister called round and nearly collapsed from the smell of a hob burner I had accidentally switched on that I realised I needed a detector that would alert me aurally to gas leaks before I blew up the street. A few bouts of food poisoning alerted me to the fact that I can eat food which would cause those with functioning nasal passages to call in the public health authorities. I now check best-before dates assiduously and treat three-day-old milk with the respect it deserves.

3 _____

I subscribe to the 'what you've never had, you never miss' school of thought but for those who lose their sense of smell, the effect on their quality of life can be enormous. Professor Tim Jacob at Cardiff University, who researches olfaction, explains 'Anosmics will have found other ways of adapting, using texture

and consistency to get information about food. But people who once relied on their sense of smell do not know how to cope without it.'

4 _____

And those are just the obvious things. As Jacob also notes: 'You lose lots of subliminal information and links with the emotional centres of the brain. Smells are inextricably linked with memories and form the backdrop to your sensory experience. The smell of your first girlfriend's perfume or boyfriend's aftershave, anything associated with strong emotion, will always trigger a rush of memory.'

5 _____

Alarmed at the thought of producing sickly babies, I enquire about treatment. For those who have lost their sense of smell through infection or damage, the news is relatively good. 'They usually regain some ability because the olfactory nerve is capable of regeneration,' says David Roberts, ear, nose and throat consultant at Guy's & St Thomas's Hospital in London.

6 _____

I will have to soldier on, and draw what comfort I can from a recent exchange with an ex-boyfriend who, as we reminisced about our relationship said wistfully, 'You were the best girlfriend in the world. You let me eat all the garlic I wanted and it didn't bother you.' I'm putting it in my next personal ad.

A Naturally, the problems of being olfactorily-challenged don't compare to those which attend blindness or deafness. Nevertheless, certain things do have to be taken into account, and certain precautions taken, which you only fully appreciate when you start living alone.

B 'The tongue can only distinguish the four basic tastes: bitter, sweet, salty, sour. Smell detects flavour and nuance, so they lose all significant sense of taste. About 17% become clinically depressed. Some become oversensitive about having body odour and are frightened of going out.'

C Steroid-based drug treatments can help further. Nasal polyps causing blockages to olfactory passageways can be treated medically and surgically. But, as one might expect, less can be done to rectify causes one is born with.

D 'It's a very emotive sense,' he explains. 'The nerves stimulated by smell send messages to one of the oldest, most primitive parts of our brain, which is why it's so integral to our lives and why people feel they cannot do without it.'

E It took until I was seven to convince my mother of this. She reluctantly acknowledged the truth of my claim after making me sniff the fumes from her bottle of nail varnish remover until I looked up hopefully and said 'My eyes are burning – is that what you mean?'

F I am beginning to feel quite intrigued by this unknown world of smells taking you back in time, but this quickly deepens into concern about what else I am missing. 'And of course you are attracted to people who smell different from you, because it suggests they have a different immunotype,' says Jacob. 'It's the evolutionary system trying to get you to pass on two sets of immunity advantages to your offspring.'

G I have also learned to stock my shelves with visitors as well as myself in mind. So I have fruit teas in the house even though they appear to be nothing more than an expensive way of colouring a mugful of hot water, and herbs, even though they are a matter of supreme indifference to me. When I cook for other people and a recipe says 'season to taste', I have to hope for the best.

Vocabulary: Smell

Adjective + noun collocations

1 **a** Complete each gap with a word from the box.

| bacon | bodies | coffee | date | fruit |
| fumes | milk | rubber | smoke | spices |

1 The **stale smell** of cigarette _____ and sweaty _____.
2 The **mouth-watering aroma** of freshly brewed _____ and sizzling _____.
3 The **acrid odour** of burning _____ and petrol _____.
4 The **rancid smell** of sour _____ and butter that has long since passed its sell-by _____.
5 The **pungent aroma** of herbs and _____ and ripe tropical _____.

b Where might you find the above combinations of smells?

Example:

1 You might experience these smells in a night club or at a party.

2 Arrange the adjectives in bold in exercise 1 into the columns below, according to their meaning. The first one has been done for you.

| **Positive** | **Negative** | **Neutral** |
| | *stale* | |

3 Add the following adjectives to the columns in exercise 2.

| fresh | faint | strong | musty | sweet |
| unmistakable | overpowering | sickly | | |

4 ⬭ Do the speaking activity on page 206.

Word formation

For questions **1–10**, read the text below. Use the word given in capitals at the end of some of the lines to form a word that fits the gap **in the same line**. There is an example at the beginning (**0**).

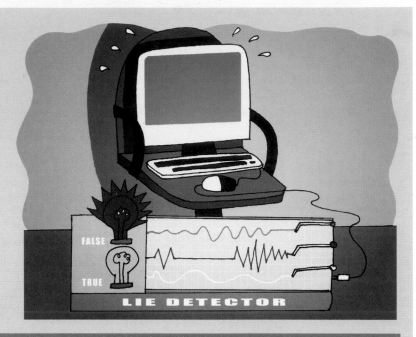

Don't forget!

- You may need to write the negative or plural form of a word.
- Check the spelling of your answers. No marks are given for a word which is misspelt.

CAN YOU TRUST THE INTERNET?

Most would agree that the golden age of the library has well and	
(**0**) _truly_ passed and that the internet has overtaken as provider	**TRUE**
of (**1**) _____ information. At the same time, there is growing	**GLOBE**
awareness and (**2**) _____ that online articles which seem to be	**SUSPECT**
based on thorough research, evidence and academic study, are not	
as (**3**) _____ as they claim. Online, a writer has the kind of	**FACT**
(**4**) _____ powers that no ordinary journalist or author would	**EDIT**
ever have, and the reader is forced to distinguish between what is	
actually (**5**) _____ or what is mere opinion. And even sites	**OBJECT**
which were once thought to be (**6**) _____ now suffer from	**RELY**
attacks carried out by internet vandals intending to cause deliberate	
(**7**) _____ with statistics, or publish personal abuse against	**ACCURATE**
a well-known person, for example. Another (**8**) _____ issue	**CONTROVERSY**
is that of writers claiming to have academic backgrounds or	
(**9**) _____ in an area when they do not. In 2007 online	**EXPERT**
encyclopedia Wikipedia admitted that one of their editors, a	
professor of religious studies who other editors believed to be	
entirely (**10**) _____, was actually a 24-year-old student	**TRUST**
called Ryan Jordan. Before he was unmasked, Jordan had made	
over 20,000 alterations to the entries people had posted on the	
encyclopedia.	

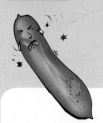

Open cloze

For questions **1–15**, complete the following article by writing **one** word in each space. The exercise begins with an example (**0**).

Don't forget!
- Always read the text through once before you start to complete the gaps.
- Look carefully at the words and sentences both before and after a gap.

LISTENING TO VEGETABLES

Scientists in Bonn have developed a method of listening to sounds from plants normally inaudible (**0**) _to_ the human ear. The basic technique (**1**) _____ developed in the Netherlands, but the German equipment is (**2**) _____ sensitive. When a leaf or stem is sliced, the plant signals pain or dismay (**3**) _____ releasing the gas ethylene over its entire surface. The gas molecules are collected in a bell jar and bombarded with laser beams, (**4**) _____ makes them vibrate. The resultant sound waves are amplified in a resonance tube, (**5**) _____ detected with a sensitive microphone. The (**6**) _____ a plant is subjected to stress, the louder the signal.

One surprising result came from an apparently healthy cucumber that was virtually shouting (**7**) _____ agony. (**8**) _____ closer study showed it (**9**) _____ developed mildew, a harmful fungus, though the symptoms were (**10**) _____ apparent. Listening to plants in this (**11**) _____ could be of great benefit to farmers as an early-warning system to detect pests and disease, and as an aid to efficient storing and transporting. Apples, for instance, give (**12**) _____ high levels of ethylene, increasing with ripeness and causing neighbouring fruit (**13**) _____ rot. Invisible differences of ripeness (**14**) _____ be detected acoustically, enabling fruit to be separated into batches in order to prolong (**15**) _____ freshness.

Key word transformations

For questions **1–8**, complete the second sentence so that it has a similar meaning to the first sentence, using the word given. **Do not change the word given.** You must use between **three** and **six** words, including the word given. Here is an example (**0**).

0 If the bank refuses to lend us money, we might have to ask your parents instead.
REQUEST
If the bank turns _down our request for_ a loan, we might have to ask your parents instead.

1 Having a holiday together was a mistake because we argued all the time.
NEVER
I wish _____ on holiday together because we argued all the time.

2 You were not supposed to tell anyone about my news!
SECRET
I'd rather _____ instead of telling everyone!

3 Although I wanted to quit smoking gradually, my doctor told me to stop immediately.
PREFER
I _____ up smoking gradually, but my doctor told me to stop immediately.

4 I would find Andy more attractive if he didn't laugh at strange things.
SENSE
If it were _____ humour, I would find Andy quite attractive.

5 If you should ever come to France, please feel free to visit us.
HAPPEN
Please feel free to visit us _____ to France.

6 Patrick is going to lose his job if he insists on arriving late to work.
KEEP
If _____ up late to work, Patrick is going to lose his job.

7 The most likely reason for the scientists getting the conclusion wrong is that they were not thorough enough with their research.
PROBABLY
If their research had been more thorough, the scientists _____ to the wrong conclusion.

8 Tom should have admitted his mistake, because the company usually gives employees another chance.
SECOND
The company might _____ if he had admitted his mistake.

Ready for **Reading**

Introduction

In Paper 1 you have 1 hour 15 minutes to answer 34 questions in four different parts. In this unit we will look at some of the techniques and approaches you should adopt in order to complete the Reading Paper in the time allowed.

Parts 1 and 3: Multiple choice

1 Both Parts 1 and 3 consist of texts followed by multiple-choice questions, which focus on a variety of aspects including details, opinions, attitudes and the author's purpose.

Part 1 contains three texts on the same theme followed by two multiple-choice questions on each text. Examples may be seen in units 3, 7 and 13.

Part 3 contains one text followed by seven multiple-choice questions. The task below is typical of those found in this part of the Reading Paper.

2 ◯ Quickly read the following magazine article, which contains an interview with the musician Chris Rea, and a review of his album *Dancing Down the Stony Road*.

Does the article encourage you to listen to or buy the record? Why (not)?

3 Read the article again. For questions **1–7**, choose the correct answer **A**, **B**, **C** or **D**. Underline the parts of the text which help you make your choices. *Example*: **1C**.

What to expect in the exam

- Each correct answer in Parts 1, 2 and 3 receives two marks.
- In Part 3 the questions follow the same order as the information in the text, although the final question may test understanding of the text as a whole.
- Many of the wrong options, or *distractors,* express ideas which are similar to, but not the same as, those expressed in the text. Each of the highlighted sections in the text expresses an idea which might cause you to choose the wrong option for the question in brackets. As you answer each question match the highlighted section to the distractor and say why it is the wrong answer. eg (1) A *He said it might be better if it were shorter. The second sentence in the next paragraph confirms this. He did **not** say it was shorter and therefore better than his other work.*

Fool if you think it's over

In hospital and facing death, Chris Rea decided it was time to make the blues music he really loved. And it's wonderful, says Mark Edwards.

I am feeling guilty as I approach Chris Rea's studios. A couple of months earlier, his record company had sent me his new album to sound out my opinion. It's fantastic, I told them, the best thing he's ever done – a collection of raw, powerful delta blues and gospel tunes that would make the world reappraise their idea of Chris Rea. And then – almost as an afterthought, in case this all sounded too gushing – (1) I added that it might benefit from being a little shorter.

After all, it was a radical change of direction from a man best known for soft-rock hits like *On the Beach* and *Road to Hell*. Perhaps a slightly shaved running length would make it less daunting? Since then I have found out that I had been sent only half of the tracks Rea wanted to release. He wanted the new album to be a double. His record company, EastWest, didn't. The disagreement proved final. Rea left EastWest and opted to release the new album, *Dancing*

Down the Stony Road, on his own label, Jazzy Blue.

As I neared his studios, I began to wonder if my throwaway comment had proved to be the final straw in the mind of some EastWest executive that a double was out of the question; or – much worse – if someone had even told Rea what I'd said. As our interview began, I confessed. (2) To my surprise and immense relief, Rea laughed and thanked me. After nearly a quarter of a century of dealing with major record labels, he was glad to be free.

While just about every musician can reel off a list of complaints about their label, Rea's label relationships have led him to be trapped in what he terms (3) 'this horrible executive rock thing' for 25 years. A man who fell in love with the delta blues of Blind Willie McTell and saw a career for himself along the lines of guitarist Ry Cooder found himself instead bracketed for his vocals alongside Dire Straits and Phil Collins, following the huge success of his early single *Fool (If You Think It's Over)*.

'I had no ambitions to be a singer,' he says. 'That was an accident, and I went along with it because it's better than being on the dole in Middlesbrough. And you think, next time around I'll slip into what I really want to do … but it never exactly happened.' Once his record company knew that he could write middle-of-the-road hits, (4) they wanted more of the same. Rea doesn't blame them; he blames himself for being too compliant. 'I always protest mitigating circumstances: an instinctive working-class fear of the suit. It's actually a failing of mine, not theirs. I've always been very keen to help get the job done. To do what's required.'

It took the prospect of his own death for Rea to finally make the album he's been dreaming of all these years. Rea has had a series of operations over the past eight years, the last of which he was told that he had little more than a 50/50 chance of surviving. As he was being wheeled into the operating theatre, he thought, 'I've got to get through this, I can't die yet because (5) the sound that the audience love when I play live I haven't actually got on record. That became the aim when I came out. I don't know how many copies the new album will sell. But what I do know is that I'll stamp my name on it.'

Quite right too. *Dancing Down the Stony Road* is a marvellous mix of moaning blues, pleading gospel tunes and raucous stomps. (6) It's the perfect setting for Rea's

gravelly voice and for his amazing guitar playing. It's easier to see Rea's connection to these songs. When the slide guitar and moans of the opening track give way to a huge, distant bass drum and an exquisite piano riff and suddenly Rea sings, 'Come on easy rider, give me something for my pain,' you know he isn't some rock star toying with the vocabulary of poor bluesmen. This is real pain he's talking about. You can also hear it in the unearthly guitar solo that rips the songs apart. 'Easy Rider,' explains Rea, 'comes from the days following the operation.'

Rea, however, believes he's always had the blues. 'When you're in Middlesbrough and your dad's ice-cream shop is four doors down from the unemployment exchange, and on a Wednesday afternoon the rest of the town shuts, but your dad won't let you shut and you only get the drunks from the unemployment exchange…' He shudders at the memory. 'I had this huge fear that I'd spend my life in that shop. I used to go upstairs to check the stock. And I'd sit there playing the guitar and it would stop me from getting frightened.' The idea of music as a way of exorcising your fears is revisited on Dancing the Blues Away, an upbeat track on the new album that – (7) don't tell EastWest – is surprisingly radio-friendly. Even playing the blues, it seems, Rea can't help creating catchy tunes.

---

1 What was the writer's first reaction to Rea's new album?
   A He preferred its length to that of his other work.
   B He liked the music but not the lyrics.
   C It would change public opinion about the musician.
   D It would appeal to a wide audience.

2 Before meeting Rea, the writer was concerned that
   A his remarks had adversely affected the musician's career.
   B the musician might have taken his remarks too seriously.
   C his opinions would be considered too superficial.
   D he might be accused of being hypocritical.

3 What does the writer say about Rea's musical career?
   A Rea treated music like any normal job.
   B Rea felt it had become too business oriented.
   C It gave Rea the chance to play with top musicians.
   D Rea was compared to musicians he had never emulated.

4 What do we learn about Rea's relationship with his former record company?
   A He felt they were demanding too much of him.
   B He was always very critical of their approach to the music business.
   C They thought he was incapable of writing any other type of music.
   D He failed to impose his own will in his dealings with them.

5 What does Rea say about his new album?
   A It was recorded during a concert.
   B He wanted the title of it to be his name.
   C He is unsure of its potential for commercial success.
   D It was delayed because of his poor health.

6 What does the writer say about the new album?
   A The beginning is rather too loud and overdramatic.
   B Rea has adapted his voice to suit the style of music.
   C It contains material which is based on personal experience.
   D The lyrics are faithful copies of those used by early blues artists.

7 The writer believes that 'Dancing the Blues Away'
   A will have popular appeal.
   B is entirely different to the rest of the album.
   C is an attempt by Rea to come to terms with his past.
   D will not please his former record company.

Part 2: Gapped text

1 Part 2 consists of a text from which six paragraphs have been removed and placed in a different order after the text. You have to decide which gap in the text each paragraph has been removed from.

This task tests your understanding of text structure and your ability to predict how a text will develop. It is important, therefore, that you first familiarize yourself fully with the base text (the main text with the gaps) in order to gain an overall idea of the structure and content of the text.

2 ⬤ Look at the headline and introductory sentence for the newspaper article. How do you think you make the perfect pizza? What could go wrong when making one?

3 Read through the base text (ignoring the questions in italics). Are any of your ideas from exercise 2 mentioned?

4 Read the base text again. For each gap in the base text, read the paragraphs on either side of it, together with the questions in italics, to help you predict the general content of the missing paragraph.

5 For questions **1–6**, choose which of the paragraphs **A–G** fit into the numbered gaps in the article. There is one extra paragraph which does not fit any of the gaps.

How to go about it

- Read all the paragraphs before you start to make any choices.
- As you decide on your answers, underline words or phrases in the base text which show links with the missing paragraphs. Relevant parts of the missing paragraphs have already been underlined to help you.
- Check your answers by reading through the whole article again to ensure that it makes sense. Check that the extra paragraph does not fit into any of the gaps.

A Francesco, on the other hand, made it all look so easy. He had trained as a baker in his native Sardinia before graduating to pizzas at home and finally in London. He showed me what to do again and I tried to take it in. The chilled dough balls, pre-weighed at 170g, were all ready in a special fridge below the work counter. The dough was sticky, and Francesco worked fast.

B There was a point away from the fire where the pizzas go when they are first put in. I plunged the long handle deep inside and, feeling the heat on my arms, brought it back sharply. The pizza slid off the paddle and landed on the target area. Francesco quickly made one of his own to act as a comparison.

C On my next attempt, I quickly got to the shaping stage with half the pizza hanging over the edge. This was where I had gone wrong. Using only the bottom edge of my hands with my fingers working the edges I started to do the breast stroke: fingers together, fingers apart, working and stretching. It began to work.

D Instead, the dough was carefully placed on the steel work surface with one half of it hanging over the edge. One hand pressed and stretched and the other pulled in the opposite direction. Before you could say 'pizza Margherita' there was a perfect circle ready to be topped.

E This became clear later when the finished item was placed in the deep oven, enduring temperatures I'd never thought possible in a kitchen. For now, though, as I waited for my base to settle, Francesco revealed one or two secrets about the whole dough-making process.

F Silently Francesco reached for his pizza paddle, scooped up my work and threw it disdainfully into the red-hot stone oven where it burnt rapidly on top of a funeral pyre of burning wood. I made up my mind that my future attempts would be more worthy of the long traditions of pizza making.

G The stage was all mine. I had been told to concentrate on the edges using the flat edge of my hand under my little finger. I started to work the dough and tried to stretch it. It did begin to take shape, but as soon as I let it go it just went back again and didn't get any bigger. I felt more and more eyes on me.

The perils of pizza making

It looks easy but it really isn't, says Chandos Elletson, whose efforts turned out far from perfect.

My first pizza was cremated. I hadn't even got to the toppings, let alone the tossing stage. I was stuck on the rolling-out bit. I fast discovered that specialist pizza chefs – pizzaioli – don't use rolling pins, they use their hands to shape the dough into perfect circles. Francesco Sarritzu, the pizzaiolo at The Park restaurant in Queen's Park, London, where I went to be a trainee for the evening, took one look at my sorry effort and sighed. It wasn't so much a circle as an early map of the world.

1

How might the author have felt at the result of his first attempt?

What do you think he did with his 'map of the world'?

For real, or original, pizza making is an age-old craft, and the pizzaiolo a true craftsman. He is at once baker, fire stoker and cook. A wood-burning oven is also an essential part of the proceedings. However, before the pizzas get to the fire they have to be properly shaped and it was this procedure that I was struggling with.

2

*In the paragraph which follows this gap, what or who does **it** in the first sentence, and **he** in the third, refer to? (These will be mentioned in the missing paragraph.)*

*Do you think **he** is 'struggling' like the author?*

First it was dropped into a large pile of flour and then it was mixed with a small handful of polenta. From here it was all hands. He pressed out the dough with his fingers all the time working in flour and pressing the edges out until a small round circle had emerged. Francesco then threw it into his hands, twirling it to shake off the excess flour. He did not toss it in the air. 'Tossing is for show,' he said disdainfully. 'It is not necessary.'

3

Do you think Francesco has finished making his pizza base yet?

Now it was my turn. I moved nervously into position and scooped up a piece of dough from its snug tray. It immediately stuck to my fingers and when I threw it at the flour it just remained stuck. I had to pull it off. The next bit is easy, or so it seems, but unless you follow the right procedure, you sow the seeds of later failure. The object is to press out the edges, not the centre, using the flour to dry out the stickiness. However, the temptation to press everything in sight to make it stretch into a circular shape is too strong; before I knew it I had thick edges and a thin centre.

I did as Francesco had done and slapped it with the palm of my hand. This made me feel better so I did it again. Next I did some twirling and the flour showered everywhere. Then I noticed, to my horror, that some customers were watching me. 'Shall we watch the man make the pizza?' a man asked his young daughter, who he was holding in his arms.

4

What might the effect be on the author of having customers watching him?

Then the worst thing of all happened: a hole appeared in the centre. 'Look Daddy. There's a hole,' the little girl said. I looked up from my work crestfallen. I was defeated. 'It's my first evening,' I admitted. Francesco stepped in with the paddle and my second pizza went where the first one had gone: on the fire. We all watched it go up in flames. I was baffled and embarrassed, but I thought I was on to something.

5

How well does the author progress in the missing paragraph for this gap?

Using the information in the paragraph before this gap, go back to gap 1 and answer the second question in italics.

Francesco noticed and applauded. My base was not perfectly round or even but it was certainly an improvement. Having topped it with a thin smear of tomato sauce and some mozzarella, it was time to get it onto the paddle. With one determined shove the pizza went on and I asked Francesco to show me the best place for it in the oven.

6

What will probably be mentioned in the missing paragraph for this gap?

*What do the pronouns **they**, **mine** and **his** in the paragraph following this gap refer to?*

When they were done we had a tasting: mine was tough and crunchy in places, not bad in others. His was perfectly crispy and soft everywhere. He said: 'The base must be absolutely even and not overworked. When you work too hard it gets tough.' Orders from the restaurant started to come in and as I watched Francesco work, Rupert, the restaurant manager, ambled over. 'You can start singing any time,' he said casually. 'What?' 'Oh, didn't we tell you? Francesco usually sings opera as he works.' It was at that moment that this trainee headed for the train.

Part 4: Multiple matching

1 Part 4 consists of a text or several short texts preceded by questions or statements which you have to match with the corresponding information in the text.

The task requires you to scan the text in order to find the specific information you need. It is **not** necessary to read every word in the text to complete the task.

2 Read through the texts on page 47 to get a general idea of their content.

What is your impression of the people who wrote the texts?

3 For questions **1–15**, choose from the ski slopes **A–E.** The slopes may be chosen more than once. Where more than one answer is required, these may be given **in any order**.

What to expect in the exam

- Each correct answer in Part 4 receives one mark.

How to go about it

- Underline key words in the statements before the text. Some of these have been done for you.
- Scan each of the texts, looking for information which matches that contained in the statements. *The statements for text A have been given. For each of these statements, underline and label the relevant section of the text, as in the example for number 2. Then do the same for texts B–E. You may need to read more than one section of a particular text to find an answer.*
- If there are any statements you have not matched, scan the texts again looking for the information you need.

In which text is the following mentioned?

a feature of the run which in other circumstances can pose problems	1 ___	
the <u>need</u> to <u>select</u> a run which is <u>not overly difficult</u>	2 _A_	
regret at not being able to take in the scenery	3 ___	
the possibility for the skier to extend the run by taking an alternative route	4 ___	
a warning about the existence of hidden dangers	5 ___	
the protection offered to skiers on one section of the run	6 ___	
the <u>main challenge</u> for skiers who have <u>just learnt the essential skills</u>	7 _A_	
the quiet location of the run	8 ___	
the extreme importance attached by the resort to the maintenance of its runs	9 ___	
the proximity of the run to a number of impressive mountains	10 ___	
the <u>sense of progress</u> experienced by the skier who completes the run for the <u>first time</u>	11 _A_	
the need to be accompanied by someone who is familiar with the run	12 ___	13 ___
the outstanding conditions towards the top of the run	14 ___	
the <u>possibility</u> of a skier's <u>confidence</u> being <u>affected</u> for a <u>long period</u>	15 _A_	

Slopes at the top of the world

Five snow professionals tell us about some of the top ski slopes, each in its own way a world-beater.

A Ali Ross – Parsenn, Davos

Once they've mastered the basics, the big hurdle for skiers is the run that gives them their first serious mountain experience. It's often a dangerous period – if they try something too hard, they could end up scaring themselves silly, and it could take them years to learn how to enjoy themselves on skis again. It's important to pick a run that isn't too tough. Parsenn, in Davos, Switzerland is a beautiful run that seems to go on for ever, all the way from the Weissfluhjoch down to Klosters. In fact, it's about 10km long, and the vertical drop is nearly 1,500m – it will take most intermediate skiers most of the morning to get up and down again. It's nice and wide, and you never feel as if it's pushing you beyond your limits. Ski it once, and you'll feel you've finally made it into the ranks of the grown-ups.

B Caroline Stuart–Taylor – Ventina, Cervinia

On the whole, Italian resorts have fairly good standards of piste preparation, but Cervinia is special. There, they are fanatical about their piste-grooming. One of the runs at this resort, the Ventina, is an absolute classic. It runs from the top of the Plateau Rosa cable car, and you can follow it for 8km down to the resort, or branch off towards Valtournenche and go even further. It's not so flat that it's boring, and not so steep that it's intimidating, and because of the grooming, there's next to no risk of any nasty surprises. It's perfect for high-speed cruising and practising your turns. Other than at weekends, it tends not to be very crowded, and the quality of the snow, especially along the upper reaches, is superb.

C Becci Malthouse – Bruson, near Verbier

The best snowboarding run I know has to be in Bruson, Switzerland. Not many people know about this place, which is tucked away across the valley from Verbier. The run is off piste, and a guide is a must the first time you attempt it. There's a fantastic view from the top back towards Verbier, and – provided nobody else has read this – you'll get a good idea of how busy it is over there compared to your side of the valley. What I love about this run is that it's got the lot: cornices, wind lips, powder fields and trees. Normally, trees can be tricky for snowboarders, but these are just right. The slope drops steeply enough that you never get stuck on flat sections, and the branches are not so close together that you have to fight your way through.

D Jamie Strachan – Pas de Chevre, Chamonix

The Pas de Chevre, in Chamonix, France, runs from the top of the Grands Montets chairlift all the way down to Chamonix, but to do it, you must have a guide to show you the way. Most of the good skiing in the area is on glaciers, so you'll need to beware of the extra hazards that this throws up, such as crevasses lurking unseen. It's an amazing run – at least 15km long – and it takes you through a landscape that doesn't seem to belong on this planet. Towering above you is the jagged tooth of the Aiguille du Dru, one of the finest peaks in Europe, and in front of you are the hanging seracs of the glacier – big pillars of ice formed as it breaks up on its way down the valley. It will leave you speechless.

E Chris Gill – Schilthorn, Murren

Every January, 1,800 amateurs queue up at the top of the Schilthorn, in Murren, Switzerland, for one of the maddest ski races: the Inferno. It runs down a 16km course with a vertical drop of more than 2,000m. One of the most difficult stretches of the course is called the Kanonenrohr – the Gun Barrel. This is a narrow shelf with a rock wall on one side and a sheer drop on the other, screened with safety nets. It's not the kind of place you start admiring the view – which is a shame, because just before you enter it, you are confronted by one of the most magnificent sights in the Alps: a dramatic close-up of the imposing Eiger, Monch and Jungfrau, which rise up on the other side of the valley. The top half of the course is one of my favourite runs; a lovely mix of groomed black sections, generous reds and challenging moguls. And that view always stops me in my tracks.

Language Focus 1: Punctuation

1 ○ Read the following quotations on the theme of work. Comment on each one with your partner, saying whether you like or dislike it, agree or disagree with it. Give reasons for your opinions.

> 1 "Work is a necessary evil to be avoided.

Mark Twain

> 2 "Hard work never killed anybody, but why take a chance."

Charlie McCarthy

> 3 "People, who work sitting down get paid more than people who work standing up."

Ogden Nash

> 4 "I like work; it fascinates me I can sit and look at it for hours."

Jerome K. Jerome

> 5 "A lot of fellows nowadays have a BA, MD or PhD. Unfortunately, they dont have a JOB."

Fats Domino

> 6 "Its not the hours you put in your work that counts, it's the work you put in the hours."

Sam Ewing

> 7 "Far and away the best prize that life offer's is the chance to work hard at work worth doing."

Theodore Roosevelt

2 Each of the quotations above contains one punctuation mistake. Find the mistakes and correct them.

ⓖ Read more about punctuation in the Grammar reference on page 218.

3 Punctuate the following newspaper article on working trends in Britain. Add capital letters where necessary.

HOME-WORKING

if you had the choice would you prefer to work from home or in an office British workers seem to be in no doubt one in four of them has given up commuting to the office in favour of a more domestic working environment and the figure is growing

the number of home-workers is likely to increase by more than 50% over the next five years claimed a spokesperson for Datamonitor the London-based market research company as a result of this trend consumers will spend a great deal less on certain goods and services transport petrol eating out and drinks moreover because home-workers usually take fewer showers the sale of personal care products such as deodorants and soap will also be affected

the study which shows that home-workers tend to be the more highly qualified professionals in a company says that firms are in danger of losing their best employees if they do not allow home-working unfortunately however there are some who abuse the trust which has been placed in them Datamonitor discovered that many like to watch television listen to the radio and drink alcohol while they work

4 Check your answer with the suggested version on page 206.

5 ○ What are the advantages and disadvantages of home-working?

Would you prefer to work from home?

Writing 1:
CAE Part 2

Formal letters: application

1 Read the following job advertisement and make a list of the characteristics the ideal candidate would possess.

2 The following is a letter of application for the job advertised in exercise 1. In questions **1–15**, **two** of the alternatives can be used in each space. Cross out the alternative which **cannot** be used. The exercise begins with an example (**0**).

Personal Assistant to Insurance Executive

A dynamic PA is required to work for this very busy Insurance Executive. Duties include correspondence, diary management and booking travel. There will also be a great deal of contact with business people at a high level. A minimum of five years' related experience is essential.

---

(0) *Dear Sir/ ~~Dear Executive~~ / Dear Sir or Madam*

I am writing in (1) *reply/apply/response* to your advertisement which appears in today's edition of the Business Times newspaper.

As you (2) *must/can/will* see from my (3) *enclosed/attached/enveloped* CV, I have spent the last six years working at the Tadwell branch of the Excel Insurance Company. I joined the branch as trainee secretary after leaving school and two years ago I was (4) *appointed/destined/promoted* to the (5) *place/position/post* of office manager, in charge of a (6) *staff/team/number* of seven. My (7) *duties/chores/responsibilities* range from the day-to-day (8) *conduct/management/running* of the office to staff training and new recruitment. I am also responsible for (9) *organizing/making/sorting* travel arrangements for management and visiting officials.

I am now interested in working in a more dynamic environment and given the experience I have (10) *acquired/gained/learned* at Excel, I consider myself well equipped to (11) *respond to/take up/rise for* the challenge offered by the post of Personal Assistant. I also feel I (12) *have/own/possess* the necessary personal qualities to (13) *meet/complete/deal with* the demands of the job; I have included in the CV the contact details of my branch manager, who would be (14) *welcome/willing/pleased* to provide you with a character reference.

I am available for interview at any time which might be convenient to you and would be able to start work after serving out the two months' notice in my (15) *actual/current/present* job.

I look forward to hearing from you.

Yours faithfully

Lara Goodrich

---

3 Write your own **letter of application** in **220–260** words for the following job, which you see advertised in an English-language magazine in your country.

Language School Receptionist

Busy and expanding language school with a reputation for professional standards and friendly service requires two receptionists for its new centre in the north of England. Successful candidates will have a genuine interest in people and be able to work under pressure. They will also be reasonably fluent in both spoken and written English. IT skills an advantage. Previous experience useful but not essential.

How to go about it

- Make notes about relevant experience, skills and personal qualities which would make you suitable for the job. Think also about your reasons for applying. Remember, you can invent information.
- Make a paragraph plan of your letter. Look back at Lara Goodrich's application; how has she organized her information into paragraphs?
- Underline any words and expressions in Lara's application which you might find useful.

Listening 1:
CAE Part 4

Multiple matching

1 ○ What advice would you give to someone going for a job interview?

Example: Dress smartly.

2 ◉ **1.11–1.15** You will hear five short extracts in which different people are talking about interviews they attended. **While you listen you must complete both tasks.**

How to go about it

- Read through both tasks carefully before you start to listen. Note that in Task One, you are listening for the **advice** the person received, not what they actually did.
- Try to predict the language you might hear for each prompt.
  Example:
  A Mind your body language - the way you sit or stand; what you do with your arms, hands and legs.
- Concentrate mainly, but not exclusively, on Task One the first time you listen. The second time you listen, give more attention to Task Two.
- Don't leave any questions unanswered.

TASK ONE

For questions 1–5, choose from the list **A–H** the advice each speaker received.

A mind your body language

B arrive early for the interview

C wear the right clothes

D show interest in the prospective employer

E hide your enthusiasm for the job

F practise the interview beforehand

G think of an unusual situation

H control your nerves

	1
	2
	3
	4
	5

TASK TWO

For questions 6–10, choose from the list **A–H** the problem each speaker encountered.

A feeling unwell

B having the wrong information

C not having the right personality

D arriving late for the interview

E having a slight accident

F not having the right qualifications

G being unable to answer questions

H being unhappy about the pay

	6
	7
	8
	9
	10

Don't forget!

- There are two questions for each speaker; one in Task One and one in Task Two. Questions 1 and 6 correspond to the first speaker; questions 2 and 7 to the second speaker, and so on.
- Three of the prompts in each task are not used.

3 ○ If you have had an interview or an oral examination, tell your partner about how you prepared for it, what you remember about the interview and what the outcome was.

If you have never had an interview, tell your partner what you would fear most about going for an interview and what you would do to overcome this fear.

Language focus 2: Gerunds and infinitives

A Review

The following sentences are all from the listening. Discuss with your partner the reasons why the words underlined are in the gerund or the infinitive.

Example:
1 *The noun 'way' is often followed by the infinitive. 'Going' is in the gerund because it follows the preposition 'by'; all prepositions take the -ing form of a verb.*

1 The best way <u>to prepare</u> for an interview is by <u>going</u> to the company's website.
2 They can <u>see</u> you've done your homework.
3 You're not <u>to get</u> all uptight and on edge.
4 <u>Projecting</u> self-confidence at an interview is vital for success.
5 I put on my best suit <u>to give</u> me that confidence.
6 I think I managed <u>to hide</u> it.
7 It's advisable <u>to lean</u> forward.
8 They recommended <u>imagining</u> the interviewer in the bath.

B Common problems

1 In **1–8** below there is a mistake in one of the two sentences. Find the mistake and correct it.

Example: *feeling*
a *You can't help ~~to feel~~ sorry for John, losing his job like that.*
b *The company says it'll help him to find another, but it's not the same.*

1 a I have been made to feel very welcome in my new job.
   b They even let me to leave early so I can pick up my son from school.
2 a It's taken me time to adjust to working in an open-plan office.
   b I still can't get used to share the same working space with the boss.
3 a It's not worth to make an effort in my job – the pay is so low.
   b And there's certainly no point taking work home at weekends.
4 a We appreciate your agreeing to give a talk at the conference.
   b We would like that you are our guest for dinner after your talk.
5 a As soon as I get to work all the phones start ringing.
   b They don't stop to ring all day.
6 a I don't mind to go to the office meal tonight…
   b … but I really don't feel like having a cocktail with the boss beforehand.
7 a I advised him to buy a new suit for his interview.
   b I also recommended to have a haircut.
8 a We were to have received a pay rise this year.
   b Management have admitted to have broken their promise to increase salaries.

Check your ideas in the Grammar reference on page 219.

2 Work with a partner. Talk to each other about something

- you would miss being able to do if you lived abroad.
- you would refuse to do under any circumstances.
- you remember doing when you were a very small child.
- you are planning to do in the next few months.
- you regret doing.
- your parents didn't let you do as a child.
- you always have difficulty doing.
- you often forget to do.

C Nouns followed by the infinitive

Each of the nouns in the box can be followed by the infinitive with *to*. For each question **1–5**, use the information in the informal sentence **a** to complete the gaps in the formal sentence **b**, using the words in the box. You should use each word once only.

effort	attempts	willingness	opportunity
	capacity	ability	decision
	determination	tendency	refusal

1 a It's very obvious that he really wants to get on in the company and he's done a lot to get over his shyness.
   b He has shown a clear _____ to make progress in the company and he has made a great _____ to overcome his shyness.
2 a She usually thinks it's her fault if work doesn't get done on time, even though I've tried to tell her several times it's not true.
   b She has a _____ to blame herself if deadlines are not met, despite my various _____ to persuade her otherwise.
3 a He never misses a chance to become a better salesman and what I admire most is the fact that he doesn't get fed up if things aren't going well.
   b He takes advantage of every _____ to develop as a salesman, and his _____ to become despondent in the face of difficulties is his most admirable quality.
4 a He also doesn't seem very capable of controlling his pupils and I think he's right to want to get out of teaching.
   b Furthermore, he seems to lack the _____ to maintain classroom discipline, and I can only support his _____ to leave the teaching profession.
5 a The best things about her are that she's prepared to take on new challenges and she can handle stressful situations.
   b Her greatest strengths are her _____ to accept new challenges and her _____ to cope with pressure.

Multiple matching

1 ⬭ What do you understand by the title of the article: 'The Fast Track to Burnout'?

What causes some employees to burn out?

2 You are going to read a magazine interview with four young executives who left their jobs. For questions **1–15**, choose from the executives **A–D**.

What to expect in the exam

- Part 4 tasks are multiple-matching tasks. There are fifteen questions in total.
- The text may be continuous or consist of a group of shorter texts, or sections of text. The following Part 4 text has been divided into sections.

How to go about it

- Re-read **How to go about it** on page 24 of Unit 2.
- To help you with numbers **1–4** below, key words in the questions have been underlined, together with the relevant parts of the text.
- Now look at numbers **5–15** and underline the key words in the questions in the same way. Then underline the parts of the text which provide the answers.

Of which young executive is the following true?

Her sense of <u>being unimportant</u> did not change once <u>she had been promoted</u>.	1 ___
Her <u>current job</u> does not provide her with a <u>regular income</u>.	2 ___
She felt that her <u>colleagues</u> were being <u>unco-operative on purpose</u>.	3 ___
A <u>project</u> that she was working on <u>did not turn out the way she expected</u>.	4 ___
She admits to showing off the things she could afford to buy with her high salary.	5 ___
She accepted the job because of the benefits that were additional to the salary.	6 ___
She suggests that her young age meant she was unable to cope with a stressful situation.	7 ___
She was trying to find a way to leave the company before she received a promotion.	8 ___
The people she worked with could not relate to a decision she had made.	9 ___
She suggests a lack of money in her childhood made a high salary more desirable.	10 ___
She believes that other people could have done her job equally well.	11 ___
She does not have any negative feelings towards the company she worked for.	12 ___
The feelings she had towards her promotion quickly changed.	13 ___
One of her qualities also disadvantaged her in a certain way.	14 ___
She wanted more freedom while she was still at a young age.	15 ___

The Fast Track to Burnout

An increasing number of young executives are giving up their corporate positions after experiencing an overload of pressure and dissatisfaction with what they imagined would be a dream career. Kate Martins talks to four young people who turned their backs on high salaries and even higher expectations. Here's how to beat it.

A Tanya Burrows bears no grudge towards the corporation that rewarded her with five promotions within the same number of years. 'At twenty-seven, I was able to buy my own luxury apartment,' she says. 'For that reason I'll always be grateful to them.' Tanya admits that the high salary that came with each promotion was irresistible. 'We weren't poor but I don't think my parents ever bought anything that wasn't secondhand. That definitely played a role in my motivation. When someone's saying you can negotiate your own salary, it's hard to say no.' So what changed for Tanya? 'Honestly, I got sick of the materialism. I got sucked in too at first – you'd make sure other people knew what designer labels you were wearing, that they could see your cell phone was top of the range … but it just wore thin for me.' Tanya decided to quit <u>and pursue her real passion for photography. 'It doesn't offer much financial security as you don't know when you'll get your next contract,</u> but I get to work in far more inspiring environments,' she says.

B Lily Tan left university with an MBA distinction and was quickly snapped up by a major retail chain. In just five years she achieved a senior management position and after receiving news of the promotion she was elated. 'I rang round just about everyone I could think of,' she laughs. 'But the next day I felt nothing. I had no inclination to get out of bed and face the constant pressure.' Despite her sudden disillusionment, she continued to persevere <u>and was the brains behind a new strategy. 'Everyone seemed to be in favour of it at the planning stage,' she says. But during the implementation stage, unforeseen problems arose</u> and eventually the strategy was abandoned. Lily's next performance appraisal gave her a really low rating which she found devastating. The whole experience was quite traumatizing and I was too emotionally immature to deal with it.' It wasn't long before Lily left and set up her own recruitment company which is now flourishing. She still regrets her discovery that there is no such thing as team spirit when one of the members makes a mistake.

C Jane Dawson graduated top of her class in a Bachelor of Business (Finance) degree and was offered a contract by three major investment companies. She accepted the one that was offering perks such as free tickets to major sporting events and a flash company car. Just like the three other young high-flyers in these interviews, Jane's potential for leadership was quickly noted and she found herself promoted to team leader within six months. But, exceptionally, in her case, she had already been looking for an escape route. 'Sure it was good money but the hours were ridiculous. I felt I should have been carefree at that age but the burden of responsibility was enormous. I felt trapped.' <u>Despite the fact that she'd been elevated to senior analyst, Jane still felt anonymous within the giant corporation. 'It was a real feeling of being the small cog in a big machine. Nothing I did really mattered.'</u> She forced herself to stay on for another year, but then nervously asked for a sabbatical. To her amazement, her department head agreed. 'I guess they knew I'd reached burnout and didn't want to lose me altogether – but there were plenty of workmates perfectly able to step into my shoes,' she admits. She spent the year travelling and working on community projects in developing countries. By the time Jane was due to return, she knew she was in the wrong job. She applied to work for an aid organization, where she says 'At last I feel I'm doing something worthwhile.'

D Natalie Copeland was signed up to work for a leading PR consultancy. She admits to being a perfectionist, an attribute which saw her rise through the ranks in no time. 'It's a weakness, too,' she says. 'It can mean that you're reluctant to delegate and end up with the pressure of doing it all yourself.' For the first few years, however, she had no problem with overtime and her performance appraisals were almost always flawless. But Natalie feels she committed 'career-suicide' by opting to getting married and have a child at twenty-five. 'My colleagues seemed utterly mystified and tried to talk me out of it.' And on her return to work Natalie felt instant resentment towards her. 'I had to leave promptly at the end of the working day to take care of my daughter Anita but would come in an hour early and work through my lunch hour. It made no difference,' she explains. 'They simply alienated me.' <u>By this she means that workmates were reluctant to update her on recent developments and withheld vital information on new projects.</u> With little support from her seniors either, and refusing to compromise her time with her family, Natalie handed in her notice and now works for a smaller PR company offering flexi-time.

◯ Reacting to the text

Do you sympathize with any of the four young executives? Why/why not?

Imagine you were a young executive. How would you feel about and react to:
- your colleagues showing off their wealth and possessions.
- a poor performance appraisal that you think is unfair.
- working much longer hours than most people you know.
- being excluded by people in your department.

Use of English:
CAE Part 4

Gapped sentences

1 In **1–8**, complete each of the collocations with a noun from the box.

favour role ranks pressure notice grudge position contract

1 to bear someone a _____ (A)
2 to play a _____ (A)
3 to achieve a (management) _____ (B)
4 to face _____ (B)
5 to be in _____ of something (B)
6 to be offered a _____ (C)
7 to rise through the _____ (D)
8 to hand in your _____ (D)

Check your answers in the reading text on page 53. The letters in brackets refer to the sections in which the collocations can be found.

2 Use context to work out the meanings of the collocations in exercise 1.

3 For questions **1–5**, think of one word only which can be used appropriately in all three sentences. All the words are either nouns or verbs from the collocations in exercise 1. Here is an example (**0**).

0 We don't take much _notice_ of the dress code at work and we tend to wear what we like.
I just saw the manager putting up a _notice_ advertising for a part-time sales assistant.
You didn't happen to _notice_ where I put that file, did you?

How to go about it

- Read all three sentences before you think of a possible word because:
  (a) this may prevent you from choosing a word that fits correctly in the first sentence but does not work in the second and/or third.
  (b) even if you have no idea what could go in the first sentence, you may be sure of the answer in the second or third.
- The word must have the same form – but could function, for example, as a noun, a verb, or an adjective, eg *a light / to light / light* (adj)

1 Karen's in a higher _____ than me at work so I don't feel I can criticize her.

Your sales figures have fallen so you're in no _____ to ask for a higher salary.

What's the company's _____ on hiring people without a suitable degree?

2 The characters in her novels _____ a strong resemblance to those in the *Harry Potter* series.

When you prepare your CV, _____ in mind that it should be informative but also concise.

I can't _____ the thought of taking on any more responsibility!

3 You need to _____ the fact that Bettina doesn't want to go out with you anymore!

The team will be attempting to climb the north _____ of the mountain today.

She was looking the other way so I asked her to turn round and _____ me.

4 The thing I like about our boss is that he never shows _____ to anyone – he treats us all the same.

If our clients want to postpone the meeting, the delay might actually work in our _____.

Thanks for answering my calls this morning – I owe you a _____.

5 The number of nurses leaving their profession is expected to _____ sharply.

The people were starving and had no choice but to _____ against the government.

In stunned silence, he watched his students _____ one by one from their seats and walk out of the room in protest.

Listening 2:
CAE Part 2

Sentence completion

1 ⬭ 'Too much to do and not enough time to do it.' To what extent does this apply to you? How well do you organize your time?

2 ◉ 1.16 You will hear part of a talk by time management expert David Markham. For questions **1–8**, complete the sentences.

Don't forget!

• Read through all the questions and predict the type of information required.

David says that the key to good time management is [1] .

It's important to have [2] expectations of what we can achieve.

David warns that [3] can prevent us achieving what we set out to do.

He recommends giving priority to [4] if we feel overwhelmed.

David advises against always trying to [5] in our work.

Housework requires the same [6] that we need to exercise at work.

David suggests we should reserve time for those pursuits we find [7] .

He says it is a mistake to think of the [8] as a form of relaxation.

3 ⬭ Do you manage 'to achieve the right balance between work and relaxation'?

Vocabulary: Time

1 Complete each gap in these extracts from the listening with a word from the box.

against	aside	for	for	in	off	up

1 … what you hope to achieve _____ **the time available**.
2 … you have to phone in sick and **take time** _____ **work**.
3 … if **time is** _____ **you**, if you're **pressed** _____ **time**, don't worry if what you produce is less than wonderful.
4 … what we all work for is to **make time** _____ **ourselves**, to **free** _____ **time for** the things we really want to do …
5 It's essential to **set** _____ **enough time** to pursue your interests …

2 The following words can all be used before the noun *time*. Add a word from the box to the appropriate group **a–f**, then discuss the possible context in which you might expect to use or hear the collocations.

half	flying	harvest	prime	record-breaking	sale	~~spare~~

Example:

free   leisure   ___*spare*___

You could use free time, leisure time and spare time when talking about what you do when you're not studying or working.

a kick-off   injury   _____
b qualifying   winning   _____
c arrival   departure   _____
d peak viewing   off-peak viewing _____
e opening   closing   _____
f sowing   milking   _____

3 Choose three of the collocations from exercise 2 and write a sentence for each, leaving a gap where the collocate of *time* should be. Then show your sentences to your partner who will try to guess the missing word(s).

Example

United scored the winning goal in the last minute of _____ time.

[Answer: *injury*]

Writing 2:
CAE Part 2

Character reference

1 The formal sentences in Section C on page 51 of this unit are all extracts from character references. Look at each one again and decide if it makes a positive or negative comment on the applicant.

2 Read the following character reference which was provided for Lara Goodrich's job application on page 49 of this unit. How strong are her chances of getting the job advertised on that page?

To whom it may concern

Lara Goodrich

As the manager of a local branch of the Excel Insurance Company I have known and worked with Lara Goodrich for nearly six years. During this short time she has progressed from her initial job as trainee secretary to her current position as office manager.

At each stage in her career here Lara has shown great enthusiasm for her work and has always managed to combine a friendly, outgoing nature with a dedicated, professional approach. Her willingness to respond to circumstances and work extra hours if required has been a major asset to the company.

She is at all times very approachable and enjoys the affection and respect of office colleagues and members of the sales team alike. She is also extremely adept at dealing with difficult customers. She can be sensitive to criticism and does have a tendency to take things to heart. However, this is a mark of her perfectionism, which generally manifests itself as a positive attribute.

Indeed, her ability to work accurately and with attention to detail is one of her greatest strengths, particularly in this field of work. She has excellent organizational skills and has been responsible for planning my own business trips, as well as making travel arrangements for visitors from other branches and Head Office. Naturally, with her experience she is familiar with all aspects of office work, and quickly assimilates new developments.

For these reasons I am confident that Lara has the right qualities for this job and have no hesitation in supporting her application.

3 a How has the character reference been organized? Summarize the content of each paragraph.
  b Underline any useful phrases which could be used in other character references.
  c Find an example of a negative quality, which is then turned to the applicant's advantage.

4 a Here is some useful language for character references. For each group of five words or phrases decide which word or phrase is different in some way from the others in the group.

Example: 1 'stubborn' is the only negative word in the group

1 have a/an
| helpful |
| sensitive |
| easy-going |
| stubborn |
| determined |
nature

2 show great
| potential |
| reluctance |
| dedication |
| ability |
| patience |

3
| lack |
| develop |
| display |
| possess |
| show |
the right personal **qualities**

4 have a (strong) **tendency to**
| be domineering |
| lose one's temper |
| become ill |
| worry over detail |
| avoid responsibility |

5 have/develop
advanced	computer
excellent	secretarial
outstanding	management
poor	parenting
the necessary	communication
skills

6 adopt a/an
| cautious |
| energetic |
| enthusiastic |
| slapdash |
| positive |
approach to one's work

b Arrange the adjectives of personality in section B on page 211 into two groups, positive and negative.

5 Read the following Part 2 writing task.

A friend of yours has applied for a job as a local guide for a London-based holiday company, which specializes in tours in your country for elderly British people. You have been asked to write a character reference for your friend, commenting on his or her previous experience, relevant knowledge and any personal qualities which might be useful for the job.

Write your **character reference** in **220–260** words.

How to go about it

- Make a list of the personal qualities, knowledge and experience that someone doing this job should have. Consider giving your friend a more negative attribute, as in the model, to add authenticity to the reference.
- Plan your answer to the question, organizing your ideas into suitable paragraphs.
- Write your answer using some of the language you have seen in this section.

④ Review

Word combinations

For sentences **1–10**, underline the correct alternative.

1 The day after his lottery win George *left out/handed in/gave up/put through* his notice at work.

2 The reason I've never hired a babysitter is that I couldn't *bear/support/agree/approve* the thought of leaving Sammy alone with a complete stranger.

3 I'm sorry, I can't deal with it now – I'm a little *delayed/pressed/late/short* for time.

4 None of the TV stations here put educational programmes on at peak *showing/sighting/seeing/viewing* times.

5 You should *give/find/set/keep* aside at least half an hour a week to read an English newspaper or magazine.

6 Write on the other side of the paper if you can't fit everything into the space *free/spare/available/providing*.

7 I was most impressed by his *way/tendency/ability/capacity* of thinking and expressing himself.

8 I *hate/avoid/admit/can't* help to say it, but I thought it was a terrible film.

9 Sarah has made *combined/predetermined/great/wide* efforts to catch up with the work she missed during her long absence.

10 We offer excellent promotion prospects and you will be given *every/much/great/all* opportunity to progress in your career.

Gerunds and infinitives

For **1–8**, complete each of the gaps with the correct form of the verb in brackets.

1 I really don't feel at all like _____ (go) out tonight, so it's no use _____ (try) _____ (get) me _____ (go) clubbing with you.

2 As soon as I stopped _____ (smoke), I started _____ (eat) more.

3 I couldn't help _____ (notice) you were wearing Gucci shoes. I hope you don't mind me _____ (ask), but how much were they?

4 I'll try _____ (not/keep) you for too long. I wouldn't like you _____ (think) I was wasting your time.

5 We really do appreciate you _____ (give) up your valuable time _____ (come) and _____ (talk) to us today, Mr Wilson.

6 I distinctly remember Steve _____ (agree) _____ (help) us with the move today. He either forgot _____ (set) his alarm, or he's found something better _____ (do).

7 The police made several unsuccessful attempts _____ (enter) the building, and even firefighters had difficulty _____ (cut) through the thick metal door.

8 He recommended me _____ (claim) compensation for unfair dismissal, but he suggested _____ (seek) legal advice first.

Key word transformations

For questions **1–8**, complete the second sentence so that it has a similar meaning to the first sentence, using the word given. **Do not change the word given.** You must use between **three** and **six** words, including the word given. Here is an example (**0**).

0 I felt that no one in the office really wanted to tell me how the new software programme worked.
RELUCTANT
I felt that everyone in the office _____was reluctant to explain_____ to me how the new software programme worked.

In this exercise, all of the target language can be found in the article *The Fast Track to Burnout*.

How to go about it

- Match the key information in the lead-in sentence with the information in the second sentence. Then decide what information is still missing from the second sentence – and how the key word can supply this.
- It is important to be accurate. For example, if the key word is a verb, you need to remember if it takes a preposition, and whether it is followed by the gerund or infinitive. If the key word is a noun, you may need to think of the verb that collocates with it.

Don't forget!

- Do not change the word given in capital letters.
- Write between three and six words.

1 My boss doesn't mind what time I start or finish work.
DIFFERENCE
It _____ what time I start or finish work.

2 It was Jane who came up with the idea for the sales promotion.
BRAINS
Jane _____ the sales promotion.

3 It's true that I like to work on tasks by myself.
BEING
I _____ a person who prefers to work alone.

4 Yesterday I informed my boss in writing that I would be leaving the company.
NOTICE
I _____ to my boss yesterday.

5 The day after I lost my job, I did not feel like getting out of bed.
INCLINATION
I _____ out of bed the day after losing my job.

6 It won't be easy for anyone to take over John's job when he retires.
SHOES
When John retires, it will be difficult for anyone _____.

7 The idea of flexi-time seemed to be popular with most of our senior managers.
FAVOUR
Most of our senior managers seemed _____ flexi-time.

8 Team spirit no longer exists after one member of a team makes a mistake,
SUCH
Once one member of a team makes a mistake there _____ as team spirit.

Long turn

- What might the people be talking about?
- How well do you think they get on with each other?

1 The photos above show people talking.

Student A:
Compare two of the pictures and say what the people might be talking about and how well you think they get on with each other.

Student B:
When your partner has finished talking about his or her pictures, compare the other two pictures in the same way.

2 Discuss together which people you think argue the most and which the least, giving reasons.

What to expect in the exam

- Student A's instructions also appear as written questions above the pictures.

Don't forget!

- Talk about the similarities and differences between the two pictures.
- Do not simply describe the pictures. Speculate about them as indicated in the instruction.
- Use a wide range of vocabulary. Look at the list of adjectives in section A on page 211 and note down those which might be useful when talking about your two pictures.

Listening 1:

Multiple choice

1 ● 1.17 You will hear part of a radio discussion about marriage in Britain. For questions **1–6**, choose the answer (**A**, **B**, **C** or **D**) which fits best according to what you hear.

1 According to Julie, why did she and Peter get married?
   A They both felt pressured to do so by their parents.
   B She felt morally obliged to accept Peter's proposal.
   C It seemed an appropriate course of action to take.
   D They hoped to inject more romance into their relationship.

2 What does Julie say was Peter's initial attitude towards the wedding?
   A He did not want a religious service.
   B He was more enthusiastic than Julie.
   C He was concerned about the expense.
   D He wanted it to be a small-scale event.

3 Bryan and Chrissie both felt that their relationship
   A did not meet with their parents' approval.
   B might have ended if they had not got married.
   C suffered as a result of financial problems.
   D could become stronger with time.

4 What does Julie say about arguments with her husband?
   A They do not have long-lasting effects.
   B They nearly ruined their honeymoon.
   C They can become quite violent.
   D They tend to go on for quite some time.

5 According to Bryan, what has created most problems in his current marriage?
   A working long hours
   B selling his business
   C living in a small flat
   D having three children

6 For a marriage to survive, Julie believes that couples need to be
   A optimistic.
   B honest.
   C flexible.
   D decisive.

2 ● Is marriage becoming more or less popular in your own country? How common is it for marriage to end in divorce?

What is your own attitude to marriage? For what reasons would/did you get married?

Do you prefer the idea of a religious wedding and 'the whole works' like Julie, or a civil ceremony, 'a quick registry-office job', like Bryan? Why?

Reading:
CAE Part 2

Gapped text

1 ○ When you are upset or have a problem, who do you turn to first for help and advice? Why?

Has this always been the case?

2 You are going to read a magazine article about the relationship between mothers and their sons. Six paragraphs have been removed from the extract. Choose from the paragraphs **A–G** the one which fits each gap (**1–6**). There is one extra paragraph which you do not need to use.

Don't forget!

- Read the whole of the base text and all the paragraphs before you start to make any choices.
- Underline words or phrases which show links between base text and missing paragraphs. Some parts of this base text have already been underlined to help you.
- Check your answers by reading the whole article through again to ensure that it makes sense. Check that the extra paragraph does not fit into any of the gaps.

MOTHERHOOD'S BEST-KEPT SECRET

One night, not so long ago, just as I was drifting off to sleep, the phone rang. It was my 19-year-old son, who is at university in Edinburgh, calling to say that he had broken up with his girlfriend at midnight and he had been wandering around the city ever since, not knowing what to do. I told him to catch the first train home. He arrived looking a wreck, but after a good sleep and some home cooking, he began to feel his old self again.

1	

Girls I knew then were fairly open with their mothers, but none of my male contemporaries would ever have admitted asking their mothers for advice. Despite all our talk about how important it was for men to let down their defences and learn how to express their feelings, most of us still secretly felt that any man who depended on his mother too much was a bit of a mummy's boy.

2	

But things don't work that way any more. In a world of short-term contracts, downsizing and redundancy, even the most promising and ambitious of our children will go through many career highs and lows during their twenties; and whenever they hit those depths, many of them will return to the nest. A typical son will continue to be at least partly dependent on his mother well past the age of 18.

3	

They're also better able to see through the mask of apparent self-confidence. When my boy was growing up, he always maintained a fairly invincible front. His early imaginary play involved sieges, ambushes and surprise attacks. His starting point, though, was always a danger against which he needed to defend himself. He used the games to convince himself that he could prevail.

4	

In his teens, he used many of these same tricks to keep me at bay. If I drove him anywhere to meet his friends, he insisted I drop him off out of sight of where they were waiting. There were girlfriends I never met, and phone conversations which were all in code. But occasionally, a confidential mood would come over him and he would tell me whatever happened to be on his mind.

5	

'And there's another important change,' she adds. 'Most of us took pains to reassure our sons that it was okay for them to show physical affection or cry when they were upset. If our boys are not so anxious now about showing their emotions, our efforts in this area have not been in vain.' This seems to be backed up by research, which shows that boys call their mothers on their mobile phones more than anyone else.

6	

What I didn't anticipate was for the same thing to happen with my son. I assumed I would lose him, just like all the experts said. It may be that they were wrong all along – that sons have always confided in their mothers – and just made sure that no one else knew. Have I stumbled on motherhood's best-kept secret? Even if I have, it doesn't diminish my sense of wonder. It's still like getting a present you never expected.

A These days, however, mothers can expect to be relied on almost indefinitely for the type of advice that calls on our experience of the outside world. A generation ago, it was accepted that sons would eventually leave their mothers to join the world of men and work. Mothers put their 18 years in and then opened the door to allow their sons to move into jobs for life.

B Friends told me that they, too, were getting the same volume of confidences. Celia Pyper says this is normal behaviour for today's boys: 'Our sons will tell us more than their fathers told their mothers, because we have brought them up to do so. Our norm has been to empathize with our children when they tell us about their actions or feelings, whereas the previous generation tended to be shocked.'

C Many of my friends are surprised at this reluctance of their 20-something sons to break away. But according to psychotherapist Celia Pyper, the mother–son intimacy is nothing new. 'Mums have always been easier to talk to,' she observes. 'They're more cuddly than their fathers, and sons realize early on that their mothers are more accepting of human frailty.'

D They are not in any doubt about how to respond to the situation. As one friend said of her rather reticent son: 'My job is to give my son courage.' And whilst we might welcome the chance to see more of our children, one does have the feeling that there is something anti-natural in all this.

E 'But don't assume that girls are any tougher than boys,' says Celia Pyper. 'Daughters need their mothers too.' Certainly, I know how much my own daughters need me. But this continuing mother–daughter bond is something I expected.

F The next afternoon he told me what had happened. Then he told me more. And more. And even more. A moment arrived when I couldn't help asking myself, should I be hearing all of this? It wasn't that I was shocked. He reminded me of myself in my own student years, but with one important difference – I would never ever have confided in my parents this way.

G As he got older and had to ride to school on a bus with other children, all too often there were situations in which he didn't. I had to teach him how to put up new defences so that his rougher classmates would not see his weaknesses.

⬤ **Reacting to the text**

To what extent have parent–children relationships changed in recent decades in your own country? Is the relationship very different for sons and daughters?

Vocabulary 1: Verb + Noun collocations

1 Find and circle the following nouns in the base text of the article on page 62. Write them in your vocabulary notebook, together with the verb which is used with each one. Record any adjectives which are used as well.

Example: maintain a fairly invincible front

front	feelings	pains
affection	emotions	

2 Find and circle the following phrasal verbs in the base text and with your partner, discuss their meaning in context.

drift off to	break up with	let down
go through	see through	

Record the verbs in your notebook, together with the noun which follows each one.

Language focus 1: Reference and ellipsis

A Reference

1 Find the following sentences in the reading text on pages 62 and 63 and decide what the words in **bold** refer to. Sentences a–d can be found in the paragraph of the base text immediately after the number given in brackets.

a Girls I knew **then** were fairly open with their mothers. (1)
b But things don't work **that way** any more. (2)
c In his teens, he used many of **these same tricks** to keep me at bay. (4)
d … our efforts in **this area** have not been in vain. (5)
e Celia Pyper says **this** is normal behaviour for today's boys. (paragraph B)
f Our sons will tell us more than their fathers told their mothers, because we have brought them up to **do so**. (paragraph B)

2 Words such as **do so** in **f** above are often called 'substitute words'; they substitute and avoid repetition of words and phrases which have already been used.
In **1–6** below, underline the correct substitute word. There is an example at the beginning (**0**).

0 She can't sing and *so/not/nor/never* can I.
1 A Do you think the weather will clear up by tomorrow?
  B I certainly hope *it/this/so/will*.
2 Can you lend me your helmet? If *yes/so/not/no*, don't worry – I'll borrow Mike's.
3 A Elaine wants to go to the beach.
  B I *want/go/am/do*, too.
4 Last Christmas it was orange trousers; this year she gave me these yellow *pair/ones/types/colour*!
5 Students passing the exam will automatically go into the next level. All *those/these/them/ones* that fail will have to repeat this *same/such/one/also*.
6 Suddenly, Brenda appeared. *Such/Then/When/This* was the moment he had been waiting for.

B Ellipsis

1 Sometimes, to avoid repetition, it is enough to simply omit a word or words. This is called ellipsis. Find the following sentences in the text and decide which word or words have been omitted.

a … and he had been wandering around the city ever since _____ . (introductory paragraph)
b Even if I have _____ , it doesn't diminish my sense of wonder. (6)
c As he got older and _____ had to ride to school on a bus with other children, all too often there were situations in which he didn't _____ . (paragraph G)

2 In **1–6** below, decide which words could be omitted to avoid repetition. There is an example at the beginning (**0**).

0 My brother was afraid of the dark but I wasn't ~~afraid of the dark~~.

1 A Do you think you'll be home before midnight?
  B I should be home before midnight.
2 I asked him to play a tune on the piano and he said he didn't want to play a tune on the piano.
3 She always comes to class on Tuesdays, but she hardly ever comes to class on Thursdays.
4 He left without saying goodbye. I have no idea why he left without saying goodbye.
5 A I have a feeling he was sacked from his last job.
  B Yes, he might well have been sacked from his last job.
6 He told me to apologize to her but I'd already apologized to her.

🔊 Read more about Reference and Ellipsis in the Grammar reference on pages 219 and 220.

3 Use substitute words and ellipsis to reduce the amount of repetition in the following text. There is an example at the beginning.

A family of teachers

her
For most of ~~my mother's~~ working life my mother taught chemistry in a secondary school. She always said the reason she had entered the teaching profession was because her father had virtually forced her to enter the teaching profession. Her father was a teacher and her mother was a teacher as well, though she herself had no intention of becoming a teacher. However, whereas my grandmother felt that my mother should only follow in their footsteps if my mother wanted to follow in their footsteps, my grandfather was determined that she should teach for a living – so she taught for a living.

She'd actually like to have become a pharmacist and run her own business, but she wasn't sufficiently qualified to become a pharmacist and have her own business. Apart from the fact that she wasn't sufficiently well qualified, she might well have had problems raising the necessary capital, and if she'd asked her father to lend her the necessary capital he probably wouldn't have lent her the necessary capital. I think my mother resented my grandfather for the pressure my grandfather had put on her, and my mother always encouraged me to make my own decisions. I made my own decisions – and now I work as a teacher, and my son works as a teacher too!

Vocabulary 2: Relationships

1 Complete each gap with the appropriate form of one of the verbs from the box. In each section **1–7**, the verb required for both spaces, **a** and **b**, is the same.

have	look	take	get	put	turn	keep

1 a Sally and my father _____ **on like a house on fire**; she loves going to see him.

b The noise from the neighbours is beginning to _____ **on my nerves**. I'm going to complain if it doesn't stop soon.

2 a His gambling problem has _____ **a great strain on** our relationship. I'm seriously thinking of leaving him.

b It was just a joke – I wasn't trying to _____ **you down**. I'd never deliberately set out to make anyone feel stupid.

3 a The maths teacher _____ **it in for me**; she was always giving me extra homework or keeping me behind after school.

b They _____ **a** fairly **rocky relationship** at first, but they're talking of getting married now.

4 a They set up in partnership in 1995, but **the relationship** _____ **sour** when Jim's love of whisky began to affect his work.

b When her father returned after nine years' absence, Sue did not have the heart to _____ **her back on him**.

5 a She'd always approved of his girlfriends before, but she never really _____ **to** Sandra.

b Sandra _____ **an instant dislike to** his mother, but she did her best to hide it.

6 a He's well liked, and a lot of the younger members of staff _____ **up to him** as a role model.

b I used to _____ **down on** art students at university, but now they're probably all earning far more than me.

7 a He _____ **himself to himself** on the holiday, eating alone and opting out of the organized excursions.

b I left over ten years ago, but I've managed to _____ **in touch with** some of my former colleagues.

2 Look at the expressions in **bold** in exercise 1 and decide whether each one has a negative or a positive meaning.

3 ⬤ Choose three of the expressions from exercise 1 and use them to talk about your own relationships, past or present.

Example:
*My cousin used to really **get on my nerves**. He was always phoning me up or coming to see me. He never gave me a moment's peace. Things are fine now – he went abroad to live so I just get the occasional letter.*

Speaking 2: CAE Part 3

Collaborative task

○ Here are some pictures showing people in different kinds of relationships.

Talk with your partner about the ways in which the two people in each relationship depend on each other. Then decide which two people depend on each other the most.

- In what ways do the two people in each relationship depend on each other?
- Which two people depend on each other the most?

Speaking 3: CAE Part 4

Further discussion

○ Discuss the following questions.

What other pairs of people are heavily dependent on one another?

What makes someone a good friend?

How far do you agree that older generations have more to teach young people than the other way round?

What are the advantages and disadvantages of working closely with the same person for a long time?

Some people prefer to spend time socializing with colleagues or friends, rather than their family. How about you?

How to go about it

- Give full answers to the questions, justifying your opinions. Remember, it is your language which is being assessed and not your ideas.
- Respond to what your partner says, as in Part 3, and develop the discussion.

Listening 2:
CAE Part 1

Multiple choice

1.18–1.20 You will hear three different extracts. For questions **1–6**, choose the answer (**A**, **B** or **C**) which fits best according to what you hear. There are two questions for each extract.

What to expect in the exam

- In Part 1 of the Listening Paper, the three extracts are all on different themes. However, for the task you are about to do, the extracts are all on the same theme of relationships.

Extract one

You hear part of an interview with an actress called Miriam Landers talking about a director she has worked with.

1 How does Miriam feel about acting in her new play?
  A She is nervous about the first night of the production.
  B She feels certain her performance will be convincing.
  C She is concerned that it will leave her feeling very tired.

2 What does Miriam say about her relationship with her director, Malcolm Rush?
  A He makes all the important decisions.
  B He always finds something to criticize.
  C He is prepared to listen to her suggestions.

Extract two

You hear two people on a film review programme talking about a new movie.

3 What do the two speakers agree about?
  A All the actors give very good performances.
  B The special effects are better than in similar films.
  C The relationship between the two characters is unoriginal.

4 What does the man say is true at the end of the film?
  A The detectives dislike each other.
  B The detectives do not trust each other.
  C The detectives decide to continue their partnership.

Extract three

You hear part of an interview with a professional rally driver.

5 What is worrying the driver about his next race?
  A the fact that he has a new co-driver
  B the possibility that he may lose control of the car
  C the risk of the car having engine failure

6 What does he say about the role of the co-driver?
  A A co-driver is supposed to keep the driver calm.
  B Many people do not appreciate what the co-driver docs.
  C It is always the co-driver's fault when accidents occur.

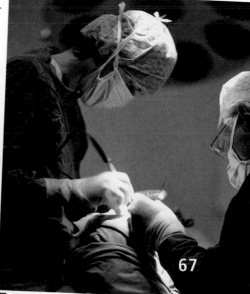

Language focus 2: Relative clauses

1 Read sentences **a–f** from the Listening. Then answer questions **1–4** below.

a It's Scott **who** has the map and the notes.

b Are you at all anxious or is opening night an occasion **which** no longer bothers you?

c You don't just learn the part, you live it, **which** takes away any fears you might have of not being able to persuade an audience you're real.

d We have two mismatched cops, one of **whom** plays by the rules and the other is a rebel.

e And the plot, **which** is actually quite sophisticated, keeps you guessing all the way through.

f Isn't this the kind of scenario we've seen too many times already?

1 What or who do each of the relative pronouns in **a–e** refer to?

2 Why are commas used before the relative pronoun in **c**, **d** and **e** but not in **a** or **b**?

3 Which of the relative pronouns could be replaced by **that**?

4 Which relative pronoun has been omitted from **f**? Why is it possible to leave it out of this sentence but not the others?

Check your ideas in the Grammar reference on page 220.

2 Complete each of the spaces with one of the words from the box. Each of the words can be used more than once. Then decide whether:

a commas are required or not

b **that** can be used instead of the word you have chosen

c the word can be omitted

who	which	whose	who's
where	why	what	

1 I went walking with my husband at the weekend _____ is something _____ we haven't done for a long time.

2 The novel is set in Kaunas _____ at that time was the capital of Lithuania. The initial chapters focus on Vitas's father _____ fiery temperament had a lasting effect on the boy.

3 _____ I'd like to know is what happened to that boxer _____ she was seeing. Are they still going out together?

4 He left all his money to a woman _____ had never shown him any affection. The reason _____ he did this has never been fully understood.

5 Her mother _____ hated city life longed to return to the village _____ she grew up in and _____ she still owned a small plot of land.

6 Is there anyone _____ got a car or _____ mum or dad could give us a lift?

Writing: **CAE Part 2**

Essays

1 Read the Part 2 task below and the model answer on page 69. Which of the three possible paragraph plans, **A**, **B** or **C**, does the essay follow?

You have recently had a class discussion on the relative importance of friends and families in modern society. Your teacher has asked you to write an essay, giving your opinion on the following statement.

Friendships have become more important than family relationships.

Write your **essay** in **220–260** words.

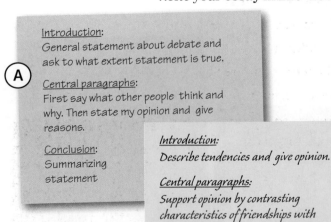

A
Introduction:
General statement about debate and ask to what extent statement is true.

Central paragraphs:
First say what other people think and why. Then state my opinion and give reasons.

Conclusion:
Summarizing statement

B
Introduction:
Introduce topic and describe tendencies.

Central paragraphs:
First describe ways in which friends are more important than family. Then describe ways in which family is more important than friends.

Conclusion:
Weigh up arguments given and state opinion. Give reason(s).

C
Introduction:
Describe tendencies and give opinion.

Central paragraphs:
Support opinion by contrasting characteristics of friendships with those of family.

Conclusion:
Restate opinion with general reason.

Friendships have become more important than family relationships.

Evidence seems to suggest that more value is attached to friendships nowadays than to family. A recent UK survey found that two-thirds of twentysomethings turn to friends first for advice. In addition, marriage is on the decline and increasingly, young people choose to live alone rather than in their parental home. Despite this, however, it would be wrong to argue that family relationships are less important than friendships.

The first point to bear in mind is that most friendships are short-lived. Many are formed at work or in clubs to which we belong: when we change jobs or cease to take part in a group activity, the friendships end. Our family, by contrast, is one of the few constants in a fast-changing world. We can be sure it will always be there.

A further point is that friendships require hard work and frequent attention, luxuries we often have little time for in our busy lives. Contact may be restricted to emails or text messages, secondary forms of communication which lack depth. Family ties, on the other hand, are based on unconditional love, guaranteeing the strength and survival of the relationship, even when regular visits are not possible.

Finally, friendships have limits. It is generally agreed, for example, that one should never lend money to friends, as this can only lead to problems. This is not, however, the case with families, who are usually more than willing to help in times of financial need.

To conclude, whilst some argue that the importance of the family has declined, it nevertheless remains the one solid relationship on which we can depend when everything else, including a friendship, fails. Clearly, the family is as important as it ever was.

2   Underline the following in the model answer.

   a   words and expressions which introduce a contrast

   b   words and expressions which introduce the writer's main points

   c   other useful words and expressions for writing essays

3   Write the expressions in the appropriate column. The first one has been done for you.

It would be wrong to argue that   There can be no doubt that
I would dispute the claim that   It is true to some extent that
It cannot be denied that   It is simply not the case that
It is my firm belief that   It is difficult to accept the idea that

Agreeing with a statement	Disagreeing with a statement
	It would be wrong to argue that

4   ⬤   Give your opinion on each of the following statements using an appropriate expression from exercise 3.

   1   Young people no longer respect their elders.

   2   It is better to live alone than in the parental home.

   3   The over-sixties have nothing to learn from the under-twenties.

   4   Marriage is no longer relevant in modern society.

   5   Parents should be punished for offences committed by their children.

   6   We have more means of communication, but we communicate less effectively.

5   Choose one of the statements in exercise 4 and write an **essay** for your teacher in **220–260** words, giving your opinion on the statement.

How to go about it

- Write a list of arguments for and against the statement.
- Decide whether you agree or disagree with the statement.
- Choose one of the paragraph plans in exercise 1 and adapt it to suit the statement you have chosen.
- Write your essay using some of the language you have seen in this writing section. Make sure you support your opinion with reasons.

Vocabulary

Complete each of the gaps with one of the words from the box. Some of the words will be required more than once.

up	down	in	on	through	to	for	with

1 I'm not surprised she feels humiliated – he's always putting her _____ in public like that.
2 You can't turn your back _____ me now, not after all I've done for you in the past!
3 The mortgage is putting a real strain ____ our finances.
4 The Brazilian striker never really took _____ his new coach and by the end of his first season he was asking for a transfer.
5 He really gets ____ my nerves. He never stops complaining.
6 My boss has always had it _____ _____ me; nothing I do is good enough for him.
7 Greta Garbo took such a strong dislike _____ her co-star Frederic March that she used to eat garlic before filming their love scenes.
8 My brother has done very well for himself, but he does tend to look _____ ____ me. Or is it my inferiority complex?
9 Samantha broke _____ _____ her boyfriend last week; they'd been going out with each other for three years.
10 Their marriage had been going _____ a bad patch and they'd decided to start divorce proceedings.

Reference and ellipsis

In each of the following sentences or dialogues there is one mistake. Find each mistake and correct it

1 We're going to buy a new washing machine – our old keeps breaking down.
2 **A** Do you think it'll rain?
   B I hope no – I haven't brought my umbrella.
3 **A** Haven't you been to see the Kandinsky exhibition?
   B No, I'm not interested in abstract art, and so isn't my wife.
4 Harry doesn't think they'll win at the next elections, but I do so.
5 Are you coming? Whether so, can you hurry up? We're already late.
6 **A** Do you think this milk is OK to drink?
   B It should – I only bought it two days ago.
7 **A** Put some salt in the potatoes, will you?
   B I've already!
8 It's a shame I can't go with you on Saturday – I'd really love.
9 We weren't consulted on this matter, and I think we should have.
10 He said he'd phone me today, but he hadn't. I'll give him a ring tomorrow.

Use of English:
CAE Part 2

Open cloze

Complete the following article by writing **one** word in each space. There is an example at the beginning (**0**).

GRANDPARENTS: THE NEW GENERATION

Always (**0**) _a_ sure source of affection, my grandparents (**1**) _____ hugely important figures in my life. They (**2**) _____ shower my sisters and me with sweets, indulgences and stories, telling tales about my parents as naughty children. When the last of (**3**) _____ died, we all wondered who would hold the family together.

People have relied on grandparents in Britain since the Industrial Revolution, (**4**) _____ whole families moved into cities from the country to get work in the new factories, taking grandmother along to look after the children. (**5**) _____ the fact that more grandmothers are working now, grandparents are still the backbone of childcare in Britain. They provide 44% of full-time care for pre-school children, (**6**) _____ makes you wonder how the country would manage (**7**) _____ them.

The traditional image of a grandparent is a smiling old person surrounded by a cohort of happy children, but (**8**) _____ doesn't match the facts. (**9**) _____ we have now is the so-called 'beanpole family', thinly stretched (**10**) _____ several generations, with fewer family members in each and with growing numbers of single-parent families. Grandparents are getting younger – more than 50% of grandparents (**11**) _____ already had their first grandchild by the age of 54.

For many of them, grandparenthood means juggling a job, involvement with grandchildren and, sometimes, the care of (**12**) _____ own parents. It is up (**13**) _____ us to balance the demands we make on them if we don't want to wear them (**14**) _____ . Grandparents are (**15**) _____ a valuable part of the family that we just cannot do without them.

Writing:
CAE Part 2

Articles

You see this announcement in an international magazine.

A Family Affair

We are planning to publish a series of articles on families around the world. We would like you, the readers, to write us an article describing your own family situation **and** comparing it to that of the typical family in your country.

Write your **article** in **220–260** words.

How to go about it

- Spend time planning your article before you write it.
- Read again the information on competition entries in Unit 1 on pages 14 and 15. The model answer on page 15 is in the format of an article.

Claude Monet

J. K. Rowling

Charles Darwin

Meryl Streep

Marie Curie

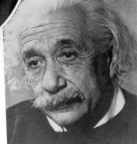

Albert Einstein

David Beckham

Speaking and reading

1 ○ Rank the people above according to how intelligent you think each one is or was: 1 = most intelligent, 7 = least intelligent.

Compare your list with your partner's, giving reasons for your decisions.

2 Read the following extract from an article on Howard Gardner's theory of multiple intelligences. How would he rank the people shown in the photos?

MULTIPLE INTELLIGENCES

1 Albert Einstein was one of the greatest thinkers the world has ever known. He formulated theories of relativity, successfully described the nature of the universe and came up with the most
5 famous equation in the world. David Beckham is the footballer whose skill and precision have made him one of the most gifted sportsmen of his generation. Who is the more intelligent?

Howard Gardner's theory of multiple intelligences
10 (MI) dares us to put these two men on neighbouring pedestals. Instead of regarding intelligence as a single quantity (g) measurable by pen-and-paper tests, Gardner, an education professor at Harvard University, divides human intelligence into no fewer than eight
15 separate categories ranging from mathematical to musical competence. His ideas have provoked vigorous debate about how one defines intelligence, about how children should be educated and how society treats those who do not sit at the top of the academic heap.
20 They have certainly divided parents – Celebration, the American town created by the Disney Corporation, based its school around Gardner's fundamental ideas. Several parents subsequently complained that their children were not being taught satisfactorily, and
25 withdrew them. Gardner's point is that g measures only one capacity, the sort of mental agility that is valued in academic achievement, and that this single number does not do justice to human potential. So he has created his own spheres of achievement.
30 Some categories are easily reconcilable with general perceptions about IQ. For example, 'linguistic' intelligence confers a mastery of language, and is the preserve of such people as poets, writers and linguists. 'Logical mathematical' intelligence marks out people
35 who take a reasoning approach to physical things, and seek underlying principles. Einstein is the standard-bearer for this group, which also includes philosophers.

These two categories are the main components of what we generally think of as 'intelligence'.

40 'Musical' intelligence characterizes musicians, composers and conductors. 'Spatial' intelligence is about being able to picture perspective, to visualize a world in one's head with great accuracy. Chess players, artists and architects would rate highly in this category.
45 Dancers, athletes and actors are lumped under the 'bodily-kinesthetic' heading; these individuals, like Beckham, are able to control their bodies and movements very carefully.

Then come two types of 'personal' intelligence
50 – intrapersonal, the ability to gauge one's own mood, feelings and mental states, and interpersonal, being able to gauge it in others and use the information. These two categories could be interpreted as emotional intelligence. Psychiatrists are particularly adept at the
55 former, while religious leaders and politicians are seen as people who can exploit the latter.

Charles Darwin is perhaps the perfect embodiment of the eighth intelligence – 'naturalist'. This label describes people with a deep understanding of the natural world
60 and its objects. Zoologists and botanists can count themselves among this group. Gardner has tentatively named a ninth, 'existential' intelligence, which characterizes those who ask fundamental questions about the universe. The Dalai Lama and
65 Jean-Paul Sartre would reside in this classification. This ninth addition, however, has yet to be confirmed to Gardner's satisfaction.

These eight (or nine) categories certainly reflect the fact that, in these areas, there is a spectrum of human ability
70 ranging from the hopeless to the brilliant. But are these really intelligences, or could these competences be more accurately described as gifts or talents?

◯ Reacting to the text

1 How would you answer the question in the final paragraph?

2 In which of the nine categories do you perform the best? What encouragement or help have you received in realizing your potential in this field?

3 Do you think children should be educated differently in the light of this theory?

Should schools focus less on traditional notions of intelligence and take more account of each individual's specific strengths?

Listening 1:
CAE Part 4

Multiple matching

1 ◉ 1.21–1.25 You will hear five short extracts in which people are talking about education and learning. **While you listen you must complete both tasks.**

TASK ONE
For questions 1–5, choose from the list **A–H** the person who is speaking.

A a researcher
B a novelist
C a teacher
D a musician
E an examiner
F a politician
G a scientist
H a parent

	1
	2
	3
	4
	5

TASK TWO
For questions 6–10, choose from the list **A–H** the attitude that each person has towards education.

A It should offer a wide range of subjects.
B It should allow students to learn at their own pace.
C It should teach students practical work-related skills.
D It should encourage a sense of responsibility.
E It should enable students to perform to their full potential.
F It should improve communication skills.
G It should encourage creativity.
H It should encourage students to join in.

	6
	7
	8
	9
	10

2 ◯ Discuss each of the views expressed in the recording, saying how much you agree or disagree with them.

How would you complete the sentence beginning 'Education should ... '?

Language focus 1: Passives 1

1 Match each of the following extracts to one of the photos on page 72. Ignore any mistakes you find for the moment.

a   She is of course famous for being written a series of books about a young wizard and his adventures at wizard school. The stories, which have being translated into more than 50 different languages, are read by children and adults of all ages all over the world.

b   And now we come to a series of pictures of Rouen Cathedral. These masterpieces of Impressionism have all been painted at the end of the nineteenth century by the man who has generally regarded as the leader of the movement.

c   In 1894 she met Pierre, the man with whom she would change the course of science. He was introduce to her by a Polish acquaintance, who thought Pierre might be able to find room in his lab for her to carry out the study she had been commissioning to do by the Society for the Encouragement of National Industry.

d   The port of Salvador, Brazil, was arrived by him aboard the HMS Beagle on 28 February 1832 and so began his five-year study of the flora and fauna of South America. During his travels there he contracted Chagas Disease and he was being plagued by fatigue and intestinal sickness for the rest of his life.

e   Personally, I think she should had been awarded an Oscar for her part in *Silkwood* (1983). This dramatic film is based on the true story of Karen Silkwood, whose complaints about radiation sickness are ignored for the management of the plutonium factory where she works.

2 In each extract there are two mistakes related to the passive. Find the mistakes and correct them.

3 The agent, the person or thing that performs an action, is often not mentioned in passive constructions. Match the reasons **a–d** to the examples **1–4**.

Reasons why the agent is not mentioned
a   to avoid the use of 'you' in official notices
b   the agent is unknown or unimportant
c   it is obvious who the agent is
d   the agent is 'people in general'

Examples:
1   *Several parents subsequently complained that their children were not being taught satisfactorily, and withdrew them.*
2   *But are these really intelligences, or could these competences be more accurately described as gifts or talents?*
3   *The stories have been translated into over fifty different languages.*
4   *All library books must be returned before the end of term.*

4 a   The use of either the active or passive is often determined by context. In English 'given', or previously mentioned information tends to come at the beginning of a clause or sentence, and new information towards the end. This is illustrated in the second sentences of each extract in exercise 1 above.

Example: a
The stories is 'given' information: they are mentioned in the previous sentence.
are read by children and adults of all ages all over the world is new information: this fact has not yet been mentioned.

Because the 'given' information, 'The stories', is not the agent of the verb 'read', then the passive form is required.

b   Circle the given information at the beginning of the second sentences in extracts **b–e**. Are the subsequent verbs in the active or the passive?

5 a   There is also a tendency in English to place long phrases towards the end of a clause. Consequently, if the agent is a long phrase, then this appears at the end of the clause and the passive form of the verb is required.

Example: a
… by children and adults of all ages all over the world.

b   Underline the agent in each of the second sentences in **b–e** in exercise 1.

(G) Read more about Passives in Parts A–C of the Grammar reference on page 220.

Practice

The extracts **1–5** below have been taken from students' written work. For each extract, consider the whole context and rewrite the second sentence if you think it would sound more natural in the passive. If you change a sentence, decide whether the agent needs to be mentioned.

I am writing with regard to an article which recently appeared in your newspaper on the subject of this year's Charity Fun Run. Steven Ward, former Olympic athlete and manager of the Hythe sports centre, which sponsored the event, wrote the item.

Many young people are now turning their backs on hamburgers in favour of their own national dishes. This development, together with the recent beef scare, has obviously caused problems for the American fast food chains here.

3

However, we feel it would be more appropriate to celebrate the school's anniversary by organizing a concert, possibly during the last week of the academic year. The 2,000-seater Mulberry Hall Function Room in Scarcroft Road is where the school could hold the event.

4

The aim of this report is to present the findings of a survey into local shopping habits and to make recommendations for improvements in facilities and services. First-year students at Holmbush Business College, who designed their own questionnaire as part of their course work, carried out the survey during the busy pre-Christmas shopping period.

5

For the past eight years I have been working at the Birmingham-based engineering firm, Holwill & Deaks plc. The management of the company has recently promoted me to the post of Chief Accounts Clerk, in charge of a staff of five.

Vocabulary 1: Intelligence and ability

1 In **a–e** underline the informal word or expression in each group.

   a a bright child/a child prodigy/a whizzkid
   b a brilliant/brainy/gifted student
   c I have a flair for languages/I have a gift for music/I'm a dab hand at painting.
   d I'm (an) ace at tennis/I'm a skilful card player/I'm a strong swimmer.
   e I'm weak at maths/I'm hopeless at cooking/I have a poor memory.

2 Tell your partner which of the words and expressions in exercise 1 could apply to you. Explain why.

3 Tell your partner about anyone you know who is

   a a competent skier.
   b a proficient typist.
   c a skilled craftsman or woman.
   d an expert cook.
   e a computer expert.
   f an accomplished musician.

4 One of the adverbs in each group does not normally collocate with the adjective in capital letters. Underline the adverb which does not fit.

a	highly	naturally	academically	practically	musically	GIFTED
b	highly	exceptionally	enormously	hugely	largely	TALENTED
c	highly	extremely	absolutely	very	quite	PROMISING

5 In the reading text we were told that David Beckham was 'one of the most gifted sportsmen of his generation'. Think of one famous person for each of the following descriptions and tell your partner about him or her.

   a a highly talented young actor
   b an exceptionally gifted musician
   c a very promising young (tennis, football etc) player or athlete

75

Writing:
CAE Part 2

Reviews

1 Can you identify the actors in the photographs?

Have you seen any of their films? Did you enjoy them?

2 Read the following Part 2 task and the model answer. Given the information in the answer, which of the two films would you prefer to see?

Self help

Do exercises 4 and 5 below in your vocabulary notebook.

An international magazine has asked its readers to send in a review for its regular arts section. Write a **review** for the magazine comparing and contrasting two books, films or music CDs. Comment on their similarities and differences, and say which of the two books, films or CDs you would recommend and why. Write between **220** and **260** words.

All in the mind

The real-life struggle of brilliant minds with paranoid schizophrenia and Alzheimer's disease may not sound like the ingredients of an entertaining afternoon's viewing. But Russell Crowe's stunning performance as mathematical genius John Nash in 'A Beautiful Mind' and Judi Dench's moving portrayal of philosopher and novelist Iris Murdoch in 'Iris', will have you rushing out to buy the books on which these two Oscar-winning films are based.

It is in their thematic content that the two films resemble each other most. Both focus on the withdrawal of the protagonists into their own inner world and the effect this has on their long-suffering but devoted marital partners. Also common to both films is the fact that we witness the two academics in their youth and old age. Hats off here to Crowe's make up team – he is remarkably convincing as the sixty-six-year-old Nash receiving his Nobel Prize in 1994.

'Iris' differs from 'A Beautiful Mind' in this respect, relying instead on other actors to play the vivacious young Iris – a very credible Kate Winslet – and her stuttering companion, John Bayley. In addition, unlike the more linear American film, flashbacks are used to good effect to switch backwards and forwards between the two contrasting stages of Murdoch's life.

The strength of 'Iris' lies in its powerful acting and mundane realism, with the novelist seen doing the shopping, or watching children's TV in her cluttered Oxford house. However, if, as I do, you favour something more visually appealing, but no less plausible, then 'A Beautiful Mind' is a definite must-see.

3 ◯ What information is contained in each paragraph? How many paragraphs include the writer's opinion?

4 Make a note of those adjectives used by the writer to express an opinion on the film or the acting. Include any accompanying adverbs or nouns.

Example: *stunning performance*

Divide the adjectives in section B on page 212 into two groups, positive and negative.

Don't forget!

- Aim to grab the reader's interest from the beginning.
- Express your opinions throughout your answer.

5 Which words and expressions are used in the model to compare and contrast the two films? Make a note of them together with any other relevant words.

Example: *the two films resemble each other*

Do the vocabulary exercise on page 206.

6 Now write your own answer to the task in exercise 2.

Use of English:
CAE Part 4

Gapped sentences

For questions **1–5** below, think of one word only which can be used appropriately in all three sentences. Use the collocates in **bold** to help you. Here is an example (**0**).

0   It was very _____clever_____ **of you to** convince our clients to buy the more expensive machine.

As well as having a vivid imagination, you need to be _____clever_____ **with your hands** to be a good sculptor.

Sylvia had always admired _____clever_____ people and Richard certainly seemed more intelligent than most men she'd met.

1   Just _____ you don't hit your head as we crawl through the entrance to the cave.

I **wouldn't** _____ volunteer**ing** to do some charity work once I graduate.

When choosing a course abroad, you should **bear in** _____ that some schools do not offer help with accommodation.

2   It was Martin that had the _____ **idea** of redesigning the company logo and it's now much more recognizable.

If Anna continues to win so many contracts, she'll have a _____ , if not **brilliant future** in this company.

The day began cloudy and cool but ended with _____ **sunshine** and warm temperatures.

3   Adults are supposed to be _____ **learners** in comparison to children.

I forgot that my **watch was fifteen minutes** _____ so I arrived late for the interview.

The first part of the **film** is terribly _____ and my wife actually fell asleep at one point.

4   When you reach the beach, _____ **towards** the tall cliffs on the right.

The crowd cheered as David managed to _____ **the ball** into the net in the last minute of the game.

When the Prime Minister retires. his deputy will _____ **the government**.

5   As we boarded the ship, **the** _____ **occurred to me** that I would probably never return to my country or see my family again.

Some people take risks while they're driving, **with no** _____ **for** the safety of other motorists.

We _____ **over** the offer very carefully and after a week or so we decided to accept.

Multiple choice

1 ⬤ Narcolepsy is a rare medical condition which causes people to fall asleep at any time and without any warning. In what ways do you think it might affect the lives of those people who suffer from it?

2 Read the following newspaper article quite quickly and compare what one narcoleptic says with your ideas in exercise 1.

MY CONSTANT FIGHT TO STAY AWAKE

Dan Butler-Morgan tells Bryony Gordon about the difficulties of living with narcolepsy.

As a teenager, Dan Butler-Morgan used to nod off during lessons at school. He thought it was just what every rebellious schoolboy did. But when Dan left school, got a job as a mechanic and continued to fall asleep during the day, he realized this wasn't normal. None of his colleagues dozed off while servicing a car or spent their lunch break snoozing in a corner. When his boss threatened him with the sack, he knew he had to find out what made him so different from everybody else. Dan's GP was equally baffled and immediately sent him to a sleep centre, where he was diagnosed as suffering from narcolepsy, an incurable sleep disorder that is known to affect at least 2,500 people in the UK.

Narcoleptics fall asleep at irregular and unexpected times. 'Most people,' says Dan, 'however tired, can stay awake if need be. But with me, it's like a blind is drawn. I can be having a conversation with the most interesting person, but inside, I am fighting a constant battle to stay awake. It's like someone switches the lights off.'

Dan once fell off his bike due to an attack, and has been thrown out of nightclubs by bouncers who thought he was drunk – sufferers are often mistakenly considered to be inebriated or lazy. This, coupled with the fact that nobody is quite sure what causes narcolepsy, makes it hard to diagnose. It is widely believed to be the result of a genetic mutation, and research has shown that sufferers have a deficiency of hypocretin, a small hormone produced in the brain which regulates the body's state of arousal.

Most narcoleptics also experience cataplexy, a sudden loss of muscular control that can cause them to fall to the floor, their heads to slump or their jaws to drop, usually after a sudden surge of emotion such as happiness, anger or fear. During the night, narcoleptics can also suffer from sleep paralysis – an inability to move just before falling asleep or just after waking up – and hallucinations.

Dan suffers from all of these symptoms. When I arrive for our interview he holds onto the door for support as his legs buckle in an attack of cataplexy, because 'I walked in and didn't recognize you, and I was a bit taken aback'. He finds it hard to describe the sleep paralysis and hallucinations, but says he begins 'to go cold from the toes up, and then get these horrible noises in my head – babies crying and a high-pitched squeal. Then I start to see things, either figures in the room or big hands coming at me from behind the curtains.'

The only person who can help Dan to snap out of the hallucinations is his 25-year-old wife, Claire, who is frequently tired as she is woken by the attacks. 'I put a hand on his shoulder and he will come round, but it can happen again and again during the night,' she says. At their worst, she estimates, the attacks can occur around 50 times a night.

Dan is remarkably fresh-faced for someone who is supposed to feel overwhelming fatigue. He puts this down to the new tablets he takes to control his condition. He used to take an amphetamine-based form of medication, but found that his moods fluctuated too much. But since he started taking amphetamine-free Modafinil, his moods have levelled out and his attacks have decreased to just five or six times a night, three or four nights a week.

He thinks that keeping busy also helps his condition. The couple have recently bought a house and Dan works on it every night after work until midnight. 'It's when I'm sitting still for any period of time that I know I'm going to go.' The couple recently went to see a horror movie, and Dan slept through most of it. 'Tiny little things that most people take for granted have been affected by my narcolepsy,' he says. 'Socially, we can never really plan anything. We go out to dinner and I can just fall asleep in my food.'

He is amazed at people's lack of knowledge about the condition, and has often encountered prejudice. He desperately wanted to join the police force, but was sent a rejection letter, saying he would be a health-and-safety risk. Another potential employer turned him down, telling him the sales assistant in his local chemist had told him Dan would probably turn up late for work all the time.

'It's not a disability,' he says, forlornly. 'But people's perceptions of it as one have led me to be a bit scared of trying to pursue any other career opportunities, in case I get turned down. And I sometimes feel like I am bringing other people down with it. It can make you feel like a nothing, a nobody.'

His attempts to control the cataplexy have changed his personality. 'I used to be this happy-go-lucky person, who was always cracking jokes, but now I can't really laugh because it sets off the cataplexy.' Despite all the obstacles that he has faced, though, Dan still manages to look on the bright side. 'Fortunately, I don't think I'll ever go back to being the teenager who slept whole weekends without ever waking up. This morning, I got up at 5 am and I'll go to the house this evening and work on it until late. In fact,' he says, grinning at his wife, 'I think Claire's more tired nowadays than I am.'

3 Now read the text again. For questions **1–7**, choose the correct answer **A**, **B**, **C** or **D**.

> ### Don't forget!
> - First, find the parts of the text which relate to each question. The questions follow the same order as the information in the text.
> - Eliminate the options which are clearly wrong and choose the best answer, underlining key phrases or sentences in the text.
> - Re-read the questions and check that the options you have chosen accurately reflect the information you have underlinded in the text.

1 Dan first knew he suffered from narcolepsy
  A when he was still at school.
  B during a visit to his doctor.
  C shortly after an incident at work.
  D when he became unemployed.

2 What do we learn about narcolepsy in the third paragraph?
  A The symptoms are not always correctly identified.
  B It can seriously affect the brain.
  C It can be brought on by drinking too much.
  D It often makes sufferers lazy.

3 When he first met the writer, Dan
  A was very angry.
  B was a little surprised.
  C fell over.
  D fell asleep.

4 The writer expresses her surprise at
  A the frequency with which he suffers attacks.
  B the form of medication he is taking.
  C his wife's ability to cope with the situation.
  D his apparent lack of tiredness.

5 Dan says he is most likely to fall asleep
  A in social situations.
  B at the cinema.
  C when he is inactive.
  D when he works late.

6 What, according to Dan, has been the main obstacle to him finding work?
  A His low self-esteem.
  B His fear of letting others down.
  C People's attitudes towards the disease.
  D The dangers involved in employing him.

7 What do we learn about his feelings in the last paragraph?
  A He finds his situation amusing.
  B He is able to remain positive.
  C He is concerned about his wife.
  D He wishes he could sleep like he used to.

Reacting to the text

In what ways do you think Dan's illness might affect those closest to him? Have you ever fallen asleep in an unexpected situation?

Vocabulary 2: Sleep

1 Look back at the first paragraph of the reading text on page 78 and find:
  a a verb which means 'to sleep for a short time, especially during the day'.
  b three verbs which mean 'to go to sleep, usually without intending to'.

2 Complete the spaces with one of the adjectives or adverbs from the box.

A

good	deep	fast	soundly

1 The kids are staying over at their cousins' so we should **get a** _____ **night's sleep**.
2 The passengers **slept** _____ in their cabins, unaware of the coming storm.
3 The doctor gave him a sedative and he **fell into a** _____ **sleep**.
4 Don't worry, you won't wake her up – she's _____ **asleep**.

B

wide	light	sleepless	rough

1 Over 2,000 homeless people are forced to **sleep** _____ in this city.
2 It's midnight and I feel _____ **awake**. I shouldn't have had that coffee.
3 My baby daughter's teething, so we've **had** a few _____ **nights** recently.
4 I've always been **a** _____ **sleeper**; I wake up at the slightest sound.

3 ⭕ Discuss the following questions with your partner.

1 How long does it usually take you to **get to sleep** once you've gone to bed?
2 Do you ever **lie awake** in bed worrying about things? Does anything else **keep you awake** at night?
3 What advice would you give to someone **suffering from insomnia**? Do you know of any remedies?
4 Certain types of music or a film after lunch **send some people to sleep**. Does anything have this effect on you?

Language focus 2: Passives 2

A Reporting verbs

1 The following structure can be used with certain verbs to give generalized opinions or facts.

an incurable sleep disorder that **is known to affect** at least 2,500 people in the UK.
Sufferers **are** often mistakenly **considered to be** inebriated or lazy.
It **is** widely **believed to be** the result of a genetic mutation.
(= *Many people believe it is the result of a genetic mutation.*)

With past reference, the perfect infinitive is used.

Jenkins **is said to have had** financial problems.
(= *People say that Jenkins had financial problems.*)
She **was thought to have fled** the country.
(= *The police thought she had fled the country.*)

2 Rewrite **a–e** below. Start the beginning of each new sentence with the underlined word or words.

a People expect that <u>the Prime Minister</u> will announce his resignation later today.
b They understand that <u>the 22-year-old striker</u> is considering a move to a Spanish club.
c There's a rumour going round that <u>the band</u> have sacked their lead guitarist.
d The police alleged that <u>he</u> had been selling stolen goods.
e One report says that <u>she</u> was paid over £2 million for her part in the film.

B *Have/Get something done*

1 What is the difference between the following sentences?

a We're painting the house at the weekend.
b We're having the house painted at the weekend.
c We're getting the house painted at the weekend.

2 What is the difference in the use of *have* in the following two sentences?

a I had my watch repaired last week.
b I had my watch stolen last week.

C Other passives with *get*

Get can also be used as an informal alternative to *be* in passive sentences.

Example:
I've applied for loads of jobs but keep getting turned down.

Get meaning 'become' is also common with the following past participles, sometimes with an object.

get stuck   get caught   get burned   get left
get lost   get dressed   get involved   get hurt

Examples:
The postman got stuck in the lift this morning.
She got her head stuck in the back of the chair.

Ⓖ Read more about the points in sections **A**, **B** and **C** above in Part D of the Grammar reference on pages 220 and 221.

Practice

1 Complete the gaps with a suitable phrase with *have* or *get*. The first two have been done for you.

a Hurry up or you'll <u>*get left*</u> behind!
b I go to a reflexologist every month <u>*to have my feet*</u> massaged.
c This is the first time I _____ cleaned since I bought it for our wedding.
d They've got a map and a compass so they're hardly likely _____ .
e I do wish you _____ tested – I really think you need glasses, you know.
f I'm seriously thinking _____ pierced.
g He _____ writing graffiti on the bus and they fined him £50.
h We ought _____ serviced – the engine's making all sorts of funny noises.
i We _____ broken into at the weekend. They took the computer, TV, video – everything.
j I think you _____ cut before your interview.

2 ⭕ Tell your partner about
• something you've had done recently.
• something you'd pay to have done if you had the money.
• something you'd never have done, ever.
• an occasion when you got lost.
• a time when you got caught doing something you shouldn't have been.

Listening 2:
CAE Part 2

Sentence completion

1 ⬤ Have you seen a hypnotist at work? What were your impressions?

Do you think hypnotism has any value apart from its ability to entertain?

2 ⬤ 1.26 You will hear part of a radio programme about hypnotism. For questions **1–8**, complete the sentences.

Dr Anton Mesmer took his new form of treatment to Paris in [___ **1**].

Mesmerism was used to cure conditions such as [___ **2**], rheumatism and paralysis.

Patients were treated in dark rooms, sitting in [___ **3**].

The English [___ **4**], James Braid, coined the word 'hypnotism' in 1841.

Hypnotists use a swinging watch to [___ **5**] the left side of the brain.

Watches, magnets and pictures of [___ **6**] have all been used as props.

Hypnotherapists say they can help people who want to overcome insomnia or [___ **7**].

Hypnosis is particularly useful with problems which are [___ **8**] in origin.

3 ⬤ Would you ever volunteer to be hypnotized? Why/Why not?

6 Review

Word formation

For questions **1–10**, read the text below. Use the word given in capitals at the end of some of the lines to form a word that fits the gap **in the same line**. There is an example at the beginning (**0**).

Amnesiacs struggle to imagine future events

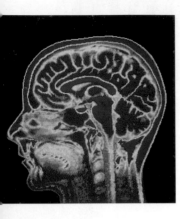

People with amnesia have difficulty imagining future events with any (**0**) ___richness___ of detail and emotion, according to Eleanor Maguire at the Wellcome Trust Centre for Neuroimaging in London, UK. She studied five patients who suffered from classic amnesia. The patients had all suffered (**1**) _____ that had damaged a brain region called the hippocampus. The damage left the subjects with no recollection of past events, and all sorts of important and precious memories were (**2**) _____ lost forever. Researchers asked the (**3**) _____ – and a control group without amnesia – to imagine several future scenarios, such as visiting a beach, and to describe what the experience would be like. They then carried out an (**4**) _____ of the subjects' descriptions, scoring each statement based on whether it involved references to (**5**) _____ relationships, emotions or specific objects. All but one of the amnesiacs were worse at (**6**) _____ future events than those without amnesia. The way they saw future events was not as a 'whole picture' where all the images fitted together and made sense, but was more likely to be (**7**) _____ , meaning they just saw a collection of very separate images. And in (**8**) _____ with their control counterparts, most amnesiacs said little about how they felt in the (**9**) _____ scenario. Although there is some anecdotal evidence to suggest that amnesiacs have problems picturing future events, Maguire is the first to study it (**10**) _____. 'The results show that amnesia patients are really stuck in the present,' she says.

	RICH
	INFECT
	FORTUNE
	PARTICIPATE
	ANALYSE
	SPACE
	VISUAL
	ORGANIZE
	COMPARE
	FICTION
	SYSTEM

Vocabulary

Underline the correct alternative.

1 I'm afraid I have a *poor/weak/light/thin* memory for faces.

2 Clearly, you need to be a *thick/hard/strong/heavy* swimmer to be a lifeguard.

3 She seems to have a natural *hand/gift/present/art* for drawing.

4 Well, that didn't work. Got any more *accomplished/competent/expert/bright* ideas?

5 He has a very *prospective/promising/provided/proficient* career ahead of him.

6 I didn't *turn/put/fall/get* to sleep until after two this morning.

7 We've been sleeping *rough/light/badly/soundly* lately. It's far too noisy in our neighbourhood.

8 I didn't hear the storm last night. I was *fast/wide/hard/deep* asleep.

9 It is his versatility that *puts/makes/sends/sets* him apart from other actors of his generation.

10 There is little to *decide/choose/separate/divide* between the two films in terms of entertainment value.

Use of English:
CAE Part 5

Key word transformations

For questions **1–8**, complete the second sentence so that it has a similar meaning to the first sentence, using the word given. **Do not change the word given.** Use between **three** and **six** words, including the word given. Here is an example (**0**).

0 It may take several months to decide on the location for the new stadium.

MADE

It may take several months before ___*a decision is made*___ about the location for the new stadium.

1 They still haven't carried out a full assessment of the effects of these changes.

FULLY

The effects of these changes have yet _____ .

2 Johnson was quite surprised when he won the election and became President.

ABACK

Johnson was rather _____ elected as President.

3 The police now think he invented the story to protect his girlfriend.

HAVE

He is now _____ up the story to protect his girlfriend.

4 My parents are planning to pay someone to repair and redecorate their house next month.

UP

My parents are planning to have their _____ next month.

5 He thinks his friends do not appreciate him.

GRANTED

He dislikes _____ by his friends.

6 They've postponed the meeting until January to give the management team longer to decide.

OFF

The meeting _____ until January to give the management team longer to decide.

7 To help us run the exhibition next month, we need at least six people.

REQUIRED

No _____ to help us run the exhibition next month.

8 A common belief is that British people cannot speak foreign languages very well.

WEAK

British people are commonly believed to _____ foreign languages.

Use of English

Introduction

In Paper 3 you have one hour to complete five different tasks. There are 50 questions in total. Part 1 (Multiple-choice cloze) and Part 2 (Open cloze) are dealt with in more detail elsewhere in this book. In this section we will look specifically at:

Part 3 Word formation
Part 4 Gapped sentences
Part 5 Key word transformations

Part 3: Word formation

What to expect in the exam

Part 3 contains a text with ten gaps, each of which has to be filled with the correct form of a word given in capital letters. In the example below, the infinitive form of the verb is needed after the modal *can*. The missing words are usually nouns, adjectives, adverbs and occasionally verbs. Sometimes the words you write will need to be in the plural, and sometimes a negative form is required. The meaning of the text surrounding the gaps will help you to decide.

1 For questions **1–10**, use the word given in capitals at the end of some of the lines to form a word that fits in the gap **in the same line**. Use the words in **bold** to help you to decide on the correct form of your answer. There is an example at the beginning (**0**).

What a pain!

We've all felt pain at some time or other, but what is its function and **how can we (0)** _minimize_ **it** in our lives?   **MINIMUM**

According to the International Association for the Study of Pain, **the (1)** _____ **of pain** is as follows: 'an unpleasant **sensory**   **DEFINE**
and (2) _____ **experience** associated with actual or   **EMOTION**
potential tissue damage.'

Our understanding of pain is influenced by **a (3)** _____ **of**   **VARY**
factors including **our (4)** _____ **state**, memories of past   **PSYCHOLOGY**
pains, and how our **cultural (5)** _____ **affect** our lives. Some   **BELIEVE**
people believe that women **should (6)** _____ **have** a much   **THEORY**
greater **(7)** _____ **for** pain than men, since they are capable   **TOLERATE**
of giving birth, which can be intensely painful. **However**, one study
conducted at the University of Bath in the UK involving men and
women submerging their arms in iced water, actually discovered
that the women found the pain **more (8)** _____ **than** the   **BEAR**
men did.

If **the (9)** _____ **of time** in which a person suffers pain is greater   **LONG**
than six months, this kind of pain is referred to as chronic. Acute pain
does not usually last as long and **it generally (10)** _____   **COMPANY**
illness, injury or surgery.

2 Describe each answer in exercise 1 using the words in the box below.

noun   adjective   adverb   verb
negative   plural   prefix   spelling change

Example (0) *'Minimize' is a verb. It requires a spelling change to form the ending 'ize'.*

3 Look at the title of the paragraph in exercise 4. What do you think the text will be about?

Read through the text quite quickly, ignoring the gaps, and check your predictions.

4 Now read the text again and for questions **1–10**, use the word given in capitals at the end of some of the lines to form a word that fits in the gap **in the same line**. There is an example at the beginning (**0**).

> **Don't forget!**
>
> Check the spelling of the words you write. No marks will be awarded for a misspelt word.

Moths count!

Renowned conservationist Sir David Attenborough is launching a campaign today called 'Moths Count', to halt the (**0**) _drastically_ declining number   **DRASTIC**
of Britain's native moths and improve their poor image. A report (**1**) _____   **TITLE**
'The State of Britain's Larger Moths' revealed last year that in many urban and
southern areas, the moth population has almost (**2**) _____ since 1968. And   **HALF**
another alarming (**3**) _____ of the long-term study showed that there has   **FIND**
been a national decrease of up to 32% in 300 larger moth species. This has led
the charity, 'Butterfly Conservation', of which Sir David is president, to develop
a new strategy which will provide opportunities for real (**4**) _____ to broaden   **ENTHUSIASM**
their (**5**) _____ and also generate appreciation among the wider public. Moths,   **EXPERT**
he insists, play an essential role in the environment. Their loss (**6**) _____ the   **THREAT**
species of birds, bats and small mammals that feed on them, and the plants that
they pollinate. 'Moths Count' campaigner Richard Fox says 'Currently there's an
an image problem, partly because there's a (**7**) _____ that moths are night   **PERCEIVE**
creatures, although many are day-flying and only about half a dozen of Britain's
2,500 species damage clothes.' Reasons for their decline include climate change
and loss of habitat linked to intensive farming. Although the (**8**) _____ of   **DIVERSE**
moths has increased with the (**9**) _____ of new species in Britain, overall their   **ESTABLISH**
numbers have dropped, and for some, extinction now seems sadly (**10**) _____ .   **AVOID**

Part 4: Gapped sentences

What to expect in the exam

- In the gapped sentences task there are five sets of three sentences.
- For each set, you need to find one word which is appropriate for the gap in each sentence.
- The word must have the same form, but might function as more than one part of speech, for example, *play* might be used as a noun and a verb; *slim* might be used as a verb and an adjective.

For questions **1–5**, think of **one** word only which can be used appropriately in all three sentences. Here is an example (**0**).

0 We took a wrong _turn_ on the motorway and got completely lost!

The clouds seem to be clearing, so it should _turn_ into a sunny day after all.

I did the washing up yesterday, so it's your _turn_ turn to do it today.

To help you answer questions **1–5** use the words in **bold** and the definitions below each set of sentences.

1 **a** Adrian's the kind of person who likes to **plan** _____ and decide how to spend each day of his holiday.

b Most people believe a good education will enable their children to **get** _____ in life.

c If you look to your left, you should be able to see our hotel **straight** _____, by the lake.

i This adverb forms a phrase which means *to think about or consider the future*.
ii The phrasal verb formed here means *to make progress or be successful*.
iii This adverb describes a location that lies directly in front of the speaker.

2 **a** We intend to _____ the magazine **at** older men, where we feel there is a gap in the market.

b Some people appear to have no _____ **in life** and go from one job to another.

c My _____ was bad and I missed the target by at least a metre.

i This verb means *to specifically design for*.
ii Synonyms for this noun might be 'ambition' or 'purpose'.
iii This noun refers to your ability to hit something.

3 **a** It's difficult to **put an exact** _____ **on** how much the museum extension will cost.

b Che Guevara was a **leading** _____ in the communist revolution in Cuba.

c The elderly _____ in the foreground standing next to the young prince is the artist's father.

i This noun means *an amount or number*.
ii Here the noun collocates with *leading* to describe a person who is well known or has been important in some way.
iii In art, the noun can be used to refer to a person in a drawing or painting.

4 **a** Sarah finally became a little more _____ with her therapist about her feelings.

b Staying out **in the** _____ air for too long can result in hypothermia, so find somewhere warm to shelter.

c The shop was badly damaged by fire and the owner does not know when it will be _____ **for business** again.

i This adjective means *to be willing to express your honest thoughts or feelings*.
ii This phrase refers to any place that is outside, rather than in a building.
iii The phrase formed here means that the public or customers are able to use a shop, service, etc.

5 **a** This new electric drill I bought seems to have **a** _____ **of its own**.

b After my grandmother died, I discovered she had **left** me her ring **in her** _____, and I still wear it today.

c Having **the** _____ **to win** is what turns good athletes into champions.

i The phrase formed with the word here means *the ability to make decisions for itself*.
ii This noun refers to the formal document in which a person writes who is to receive their possessions, land or money after they die.
iii This phrase describes the determination that is needed to succeed in something difficult.

Part 5: Key word transformations

For questions **1–8**, complete the second sentence so that it has a similar meaning to the first sentence, using the word given. **Do not change the word given.** Use between **three** and **six** words, including the word given.

How to go about it

- Read the first statement, the key word and the second statement.
- Answer the questions in *italics* after each transformation before you write your answer.

1 Karen's shyness means that she tries not to speak about anything personal in front of other people.
   HERSELF
   Karen prefers to avoid _____ public, as she is terribly shy.
   Which key verb in the first question is missing from the second?
   Is 'avoid' followed by a gerund or infinitive?
   What preposition goes before 'public' so that it means 'in front of other people'?

2 It would be a good idea if you could lose a couple of kilos.
   WEIGHT
   I don't think that _____ you any harm.
   To form the subject of the clause after 'I don't think that', do we use the gerund or infinitive?
   What common verb begins the expression '…you any harm'?

3 We had expected Pedro to get promoted.
   SURPRISE
   Pedro's promotion came _____ to us.
   In the first sentence, does the speaker say that the promotion is a surprise or not?
   What part of speech is 'surprise'? Look at the surrounding text in the second sentence to help you.

4 I think this report needed to be written more carefully.
   CARE
   You should _____ writing this report.
   Is the speaker referring to past, present or future?
   What verb often collocates with 'care'?

5 Since the director could not speak at the awards ceremony himself, one of the actors took his place.
   BEHALF
   One of the actors made _____ the director at the awards ceremony.
   What noun is formed from the verb 'speak'?
   What two prepositions go on either side of 'behalf'?

6 After the noise from the machine has stopped, you can open the lid.
   UNTIL
   Do not open the lid of the machine_____ that noise.
   Which of the following structures means that the verb/activity no longer happens:
   stop + gerund   or   stop + infinitive
   What verb often collocates with 'noise'?

7 I regret not concentrating more on what the teacher said during my French lessons.
   ATTENTION
   I now wish _____ the teacher during my French lessons.
   What structure comes after 'wish' to refer to a past regret? (See Unit 3)
   Which verb often collocates with 'attention'?
   What preposition follows 'attention'?

8 Rene's performance in last week's test was nowhere near as good as it was in today's.
   CONSIDERABLY
   Rene performed _____ he did in last week's.
   In which test did Rene have good results – today's or last week's?
   What part of speech is 'considerably'?
   What parts of speech can it precede and describe?

Multiple choice

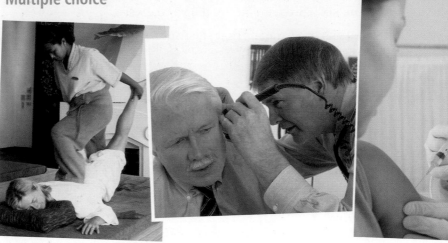

1 ⬤ What is your reaction to the images of medical treatment shown in the pictures?

2 The three extracts below are all concerned in some way with health. Read them through quickly and match each text **A–C** to one of the pictures.

3 Read the texts again and for questions **1–6**, choose the answer (**A**, **B**, **C** or **D**) which you think fits best according to the text.

A ADVERTISEMENT

ATTENTION ALL STUDENTS!

Do you need to earn money while you study but can't spare the hours for a regular job?

MINERVA PHRAMACEUTICALS is currently carrying out tests on a range of new products aimed at combating the influenza virus. They are looking for young people who are willing to take part in a series of medical trials which will ascertain the effectiveness of the new products.

To become a test subject, you should be between the ages of 18–25. Anyone suffering from chronic medical conditions, or a person who has a family history of high blood pressure cannot be permitted to participate in the tests. You must be willing to undergo a thorough medical examination to ensure you are in good physical condition before the trials can begin, and then attend trial sessions on the 1st and 15th of next month. A final compulsory examination will also be set up for the fourth week. It is vital that you are able to keep daily records of your health and any side effects of the products that you may observe.

Some subjects may experience mild allergic reactions to the test products and should make an appointment with a Minerva Pharmaceuticals doctor, who will suggest the best course of action. In the highly unlikely event that a severe reaction should occur, subjects should seek urgent attention at hospital and arrange for Minerva Pharmacueticals to be contacted. All hospital-related costs will be fully borne by the company. Such an outcome, however, has been known to occur only in exceptional   line 27 circumstances.

1 In order to participate in the medical trials, a person must be
   A healthy.
   B on a low income.
   C taking a medical degree.
   D able to report to the company every day.

2 Which phrase is echoed by the words 'to occur only in exceptional circumstances' (line 27)?
   A the best course of action
   B in the highly unlikely event
   C should seek urgent attention
   D will be fully borne by

B EXTRACT FROM A MAGAZINE ARTICLE

`I get very stressed and often have a blinding headache when I leave school. Like most teachers, I crash during the first week of the holidays and get throat infections. I don't know much about complementary medicine - my local beauty salon offers Indian head massage, and I've always promised myself I'd book an appointment, but I've never got round to it. But recently a colleague passed on an article on Thai yoga massage. It is said to work on the energy meridians, relieve physical strain and stretch your limbs. I made an appointment.

I was a little taken aback at first - it is certainly not massage as we know it. It involves much harder pressing and it felt like I was a piece of dough being kneaded. When the practitioner was massaging me I sometimes thought, "Oh please, don't do that any more." He didn't actually talk to me, apart from at the beginning when he answered my questions and when he gave instructions, which was a bit eerie. If he'd spoken to me more, I would have felt more at ease.

I felt I could have run up and down hills after the session, but the next day I was back to normal and I never got that sensation of instant energy again. As the treatments went on, the headaches began to ease off and things didn't seem to get on top of me the way they used to. I don't know if this can necessarily be put down to the treatment, though, because stress depends on so many things.'

3 The writer decided to try Thai Yoga Massage
  A as a result of another teacher's experience.
  B to compare it with Indian Head Massage.
  C after getting some background information.
  D to stop herself from becoming stressed.

4 In this piece, the writer is generally
  A convinced that alternative therapies are useless.
  B impressed by the manner of the therapist.
  C sceptical about the effects of Thai Yoga Massage.
  D optimistic that her health problems will disappear.

C EXTRACT FROM A NOVEL

Dr Iannis tilted the old man's head and peered into the ear. With his long matchstick he pressed aside the undergrowth of stiff grey hairs. There was something spherical within. He scraped its surface to remove the hard brown cankerous coating of wax, and beheld a pea. It was undoubtedly a pea; it was light green, its surface was slightly wrinkled, and there could not be any doubt in the matter. 'Have you ever stuck anything down your ear?' he demanded.

'Only my finger,' replied Stamatis.

'And how long have you been deaf in this ear?'

'Since as long as I can remember.'

Dr Iannis found an absurd picture rising up before his imagination. It was Stamatis as a toddler, with the same gnarled face, the same stoop, the same overmeasure of aural hair, reaching up to the kitchen table, and taking a dried pea from a wooden bowl. He stuck it into his mouth, found it too hard to bite, and crammed it into his ear. The doctor chuckled, 'You must have been a very annoying little boy.'

'He was a devil.'

'Be quiet woman, you didn't even know me in those days.'

'I have your mother's word, God rest her soul,' replied the old woman, pursing her lips and folding her arms, 'and I have the word of your sisters.'

5 When Dr Iannis examined Stamatis's ear
  A he was not surprised when he found a pea.
  B he realized the cause of Stamatis's hearing problems.
  C he believed the pea had only recently got stuck.
  D he was angry that Stamatis had wasted his time.

6 The old lady refers to the young Stamatis as 'a devil' to emphasize
  A his tendency to distort the truth.
  B the way his family saw him as an outsider.
  C his ability to trick other people.
  D his habit of causing trouble.

Reacting to the texts

Would you ever consider taking part in medical trials? Why/why not?

Do you think alternative therapies provide a useful and effective alternative to mainstream medicine? Why/why not?

When you were a child, did you ever require medical assistance because of something unusual you did?

Vocabulary: Health

A Health problems

1 a In **1–5** complete each of the expressions in bold with a word from the texts. Check your answers in the relevant extracts shown in brackets.

1 What is the difference between **an acute condition** and **a _____ condition**? (A)

2 What are the main causes of **high blood _____** ? (A)

3 What might a **mild _____ reaction** be? (A)

4 What do you do if you **have a _____ headache**? (B)

5 Do **throat _____** ever cause you to lose your voice? (B)

b ⬤ Work with a partner and discuss each of the questions in **a**.

2 a For each of the adjectives on the left, underline the noun or nouns on the right which collocate with it. You may need to underline one, two or all three nouns. There is an example at the beginning (**0**).

0	torn	<u>muscles</u>/<u>ligaments</u>/cheeks
1	chipped	tooth/stomach/bone
2	sprained	nail/ankle/wrist
3	blocked	toe/nose/neck
4	dislocated	shoulder/hip/jaw
5	bruised	ribs/thigh/tooth
6	swollen	glands/lips/feet

b ⬤ Which of the complaints and injuries in **a** have you suffered? Tell your partner about them.

B Phrasal verbs

1 Complete each of the gaps with the correct form of a phrasal verb. The phrasal verb should have the same meaning as the definition in brackets.

1 MINERVA PHARMACEUTICALS is currently (*performing*) _____ tests on a range of new products. (A)

2 A final compulsory examination will also be (*arranged*) _____ for the fourth week. (A)

3 I promised myself I'd book an appointment but I never (*did what I had been intending to*) _____ to it. (B)

4 I was a little _____ (*surprised*) at first – it is certainly not massage as we know it. (B)

5 As the treatments went on, the headaches began to (*become less intense*) _____. (B)

6 I don't know if this can necessarily be (*attributed*) _____ to the treatment. (B)

2 Check your answers in the relevant reading extract.

> ### Don't forget!
>
> Add the words and phrases in Sections A and B to your vocabulary notebook.

Use of English:
CAE Part 1

Multiple-choice cloze

1 Read the following text quickly, ignoring the gaps for the moment. Have you seen this phenomenon in your own language?

2 For questions **1–12**, read the text again and then decide which answer (**A**, **B**, **C** or **D**) best fits each space. There is an example at the beginning (**0**).

VIRTUAL DOCTORS

Clare Harrison rarely (**0**) _____ ill and hates going to the doctor's when she does. So when she recently (**1**) _____ out in a painful rash down one side of her body she emailed her symptoms, which also included a (**2**) _____ fever, to e-doc, the Internet medical service. Two hours later she was diagnosed as having shingles (*Herpes Zoster*) by her online doctor, who (**3**) _____ a special cleansing solution for the rash and analgesics to help (**4**) _____ the pain.

Health advice is now the second most popular topic that people search for on the Internet, and online medical (**5**) _____ is big business. Sites (**6**) _____ enormously in what they offer, with services ranging from the equivalent of a medical agony aunt to a live chat with a doctor via email. They are clearly (**7**) _____ a demand from people who are too busy or, in some cases, too embarrassed to discuss their medical (**8**) _____ with their GP.

Dr Ron Zeronis (**9**) _____ with the idea for e-doc when he (**10**) _____ a particularly dangerous form of malaria whilst travelling in a remote part of Africa. With only very basic medical facilities available, Dr Zeronis resolved there and then to launch his site and (**11**) _____ a service for others who found themselves in a similar situation. Not all practitioners, however, are in favour of sites such as e-doc; many point to the potential dangers of online medical advice, particularly in the case of more (**12**) _____ illnesses.

Self help

There are several phrases related to health and medicine in the text. Add them to your vocabulary notebook, eg *fall ill*.

0	**A** falls	**B** stays	**C** goes	**D** turns
1	**A** came	**B** passed	**C** worked	**D** ran
2	**A** small	**B** weak	**C** mild	**D** calm
3	**A** determined	**B** concluded	**C** prescribed	**D** intended
4	**A** relieve	**B** disappear	**C** improve	**D** lighten
5	**A** attendance	**B** appointment	**C** meeting	**D** consultation
6	**A** alter	**B** distinguish	**C** change	**D** vary
7	**A** meeting	**B** serving	**C** creating	**D** establishing
8	**A** complaint	**B** story	**C** hardship	**D** harm
9	**A** got on	**B** thought over	**C** came up	**D** put forward
10	**A** received	**B** contracted	**C** gained	**D** acquired
11	**A** supply	**B** distribute	**C** provide	**D** deliver
12	**A** important	**B** deathly	**C** serious	**D** endangered

3 ⬤ What do you think are 'the potential dangers of online medical advice'?

Do you/Would you consult a medical service on the Internet?

Speaking 1:
CAE Part 3

Collaborative task

○ Concerned at the negative effects of modern-day living, the government has announced plans to launch a poster campaign aimed at encouraging a healthier lifestyle and a greater sense of wellbeing amongst the population.

The illustrations below are the first drafts of the posters representing the main issues that the government wishes to address.

Talk to each other about how important each issue is to our health and wellbeing, and then decide which three posters would be the most effective.

Useful language

1 **a** Which of the following adverbs is not normally used with the adjective *important*?

> | *fairly* | *relatively* | *especially* | *particularly* | *utterly* | important

b Which of the following adjectives **cannot** be used to mean *very important*?

> | *crucial* | *vital* | *essential* | *elementary* | *fundamental* |

2 Circle the collocate in italics which is different in some way to the other three and complete the gap with an appropriate preposition.

a This poster would have a *short-term/minimal/significant/limited* effect ____ people's behaviour.

b It would be *highly/reasonably/particularly/extremely* effective ____ changing people's attitudes.

3 Underline the correct verb in italics and complete the gap with an appropriate preposition.

a I (don't) think people would *lend/pay/have/draw* a great deal of attention ____ this poster.

b I don't think people would *take/give/serve/bring* much notice ____ this one.

Speaking 2:
CAE Part 4

Further discussion

⬤ Discuss the following questions.

Would you make any changes to the posters you have chosen?

Are there any other issues which you think need addressing?

How necessary is it for governments to become involved in campaigns such as the one above?

Are we too obsessed with healthy eating and physical fitness nowadays?

To what extent does the way you dress influence the way you feel?

How far do you agree that the reason we sometimes help others is to make ourselves feel better? Give examples.

What are the positive effects of modern-day living? In what ways are we happier than previous generations?

Listening:
CAE Part 3

Multiple choice

1 ⬤ You will hear a radio programme about a treatment for removing frown lines and wrinkles from the forehead.

What do you think motivates people to have this type of treatment?

2 ⦿ 1.27 For questions **1–6**, choose the answer (**A**, **B**, **C** or **D**) which fits best according to what you hear.

1 Dr Evans says most of his patients prefer receiving the treatment at parties because
   A it is not complicated to administer.
   B they do not want to risk being seen by the media.
   C they are too busy to go to his surgery.
   D they enjoy socializing.

2 What do we learn from Lynnie about the injections?
   A The effects are temporary.
   B They are quite painful.
   C There are no side-effects.
   D They can lead to addiction.

3 Dr Evans says that he has botulism injections himself in order to
   A advertise his business.
   B look good for his wife.
   C help him feel more confident.
   D impress the media.

4 Lynnie says of the treatment that it
   A is comparable to meditation.
   B is beyond the means of most people.
   C offers good value for money.
   D has become a routine.

5 How have other people reacted to Lynnie's treatment?
   A They cannot understand why she has the injections.
   B They have become accustomed to her appearance.
   C They are glad it has helped her overcome depression.
   D They have apologized for comments they made earlier.

6 Dr Evans says that people at the parties
   A are normally more talkative than usual.
   B compliment him on his appearance.
   C are surprised at how hard he works.
   D are unaware how tired he feels.

3 ⬤ Lynnie says of the treatment: *It's a way of growing old gracefully. We all use moisturizer, we all take care of ourselves. I think it's just an extension of that.* To what extent do you agree with her?

Under what circumstances, if any, would you have either this type of treatment or cosmetic surgery?

Language focus: Reported speech

A Direct and reported speech

1 In the following example, an extract of direct speech from the listening has been reported. What tense changes have been made after the reporting verbs in **bold**?

Presenter: 'Have other people noticed the effects?'
Lynnie: 'Yes, they have. And they've grown used to my new look now.'
The presenter **asked** Lynnie if other people had noticed the effects and she **replied** that they had, and **added** that they'd grown used to her new look.

What other changes do you notice?

Read more about these changes in Part A of the Grammar reference on page 221.

2 For questions **1–4** below, refer to the direct speech to help you complete the gaps in the reported version. Use the reporting verbs in the box. **Do not write more than two words in each gap.** The exercise begins with an example (**0**).

> warned announced reminded ~~repeated~~
> pointed out predicted ~~conceded~~
> admitted stressed concluded

0 'Yes, I do accept the situation is critical, but let me say once again that we are doing our best to find a solution.'
The Prime Minister _conceded_ that the situation _was_ critical, but _repeated_ that the Government _was doing_ its best to find a solution.

1 'Yes, I did sell the stolen paintings, but I would like to mention that I have given all the proceeds to charity.'
The defendant _____ that she _____ the stolen paintings, but _____ to the court that she _____ all the proceeds to charity.

2 'I think there'll be more than 250,000 taking part in the protest. There might be some violent activists – so be careful!'
The police chief _____ that there _____ over 250,000 taking part in the protest. He _____ his men that there _____ some violent activists and urged them to be careful.

3 'The result of all this is that we must increase profits. Remember – if we don't, the company will go bankrupt.'
The Managing Director _____ that they _____ increase profits and _____ the board that if they _____ , the company _____ bankrupt.

4 'I'd just like to tell everyone that I intend to resign at the end of this season. I should emphasize that I have not been asked to leave.'
The manager has _____ that he _____ to resign at the end of this season. He _____ that he _____ been asked to leave.

B Alternative verb patterns

1 Many reporting verbs can be followed by alternative verb patterns to the 'that' clause seen in section **A**.

Example:
'I should have started younger,' said Dr Evans.
Dr Evans regretted that he had not started younger.
Dr Evans regretted not starting/having started younger.

2 Match the groups of verbs **A–D** with the corresponding verb patterns **1–4**.

1 doing something
2 to do something
3 someone to do something
4 (that) someone (should) do something

A	C
urge	suggest
remind	deny
warn	admit

B	D
promise	suggest
agree	insist
refuse	agree

3 Add each verb in the box to the appropriate group **A**, **B**, **C** or **D**. Some verbs belong to more than one group, as with *suggest* in groups **C** and **D**.

> threaten recommend persuade
> ask encourage demand offer

C Verbs and dependent prepositions

Complete each of the gaps with an appropriate preposition. Use the same preposition for both gaps in each sentence.

Example:
0 Management were able to discourage workers _from_ going on strike, but the union would not be dissuaded _from_ taking legal action.

1 I apologized ____ arriving late, but she thanked me ____ turning up at all.
2 He congratulated me ____ passing my driving test and insisted ____ buying me a drink.
3 She accused him ____ deception and spoke ____ reporting him to the police.
4 The union protested ____ the decision to sack him, but his own colleagues supported the move and argued ____ reinstating him.
5 She consented ____ the interview but objected ____ being photographed.

Read more about the points in sections **B** and **C** above in Part B of the Grammar reference on page 221.

Practice

1 a 🔘 **1.28–1.29** Listen twice to two doctors giving their opinions on the effects of passive smoking. Make notes as you listen.

Example:
non-smokers living with smokers/small amounts nicotine/risk to health

b For each speaker, choose two of the points in your notes and use reported speech to explain them.

Example:
The man claimed that smokers threatened the health of non-smokers who lived with them by causing them to breathe in small amounts of nicotine.

2 🔘 Compare your sentences with another student's. Did you report the same points?

3 🔘 Which of the two doctors do you agree with?

Word formation: Verbs

The following verbs from the listening are formed using the affixes *-ize*, *-ify* and *en-*.

social + -ize	*they enjoy <u>socializing</u>*
pure + -ify	*the botulism toxin which is <u>purified</u>*
en- + able	*to <u>enable</u> them to get work on television*

1 In **1–5** below, the affix at the beginning of each line can be used to form verbs with all of the words in the line, except one. Underline the odd one out and write down the verb forms of all the words. The exercise begins with an example (**0**).

0	**-ize**	special	summary	<u>valid</u>	modern	commercial
		specialize	*summarize*	*validate*	*modernize*	*commercialize*

1	**-ify**	class	example	simple	identity	general
2	**-ate**	difference	qualification	captive	value	assassin
3	**-ize**	character	stable	familiar	dominant	computer
4	**-en**	strong	sad	rich	deaf	high
5	**en-**	large	wide	sure	danger	courage

2 For each of the verbs in box **A** below, decide which of the prefixes in box **B** can be used to form new verbs.

Example:
cook – <u>recook</u> (cook again), <u>overcook</u> (cook too much)

A

cook	appear	read	number	load	hear	use

B

re-	dis-	over-	un-	mis-	out-

3 Complete each gap with an appropriate form of the word in capitals at the end of the line. The exercise begins with an example (**0**).

0 I see they've finally got round to <u>*widening*</u> the Shoreham road. **WIDE**

1 Each employee's performance is _____ at least once a year. **VALUE**
2 We could barely hear ourselves speak above the _____ roar of the sea. **DEAF**
3 He was fined £500 and _____ from driving for three years. **QUALIFY**
4 They lost the battle, despite _____ the enemy by two to one. **NUMBER**
5 I spent my first two weeks back at work _____ myself with all the new procedures. **FAMILIAR**
6 Arnold died in 1953: his wife, who _____ him by almost half a century, passed away on the last day of the millennium. **LIVE**
7 Before enrolling on a course, you should first ensure that it has been _____ by an officially recognized body. **VALID**
8 New 'Deluxe' moisturizing cream smooths out wrinkles and _____ that your skin stays young-looking **SURE**

4 Write similar gapped sentences for three more of the words in exercises 1 and 2. Then give your sentences to your partner to complete.

Letter

1 Read the following advertisement. Would you consider becoming a member of a club like this?

Warden Park Health & Fitness Club –

Making Fitness Fun

We offer a wide range of facilities aimed at promoting fitness, health and well-being through physical activity, rest and relaxation.

Gym: fully equipped with cardiovascular machines, including cycles, treadmills and rowers, to burn off those excess calories.

Treatment Room: for massage, manicures and waxing, to pamper yourself from head to toe.

Sauna: wonderful for unwinding after a stressful day at work.

Pool: with a special roped-off area for aquarobics.

Squash: for those who prefer more competitive activity.

Classes: our fitness studio provides classes in Step, Body Pump and Spinning.

For more information email us at info@wpark.net.

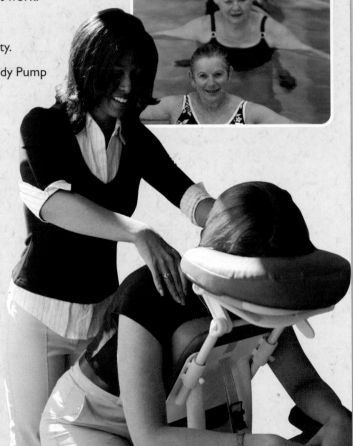

2 Read the following Part 1 task. Is a more formal or informal register appropriate for the required letter?

You belong to a health and fitness club. The General Manager has recently written to members inviting them to comment on proposed improvements to the club. Read the extracts from the General Manager's letter and from your notepad, and write a letter to the General Manager commenting on the proposed changes and offering alternative suggestions.

and would be grateful for your comments on the proposed changes, which I have summarized below.

- Building of a second sauna in the area adjacent to the swimming pool. *nice idea, but more urgent needs*

- Purchase of additional equipment (cycles, treadmills, etc) for the Gym. *no need – no room*

- Wide screen TV, broadcasting Global Sports Channel, for the snack bar. *Definitely not!*

Kind regards.

Bruce Roberts

Bruce Roberts
General Manager

Alternative suggestions
- *Take on extra instructors for classes – more variety needed (yoga, aerobics, kickboxing. etc)*
- *Extend changing room next to pool – too small*
- *Better cooking facilities for snack bar – one microwave not enough!*

Write your **letter** in **180–220** words. You do not need to include postal addresses.

3 Which of these words describe the tone or attitude you should adopt in your letter?

abrupt	appreciative	negative	constructive
complaining	polite	friendly	derisive

4 Match each of the General Manager's proposals to a corresponding alternative suggestion.

Example: *Wide screen TV for the snack bar/Better cooking facilities for snack bar*

Each pair of proposals might be dealt with at the same time in your letter.

5 Now write your answer to the question.

Useful language

1 Which of the following verbs would you **not** use when expressing your opinions and making alternative suggestions?

recommend	demand	suggest	reckon	point out
insist		agree	warn	feel

2 For **1–3**, cross out the word in *italics* which does **not** collocate with the words in **bold**.

1 a more *useful/practical/attractive/suited/popular* **option/alternative**
2 a/an *serious/general/short/distinct/obvious* **lack of** facilities/space
3 a/an *greater/clear/real/complete/urgent* **need for** more facilities/space

Use of English:
CAE Part 3

Word formation

For questions **1–10**, use the word given in capitals at the end of some of the lines to form a word that fits in the gap **in the same line**. There is an example at the beginning (**0**).

HOLDING BACK THE YEARS

No need to suffer (**0**) ____painful____, expensive cosmetic surgery. Here are five tips to combat the ageing process and make you look and feel better. — **PAIN**

Drink the right liquids
Drinking two litres of water a day helps fight (**1**) _____ , headaches, stiff joints and dry skin and eyes – especially if you work at a computer. Juices — **TIRE**
made with (**2**) _____ of fruit and vegetables such as carrot and apple — **COMBINE**
will also give you a lift and your energy levels will increase (**3**) _____. — **NOTICE**

Detox diets
Regularly cleaning up your diet to clear out (**4**) _____ toxins is the best — **WANT**
way to wash away the blues. A detox diet (**5**) _____ and re-energizes — **PURE**
your body, (**6**) _____ your mind and works wonders for your skin. — **SHARP**

Fight wrinkles
If you're worried about wrinkles, use a (**7**) _____ cream every day, — **MOISTURE**
especially during the summer months. They won't 'disappear before your very eyes', but you should notice a marked improvement.

Scalp treatment
Regular massaging of your head releases tension, helps circulation and
hair (**8**) _____ . Try it when washing your hair. — **GROW**

Learn to laugh
Laughter beats stress, boosts (**9**) _____ and improves your ability to — **IMMUNE**
learn and (**10**) _____ facts, say scientists. — **MEMORY**

Vocabulary: Health crossword

Across
 2 a minor medical _____
 6 a swollen _____
 7 a sprained _____
 9 a blinding _____
11 come out in a _____
12 a bruised _____
13 a blocked _____

Down
 1 an upset _____
 3 relieve the _____
 4 a chipped _____
 5 fall seriously _____
 6 a mild _____
 8 a torn _____
10 prescribe a _____

Reported speech

1 In each of the following sentences there is one grammatically incorrect word. Underline the unnecessary word. There is an example at the beginning (**0**).

   0 Paul said that if he had known we were moving house last week, he would have offered <u>us</u> to come and help.

   1 She confessed to being a little unfit and in need of exercise, and she agreed to having run in the local half marathon in April.
   2 He complained about he was suffering from hay fever and claimed that a vase of flowers in the school entrance had brought it on on Monday.
   3 The teacher reminded us that we should read more and virtually insisted we need buy an English newspaper; I haven't got round to doing it yet, but I will.
   4 The Transport Minister commented to reporters on the need for greater safety on the roads and pointed them out that a number of measures were about to be taken.
   5 Mrs Jacobs mentioned that she had had the car repaired five times in the last year and added that she regretted of ever having considered buying one in the first place.

2 Report the following sentences without using the verbs *say* or *tell*. The exercise begins with an example (**0**).

   0 'I didn't take your pen so please don't shout at me.'
      He denied taking her pen and asked her not to shout at him.

   1 'You really must come and visit us some time. You'll love it here, you can be sure of that.'
   2 'I'm sorry I haven't phoned earlier   I've been very busy.'
   3 'It's a very dangerous part of town, so please, please, don't go there on your own.'
   4 'You ought to wear your gloves on the run tomorrow, and don't forget to do some warm-up exercises beforehand.'
   5 'It might rain at the weekend, but if it doesn't, I'll take you all to the funfair.'

Listening 1:
CAE Part 2

Sentence completion

1 ◯ If you have a mobile phone, how much use do you make of it?

If you don't have a mobile phone, why not?

2 ◉ 1.30 You will hear part of a radio programme about mobile phones. For questions **1–8**, complete the sentences.

The first category of mobile phone user is described as [ ] **1** .

'Style bandits' see their phone as a type of [ ] **2** .

'Hedonists' and 'resisters' share an interest in simplicity and [ ] **3** when buying a mobile phone.

Mobile phones come in different colours to match the [ ] **4** of each user.

Food colours can remind us of our [ ] **5** .

More than [ ] **6** of UK teenagers have paid for a ring tone.

Ring tones of music which is [ ] **7** are popular with teenagers.

High prices are paid for numbers which people find [ ] **8** .

3 ◯ Which, if any, of the four types of user are you?

What, if anything, do you think the model, colour and ring tone of your mobile phone say about you? If you don't have a mobile phone, which of those pictured would you choose?

Do you think we attach too much importance to mobile phones? Would life be better or worse without them? Give reasons.

Language focus 1: Determiners and pronouns

1   Complete each of the gaps in the following extracts from the recording with one of the words in the box. You will need to use some of the words twice.

one	another	many	every	both

The 'hedonists' and 'resisters' are similar in (1)_____ respect, but very different in (2)_____. (3)_____ want easy-to-use phones at low cost…
'Resisters' are against mobile phones but feel they have to own (4)_____.
(5)_____ people are attracted by food colours.
Ring tones cover (6)_____ musical genre.
At the top end of the market there's (7)_____ type of personalization available to users.

2   **Determiners**, which come before nouns, are often used to talk about quantities and amounts.

   Example:
   *I think we've got **enough** milk for today.*

   Many words which are determiners can also be used on their own as **pronouns**. Pronouns are used instead of nouns.

   Example:
   *I'm going to buy some milk. We haven't got **enough**.*

   Look at the extracts in exercise 1 and decide whether each of the words you have written is used as a determiner or a pronoun.

3   a   Determiners can be used before either singular nouns, plural nouns, uncountable nouns or nouns of more than one type. In **1–3** cross out the grammatically incorrect word. There is an example at the beginning (**0**).
       0   '*All/Much/Some/No* mobile phones have this facility.'
       1   '*No/Each/All/Neither* player is allowed to handle the ball in this game.'
       2   'This happens on *many/very few/every/most* days of the year in my country.'
       3   '*A lot of/Very little/Several/No* fruit is this colour.'

   b   ⬤   For each correct alternative in the sentences in **a**, discuss what the speaker might be referring to.

       Example:
       '*All mobile phones have this facility.*' All mobile phones can be used to speak to people and send text messages.

4   a   Sometimes more than one determiner can be used before a noun. In **1–3** cross out the incorrect alternative.
       1   I go swimming *every many/every few* weeks.
       2   I'll be on holiday in *another one month/another few months*.
       3   There are *no other/no many* languages I'd like to learn.

   b   ⬤   How true are the sentences in **a** for you?

   ⬤   Read more about Determiners and Pronouns on pages 221 and 222 of the Grammar reference.

Practice

1   Each of the paragraphs **1–4** contains **two** mistakes in the use of pronouns and determiners. Find the mistakes and correct them. You will need to change the pronoun or determiner, or one of the words which follows.

   Example:
   I tried on no fewer than ten coats, and didn't buy ~~either~~ of them. Each one ~~were~~ either too long or too short and none of them would have been suitable for work.
   (any / was written as corrections)

   1   Every other years I meet up with a few of my old school friends. All of us are married with children now and we have very little free time, but we do our best to keep in touch with each another.
   2   This is one of the few pubs where you can still have a quiet drink. There are quite a few others I enjoy going to, but most of they play loud music and neither is very welcoming.
   3   Alan's been working at Crabtree's for some thirty years, and there's all likelihood he'll be there for another twenty. Most people in his profession change company every five years or so but he has none intention of moving on.
   4   Both of my daughters use the computer, but they're each restricted to an hour a day on it. Several of my friends' children, on another hand, spend as most as twenty hours a week playing games or surfing the Net.

2   Fill each of the gaps with one word from the box to complete the common expressions in **bold**.

all	lot	none	any	one
few	little	most	each	every	either

   1   We've got **an awful** _____ to do and **precious** _____ time to do it in, so let's get started now!
   2   The service in the restaurant is first class and the quality of the food **second to** _____ .
   3   He gave five concerts in London and I went to _____ **single one** of them.
   4   You can get there by bus or train. _____ **way**, it'll cost you a lot of money.
   5   _____ **too often** students fail to read the instructions properly, and **few, if** _____ , get full marks.
   6   We had to queue **a good** _____ hours to get the tickets, but we **made the** _____ **of** our time, reading, talking and playing cards.
   7   She turned the pages _____ **by one**, carefully studying the information on each one.
   8   I'd like to thank _____ **and every one** of you for all your hard work.

3   ⬤   Choose four of the expressions in exercise 2. Have a three-minute conversation with your partner on one of the topics on page 206, aiming to include all four expressions. At the end of the three minutes, tell your partner which expressions he or she has used.

Vocabulary 1: Amount

1 The underlined words in the following sentences from the listening refer to cost or amount.

Both want easy-to-use phones at <u>low cost</u>.
Companies are paying <u>huge sums</u> for mobile phone numbers.
<u>High prices</u> are paid for numbers.

> **Don't forget!**
> • Nouns are far more frequent in formal English than in conversation (see page 25).

In **1–6** below, use the information in the first sentence to complete the gaps in the second, more formal sentence. You should write two words in each gap; one from box **A** and the other, a noun, from box **B**. The exercise begins with an example (**0**).

A	small	~~extra~~	full	great	high	large	no

B	limit	cost	deal	refund	number	~~charge~~	discount

0 We can do this if you pay a little bit more.
This can be arranged for a small ___*extra charge*___ .

1 You can send in as many entries as you like.
There is _____ to the number of entries that can be submitted.
2 If so, we'd give you all your money back.
If this were the case, you would be entitled to a _____ .
3 The press are really interested in the event.
The event has attracted a _____ of media interest.
4 It's a bit cheaper if you pay cash.
We offer a _____ if you pay cash.
5 We've put up the price because it's very expensive to send it by rail now.
The current _____ of rail transport has resulted in a price increase.
6 A lot of customers have complained.
We have received a _____ of complaints from customers.

2 ◯ For **1–6** above, discuss with your partner the possible context for each of the sentences you have completed.

Example:
0 *This could be an announcement by a company or a shop which charges extra for delivery of products or purchases.*

Use of English: CAE Part 4

Gapped sentences

For questions **1–5** below, think of one word only which can be used appropriately in all three sentences. In this exercise, the words required can be found in boxes **A** and **B** on page 102. Here is an example (**0**).

0   The police do not have enough evidence to ____charge____ anyone with the murder.

The hotel receptionist tried to __charge__ me for the broken lamp in my room but I refused to pay.

The bull lowered its horns and began to __charge__ towards the people in its path.

1   I could see the horse galloping at _____ speed towards the fence with the rider shouting for help.

My grandmother lived a _____ life and everyone at her funeral had a different story to tell about her adventures.

The bill for the repairs needs to be paid in _____ before the end of this month.

2   The only aspect of the job I dislike is having to _____ with customer complaints.

Greenpaper was one of the first stationers to _____ exclusively in recycled paper products.

If you want to work in a casino, you need to be able to _____ cards rapidly and accurately.

3   When Andrew's boss found out that he had lied on his CV, it _____ him his job.

He is the kind of person who aims to win at any _____ and he won't help anyone else in the competition.

If we build an airport on this land, the _____ to the environment will be enormous.

4   Our car is always breaking down and it's _____ time we bought a new one.

The standard of the entries in this year's wildlife photography competition was extremely _____.

After Jack received news of his promotion, he was in _____ spirits for the rest of the day.

5   Eric's constant interruptions during the meeting pushed my patience to the _____.

We _____ classes to ten students so everyone can receive individual attention.

Parents should set a _____ on the amount of television their children can watch.

Reading:
CAE Part 2

Gapped text

1 ○ If you have a computer:
- how often do you use it and what for?

If you don't have a computer:
- in what ways, if any, do you think your life would improve if you had one?

2 You are going to read an article about someone who does not have a computer. Six paragraphs have been removed from the extract. Choose from the paragraphs **A–G** the one which fits each gap (**1–6**). There is one extra paragraph which you do not need to use.

UNPLUGGED

Martin Newell explains why he shuns computers and remains a devotee of 'snail mail'.

I am an Internot. That is, I have no desire to be on the Internet. I am, of course, well aware of the Internet. Boy, am I aware of the Internet! The world is being overrun by people setting up websites, talking www-slash-dot.coms and worrying about updating and upgrading.

1 [   ]

In fact, if I wanted to, I could sit in front of the computer, ordering whatever I wanted, whenever I wanted, 24 hours a day, and pay for it all electronically. But I don't have a computer. My friends, who look upon me as a 'technological oddity', find it hard to believe that I can still find work. I can't drive a car, won't fly and won't travel abroad any more. I don't even have a mobile phone.

2 [   ]

As a congenital sender and receiver of snail mail, I can only remember about two occasions in twenty-odd years when a letter has gone astray. Exactly how many bits of info has your machinery swallowed this month, brave internaut? There is the access to information, though. While doing some research on a fairly esoteric subject earlier this year, I was told by a friend that 37 Internet pages existed upon the matter. He downloaded them for me.

3 [   ]

As for the actual equipment itself, computers are so unattractive and bulky. Buying a laptop I can understand, because you can put it away. But all that dreadful grey-white office junk in your living space?

4 [   ]

I almost upgraded to a computer once but decided that a piano would be more fun, so I spent the money having one fork-lifted up into my first-floor living room. While others are getting neck-ache and headaches and running up their phone bills, I've almost figured out how to play the first few bars of 'Return to Sender.'

5 [   ]

It strikes me, though, that the main reason the Internet exists is not as a medium for spreading the joys of music, but more for the purpose of shopping and advertising. Now I know a little bit about shopping, because I get on my bicycle and go to the greengrocer's every once in a while.

6 [   ]

But perhaps by doing things in this quaint, old-fashioned way, I'm missing out on some of the financial benefits of the whole computer culture. Companies are constantly undercutting each other. Full-page newspaper ads are currently offering me the whole kit and caboodle and telling me that I can get myself connected and surfing, all for under a thousand pounds. Wow! What a bargain. I could get an electric organ fork-lifted up here for that.

Seriously, though, there is, I suppose, an outside chance I will be forced onto the Internet one day. By that time, however, it will have devolved into one tiny little module about the size of an answering machine, cost about fifty quid, and be instant, as well as idiot-proof for people like me.

A There's also this marvellous little alternative to buying books on the Net: it's called my local bookshop. It has human beings working in it. Whenever I want a particular book, I just walk down there or telephone them, and they find it for me. Within a day or two I always have it.

B The information was largely superficial and in one or two cases, written by someone who I suspect was not entirely of this planet. In the end I went to the local reference library, where a reassuringly stern librarian plonked a huge pile of books on the table in front of me and said: 'That should be a start.' I had everything I needed within an hour.

C It has not escaped my attention that you can buy and sell houses on the Internet. You can book holidays, buy a pool-table and, so I hear, even get a divorce on the Internet. Were my dog to fall seriously ill, I could even consult a vet on the Internet. Or maybe he's called the Intervet.

D Friends like these will spend hours, days even, in front of their ugly state-of-the-art computers. As they listen to music being broadcast online from all four corners of the globe, they are subjected to a constant bombardment of advertisements encouraging them to buy, buy, buy. Well, bye bye, friends.

E While we're on the subject, I hear that we can now download our music from the Net. I have only recently completed the costly operation of replacing my vinyl record collection with CDs. I hope this does not mean that these, too, will soon be obsolete.

F My own word-processor, with VDU, keyboard and printer all in one unit, is much more compact. It can be quickly shoved in the cupboard when I'm not using it. In fact, even this is too ugly for me so I glued a piece of tapestry on the space between the keyboard and the screen to make it look more homely.

G 'But how will we get hold of you?' people ask, in a tone I usually associate with anguished parents pleading with a runaway daughter calling from a phone-box. Well, you can telephone me. Or fax me. Or you could try writing me a letter.

○ Reacting to the text

Do you agree with the writer's stance? Why/Why not?

Which of the following are best done with a computer and which in the *'quaint, old-fashioned way'*? Give reasons for your opinions.

consulting reference works   shopping
writing letters   booking holidays
storing photographs   playing games

'By that time, however, it will have devolved into one tiny little module about the size of an answering machine…' How do you think computers will develop in the future?

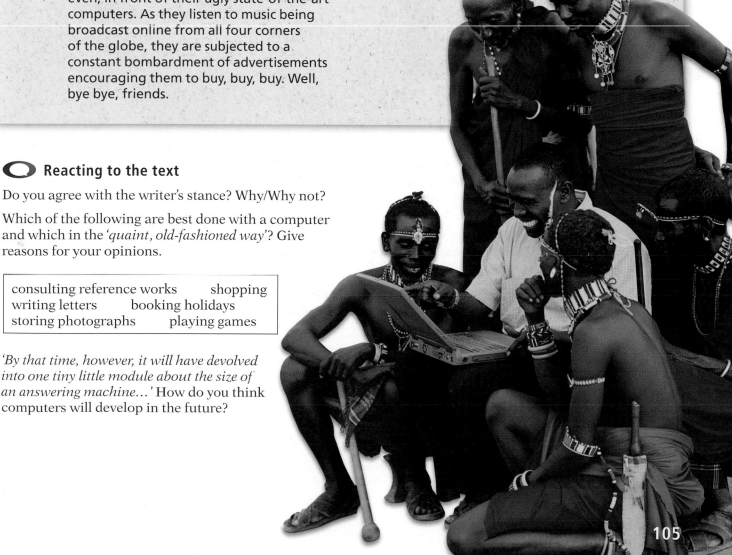

Vocabulary 2

Verbs formed with *up, down, over* and *under*

Up, down, over and *under* can be used to form a number of verbs.

Examples:
*The world is being **overrun** by people … worrying about **updating** and **upgrading**.*
*We can now **download** our music from the Net.*
*Companies are constantly **undercutting** each other.*

Complete each of the gaps with the correct form of one of the verbs in the box.

uproot	uphold	overthrow	overrule	~~overhear~~
downplay	downsize	undergo	undertake	

Example:
We closed the door to prevent anyone _overhearing_ our conversation.

1 The military government was _____ by a popular uprising and democratic elections were held.
2 The American-based company has been _____ its operations, leading to the closure of a number of European factories.
3 The Court of Appeal had been expected to _____ the judge's decision, instead of which it was _____ and Jenkins had to serve out his sentence.
4 The two leaders _____ to find a peaceful solution to the crisis and arranged to meet again.
5 The 28-year-old actress is rumoured to have _____ emergency surgery, although doctors are _____ the seriousness of the problem, suggesting she will be out of hospital soon.
6 During the war, thousands of children were _____ , forced to leave family, home and school.

Language focus 2: Modal verbs 2

Will, shall and would

1 The following examples from the reading text on pages 104 and 105 show three different uses of *will/won't*.

Habit
Friends like these *will* spend hours, days even, in front of their ugly state-of-the-art computers.

Refusal
I …*won't* fly and *won't* travel abroad any more.

Prediction
There is, I suppose, an outside chance I *will* be forced onto the Internet one day.

2 The sentences in **1–6** all contain the modal verbs *will, shall* or *would*. Match each pair to the idea they both express.

Assumption	Habit	Annoying behaviour
Request for advice/instructions		~~Offer~~
Willingness	Refusal	

Example:
0 *I'll set it up for you if you like. It's the same as the one I use at work.*
__Shall__ I show you how to draw graphs on it? __Offer__

1 It <u>won't</u> start – I think the battery's flat.
I asked him to park **it** somewhere else, but he <u>wouldn't</u> move **it**.
2 I wish he <u>would</u> turn **it** down.
We can watch the match on the balcony if you'<u>ll</u> just help me take **it** out there.
3 It <u>would</u> keep her amused on long car journeys – but we insisted she have the sound off.
He'll play with **it** all morning, his eyes glued to the tiny screen.
4 That'<u>ll</u> be Mike. Don't answer **it**!
They'<u>ll</u> have got there by now. Give **it** to me – I know their number.
5 He <u>will</u> keep forgetting to turn **it** off. It gets so hot in the kitchen!
It <u>would</u> go wrong now, wouldn't **it**! Just as I put the meat in to roast.
6 There's no more room in **it**. Where <u>shall</u> I put the chicken?
<u>Shall</u> I defrost **it** now or when we come back?

3 What do you think **it** might refer to in each pair of sentences in **1–6** above?

Example:

0 *computer*

Read more about the modal verbs *will, shall* and *would* on page 222 of the Grammar reference.

4 a Think of three domestic appliances, machines or other electronic devices and write two sentences for each, without mentioning the name of the object. Each sentence should include one of the above uses of either *will, shall* or *would*.

b Show your sentences to your partner, who will:
- say which three objects you have written about.
- tell you the idea expressed by the modal verbs.

Writing:
CAE Part 1

Reports

1 How useful do you think computers are for language learning?

What other technological aids are used in language learning? How important are they?

2 Look at the following page from a college website. Would you make use of a Multimedia Centre like this?

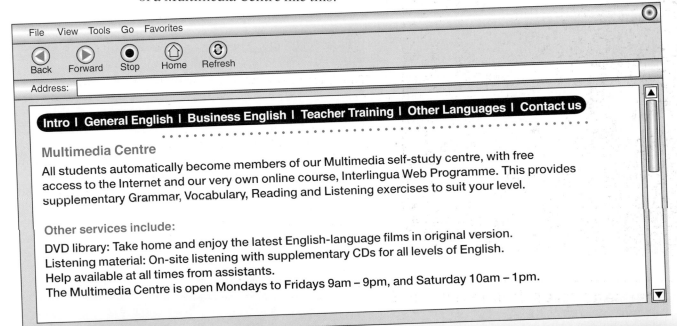

File   View   Tools   Go   Favorites

Back   Forward   Stop   Home   Refresh

Address:

Intro | General English | Business English | Teacher Training | Other Languages | Contact us

Multimedia Centre

All students automatically become members of our Multimedia self-study centre, with free access to the Internet and our very own online course, Interlingua Web Programme. This provides supplementary Grammar, Vocabulary, Reading and Listening exercises to suit your level.

Other services include:

DVD library: Take home and enjoy the latest English-language films in original version.
Listening material: On-site listening with supplementary CDs for all levels of English.
Help available at all times from assistants.
The Multimedia Centre is open Mondays to Fridays 9am – 9pm, and Saturday 10am – 1pm.

3 Read the following Part 1 task and discuss with your partner possible suggestions for improvements to Highford Academy's multimedia centre.

You help out in the multimedia centre at a language school called Highford Academy. The school's director has asked you to write a report on the centre with a view to making improvements. Read the extract from the director's email and the comments written by students, and write a report for the director incorporating students' opinions **and** making suggestions for improvements.

I expect by now you will have received some answers to the questionnaire you asked users of the centre to complete. I would therefore be grateful if you could write a report summarizing what they say and suggesting ways in which the centre could be improved.

Many thanks for your help.

Regards

Alan Shields

Like the DVD library, but most of the films are American.

Too hot, too crowded, too noisy!

You can't always get on a computer – some people spend hours writing emails.

Some excellent listening material – shame the CD players are so bad.

How to go about it

- List possible suggestions for improvements, based on your discussion in exercise 3.
- Decide on the appropriate register.
- Look again at the sections on writing reports in Unit 3.
- Refer to the Useful language section on page 201 of Ready for Writing.

4 Now write your **report** in **180–220** words.

Listening 2:
CAE Part 4

Multiple matching

1 ○ How far do you agree with each of the statements **A–H** in Task One below? Consider the future fifteen years from now when giving your opinions.

2 ⊙ **1.31–1.35** You will hear five short extracts in which different people are predicting what life will be like in fifteen years' time. **While you listen you must complete both tasks.**

Don't forget!
- Concentrate mainly, but not exclusively, on Task One the first time you listen.
- The second time you listen, give more attention to Task Two.

TASK ONE
For questions 1–5, choose from the list **A–H** the prediction each speaker makes.

A We will live longer.
B Houses will be smaller.
C Life in the workplace will be very different.
D There will be more technology in the home.
E There will be too many people.
F Technology will be smaller.
G We will lead healthier lives.
H There will be less traffic congestion.

1
2
3
4
5

TASK TWO
For questions 6–10, choose from the list A–H the feeling aroused in each speaker by the future they predict.

A amusement
B annoyance
C worry
D nostalgia
E amazement
F enthusiasm
G distrust
H indifference

6
7
8
9
10

3 ○ What are your own feelings about the future? How optimistic are you?

Language focus 3: Talking about the future

Both *will* and *going to* can be used when making predictions.

Examples:
It's *going to* change the way they do things here completely.
Life in the workplace *will* be very different.

1 In the following sentence from the listening, which of the verb forms in *italics* refers to:
a an activity that will be in progress at a certain time in the future?
b an event that will be finished before a certain time in the future?

Of course, *I'll have left* long before then, and *I'll probably be enjoying* a long, and healthy retirement somewhere.

2 For each pair of sentences 1–8, decide if the meaning is similar (**S**) or different (**D**). If the meaning is different, explain what is meant by each sentence.

1 I hope she passes.
  I expect she'll pass.
2 We're going to meet at seven.
  We're meeting at seven.
3 Will you come to the show on Friday?
  Will you be coming to the show on Friday?

4 The parcel should arrive tomorrow.
  The parcel might arrive tomorrow.
5 The Brighton train is due to leave at 6.20.
  The Brighton train leaves at 6.20.
6 I'm about to lose my temper.
  I'm on the point of losing my temper.
7 She's bound to get the job.
  She's likely to get the job.
8 He's confident of success.
  He's assured of success.
9 They're thinking of getting married.
  They're planning on getting married.
10 The Government is to spend £45 million on health care.
  The Government is expected to spend £45 million on health care.

G Read more about ways of talking about the future on pages 222 and 223 of the Grammar reference.

3 Write five true sentences using different structures from exercises 1 and 2.

4 ○ Discuss your sentences with your partner.

Determiners and pronouns

For **1–10**, complete each of the gaps with a word from the box. You do not need to use all the words.

little	few	other	others	another
much	many	all	either	neither
both	each	every	any	

1 I've nearly finished it – I just need _____ couple of weeks.
2 My computer class is every _____ day: Monday, Wednesday and Friday.
3 This is my favourite cheese, but there are one or two _____ I really like as well.
4 It took us a good _____ hours to drive to Leeds.
5 I was very tired, but there seemed _____ point in going to bed until the storm had passed.
6 I have to go to the dentist's three times a year, about once _____ four months.
7 I've got two brothers and _____ of us is different in some way.
8 Where have you been _____ this time? We've been worried sick!
9 You can pay as _____ as £20,000 for a mobile phone number.
10 Has _____ of you two got a pen you could lend me?

Use of English:
CAE Part 5

Key word transformations

For questions **1–8**, complete the second sentence so that it has a similar meaning to the first sentence, using the word given. **Do not change the word given.** Use between **three** and **six** words, including the word given.

1 Jake used his month's free membership really well by going to the gym every single day.
   MOST
   Jake _____ his month's free membership by going to the gym every single day.
2 The Japanese are the best at making pocket-sized technology.
   SECOND
   The Japanese _____ when it comes to making pocket-sized technology.
3 To reduce the amount of traffic, the government is proposing that drivers should only use their cars on alternate days.
   OTHER
   To reduce the amount of traffic, the government is proposing that cars should only _____ day.
4 Each and every one of our employees has contributed to the great success of our company.
   SINGLE
   The great success of our company is due to the contribution _____ our employees.
5 Can we please stay on one channel when we're watching TV?
   KEEP
   I wish you _____ the channel when we're watching TV.
6 During our summers at the beach, we often used to compete with each other to see who could collect the most shells.
   WOULD
   During our summers at the beach, we _____ another to see who could collect the most shells.
7 It's likely they were delayed in a traffic jam.
   PROBABLY
   They will _____ up in a traffic jam.
8 The company does not intend to create any redundancies amongst employees even though profits are down.
   NO
   Even though profits are down, the company _____ any of their employees redundant.

Use of English:
CAE Part 1

Multiple-choice cloze

For questions **1–12**, read the text and decide which answer (**A**, **B**, **C** or **D**) best fits each gap. There is an example at the beginning (**0**).

GADGETS FOR THE FUTURE

This year's Future Product of the Year Award has attracted a number of unusual entries, including the Inculpable Mousetrap and an alarm-clock duvet and pillow. Stuart Penny and Gianni Tozzi, both 29, **(0)** ____ the Inculpable Mousetrap as an 'exercise in morality' and accept it is unlikely to **(1)** ____ commercial success. You **(2)** ____ the trap, wander off to the pub and wait to see what happens. If a mouse approaches the trap, a transmitter **(3)** ____ to it sends a signal to your mobile phone. You are then **(4)** ____ to decide whether to activate the trap or not. You send back your answer as a text message and the trap's metal bar slams down or **(5)** ____ open accordingly.

Rachel Wingfield's alarm-clock duvet and pillow could **(6)** ____ the end for alarm clocks. They use pulsating light beams to wake sleepers and can be used individually or together. The sleeper **(7)** ____ programmes the alarm clock on their mobile phone, plugs it into a socket on the duvet or pillow and is woken at the correct time – with light. The whole effect is **(8)** ____ to replicate the break of **(9)** ____ . The duvet and pillow are woven through with electro-luminescent cords. At the **(10)** ____ time the mobile phone sends a tiny electric current through them and they begin to glow. Rachel, 24, says: 'Alarm clocks needlessly wake **(11)** ____ households. I wanted to design something **(12)** ____ at the individual sleeper.'

	A	B	C	D
0	projected	held	conceived	evaluated
1	favour	enjoy	appreciate	support
2	fix	put	set	shut
3	enclosed	attached	collated	united
4	offered	asked	urged	let
5	stays	holds	rests	lasts
6	say	speak	write	spell
7	uniquely	simply	plainly	purely
8	pretended	assumed	supposed	suggested
9	light	sunrise	dawn	fast
10	said	stated	announced	specified
11	full	total	whole	high
12	intended	targeted	planned	thought

9 Going places

Reading: CAE Part 4   Multiple matching

1 ◯ Have you ever been on holiday alone? If so, what was it like?

What are the advantages and disadvantages of a holiday spent on your own?

2 You are going to read an article about people going on holiday alone. For questions **1–15**, choose from the people **A–E**. The people may be chosen more than once. When more than one answer is required, these may be given in any order.

Which person/people...

started a relationship during the holiday?	**1** ____	**2** ____
did not enjoy everyone's company?	**3** ____	
has higher expectations of a holiday than he/she used to?	**4** ____	
had never felt the need to travel?	**5** ____	
enjoyed everyone's company?	**6** ____	
benefited from someone else's misfortune?	**7** ____	
intends to have the same type of holiday again?	**8** ____	**9** ____
liked the fact there was a mix of different people?	**10** ____	
gave up his/her job to travel?	**11** ____	
set out to do something before someone else?	**12** ____	
enjoyed the hard work involved?	**13** ____	
did not enjoy his/her first experience of holidaying alone?	**14** ____	
particularly appreciated the variety offered by the holiday?	**15** ____	

GOING IT ALONE

Want a trip you'll never forget? Go solo. With nobody but yourself to please, you can pick your dream holiday – and make some great friends into the bargain. Peter Hodson talks to five single travellers who blazed their own trail.

A Dominic

I'd never been away by myself or had any urge to see the world, but I'd begun to think there must be more to life than working all week and going out at the weekends. So I handed in my notice and went abroad. I started by taking a three-month overland trip from Kenya to South Africa in a truck with twenty other people.

It was tough at times, but that was part of the fun of it all. Everyone had to muck in and do their bit. If you were on cooking duty, you might have to get up at 4.30 am, and there were times when you'd have to dig the truck out of the mud. The other great thing about the trip was Cassandra. We took to each other straightaway and were a couple after a week or two. We didn't let it disrupt the dynamics of the group, though.

B Jim

A year after I was widowed I went on my own to Tenerife to a hotel that my wife and I had always enjoyed. I seemed to be the only single person there, surrounded by loving couples, and I couldn't wait to get home.

Then last year, some friends suggested I go on a singles holiday with a specialist tour operator to Turkey. I wasn't sure at first, but it turned out to be a great idea. The group really gelled, and we all got on like a house on fire. Although nobody went on the holiday looking for romance, a couple of relationships started. We did some sightseeing, went to nightclubs and organized nights in at the hotel.

I've already got myself a copy of the company's brochure for this year – it's just a question of where and when. After all, my sons are both grown up, so I don't have to worry about them any more.

C Hélène

I'd just split up with a man whose ambition had always been to get to the top of the 7,000-metre Mount Aconcagua in South America. Some months later I booked myself on to an expedition to do the climb myself. I just wanted to beat him to it, I guess.

It's a three-week expedition because you need to acclimatize, so there was quite a bit of time to get to know the other people. Everyone had come independently: two young guys aged 21 and 23, a man of 64 and a woman of 64, who I took an instant dislike to. She tired very quickly and didn't make it past second camp, which was a relief and meant I had a tent to myself. Then some of the others began to experience altitude sickness.

At the final camp the younger men pulled out and I went on with Barry, the older man. In the end we made it and came down to a very emotional reunion with the others.

D Alex

I hadn't had a holiday in three years and realized I needed to get away, so I booked a trip last Easter to Jordan. There were about sixteen people in the group, with a mix of singles, couples and a few friends who'd come along together. I certainly wasn't looking for a girlfriend – I just needed a break from work – but I hit it off with someone else in the group and we're still seeing each other.

These types of holidays are all about interacting with others, and the great thing is that you meet people from a variety of backgrounds and walks of life. The trip itself combined culture, relaxation and travelling, which suited most people, but I think next year I'll go for a higher proportion of relaxation.

E Miti

Ten years ago, I went around the world with a backpack and I got a real buzz out of travelling alone. I found that if you were single you could easily tag along with another group and strike up conversations, even friendships, with people. Since then, it's not been so easy. I no longer want to rough it – I work hard and I think I deserve a bit of pampering, but on most beach holidays you're surrounded by couples. You're just glad you've brought along a good pile of books.

Last year, though, I went to LaSource in Grenada, which combines sports, spa, good food and relaxation – and it was the best holiday of my life. The great thing about LaSource is that you can spend all day just lying by the pool and getting facials and manicures, or you can go off on boat trips or explore the beautiful island. There were plenty of couples there, but they tended to split up and do their own thing as individuals during the day, so it was easier to get to know them. I came back feeling fantastic, and, although I'm in a fairly steady relationship now, I can't wait to go back.

⬤ **Reacting to the text**

Rank the five holidays in order of preference, assuming that you had to go alone. Then explain your list to your partner.

Vocabulary 1: Doing things alone

1 Complete each of the gaps with an adjective from the box.

> single-handed   self-reliant   self-made   solitary

1 At one time Bill Gates was the youngest _____ billionaire in history.
2 15-year-old Seb Clover is the youngest person to sail across the Atlantic _____ .
3 The job taught me to be _____ ; to make decisions by myself without depending on others.
4 He was a shy, _____ man, who preferred the company of his cat to that of people.

2 Cross out the preposition that does not collocate with the words in bold.

1 Confident that I was capable of **fending with/for myself**, my parents went away for the weekend, **leaving me to/with my own devices**. I had the whole house **at/to myself** for the first time, and I could do whatever I wanted!
What would you have done in this situation?

2 As a child her parents encouraged her to **think for/by herself** rather than depend on them to make her decisions. She's clearly **got a mind of/on her own** now and will always do whatever *she* thinks is best.
How good are you at making your own decisions?

3 He was always a bit of a loner at school, **keeping himself very much to/with himself**. Even now he seems to prefer to be **on/by his own** most of the time.
Do you prefer your own company to that of others?

3 ◯ Answer each of the questions in italics in exercise 2.

4 ◯ Under what circumstances, if any, do you prefer to do each of the following alone?

> go to the cinema   listen to music   go shopping
> watch television   go for a walk   eat

Listening 1:
CAE Part 2

Sentence completion

1 ◯ Do you and your family usually go on package holidays, or do you prefer to organize your own? Give reasons.

2 ◉ 1.36 You will hear a radio programme about the travel pioneer, Thomas Cook. For questions **1–8**, complete the sentences.

Thomas Cook (1808–1892)

For his second job, Thomas Cook worked as a [_____ **1**].

At the age of 20 he became a Bible-reader and a [_____ **2**].

Thomas Cook had the idea of using the [_____ **3**] to help promote temperance.

In 1841 he organized a trip to attend a temperance [_____ **4**] in Loughborough.

Four years later Thomas Cook arranged the first [_____ **5**].

He later organized European holidays for English travellers from the [_____ **6**].

He provided travellers with an early version of [_____ **7**].

In the 1880s Thomas Cook was in charge of [_____ **8**] and military transport, both at home and in Egypt.

3 ⬤ Thomas Cook saw tourism as a way of providing opportunities for people to enrich themselves culturally and morally. To what extent do you think modern-day tourism achieves this?

We speak of *hordes of tourists, armies of tourists and tourist invasions*. How fair is this? What benefits can tourism bring?

What is the future of tourism in your country? How will people be spending their holidays in fifteen years from now?

Language focus: Creating emphasis

1 ⬤ 1.37 Listen to these three extracts from the listening and write the missing words in each gap.
a **What** many people don't know about Thomas Cook, though, is that _____ .
b **It** was _____ that led him to become a member of the Temperance Society.
c **It** _____ that he actually thought about making a profit from his idea.

2 The words you wrote in exercise 1 are given emphasis by the use of *What* and *It*. Sentence **a** without emphasis would be as follows:
Many people don't know that Thomas Cook was a very religious man.
Now rewrite sentences **b** and **c** without emphasis.

3 Here are some other ways of creating emphasis. Complete each of the explanations by writing one item from the box in each gap.

| a noun   a moment in time   a prepositional phrase |
| an action or series of actions   'the only thing that' |

a *What* can be used to emphasize _____ ;

Examples:
I couldn't find my key, so…
what I did was (to) *try and climb in through the window, but…*
what happened was (that) *a passer-by saw me and phoned the police.*

or _____ ;

Example:
What I need is *a cup of strong, black coffee.*

b *All* can be used instead of *What*, meaning _____ ;

Examples:
Don't make a fuss. **All I did was (to)** *spill some milk.*
He's so boring. **All he (ever) talks about is** *football.*

c *It* can be used to emphasize _____ ;
Example:
It was in France, *not their native England,* **that** *they first became famous.*
or with *when* to emphasize _____ ;

Example:
It was only when I got home that *I realized someone had stolen my wallet.*

4 Transform the following, emphasizing the part of the sentence which has been underlined. There is an example at the beginning (**0**).

Example:
0 *I find it amazing that <u>he can't even fry an egg.</u>*
What <u>I find amazing is that he can't even fry an egg</u>.

1 <u>How old is she?</u> That's what I'd like to know.
What _____ .
2 He lost his job, so <u>he started up his own business.</u>
He lost his job, so what he _____
_____ .
3 What I enjoyed most about the film was <u>the music.</u>
It _____ .
4 They got married <u>in June</u>, not July.
It _____ .
5 I didn't recognize him <u>until he took his hat off.</u>
It was only _____ .
6 I only found out she'd moved <u>when I spoke to Jerry.</u>
It wasn't _____ .
7 I don't know what that noise is. <u>I just switched it on</u>, that's all.
I don't know what that noise is.
All _____ .
8 He thinks about <u>his precious car</u> and nothing else.
All _____ .

⬤ Read more about creating emphasis on page 223 of the Grammar reference.

5 Complete each of the following sentences so that they are true for you.
a What worries me is…
b What I like most/least about school/my job is…
c What I'd like to know about… is…
d It was in… that I…
e I didn't enjoy… lessons at school. All we ever did was…

6 ⬤ Compare and discuss your sentences with another student.

Contributions: guidebook entry

1 ⬭ Do you enjoy visiting cities on holiday? Why/Why not?

2 ⬭ Read the following extract from a brochure on Edinburgh. Which of the places would you be most tempted to visit? Give reasons.

EDINBURGH
OFF THE BEATEN TRACK

Wander away from the city centre in any direction and you'll soon find yourself in another world of countryside and coastline, villages and hills – a region of endless variety, making the world of difference to Edinburgh as a quite unique holiday
5 destination.

Dean Village
Enter tranquil Dean Village from the New Town by steep Bell's Brae, and the bustle of city life is immediately left behind. Nestling contentedly in the valley of the Water of Leith, this
10 former milling community is now a popular residential area. From here, a leafy riverside walkway takes you into colourful Stockbridge, well known as a centre for antiques.

Cramond
Cramond lies at the mouth of the River Almond. In summer,
15 a daily ferry links this village of whitewashed cottages with Dalmeny Woods, an idyllic spot for a picnic. Stroll along the promenade towards Silverknowes or, when the tide is right, take the rocky causeway out to Cramond Island for spectacular views of the Forth Bridges in the distance. Follow
20 the path upstream of the river and you'll come across the overgrown ruins of old water mills. Further evidence of the village's long and eventful past can be seen in the remains of Roman fortifications in the grounds of Cramond Parish Church.

Portobello
25 Portobello takes its name from Puerto Bello in Panama, captured in the year this pleasant seaside resort was founded, 1739. This suburb of the city boasts a fine swimming complex with two pools and Turkish baths. There are two miles of golden sands to enjoy in the invigorating sea air against an
30 evocative background of typical Georgian and Victorian resort architecture.

George Square
Within easy walking distance of the city centre, George Square is at the heart of the University of Edinburgh.
35 A traditional meeting place for the city's student population, this peaceful garden oasis of manicured lawns and colourful blooms invites all to linger awhile and enjoy a few precious moments away from the hustle and bustle of everyday life.

Holyrood Park
40 No trip to Edinburgh would be complete without a walk in the magnificent parkland that is Holyrood Park. A network of paths ranging
45 from the gently sloping to the steep and craggy cut across the Park in every direction, leading the most energetic to the windswept summit of Arthur's Seat with its superb views.

Morningside and Braid Hills
The lively residential suburb of Morningside lies in the shadow
50 of the magnificent Braid Hills, acquired by the town council for use as a public golf course. The area of unspoilt countryside linking the Braid Hills with Blackford Hill is the Hermitage of Braid, a peaceful wooded public walk along the valley of Braid. At 539 feet, Blackford Hill towers over Southern
55 Edinburgh, its tracks and trails offering breathtaking views and unusual perspectives of Edinburgh and the Castle. The Royal Observatory (open to the public) sits in splendour at the top.

For further information on these areas contact the Edinburgh and Lothians Tourist Board

3 The extract contains a number of expressions which are typical of tourist brochures.

Use the nouns in the box to complete each of the expressions **1–10 as they were used in the extract**. Complete as many as possible from memory before checking your answers in the extract. There is an example at the beginning (**0**).

life	picnic	air	distance	~~variety~~	walkway
countryside	past	views	sands	destination	

0   a region of endless   *variety*

1   a quite unique holiday   _____
2   a leafy riverside   _____
3   an idyllic spot for a   _____
4   spectacular   _____
5   the village's long and eventful   _____
6   two miles of golden   _____
7   the invigorating sea   _____
8   within easy walking   _____
9   the hustle and bustle of everyday _____
10 an area of unspoilt   _____

4 Cover up the words on the right in exercise 3. How many can you remember now?

5 Underline any more words and expressions in the text which you feel might be useful when writing entries to other tourist brochures.

6 Read the following Part 2 task.

A guidebook is being produced in English for foreign visitors to your area, and you have been asked to write an entry for the section entitled 'Off the Beaten Track'. This section will include information about three places which are away from any city centre and not often visited by foreign tourists. You should:

- describe the places, saying why they will appeal to visitors.
- mention the kind of things they can expect to see and do there.
- include any historical information, if appropriate.

How to go about it

- Write down the names of *at least* four places **in your area** you could write about.
- For each place make notes according to the three bullet points in the task. Include any relevant vocabulary from the extract on Edinburgh and page 199 of Ready for Writing.
- Select three of the places. When choosing, consider how much you have to say and the range of language you could use.
- Write your answer, remembering to include a brief introduction and give each paragraph a heading.

Now write your **contribution to the guidebook**.

Don't forget!

You should write between 220 and 260 words, roughly half the length of the extract from the brochure on Edinburgh.

Listening 2:
CAE Part 3

Multiple choice

1 ⬭ Read the dictionary definitions and the newspaper headlines.

Why do you think people become so aggressive in cars and aeroplanes?

Have you witnessed or read about any examples of road and air rage?

air rage *n* [U] an airline passenger's verbal or physical assault of crew members or other passengers

road rage *n* [U] the uncontrolled anger of a motorist incited by the actions of another driver and expressed in aggressive or violent behaviour

Driver accused of 'road rage' shooting

Passenger faces two-year jail sentence for headbutting steward

2 ⊙ 1.38 You will hear a radio interview with a road safety expert on the topic of road rage. For questions **1–6**, choose the answer (**A**, **B**, **C** or **D**) which fits best according to what you hear.

1 James says that drivers become angry if
   A they think they will be delayed.
   B other drivers threaten them.
   C other people don't drive as well as they do.
   D they lose control of their car.

2 Revenge rage can lead motorists to
   A chase after dangerous drivers.
   B become distracted whilst driving.
   C deliberately damage another car.
   D take unnecessary risks.

3 Most 'revenge ragers' are
   A young male drivers.
   B drivers of large vehicles.
   C inexperienced drivers.
   D people who drive little.

4 James says that passengers become angry when buses are
   A slow.
   B expensive.
   C crowded.
   D uncomfortable.

5 What, according to James, does the experiment with grass show?
   A People living in country areas are better drivers.
   B Strong smells help us drive more safely.
   C Our surroundings can affect the way we drive.
   D Regular breaks on a journey keep drivers calm.

6 James thinks the hi-tech car
   A sounds less irritating than a passenger.
   B is not very reliable.
   C could cause further anger.
   D would be difficult to control.

3 ⬭ Do you have any suggestions for keeping calm in the car?

Does the public transport system in your area provide a viable alternative to the car?

How might the problem of traffic congestion in cities be solved?

Vocabulary 2: Anger

1   The following expressions were used in the listening to talk about people getting angry.

    Which two are more informal?

lose one's temper	blow a fuse	get worked up	become irate

2   Complete each of the gaps with an adjective from the box. The words in bold are common collocates of the adjectives.

seething	cross	heated	berserk	irate

1   They had a rather _____ **argument** about hunting, each with very different views on the topic.
2   The waitress was attempting to calm an extremely _____ **customer** who was complaining loudly about his bill.
3   Mummy's a little bit _____ **with you**, Peter. You know you shouldn't tell lies.
4   Her face showed no emotion, but inwardly she was absolutely _____ **with anger and indignation**.
5   He **went** completely _____ , shaking his fist at me and screaming blue murder.

3   Complete each of the gaps with a noun from the box.

outburst	rage	steam	tantrum	top

1   My dad would **blow his** _____ if he found out I'd been smoking.
2   When I refused his request, **he flew into a** _____ and stormed out of my office.
3   I was taken aback by her **sudden** _____ **of temper**.
4   I was furious; I had to go for a long walk to **let off** _____ .
5   If she doesn't get what she wants, she **throws a** _____ , stamping her feet and screaming her head off.

4   ⬤   What sort of things make you angry?

    What do you do when you lose your temper?

    What do you do to calm down?

Long turn

Look at these pictures. They show people who are angry for various reasons.

Student A:
Compare two of the pictures, and say what might have happened to make these people angry and what might happen next.

Student B:
When your partner has finished talking about the pictures, say which of those situations is the most unpleasant for the person on the receiving end of the anger.

Now change roles. Follow the instructions again using the remaining pictures.

Before you do the task, complete the exercises at the top of page 121.

> • What might have happened to make these people angry?
> • What might happen next?

What to expect in the exam

• One student speaks for a minute about two pictures from a set of three. The other student has about 30 seconds to answer an additional question on the same set of pictures.
• Both students are then given a second set of pictures and the roles are reversed

Useful language

1 For each picture, decide which of the words and expressions from the Vocabulary section on page 119 you could use when talking about it.

2 Complete each of the gaps with one of the pairs of words in the box. There is an example at the beginning (**0**).

> looks as   looks like   may well   ~~seems quite~~
>   very likely   fair chance   might have

0 She _seems quite_ cross.

1 He _____ been put in the wrong room.
2 She _____ have done something dangerous.
3 He _____ if he's about to burst into tears.
4 There's a _____ they'll come to blows.
5 They're _____ to go their own separate ways.
6 It _____ an example of road rage.

Word formation: Alternatives from the same prompt word

In these two extracts from the listening on page 118, the underlined adverbs are both formed from the same root, *consider*.

On country roads there is <u>considerably</u> less traffic.
It also praises them when they are driving <u>considerately</u>.

1 Which other noun, apart from the one underlined, can be formed from the word in capitals?

  …suggestions as to how we can maintain our <u>composure</u> in the car   **COMPOSE**

2 Underline the appropriate alternative in the following sentences. Each alternative is formed from the same prompt word given in capitals at the end of the sentence. Pay attention to the words in bold; these words are collocates of the correct alternative.

Example:
First prize is **the not** *inconsiderate/<u>inconsiderable</u>* **sum** of £500,000.   **CONSIDER**

1 'The Lord of the Rings' is *a timeless/an untimely* **classic**, as fresh today as it was when it was first published.   **TIME**
2 I grew up in England but Spain has become my *adopted/adoptive* **country**.   **ADOPT**
3 **Appearances** can be very *deceitful/deceptive*.   **DECEIVE**
4 He produced a wealth of *supporting/supportive* **evidence** to substantiate his claim.   **SUPPORT**
5 There has been **an** *appreciative/appreciable* **increase** in global temperatures over the last two decades.   **APPRECIATE**
6 Police have refused to **reveal the** *identification/identity* of the man detained in connection with the murder.   **IDENTIFY**
7 The appointment with my GP was at 8.30, but it wasn't until 9.15 that I was finally shown into her *consulting/consultative* **room**.   **CONSULT**
8 The Macmillan English **Dictionary** for advanced learners contains over 100,000 *entrances/entries*.   **ENTER**
9 Millions of innocent civilians **suffered great** *hardness/hardship* as a result of the war.   **HARD**
10 He's retired and now works for the company **in an** *advisory/advisable* **capacity**.   **ADVISE**
11 The gardens contain a wealth of plants and flowers **of every** *imaginary/imaginable/imaginative* **colour**.   **IMAGINE**
12 My two brothers, Pat and Eric, were both given heavy prison sentences **for their** *respectable/respective/respectful* **crimes**.   **RESPECT**

Word formation

For questions **1–10**, use the word given in capitals at the end of some of the lines to form a word that fits in the gap **in the same line**. There is an example at the beginning (**0**).

ANGER

We've all felt anger at some time, whether as faint (**0**) _annoyance_ or blind rage.   **ANNOY**
Anger is a normal, sometimes useful human emotion, but uncontrolled outbursts of
temper can be (**1**) _____ . 'People who give free rein to their anger,   **DESTROY**
(**2**) _____ of the offence this may cause, haven't learned to express themselves   **REGARD**
constructively,' says Martin Smolik, who runs weekend (**3**) _____ courses in   **RESIDENCE**
anger management. 'It is important to maintain your (**4**) _____ and put your   **COMPOSE**
case in an assertive, not aggressive, manner without hurting others. Being assertive
doesn't mean being pushy or demanding; it means being (**5**) _____ of yourself   **RESPECT**
and other people.' He adds that people who are (**6**) _____ angered are   **EASY**
intolerant of frustration, (**7**) _____ or irritation and, not surprisingly, find   **CONVENIENT**
(**8**) _____ to other people very difficult. But what causes people to behave like   **RELATE**
this? It seems there is evidence to support the idea that some children may be born
(**9**) _____ and prone to anger and this tendency is sometimes apparent from a   **IRRITATE**
very early age. However, research also suggests that a person's family (**10**) _____   **GROUND**
may have an influence. Very often, people who are quick-tempered come from
disorganized and disruptive families who find it difficult to express their emotions.

Vocabulary

1 In **A** and **B**, form expressions by matching each of the verbs **1–6** with an appropriate ending **a–f**. The first one has been done for you.

A Anger
1 lose   **a** off steam
2 fly   **b** a tantrum
3 let   **c** your temper
4 throw   **d** berserk
5 blow   **e** into a rage
6 go   **f** a fuse

B Doing things alone
1 do   **a** it alone
2 fend   **b** your own thing
3 leave   **c** yourself to yourself
4 keep   **d** a mind of your own
5 have   **e** you to your own devices
6 go   **f** for yourself

2 Complete sentences **1–5** using the expressions in exercise 1. You may need to change some of the words.

Example:
0 *Those who do not wish to come on this afternoon's excursion are quite welcome to go off and* _do their own thing_ .

1 I have a large cushion at work, which I punch every time I need to _____ .
2 Because of old age and ill health she could no longer _____ and she had to go into a nursing home.
3 All I did was ask him how old he was and he _____ absolutely _____ .
4 I don't know him very well; he's very quiet and he _____ .
5 Rather like a small child who _____ , she will scream, shout and stamp her feet to get what she wants.

Use of English:
CAE Part 4

Gapped sentences

For questions **1–5**, think of one word only which can be used appropriately in all three sentences. Here is an example (**0**).

0 I share a flat with two friends but we all do our ___own___ cooking.

My grandfather used to ___own___ a cat called Charlie that hissed at every visitor to the house.

When Mrs Brindle demanded to know who'd broken the window, none of the students would ___own___ up.

1 We went on a coach tour and visited several local beauty _____ .

The day after the injection she came out in _____ and had to go back to the doctor's.

As soon as she _____ another dog, Molly starts barking and pulling at the lead.

2 All members of the History Society have free _____ to over 200 castles and monuments throughout the country.

The closing date for the competition is Friday May 8th and the winning _____ will be published in the July issue of *The Traveller*.

Each dictionary _____ contains detailed information about the etymology, or origins, of the word.

3 The television company _____ in close collaboration with teachers to devise the series of educational programmes.

My sister gets _____ up if I borrow her clothes without asking her first.

The modem _____ perfectly the first time I tried it, but it's not showing any signs of life now.

4 We do not share the governments _____ that the minimum voting age should be reduced to sixteen.

They watched the plane take off and gradually disappear from _____.

We had a breathtaking _____ of the mountains from our hotel room.

5 The researchers interviewed a wide _____ section of society for the survey.

I heard that in some countries it's considered rude to _____ your legs when other people are present.

I get very _____ with her when she tells lies.

Introduction

Paper 4 lasts approximately 40 minutes and contains four parts. In all four parts the recordings are heard twice. At the end of Paper 4 you will have five minutes to transfer your answers onto the separate answer sheet. Each correct answer is awarded one mark.

Part 1: Multiple choice

1 In Part 1 you will hear three short extracts from conversations between two or more people. The recordings, which are all on different themes, may be taken, for example, from radio broadcasts, interviews or discussions. There are two multiple-choice questions for each extract. You will hear the same extract twice before moving on to the next one.

2 ● 2.1–2.3 You will hear three different extracts. For questions **1–6**, choose the answer (**A**, **B** or **C**) which fits best according to what you hear.

Extract One

You hear part of an interview with a lecturer in journalism talking about the issue of global warming.

1 Why does the lecturer compare articles on war with articles on global warming?
   A to show that journalism is not truly objective
   B to emphasize that global warming has dangerous consequences
   C to suggest that public protest is growing

2 The lecturer says that people will do less harm to the environment when
   A reporters and writers present accurate information.
   B they see how they can personally benefit from it.
   C the government passes laws to make them.

Extract Two

You hear part of an interview with Andy Marsden, the owner of a chocolate manufacturing company and shop.

3 What made Andy decide to buy Kiss Chocolates?
   A He had once been employed there.
   B His wife and the owner were old friends.
   C He thought it would provide a safe future.

4 What does Andy like most about working at Kiss Chocolates?
   A testing the chocolates
   B dealing with customers
   C making a steady profit

Extract Three

You hear two people on a book review programme talking about a book called *The Children of Hurin*.

5 The two speakers agree that *The Children of Hurin*
   A is hard to put down.
   B has a sad feel to it.
   C ends in a surprising way.

6 What slight criticism does the man make about the book?
   A It contains different styles of writing.
   B The characters are not complex enough.
   C The themes may not appeal to modern readers.

3 Check your answers by looking at the listening script on pages 233 and 234. Underline the part or parts of each extract which indicate the correct answer.

Part 2: Sentence completion

1 In Part 2 you will hear a monologue lasting approximately three minutes. The recording will be taken from one of a possible number of sources including radio broadcasts, speeches, talks, lectures, anecdotes and announcements.

There are eight questions testing your understanding of specific information and people's opinions. You are required to complete sentences with numbers, single words or short phrases, usually of no more than three words.

2 ◉ 2.4 You will hear part of talk by Amanda Tyler, who is a waxwork sculptor. For questions **1–8**, complete the sentences.

What to expect in the exam

- For Part 2 tasks you have 45 seconds to read the questions. Use this time to think about the kind of information you might hear and the language structure you might need to complete each question.
  eg 1 A noun will be needed here, possibly preceded by an adjective. It will probably be a part of the building, but the preposition 'in' can't be followed by 'first floor', 'second floor', etc.
- For some of the questions you will hear distractors, words which might at first seem relevant, but which do not complete the questions correctly. For question 2, for example, you will hear Amanda mention two courses she took. Only one of these, however, is a degree course; the other is a distractor.
  As you read each question, underline key words to help you focus on the exact information required. The first two have been done for you.

WAXWORK SCULPTOR

Amanda's <u>studio</u> is situated <u>in the</u> [＿＿＿＿＿ **1**] <u>of the</u> wax <u>museum</u>.

She took a <u>degree course</u> called [＿＿＿＿＿ **2**].

She particularly enjoys the part of her job which requires her to

[＿＿＿＿＿ **3**] of a subject.

She uses the clay model of a famous television [＿＿＿＿＿ **4**] to

explain how a waxwork figure is made.

The frame of a figure consists of wire netting and rods made out

of [＿＿＿＿＿ **5**].

The figure Amanda is currently working on will be in a characteristic

[＿＿＿＿＿ **6**] position.

She can take up to [＿＿＿＿＿ **7**] to complete a waxwork figure.

The make-up artist applies a combination of [＿＿＿＿＿ **8**] and

cosmetics to colour the wax head.

3 On page 207 you will find one student's answers to the listening task above together with relevant advice about what to do and what not to do.

Did you make any similar mistakes?

Part 3: Multiple choice

1 Part 3 consists of a conversation between two or more speakers lasting approximately four minutes. There are six multiple-choice questions, mostly testing your understanding of the attitudes and opinions of the speakers. The questions follow the same order as the corresponding information in the recording.

> ### What to expect in the exam
>
> - For Part 3 tasks you have one minute to read through the questions.
> - As with the other Parts of Paper 4, you will hear words and ideas which may cause you to choose the wrong answer.

2 You will hear an interview with Sandra Peyton and David Sadler, who work as partners in the media company, Advert Eyes, making TV commercials. For questions **1–6**, choose the answer (**A, B, C** or **D**) which fits best according to what you hear.

3 Before you answer questions **1–6**, here is an example (**0**). Read the question and the shaded section of the recording on page 234. Decide on the correct answer, underlining the part or parts of the text which justify your choice.

0 Why did Sandra leave her job with the satellite TV company?
  A She was unhappy with the salary.
  B She felt she was too old for the job.
  C She predicted she might lose her job.
  D She did not get on with her colleagues.

4 With your partner, explain with reference to the text why the other options are wrong.

5 👁 2.5 Now read questions **1–6**. Then listen to the recording and choose the correct answers.

1 What did David learn from his time with Trenton TV?
  A the need to work as part of a team
  B the importance of having a positive outlook
  C the advantages of working under pressure
  D the need to question existing practices

2 What impressed Sandra about David when they first met?
  A his experience
  B his appearance
  C his future plans
  D his enthusiasm

3 What made David accept Sandra's proposal to go into partnership?
  A He had always enjoyed taking risks.
  B He felt they had a similar way of thinking.
  C She had relevant directing experience.
  D She was familiar with the business world.

4 How did Sandra feel when she was having problems raising money for the business?
  A puzzled
  B depressed
  C angry
  D worried

5 What does David consider to be a drawback of directing TV commercials?
  A He does not achieve enough recognition for his work.
  B He does not have enough control over content.
  C Money has too great an influence on the process.
  D Many clients have unrealistic expectations.

6 What do Sandra and David say about the future of their company?
  A They would prefer to keep their plans a secret.
  B Their aim is to expand at some time in the future.
  C They are unsure how the company will develop.
  D They hope to move into other areas of directing.

6 Look at the listening script on pages 234 and 235 and for questions **1–6** follow the same procedure as in exercises **3** and **4** above.

Part 4: Multiple matching

1 In Part 4 you will hear five short monologues which are all related in some way. For each speaker there are two separate tasks. For each task you are required to select the correct option from a choice of eight.

2 ◉ 2.6–2.10 You will hear five short extracts in which different people are talking about living abroad. **While you listen you must complete both tasks.**

Concentrate mainly, but not exclusively, on Task One the first time you listen. The second time you listen, give more attention to Task Two.

What to expect in the exam

- You have 45 seconds to read through the tasks.
- Listen to the whole of each monologue to find the answers to both tasks. You may hear the answer to Task Two before the answer to Task One. This is the case with Speaker 4 below.
- Once again, you will hear distractors.

TASK ONE

For questions 1–5, choose from the list **A–H** the main reason why each speaker went to live abroad.

A to be with his/her partner   ☐ 1

B for health reasons

C to speak the language   ☐ 2

D for work reasons

E to earn more money   ☐ 3

F to run away from a problem   ☐ 4

G for a change of routine

H to study   ☐ 5

TASK TWO

For questions 6–10, choose from the list **A–H** what the speaker says about living abroad.

A I miss my family.   ☐ 6

B The weather can be depressing.

C I go home regularly.   ☐ 7

D Life is more exciting here.

E I regret coming here.   ☐ 8

F It's a cosmopolitan place.   ☐ 9

G I feel like an outsider.

H I won't stay here for ever.   ☐ 10

---

3 Check your answers using the listening script on page 235. Underline those parts of each extract which guide you to the correct answers.

4 One student wrote the following **incorrect** answers for questions **6–10** in Task Two.

   6 D   **7** A   **8** C   **9** B   **10** H

Identify the distractor in each extract which may have caused the student to choose the wrong answer.

Example:
6 Speaker 1: *Plus it seemed so exciting when I came here two years ago.*

Vocabulary 1: Describing rooms and houses

1 Some adjectives for describing rooms are often used in partnership with others which have a similar or related meaning. Match each adjective **1–6** with another **a–f** to form appropriate partnerships. The first one has been done for you.

1	bright and		**a**	tidy
2	light and		**b**	dingy
3	neat and		**c**	cheerful
4	dark and		**d**	cosy
5	warm and		**f**	cluttered
6	cramped and		**e**	airy

2 All three adverbs in each group **a–e** below collocate with one of the adjectives in the box. Write an appropriate adjective from the box in each space.

> furnished   built   situated   decorated   lit

a dimly
   brightly   _____
   softly

c tastefully
   newly   _____
   richly

e conveniently
   ideally   _____
   pleasantly

b comfortably
   sparsely   _____
   elegantly

d recently
   poorly   _____
   solidly

3 ⬤ Using the adjectives and adverbs from exercises 1 and 2, describe your:
• home and its location   • bedroom   • living room

Example: I live on the outskirts of the city in a rented flat. It isn't very conveniently situated – there are no shops nearby and as the underground doesn't go out that far, I have to walk or get the bus everywhere. It's solidly built, but the stairwell is rather dark and dingy…

4 ⬤ Work with a partner. Each describe one of the rooms in the pictures below, saying what type of person the room might belong to and how you would feel about living there.

Use of English 1: Open cloze
CAE Part 2

1 ⬤ Why do many people hate doing housework?

2 Read the following text, ignoring the gaps for the moment. According to the text, why is housework so depressing?

HOUSEWORK GETS YOU DOWN

It may come (0) _as_ no surprise to learn that household chores can make you feel depressed. There is evidence (1) ____ suggest that the more housework men and women do, the more likely they (2) ____ to suffer from mood swings. 'Any form of repetitive cyclical work (3) ____ bound to be depressing,' says psychologist Nicholas Emler. 'Domestic chores are open-ended tasks, so there is no defined end point. People prefer tasks they can complete, and (4) ____ a satisfactory conclusion they become stressed.'

Work in the home has no job description and family members rarely appreciate just (5) ____ much work has gone into preparing an evening meal or cleaning the bathroom. Women still take responsibility (6) ____ the lion's share of domestic chores, but with many in full-time jobs they can (7) ____ longer pride themselves on having a spotless home. 'The concept of being house-proud is out of fashion,' says Prof Emler, who points (8) ____ that the vast majority of men continue to shy away (9) ____ doing the dishes. In other situations financial reward can go (10) ____ way to compensating for dull, repetitive work, but housework is a strenuous job with no pay.

Writer Tracy Kerry believes that many people nowadays just don't know how to do housework. 'There are an awful (11) ____ of inexperienced people whose mothers were (12) ____ busy working to show them. Sweeping a room (13) ____ seem an easy enough task to perform, but there's a right way and a wrong way to do it. To make housework easier she suggests (14) ____ get rid of possessions that are of no use to us any more. 'Keep clutter (15) ____ control and you will feel more able to cope.'

---

3 Read the text again and complete each gap with **one** word. There is an example at the beginning (0). Use the questions and advice in the box to help you.

1	Why is a relative pronoun not possible here?
2/3	See page 222 for the grammar of 'likely' and 'bound'.
4	Will the missing word have a positive or negative meaning?
5	Overall context and 'just' before the gap will help you make your choice.
6	Which preposition is required after 'responsibility'?
7	Look at the surrounding context. Can women 'pride themselves on having a spotless home' now?
8	This phrasal verb appeared on page 94.
9	A preposition is required to complete this phrasal verb.
10	Why is an adjective *not* possible here before the singular countable noun 'way'?
11	See page 101 for the expression 'an awful ____ of'.
12	Note the infinitive later in the sentence.
13	Note that 'seem' is the infinitive form of the verb, not the third person singular. What does this tell you about the type of word required in the gap?
14	See page 221 for the grammar of 'suggest'.
15	Which preposition is used in the expression 'keep something _____ control'?

4 ⬤ Who does 'the lion's share of domestic chores' in your house? Why?

To what extent are you/your parents house-proud?

Do you follow the advice in the last sentence of the text? What other advice would you give to make housework less depressing?

Reading:
CAE Part 3

Multiple choice

1 ◯ In what ways would your life be different if your house had no running water, no electricity and no central heating? How would you cope?

2 Read through the text quickly and anwer the following questions:
What is your initial reaction to the story of Albert Juttus?
Do you feel sympathy for him? Why (not)?

3 Now read the text again and for questions **1–7** on page 131, choose the correct answer **A**, **B**, **C** or **D**.

THE JOY OF PLUMBING

I'm driving along a road in Leicestershire, in the tidy heart of the English countryside, where slick green fields roll out on either side to the horizon. I drive through the village of Shenton, a quiet place without
5 so much as a pub, past prosperous-looking farms and neat brick houses. And then I pull up outside a rather shabby bungalow. Around the bungalow is a sea of mud. Between the road and the bungalow there is a ditch, choked with weeds, with a little muddy stream trickling
10 along it. I push open the door of the bungalow to find Albert Juttus, a gentle-looking 73-year-old, sitting in his front room before a tiny heater running off a cylinder of Calor gas. He's lived in this house for 46 years, and in all that time his only source of water has been that muddy
15 ditch.
'I'm on the move from the 17th century,' he says. 'They're putting me right in the 21st century.' He had lived his life in total obscurity until last week, when the local council awarded him its biggest-ever grant, over
20 £40,000, to transform his tiny property. It will now be connected to running water, given a new roof, windows and doors, as well as a lavatory, a sink and a shower. His wife, Grace, has moved temporarily into a nursing home while the work is in progress. Since the announcement
25 of that grant, the council has been rather embarrassed by the interest that Albert Juttus's belated journey into the 21st century has attracted: front-page coverage in the local paper and visits to his humble dwelling by television journalists.
30 But Albert Juttus's life isn't just an odd curiosity: it says something about communities and how they work, or don't work, in Britain today. Having become rather frail and vulnerable in the last few years, he and his wife were heavily reliant on the good nature of one
35 neighbour, who declines to be named. Her tales of their neglected life strike a chill into your heart. 'Every time I came back from seeing them my son would say, 'you've been down at Albert's'. The stink was so bad in their house it would get in my clothes.'
40 For two people in their seventies, coping without running water and electricity had already become too much many years ago. The couple, who have no family, did not realize they were entitled to an improvement grant. 'We have never had very much, but we have
45 always had each other,' said Albert, 'and that's all we ever wanted. We've never been comfortable with the idea of handouts.' The local council said they'd have acted sooner, had they known about the Juttuses, but the couple had obviously been slipping through the net for
50 a long time.

And it would be wrong to see Albert Juttus as just someone to be pitied. In many ways he's a real survivor. Fleeing from Estonia in 1946, he came to Britain without knowing a word of English. After a succession
55 of low-paid jobs on farms and in mills, he found work in a nearby tyre factory. He had friends there, but although he knew he was the only one without running water and electricity, his only thought was of the bills they must have had to pay each month. 'I didn't think I could
60 deal with those big bills,' he remembers. And didn't they tell you to get your life together? Juttus looks a little shocked. 'They wouldn't speak out of turn,' he says quietly. So this man, living on a labourer's wage, with a wife who didn't work, clearly believed he was just
65 locked out of the lifestyle that everyone around him took for granted.
So how did change ever come to this little house lost in time? Albert Juttus, in his bizarrely modest but oddly practical way, decided that it was indeed pretty
70 hard getting water out of the ditch, but that it would be easier if he had a proper well. So some time ago he asked a health worker whether they could get someone to dig a well and their case was referred to a charity called Care and Repair. Shocked beyond belief by what they saw
75 when they visited the house, these people began to put pressure on the council to rectify the situation.
Doesn't Mr Juttus wish he'd managed to change it all much earlier? 'It's too late to wish now,' he says, stubbing out a cigarette. 'Times never return.' And clearly
80 something in him even feels ambivalent about the new life that looms ahead. 'It's easy, isn't it, you just switch a button or turn a tap, it all just happens. But, I'll get spoilt. They'll be bringing me slippers and a pipe next.'
It would have been a lot easier for the council if he
85 had agreed to move into a spanking new home on a smart estate, but he wouldn't do that. At the back of his house the view sweeps on and on over green fields and to the soft surge of low hills fringed with trees. 'That's the good thing about the country,' he says, looking out
90 over the familiar prospect. 'You see long distances. I can sit out before sunset, when the birds start singing. I wouldn't like to move. What for?'

1 On arriving at the Juttuses' bungalow, the writer was struck by

   A its isolation from the rest of the community.
   B the ease with which she entered it.
   C the contrast it made with the surrounding area.
   D the beauty of the countryside in which it was situated.

2 What had recently changed for Albert Juttus at the time of the writer's visit?

   A He had achieved a certain amount of fame.
   B His house had been completely renovated.
   C He had had new lighting installed.
   D He had inherited a large sum of money.

3 The Juttuses went so long without basic amenities because

   A they had not previously qualified for a grant.
   B they had refused offers of financial aid.
   C the authorities were unaware of their situation.
   D they had always received help from local people.

4 What does Albert imply about his workmates in the tyre factory?

   A They were probably earning more than he was.
   B They did not appreciate how lucky they were.
   C They had more right to running water and electricity than he did.
   D They were not the type of people to interfere in the affairs of others.

5 What led to the Juttuses receiving an improvement grant?

   A They applied to a charity for some money.
   B They complained about the health risks.
   C Other people decided to act on their behalf.
   D Albert came down with a serious illness.

6 What does Albert feel about the changes to his house?

   A He regrets not making them before.
   B He is uncertain whether he will like them.
   C He thinks the council could do more.
   D He cannot believe how fortunate he is.

7 In the last paragraph we learn that Albert does not want to leave his house because

   A a suitable new home has not yet been offered to him.
   B he is mistrustful of the local authorities.
   C the view reminds him of where he used to live.
   D he is very attached to his surroundings.

⬤ Reacting to the text

How common is it for people in your country to live in conditions like those of the Juttuses? What do local authorities do to help such people?

'He came to Britain without knowing a word of English.' What difficulties would someone in this situation face? Would you be able to cope?

'I wouldn't like to move. What for?' How true is this for you? Where would you prefer to live if you had to move:
a to another part of your town or city?
b to a different part of your country?
c abroad?

Vocabulary 2: Metaphorical meanings

1 Words can often have a metaphorical meaning in addition to their literal meaning.
Compare the use of 'icy' in these two sentences:

The pavement was <u>*icy*</u>.   Literal meaning: 'covered with ice'.
Her eyes met his <u>*icy*</u> *stare*.   Metaphorical meaning: 'unfriendly; cold, like ice'.

2 The underlined words in the following extracts from the text are used metaphorically.
What is the meaning of these words:
a as they are used in the extract?
b in their literal sense?

green fields <u>*roll out*</u> *on either side*   *the view* <u>*sweeps*</u> *on and on over green fields*
a ditch, <u>*choked*</u> *with weeds*   *low hills,* <u>*fringed*</u> *with trees*
a <u>*sea*</u> *of mud*   *the tidy* <u>*heart*</u> *of the English countryside*

3 In each of the exercises **A** and **B**, complete the gaps with one of the words from the box.

A Verbs

nestles	towers	thunders	stretches	sits	hugs

1 Every time **a lorry** _____ **past**, the house shakes.
2 **The mountain** _____ **above** the city's eastern suburbs.
3 **The house** _____ **proudly on top of** a hill overlooking the river.
4 **The road** _____ **the coast** for a mile before heading off inland.
5 **The village** _____ **cosily** in an unspoilt alpine valley.
6 **The town** _____ **along** the river valley towards the sea.

B Nouns

nightmare	tide	eyesore	stream	patchwork	roar

1 There is mounting anxiety about **the rising** _____ **of crime** in our town.
2 **The deafening** _____ **of the sea** makes it difficult to speak in the garden.
3 There's **a constant** _____ **of cars**, all making their way to the new shopping complex.
4 Trying to find a place to park around here is **a real** _____ .
5 The new office block is **a major** _____ : it completely ruins the view.
6 As you come into land you fly over **a** _____ **of green fields** and stone walls.

4 ⬭ Describe the picture on this page using some of the words from exercises 2 and 3.

5 ⬭ Write sentences using four of the words from exercises 2 and 3 in their metaphorical sense to describe places in your region. Read out each sentence without saying the name of the place. Can your partner guess which place you have described?

Language focus: Participle clauses

1 Participle clauses are clauses which begin with a present or past participle. They help to express ideas concisely and are more commonly used in written English.

Participle clauses can be used instead of relative clauses, as in this example from the reading text:

Between the road and the bungalow there is a ditch, (which is) choked with weeds…

Which words have been omitted from the following sentence to create a participle clause?

So this man, living on a labourer's wage, clearly believed he was just locked out of the lifestyle.

2 Conjunctions like *and, so, because, as, when, after* and *if* can also be omitted to create participle clauses. Underline the sentences in the reading text which express the same ideas as **a–d** below.

a *Because* they had become rather frail and vulnerable in the last few years, he and his wife were heavily reliant on the good nature of one neighbour.

b He fled from Estonia in 1946 *and* came to Britain.

c These people were shocked beyond belief by what they saw when they visited the house, *so* they began to put pressure on the local council.

d 'That's the good thing about the country,' he says, *as* he looks out over the familiar prospect.

3  Explain the difference in meaning between the following pairs of sentences. Which sentence in each pair is more likely?

1 a Driving home from the pub last night, the police stopped him.
  b Driving home from the pub last night, he was stopped by the police.

2 a The manager being ill, Elisa took over all his responsibilities for the week.
  b Being ill, Elisa took over all the manager's responsibilities for the week.

Read more about participle clauses on page 223 of the Grammar reference.

Practice

1 Sentences **1–6** contain participle clauses. Rewrite each one using conjunctions or relative pronouns. There is an example at the beginning (**0**).

0 Not wanting to wake anyone up, she took her shoes off and tiptoed up the stairs.
She didn't want to wake anyone up, so she took her shoes off and tiptoed up the stairs.

1 Having won the silver medal in the 100 metres, he went on to take gold in the 200 metres and long jump.

2 Don't look now, but the woman sitting next to you is wearing shoes made of crocodile skin.

3 Drunk in moderation, red wine is thought to protect against coronary disease.

4 Wrapped in a blanket and looking tired after his ordeal, Mr Brown was full of praise for the rescue services.

5 Reaching for the sugar, he knocked over his glass, spilling wine over her new dress.

6 Having never been abroad before, Brian was feeling a little on edge.

2 Rewrite the following sentences using participle clauses.

1 Because I live within walking distance of the centre, I rarely use the car.

2 When I was cycling in to work the other day, I saw a deer.

3 As we'd never had so much peace and quiet before, we found living here a little strange at first.

4 Our bedroom, which is situated at the back of the building, has some superb views over the rooftops towards the docks.

5 If you play it at full volume, it really annoys the neighbours.

6 The house is a little off the beaten track, so it's not that easy to find.

7 After the children had all left home, we decided to move away from the hustle and bustle.

8 Although it is not known for its tourist attractions, our neighbourhood does have one or two treasures which are waiting to be discovered.

3 For each of the sentences in exercise 2, say whether you think the speaker lives in a rural area or a city. Which would you prefer to live in? Give reasons.

Self help

Appropriate use of participle clauses in your answers in the Writing Paper will add variety to your writing and help create a good impression.

Use of English 2:
CAE Part 1

Multiple-choice cloze

1 ⬤ How often do you talk to your neighbours? What do you talk about?

2 For questions **1–12**, read the text and decide which answer (**A**, **B**, **C** or **D**) best fits each gap. There is an example at the beginning (**0**).

Don't forget!

- Read the text through first before making your choices.
  Answer these questions as you read:
  What has caused the decline in communication between neighbours in Britain?
  What has been one of the effects of this decline?

A LACK OF COMMUNICATION

Recent research has **(0)** ____ that a third of people in Britain have not met their **(1)** ____ neighbours, and those who know each other **(2)** ____ speak. Neighbours gossiping over garden fences and in the street was a common **(3)** ____ in the 1950s, says Dr Carl Chinn, an expert on local communities. Now, however, longer hours spent working at the office, together with the Internet and satellite television, are eroding neighbourhood **(4)** ____. 'Poor neighbourhoods once had strong kinship, but now prosperity buys privacy,' said Chinn.

Professor John Locke, a social scientist at Cambridge University, has analysed a large **(5)** ____ of surveys. He found that in America and Britain the **(6)** ____ of time spent in social activity is decreasing. A third of people said they never spoke to their neighbours at **(7)** ____. Andrew Mayer, 25, a strategy consultant, rents a large apartment in west London, with two flatmates, who work in e-commerce. 'We have a family of teachers upstairs and lawyers below, but our only contact comes via letters **(8)** ____ to the communal facilities or complaints that we've not put out our bin bags properly,' said Mayer.

The **(9)** ____ of communities can have serious effects. Concerned at the rise in burglaries and **(10)** ____ of vandalism, the police have relaunched crime prevention schemes such as Neighbourhood Watch, **(11)** ____ on people who live in the same area to **(12)** ____ an eye on each others' houses and report anything they see which is unusual.

0 A exhibited	**B** conducted	**C** displayed	**D** <u>revealed</u>
1 A side-on	**B** next-door	**C** close-up	**D** nearside
2 A barely	**B** roughly	**C** nearly	**D** virtually
3 A outlook	**B** view	**C** vision	**D** sight
4 A ties	**B** joints	**C** strings	**D** laces
5 A deal	**B** amount	**C** number	**D** measure
6 A deal	**B** amount	**C** number	**D** measure
7 A least	**B** once	**C** all	**D** most
8 A concerning	**B** regarding	**C** applying	**D** relating
9 A breakout	**B** breakthrough	**C** breakdown	**D** breakaway
10 A acts	**B** shows	**C** counts	**D** works
11 A asking	**B** calling	**C** inviting	**D** trying
12 A put	**B** keep	**C** hold	**D** give

3 ⬤ What findings do you think similar research in your own country would reveal? Do you agree with Dr Chinn that 'prosperity buys privacy'?

Multiple matching

1　🔘 2.11–2.15 You will hear five short extracts in which people are talking about noise from the neighbouring house. **While you listen you must complete both tasks.**

TASK ONE	TASK TWO
For questions 1–5, choose from the list **A–H** what the cause of the noise was.	For questions 6–10, choose from the list **A–H** what the speakers say about the effect the noise had on them.

TASK ONE

For questions 1–5, choose from the list **A–H** what the cause of the noise was.

A　birds

B　people talking

C　construction work

D　a television set

E　music equipment

F　cars

G　a baby crying

H　singing

Speaker 1 [| 1]

Speaker 2 [| 2]

Speaker 3 [| 3]

Speaker 4 [| 4]

Speaker 5 [| 5]

TASK TWO

For questions 6–10, choose from the list **A–H** what the speakers say about the effect the noise had on them.

A　It changed my personality.

B　It taught me to be more tolerant.

C　My health was affected.

D　I was forced to move house.

E　It destroyed a friendship.

F　It didn't bother me.

G　It prevented me from working.

H　I was forced to take legal action.

Speaker 1 [| 6]

Speaker 2 [| 7]

Speaker 3 [| 8]

Speaker 4 [| 9]

Speaker 5 [| 10]

2　🔘 Which of the speakers do you have most and least sympathy with? Why?

Have you had any similar problems with neighbours? Are you a noisy neighbour?

What, if anything, can or should be done to help victims of noisy neighbours?

Vocabulary 3: Noise and sound

1　Look at the following extracts from the recording. What type of noise is indicated by all three underlined words?

a　*The din was unbearable …*

b　*… it would start at 5, this awful racket and it'd wake up the baby.*

c　*Night after night he'd have it blaring out at full volume.*

2　In **1–3** below, each of the adjectives collocates with the noun in capital letters at the end of the line. Underline the adjective in each group of three which has a very different meaning to the other two. There is an example at the beginning (**0**).

0	squeaky	high-pitched	deep	**VOICE**

'Deep' describes a voice with a low pitch; the other two adjectives describe a voice with a high pitch.

1	loud	booming	hushed	**VOICE**
2	distant	unmistakable	muffled	**SOUND**
3	excessive	incessant	constant	**NOISE**

3　Cross out the word which does not normally collocate with the noun or adjective in capital letters at the beginning of each line. There is an example at the beginning (**0**).

0	**DOGS**	growl	~~roar~~	whine	

Noun + verb

1	**NOISE**	dies down	fades away	goes off	
2	**DOORS**	slam shut	rustle open	creak open	
3	**BELLS**	hoot	tinkle	chime	

Adjective + noun

4	**ROWDY**	behaviour	fans	engine	party
5	**PIERCING**	groan	cry	scream	shriek
6	**DEAFENING**	applause	cheer	silence	ear

4 Complete each of the gaps in **1–6** below with a collocation from exercises 2 and 3. There is an example at the beginning (**0**).

0 'Come in,' he said in a high ___squeaky voice___ that made him sound like a little mouse.

1 She spoke in a _____ , anxious not to wake anyone up.
2 We could hear the _____ of Bob's tractor in the valley below; it was faint, but unmistakable.
3 Wait until the _____ a little before you give your speech, otherwise you'll have to shout.
4 Police arrested several _____ who had clearly been drinking before the match.
5 His shock announcement that he was resigning met with _____; no one knew quite what to say.
6 There was a sudden gust of wind and the _____ behind her; she thought at first a gun had been fired.

5 👁 **2.16** You will hear a sequence of sounds. Make notes as you listen.

6 💬 Discuss with your partner what might have been happening. Wherever possible, use the vocabulary from exercises 2 and 3 to describe the sounds.

7 💬 What are your favourite sounds? Which sounds do you not like? Give reasons.

Writing: CAE Part 2

Information sheets

1 Read the following Part 2 task and the sample answer. Does the answer address all the points in the writing task?

You work as a secretary in a language school in your country. Every year new teachers come from abroad to work at the school and you have been asked to produce an information sheet in English giving information and advice on finding accommodation. You should:

- describe the different types of accommodation available and advise on the best areas to live in

- include suggestions on how to go about finding accommodation

- give practical information and advice which might be useful to teachers once they have decided where to live.

Write your **information sheet**.

Finding Accommodation: a teacher's guide

Looking for accommodation in unfamiliar surroundings is no easy task, so here is some practical information and advice to help you on your way.

What's available?

Most teachers live in flats, as rented houses are hard to come by and usually outside their price range. It's also common to share, as a place of your own can cost as much as 450 euros a month. Another less expensive option for new teachers is to spend the first few weeks lodging with a family — it's simple to arrange and can provide a friendly introduction to the city.

Which area you decide on is obviously a matter of personal choice, though the vast majority of teachers live within easy walking distance of the school. Flats here may be slightly more expensive, but you save on daily travel costs to work.

Where do I look?

You could:
- talk to other teachers
- look at the noticeboard in the school clubroom
- read the local English language magazine 'The Word'
- buy the property magazine 'Casa Blanca' every day
- go to our student accommodation office if you want to live with a family

What happens next?

Before you move in, you will have to pay a deposit of one month's rent. Your landlord/lady is supposed to refund this when you leave, so be sure to ask for a receipt.

The law also requires you to sign either a one- or five-year contract. We would advise against making a long-term commitment since things might not work out as planned and the flat may not live up to your expectations.

Finally, if you do share, insist on having an itemized telephone bill, as long-distance calls can often lead to bitter disputes!

---

2   To obtain a high mark in the CAE examination, you need to use a wide range of relevant vocabulary and structures. To what extent does each section of the sample answer achieve this? Give examples.

3   Is the register of the example answer more formal or informal? Give examples.

How appropriate is it for the task?

4   Underline those words which are used to link ideas.

Example:

… is no easy task, <u>so</u> here is some practical advice…

5   Choose **one** of the following Part 2 tasks and write your **information sheet**. You should write **220–260** words.

1   You are a member of the students' committee at a college where students from all over the world study. The committee organizes a number of events in the first week of each academic year, aimed at welcoming new students and helping them to integrate into the social life of the college. You have agreed to write an information sheet which:
   - informs students about the planned events for this year's opening week
   - offers further advice on how to meet new people throughout the year.

2   You have been asked by your college to write an information sheet in English giving advice to students from abroad on coping with stress. You should alert students to the causes of stress in the college environment and offer practical suggestions on how to deal with it.

> ### How to go about it
>
> - When choosing your task, ensure that you have sufficient ideas and can offer a range of language relevant to the topic.
> - Plan your answer so that it addresses all the points in the task appropriately.
> - Use clearly defined paragraphs of an appropriate length. If you use bullet points, do not limit your language to a series of simple sentences or a list of phrases.
> - Give your information sheet a title and section/paragraph headings.
> - Check your completed answer for mistakes.

Vocabulary

Match each of the sentence beginnings **1–8** with an appropriate ending **a–h**. The items in bold are all common collocations.

Example:
1 c

1 The words of the Prime Minister were drowned out by the **deafening**
2 The Sports Minister has announced measures to **deal with the rising**
3 The former headmaster was an imposing figure, with a **big booming**
4 He moved nervously towards the door, with one eye on the **growling**
5 They walked through a landscape of fast-flowing rivers and **roaring**
6 The village is hidden away in a valley, surrounded by **gently rolling**
7 The full moon lit up his monstrous face, and Edna **let out a piercing**
8 She quickly fell asleep, only to be woken soon after by the **chiming**

a **hills** and green fields dotted with white sheep.
b **voice**, which struck fear into the children.
c **cheers** of some 3,000 jubilant supporters.
d **waterfalls**, fed by the recent torrential rains.
e **clock** in the hallway as it struck midnight.
f **tide of violence** at football matches.
g **dog** that was chained to a post in the garden.
h **scream**, which cut through the silence of the night.

Participle clauses

Rewrite the following story using participle clauses and replacing the word 'and' to combine ideas.

Example:
Having grown up in the countryside, Charlie wanted to go back there to spend his retirement.

Charlie had grown up in the countryside **and** he wanted to go back there to spend his retirement. He looked through a newspaper one day **and** he saw a cottage for sale in a picturesque rural area. It was situated in a small village near the church **and** it had a conservatory and a large garden **and** the garden contained fruit trees; it seemed perfect. Charlie was not known for his decisiveness **and** he surprised everyone by putting down a deposit on it the very next day. He saw it once **and** he immediately made up his mind to buy it.

However, he moved into the cottage **and** he soon realized it was not the peaceful rural idyll he had expected. The church bells chimed every hour on the hour **and** kept him awake at night. Also, the village was in an area of outstanding beauty **and** coachloads of tourists arrived every weekend **and** disturbed the peace and quiet. Worst of all, the locals objected to the presence of outsiders in the village **and** they were very unfriendly towards him. Charlie lived there for six months **and** he decided to move back to the city.

Use of English: CAE Part 3

Word formation

For questions **1–10**, use the word given in capitals at the end of some of the lines to form a word that fits in the gap **in the same line**. There is an example at the beginning (**0**).

IRONING

Many people hate ironing and seek out modern fabrics that (**0**) _conveniently_ **CONVENIENCE**
do not crease, but is it really such a tedious and (**1**) _____ chore? When **AGREE**
done in the (**2**) _____ and warmth of a cosy kitchen with the radio on, it can **PRIVATE**
be a fairly pleasant way of spending your time. And when it's finished, there's
always something rather (**3**) _____ about a pile of neatly ironed clothes. **SATISFY**
Anyway, love it or loathe it, here are a few guidelines:

- Before you start, (**4**) _____ you have enough wardrobe space to allow **SURE**
  your clothes to hang (**5**) _____ once they have been ironed. **FREE**

- Plug the iron in close to the ironing board. A length of cord stretched across
  a room represents a serious (**6**) _____ hazard. Also keep cords beyond the **SAFE**
  reach of children, whose natural (**7**) _____ may lead them to pull the **CURIOUS**
  cord – and the iron – onto themselves.

- Read the care label on each garment for the recommended ironing (**8**) _____ **PROCEED**
  and the appropriate temperature (**9**) _____. If in doubt, start with a cool iron. **SET**
  If this proves to be (**10**) _____ and the clothes remain creased, increase **EFFECT**
  the temperature as necessary.

- Iron clothes while they are
  still slightly damp.

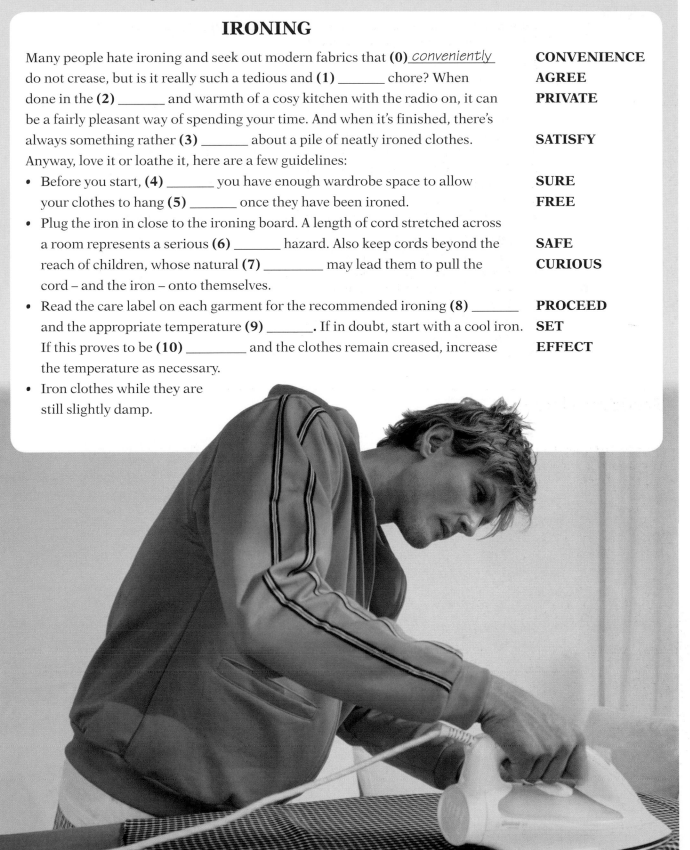

Multiple choice

1 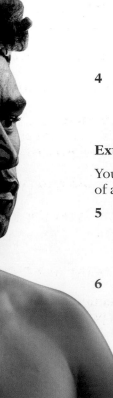 Discuss the following questions about the photographs.
In which English-speaking countries do you think they were taken?
What significance might the tattoos have for the young man?
What hardships do you think the Chinese gold miners had to face?
How do you think the children are feeling?

2 **2.17–2.19** You will hear three different extracts. For questions **1–6**, choose the answer (**A**, **B** or **C**) which fits best according to what you hear. There are two questions for each extract.

Extract one

You hear part of an interview with Diane Grossman, the organizer of a recruitment fair for Summer Camps USA.

1 According to Diane, non-Americans working at summer camp may
  A arrange to visit friends in their countries.
  B recognize similarities between nationalities.
  C understand more about the American lifestyle.

2 Diane compares summer camp to a military camp to suggest that
  A there are strict rules.
  B the facilities are basic.
  C the working hours are long.

Extract two

You hear part of an interview with James Lee, a writer who took part in a documentary about the history of Chinese migration to Australia.

3 The documentary helped James to realize
  A that he was more Chinese than Australian.
  B how fortunate he was compared to other Chinese Australians he knew.
  C what his ancestors had done for him.

4 According to James, Chinese Australians are now
  A working in a greater range of professions.
  B regarded as real Australians.
  C better educated than other ethnic groups.

Extract three

You hear part of an interview with Jeremy Mitchell, the organizer of an exhibition on the art of tattooing.

5 Jeremy says that an aim of the exhibition is to
  A change people's attitudes towards tattoos.
  B show how much variety of design there is in tattooing.
  C explain the value of tattoos in different social groups.

6 According to Jeremy, in Maori culture tattoos are worn
  A only by powerful men.
  B to indicate social status.
  C mainly on the face.

3 ⬭ In what ways might children benefit from attending a summer camp? What can they learn?

How well have immigrant workers in your country integrated into the local culture?

If you were to have a tattoo, where on your body would it be, what would it show and why?

Vocabulary 1: Sight

1 Underline the correct alternative in the following extracts from the recording.

   a They should *look/see* out for our advertisements in *The Globe*.

   b Our communities used to be hidden from *show/view*.

   c You've now also got Chinese Australians performing as musicians, artists, writers – that was a rare *vision/sight* not so long ago.

   d The exhibition really does provide a fascinating *look/view* at the history of tattooing.

   e There's also a collection of tools on *view/sight*.

2 Complete each gap with one of the nouns from the box. In each section **1–5**, the noun required for both spaces, **a** and **b**, is the same.

> vision   sight   view   look   eye

1 a Looking out across the bay, she suddenly **caught** _____ of a dolphin.

   b Stay here, don't say a word and **keep out of** _____ !

2 a A movement in the bushes **caught my** _____ and I moved closer to investigate.

   b You'll need a good telescope, as the star is not normally **visible to the naked** _____ .

3 a He sprayed anti-government slogans on the ministry building **in full** _____ **of** the security guards.

   b As we turned the corner the house **came into** _____ .

4 a You've probably sprained it or something. Let me **have a** _____ **at** it.

   b Now it's time for *In Depth*, in which we **take a closer** _____ **at** an issue in the news.

5 a The mole, which spends most of its life underground, has very **poor** _____ . Nor can it hear or smell very well.

   b Many of his short stories offer a dark and terrifying _____ **of the future**.

3 ⬭ Talk to your partner about:

   a **a familiar sight** in your town or the surrounding countryside at this time of year.

   b **a breathtaking view** you have seen.

   c someone **in the public eye** whom you admire.

   d a radio or television programme you know which provides **an in-depth look** at current affairs.

   e the advantages and disadvantages of having **x-ray vision**.

Gapped text

1   ⬤   How often do you go to see a performance of a play, a classical music concert or an opera?

Are members of the audience expected to behave in a certain way?

What type of behaviour might other members of the audience find annoying?

2   You are going to read an article about the way people sometimes behave in the theatre or concert hall. Six paragraphs have been removed from the article. Choose from the paragraphs **A–G** the one which fits each gap (**1–6**). There is one extra paragraph which you do not need to use.

THE TROUBLE WITH MODERN AUDIENCES

Stephen Pollard believes that many of us need to be educated in the norms of social conduct – in particular, concert etiquette.

According to the reviews, the performance of Mahler's Sixth Symphony that I went to last week was 'transcendent', 'emotionally perfect' and 'violently good'. A friend called me the following morning and told me that it was one of the most powerful experiences of her life.

1	

Sitting in the row in front of me, you see, was the family from hell. I don't know their names, but let's call them the Fidget-Bottoms. Mr and Mrs Fidget-Bottom spent the entire time stroking and kissing their kids, mock conducting, stretching out their arms across the back of their seats as if they were on the sofa at home and, just for good measure, bobbing their heads up and down in time with the music.

2	

I planted a well-aimed kick in the back of the seat. Nothing. A killer combination of the family's total self-absorption, and the seat's wooden solidity, meant that the only effect was a painful toe. So I resorted to another equally fruitless tactic; that of seething with righteous indignation.

3	

Now there is a more *laissez-faire* attitude, which, whilst opening up cultural institutions to millions, has its own drawbacks. Today, you come as you please, and behave as you please. It's your right. If you want to flick through your programme, fine. If you want to use it as a fan, fine. If you want to cough, fine.

4	

But we are not at home. The very point of the theatre is to be out of the house, and part of a crowd. And being part of a crowd has obligations – not shouting 'fire' out of mischief, for example, in a crowded room. When travelling by bus, I do not sing arias from Handel's *Messiah*. Nor do I whistle along to the music at weddings. I behave as is expected of me.

5	

As a result we have forgotten – or more truthfully, never learned – how to listen. When the *St Matthew Passion* was written it was heard at Easter, once every very few years. A performance was an event, an event which we had no way of even attempting to recreate. Today, we can record the performance and then listen to it in the bath. We can have its choruses playing as background music while we eat.

6	

It's hardly surprising that we take that behaviour, and that attitude, into the concert hall with us. Mr and Mrs Fidget-Bottom, and the little Fidget-Bottoms, certainly ruined my concert last week, and I am fairly sure they are going to ruin quite a few others as they get older.

A This particular family may have been especially horrific, but they are merely grotesque extensions of the downside of the increasing accessibility of culture. The old formal rules of behaviour at the theatre, concerts and opera – dressing up in black tie and all that, and the feeling that unless you were part of a closed circle then it wasn't your business to attend – were indeed far too stifling.

B Rarely, if ever, do we sit down in our own home to listen to a full performance of a piece of music, with no other distractions. And if we do make an attempt, then no sooner have we settled into our armchair than we think of something else we could be doing – and we do it.

C Which is more than can be said for the Fidget-Bottoms of this world, who seems oblivious to the norms of social conduct. The problem stems from the fact that culture is now too readily accessible. We no longer need to make an effort with it. You wanna hear Beethoven's Ninth? Pop on a CD. Fancy Vivaldi's *Four Seasons*? Which version?

D I felt then, as I do now, that my outburst of temper was fully justified. What these people, and people like them clearly need, is an education in how to behave in public, beginning with a basic introduction to concert etiquette. On no account should you kiss your children once the concert has started. Indeed, save that for when you get home.

E I wouldn't know. My body was in the concert hall, and my ears are in full working order. But neither were any use to me. The London Symphony Orchestra might as well have been playing *Chopsticks* for all the impact the Mahler had on me.

F Unwrapping sweets, fidgeting, wandering off to the toilet and chatting are also on the list of things you can do during a performance. When going out is as easy, and as normal, as staying in, then we behave the same in the theatre or the concert hall as we do in the living room. And so we don't have a thought for those around us.

G They were cocooned in their own world, with not the slightest concern for anyone around. I doubt that it even crossed their mind that they were doing anything wrong, so unabashed was their behaviour. The situation called for action.

◯ Reacting to the text

Do you agree with the writer's views? Why/Why not?

There has been much debate in Britain in recent years about the 'dumbing down' of culture, a reduction in the quality and/or educational value of television and the arts, brought about by the desire to make them more accessible.

How true is this in your country? Do you think young people have greater or less cultural knowledge than previous generations?

Language focus: Inversion

1 Comment on the word order in sentences **a–d**, which are taken from the reading.
What effect is the writer hoping to achieve by placing the words which are written in bold at the beginning of the sentence?

   a **Rarely**, if ever, do we sit down in our own home to listen to a full performance of a piece of music…
   b **No sooner** have we settled into our armchair than we think of something else we could be doing…
   c **On no account** should you kiss your children once the concert has started.
   d When travelling by bus, I do not sing arias from Handel's *Messiah*. **Nor** do I whistle along to the music at weddings.

2 Rewrite **a–d** in exercise 1 so that the words in bold do not appear at the beginning of the sentence.

   Example:
   a We rarely, if ever, sit down in our own home to listen to a full performance of a piece of music.

   🅖 Read more about inversion on pages 223 and 224 of the Grammar reference.

Practice

1 Rewrite the following sentences, beginning with the words given. There is an example at the beginning (**0**).
   0 As soon as Springsteen had gone on stage, it started to rain.
   No sooner _had Springsteen gone on stage than it started to rain._

   1 We only very rarely go to the cinema these days.
   Only very rarely _____ .
   2 I have never seen such a terrible performance of *Hamlet* before.
   Never before _____ .

3 Bags must not be left unattended at any time.
   At no time _____ .
4 The identity of the murderer is not revealed until the very last page.
   Not until _____ .
5 They only realized the painting had been hung upside down when someone complained at reception.
   Only when _____ .

2 Rewrite sentences **1–5**, beginning with the word in *italics*.

   1 He would *never* play in front of a live audience again.
   2 She had *hardly* sat down to watch her favourite programme when the phone rang.
   3 You will not be allowed to enter the auditorium *under* any circumstances once the play has started.
   4 We *not* only went to the National Gallery, but we also saw a West End musical.
   5 Amy had *not* enjoyed herself so much since she went to the circus as a child.

3 Complete the following sentences so that they are true for you.

   a Only very rarely do I _____ .
   b Under no circumstances would I _____ .
   c Never again will I _____ .
   d Not once in my life have I _____ .
   e Not since _____ have I _____
   _____ .
   f Not until _____ did I _____
   _____ .

4 ⬭ Comment on and discuss your sentences with your partner.

Word formation: Nouns formed with *in, out, up, down, back*

1 The words *in, out, up, down* and *back* can be used to form nouns, as in this example from the text:

*They are merely grotesque extensions of the **downside** of the increasing accessibility of culture.*

Complete the underlined words in the following sentences. Then check your answers in the text.

   a Now there is a more *laissez-faire* attitude, which, whilst opening up cultural institution to millions, has its own _draw_____ . (4ᵗʰ paragraph of base text)
   b We can have its choruses playing as _____ground_ music while we eat. (6ᵗʰ paragraph of base text)
   c I felt then, as I do now, that my _____burst_ of temper was fully justified. (paragraph D)

2 Complete each gap with an appropriate noun form of the word in capitals at the end of the line. Each of the nouns should be formed using one of the words in the box. The exercise starts with an example (**0**).

in   out   up   down   back

0 Organizers blamed the bad weather for the **low** _turnout_ ; fewer than 2,000 people attended this year's festival.   **TURN**

1 A **heavy** _____ before the start of the match left the pitch looking rather like a swimming pool.   **POUR**

2 News of a **sharp** _____ **in** property prices will not please first-time buyers.   **TURN**

3 The new tax legislation is designed to help those **on low** _____ .   **COME**

4 There has been a **serious** _____ **of** cholera on the island, infecting over 50,000 people.   **BREAK**

5 The exhibition **provides a fascinating** _____ **into** traditional farming methods.   **SIGHT**

6 Whilst the Government seems confident of victory, it is still too early to **predict the final** _____ of the election.   **COME**

7 The Government **suffered a severe** _____ in the election, losing its overall majority in the National Assembly.   **SET**

8 There has been a 5% **fall in industrial** _____ this year, in contrast to agricultural production, which has risen by 3%.   **PUT**

9 His parents were firm believers in discipline and **he had a very strict** _____ .   **BRING**

10 There has been a **complete** _____ **in** law and order in the capital, with reports of widespread looting and violence.   **BREAK**

Listening 2:
CAE Part 2

Sentence completion

1 👁 **2.20** You will hear part of a radio programme in which a writer makes a confession. For questions **1–8**, complete the sentences.

Gaby says she spends a lot of time in [**1**] for research purposes.

As a teenager she always had problems with her [**2**] .

Most people attributed her A level failures to [**3**] rather than lack of effort.

Gaby thinks that after leaving school she probably appeared quite [**4**] .

Her reading helped her to develop an interest in different features of [**5**] .

Some of her friends are in jobs which have a negative effect on [**6**] .

She thinks her lifestyle causes some of her friends to have feelings of [**7**] .

A problem for many graduates is that they begin their working lives in [**8**] .

2 ⬭ To what extent is having a degree in your country a guarantee of higher earnings?

What are the advantages and disadvantages of going to university?

Should university education be paid for by student loans or government grants? Why?

Vocabulary 2: *Read* and *write*

1 ⬭ What do the underlined words mean in these two extracts from the listening?

… the most versatile and <u>prolific writer</u> of her generation.
I also <u>read voraciously</u> and always seemed to have a book in my hand.

2 Complete each of the gaps with one of the words from the box.

neatly	widely	well	aloud	rough	plain	avid	good

1 My poem was **read** _____ to the whole class. It was so embarrassing!
2 My wife and I are _____ **readers** of your magazine and eagerly look forward to each month's issue.
3 This book's **a** very _____ **read** – I'd definitely recommend it!
4 As a student he **read** _____ and voraciously on a whole range of subjects from algebra to zoology.
5 Reproducing Goethe's style in English is no easy task, but this translation **reads** rather _____ .
6 I'd like you to **write a** _____ **draft** of the letter in this class, then you can **copy it** _____ into your notebook for homework.
7 I do wish these documents were **written in** _____ **English** – they're far too complicated to understand.

3 Do the speaking exercise on page 208.

Reading and speaking: Gap year

1 ⬭ Read the following paragraph about gap years. Why do you think many universities and employers prefer students who have taken a gap year?

> Many young people in the UK take a gap year between leaving school and starting university in order to do something different before continuing with their studies. There are various options open to them, either in the UK or abroad, including travel, teaching, caring and conservation work, as well as academic and cultural study courses.

2 Read the following opinions, which were posted on a gap year website, and compare them with your ideas in exercise 1.

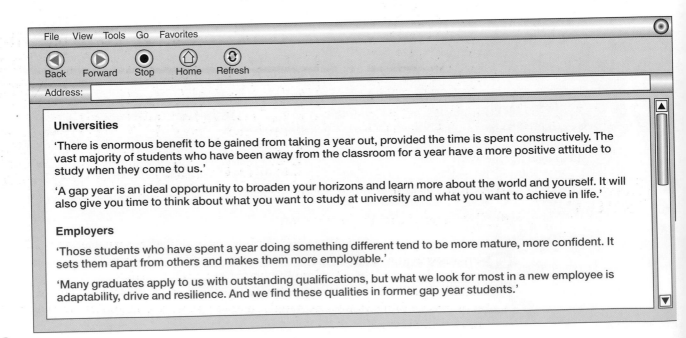

File View Tools Go Favorites

Back Forward Stop Home Refresh

Address:

Universities

'There is enormous benefit to be gained from taking a year out, provided the time is spent constructively. The vast majority of students who have been away from the classroom for a year have a more positive attitude to study when they come to us.'

'A gap year is an ideal opportunity to broaden your horizons and learn more about the world and yourself. It will also give you time to think about what you want to study at university and what you want to achieve in life.'

Employers

'Those students who have spent a year doing something different tend to be more mature, more confident. It sets them apart from others and makes them more employable.'

'Many graduates apply to us with outstanding qualifications, but what we look for most in a new employee is adaptability, drive and resilience. And we find these qualities in former gap year students.'

Speaking 1:
CAE Part 3

Collaborative task

◯ Read the advertisements below.

Talk to your partner about what you might learn and the problems you might encounter in these situations. Then decide which situation would provide the most worthwhile learning experience.

Useful language

When talking about the problems you might encounter, try to use some of the vocabulary in section A of the Wordlist on page 209.

- What might you learn and what problems might you encounter in these situations?
- Which situation would provide the most worthwhile learning experience?

Conservation International

Conservation and research work with teams of volunteers on nature reserves in South America and Africa. Projects include monitoring wildlife, path building and water and soil conservation.

Language Teachers Abroad

Teach your own language or English in almost any country in the world. Class sizes vary from one to one hundred and resources can be basic, but your students will welcome you with open arms.

In-Company Experience

Challenging posts in industry for gap year students. Use your academic and interpersonal skills to improve a product or service provided by a top name company – and get paid for it!

Camp World

Work in camps for young people in one or more of the five continents. You help organize sports activities and other outdoor pursuits and you could end up with a qualification as an instructor.

Community Care

Volunteer work at home and abroad with the physically and mentally handicapped, the homeless, the elderly and orphans. You will need to be committed, patient and sensitive to others.

Academic Study Year

Spend a whole year studying at a foreign university in Europe, the USA or even further afield, without the pressure of exams. Accommodation with local families. Grants available.

Speaking 2:
CAE Part 4

Further discussion

◯ Discuss the following questions.

- How might parents feel about their children spending their gap year abroad?
- Do you agree that 'Experience is the best teacher'? Why/Why not?
- What has been your most valuable learning experience to date?
- What things can we learn from elderly people and what can we teach them?
- Some people think that young people have too many opportunities nowadays. What would you say to them?

Writing:
CAE Part 1

Proposals

1 Read the following Part 1 task, underlining key words in the instructions and input material.

The committee of your school's Arts Club, of which you are a member, has decided to publish a monthly arts magazine for students. Read your notes below, and the replies from people you have contacted, and write a proposal for the committee suggesting four ideas for inclusion in the first issue and giving your reasons.

IDEAS FOR FIRST ISSUE

NB aim for variety

FILM REVIEWS   what's on at local cinema?

BOOK REVIEWS   contact Derek.

LOCAL EVENTS · art exhibition in Town Hall
· circus in Wigmore Park

CLUB ACTIVITIES next month's trip to see
musical in London

INTERVIEWS · offer from Hadley Norris —
curator of local art Museum.
· Audrey Perham — actor?

COMPETITIONS   writing competition? film quiz?

I've enclosed reviews on three art history books - hope that's OK.

Derek Turner, Turner's bookshop

not possible as I'm busy rehearsing for my next production. However, here are four free tickets to offer as prizes.

Audrey Perham

as it's the school holidays we'll be showing mostly cartoons and action films.

Peter Tulley, Manager, ABC cinema

Write your **proposal** in 180–220 words.

2 Which four ideas would you include in your proposal, and why?

3 Read the following answer to the task and comment on the following:

- the overall length of the answer
- the writer's use of the input material
- the appropriacy and consistency of the register
- the quality and range of the language
- the organization of ideas and use of linking devices.

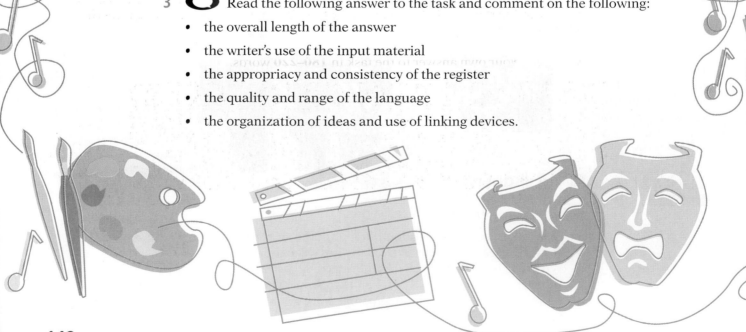

Proposal for contents of first issue of arts magazine

Introduction

I would like to make suggestions for the contents of the first issue of the new Arts Club magazine.

Reviews

One possibility is to have reviews of films which are on at the local cinema but as it's the school holidays they're going to be showing mostly cartoons and action films so I don't think it's a good idea. Also we could have reviews of books – Derek Turner, the owner of Turner's bookshop and a good friend of mine, has enclosed reviews on three art history books, but an excess of art is not desirable, especially as we can do an interview with Hadley Norris of the local art museum (see below), so perhaps we could have some alternative reviews from Derek or someone else in the second issue instead of this one.

Events and Activities

I suggest you to include some stuff about local events, too. Next month there is an art exhibition in the Town Hall and an international circus in Wigmore Park. They will be interesting for loads of different people and it's an important thing to aim for variety when we decide what to put in the first issue. Also I recommend to inform students about club activities eg next month's club trip to see the musical 'Rats' in London. Why don't we include a review, too?

Interviews

It was my firm intention to include an interview with Audrey Perham, the actor who lives near the college, but she is busy at the moment rehearsing for her next production. The good news is that she has given us four free tickets to go and see it. We might consider offering these as prizes for the competition (I shall say more about that later). Anyway, we've got an offer from Hadley Norris, the curator of the local art museum, so that's good and means we can have at least one interview.

Competitions

A film quiz is better than a writing competition because more people would enter. It is more fun. We can offer the tickets given to us by Audrey Perham as prizes.

Conclusion

So, for all the reasons I mention above, I think we should have: information about local events, information about club activities (with a review of 'Rats'), an interview with Hadley Norris and a film quiz.

4 The verbs *suggest* and *recommend* have been used incorrectly in the paragraph entitled 'Events and Activities'. Re-read page 221 of the Grammar reference and correct the mistakes.

5 Now write your own answer to the task in **180–220** words.

Don't forget!

- Plan your answer, selecting appropriately from the information in the input material.
- Expand on one or two of the points in the input material, adding relevant information of your own.
- Use an appropriate register consistently.
- Do not lift whole phrases from the input material.

11 Review

Word formation

For questions **1–10**, use the word given in capitals at the end of some of the lines to form a word that fits in the gap **in the same line**. There is an example at the beginning (**0**).

ANTHONY MASTERS

Anthony Masters was a writer of (**0**) _exceptional_ gifts and prodigious   **EXCEPTION**

energy. He began his (**1**) _____ and versatile career as a teenager,   **EVENT**

when he was expelled from school for organizing a revolt against the

school uniform. In order to earn a living, he fulfilled his (**2**) _____   **CHILD**

ambition and took up writing. In 1964, at the age of 23, he published

A Pocketful of Rye, a collection of short stories whose (**3**) _____   **FRESH**

of style earned him the distinction of being runner-up in the John

Llewellyn Rhys Memorial Prize, an established and prestigious British

-based (**4**) _____ award. He won the award two years later with   **LITERATURE**

his novel *The Seahorse,* after which he continued to display his (**5**) _____   **CONSIDER**

talent by writing both fiction and non-fiction. The (**6**) _____ for   **INSPIRE**

many of his novels came from his experience helping the (**7**) _____   **SOCIAL**

excluded: he ran soup kitchens for drug addicts and campaigned for the

civic rights of gypsies and other ethnic (**8**) _____ . His non-fiction   **MINOR**

(**9**) _____ was typically eclectic, ranging from biographies to social   **PUT**

histories, but it was as a writer of children's fiction that Masters outshone

his contemporaries. His work contains a sensitivity which remains

(**10**) _____ by any other writer of the genre.   **EQUAL**

Vocabulary

Complete each of the gaps with the correct form of one of the verbs from the box. There is an example at the beginning (**0**).

look	turn	catch	come	read	~~have~~
suffer	take	keep	break	write	

0 Her parents were both lawyers and she _had_ a very comfortable middle-class upbringing.

1 One of the best ways to improve your English at this level is to _____ widely.

2 On tonight's programme we'll be _____ a critical look at education.

3 I've done the homework in rough – I'll _____ it out neatly tonight and hand it in tomorrow.

4 _____ out for a present for Luke when you go shopping tomorrow.

5 Their hopes of winning the championship _____ a serious setback on Sunday, when they lost at home to United.

6 She peered out into the audience, hoping to _____ sight of her mother.

7 A cheer went up on deck as the harbour _____ into view.

8 Toys should be _____ out of sight all the time a child is eating.

9 Thousands of people _____ out to catch a glimpse of the President as he toured the region.

10 Tensions grew between the two nations until finally war _____ out in March.

Open cloze

For questions **1–15**, read the text below and think of the word which best fits each gap. Use only one word in each gap. There is an example at the beginning (**0**).

PHOTOGRAPHIC PORTRAITS

The most famous portraits are now created by photographers rather **(0)** _than_ painters, and the people **(1)** _____ the lens are as celebrated as the sitters in front. But are the images they produce **(2)** _____ celebrities like Madonna or Kate Moss worthy of serious art exhibitions? Will they **(3)** _____ looked back on as a true record of the age? Critics say fashion photographers lack artistic depth and integrity, **(4)** _____ of which are necessary to be a true artist. Their defenders say their approach is little different from **(5)** _____ of respected portrait artists throughout the ages, from Holbein to Reynolds. Just **(6)** _____ court artists in the past, photographers work to a tight timetable and commercial constraint and often have a very short time in **(7)** _____ to get to know their sitter. For a painter like Reynolds, this was very **(8)** _____ the case. It is known that he **(9)** _____ hold up to eight sittings in a day to finish a work on time. Not **(10)** _____ the nineteenth century did the idea emerge that art should not be commercially based. But artist Sue Dent accuses many photographers of overfalsifying reality **(11)** _____ using technology to cover up spots and wrinkles. 'The emphasis **(12)** _____ on creating perfection and beauty, but in fact **(13)** _____ you end up with is a face without emotion, so **(14)** _____ of seeing anger, fear or tenderness, you're just presented with a blank look in the sitter's eyes. And **(15)** _____ it is true that flattery has always been a feature of portraits, it somehow seems worse in photographs.'

Sentence completion

1 ⬭ If you have been in a desert, what were your impressions? If you haven't, would you like to visit one? Why/Why not?

What strategies do you imagine desert wildlife has for coping with the heat and lack of water?

2 ⊙ **2.21** You will hear part of a radio documentary on desert wildlife. For questions **1–8**, complete the sentences.

DESERT WILDLIFE

Plants

The leaves of the desert holly release [_____ **1**] in order to reflect heat.

The saguaro cactus is able to [_____ **2**] in its trunk.

Some saguaro cacti are as much as [_____ **3**] feet tall.

Birds

The road runner uses its [_____ **4**] to protect it from the sun.

Birds are also protected from the heat by [_____ **5**].

Mammals

The jack rabbit and fennec fox have very [_____ **6**] to help cool their blood.

Camels' toes have [_____ **7**] between them.

Camels can last four times as long as a [_____ **8**] without water.

3 ⬭ The presenter asked the following question: 'What purpose does the hump on a camel serve?' Do you know the answer?

What strategies do you have for coping with the heat?

Vocabulary 1: Words with more than one use

1 ⬭ In the following extracts from the recording, which part of what plant or animal do each of the words in italics refer to?

… bringing *it* forward over its head to create shade, thus enabling the bird to **keep cool**.
… *their* main function is to **keep external heat out**.
… *This* spreads out as they walk on soft sand and **keeps them from sinking into it**.

2 ⬭ The verb *keep* has several different uses. Explain the meaning of each of the phrases in bold in exercise 1.

3 ⬭ For questions **1–5** below, choose a word from the box which can be used appropriately in all three sentences. There are some words you do not need to use.

pay get wish give know like make meet hear welcome

Here is an example (**0**).

0 a I'm afraid I don't think I'll be able to ___make___ **it to** the meeting.
  b The pay rise will ___make___ **it possible for** us to buy a new car.
  c I don't want to ___make___ **trouble,** but I think someone in the office has been a taking a lot of stationery home.

1 a They said they would **let her** _____ in writing of their decision.
  b He's very friendly once you **get to** _____ him.
  c **Do you** _____ **the names of** five birds, five fish and five trees in English?

2 a We would _____ **your suggestions** for future editions of the magazine.
  b We are **delighted to** _____ Toby Gray, who is on a visit from Head Office.
  c Are spring flowers **a** _____ **sight** for you or do you suffer from hay fever?

3 a **It doesn't** _____ **to** cheat or tell lies – it's much better to be honest.
  b It's unusual for my children to _____ **me a compliment** like that.
  c Do you _____ **much attention to** what's going on in the world?

4 a When you arrive in Paris, I'll _____ **you off the train** and take you to my flat.
  b I doubt this attempt to settle the dispute will _____ **with any success**.
  c Will the world be able to _____ **the challenge** of fighting global warming?

5 a I don't _____ **to be rude** but I'd rather just read my book during the flight.
  b I'd like to thank Linda for all her hard work and _____ **her all the best** in her new post.
  c If you could be **granted one** _____, which of the world's problems would you ask to be solved?

4 ⬭ Explain the meaning of the phrases formed by the words in bold and the verbs you have inserted in exercise 3.

Example: **0 a** *attend, come to*
     b *enable*
     c *cause problems*

5 ⬭ Discuss the questions in each of the **c** sentences in **1–5** of exercise **3**.

Use of English 1:
CAE Part 1

Multiple-choice cloze

1 ⬭ Do you think wild animals should be farmed for their skin or meat? Give reasons for your views.

2 Read the text below, ignoring the gaps for the moment.
Why did Andy Johnson start his farm?
What objection does Dr Clifford Warwick raise?

3 For questions **1–12**, read the text again and decide which answer (**A**, **B**, **C** or **D**) best fits each gap. There is an example at the beginning (**0**).

CROCODILE FARMS

When Andy Johnson **(0)** ___ Britain's first ever crocodile farm in 2006, he **(1)** ___ under fierce criticism from animal rights groups, opposed to the factory farming of wildlife. However, Johnson, who also farms cattle, pigs and lambs, **(2)** ___ that his motivation for starting a crocodile farm was for **(3)** ___ environmental reasons. He wants to protect wild crocodiles from being poached, and he is primarily interested in their meat, not their skins. 'By supplying Europeans with home-produced crocodile, we can **(4)** ___ the market value of illegally supplied crocodile meat,' he claims.

Johnson says the meat 'has a mild flavour – it's low fat, high protein, very healthy and humanely produced'. His crocodiles are housed in a tropically heated room that **(5)** ___ around 20 by 30 metres, so they have plenty of room. However, Dr Clifford Warwick, a reptile biologist, **(6)** ___ concern: 'Their biology and behaviour do not **(7)** ___ themselves to a captive life. The animals may seem peaceful and relaxed, but an animal behaviourist can see that they are stressed.'

In the last century, many species of crocodiles were hunted to the **(8)** ___ of extinction as trade in their skins flourished. Some 300,000 Australian saltwater crocodiles were killed between 1945 and 1972. The alligator suffered a similar **(9)** ___, although both species are now protected and their **(10)** ___ are slowly rising. Worldwide, the legal trade in crocodilian skins (crocodiles, alligators and caymans) has roughly tripled since 1977, rising to a million or **(11)** ___ animals by 2002. The majority of these are farmed animals, but upwards of 90,000 are killed annually in the **(12)** ___.

	A	**B**	**C**	**D**
0	put out	gave off	<u>set up</u>	brought about
1	came	went	met	put
2	insists	ascertains	insures	convinces
3	finely	utterly	cleanly	purely
4	downsize	downplay	undercut	undergo
5	rules	measures	ranges	sizes
6	speaks	gives	expresses	arises
7	lend	owe	make	let
8	frontier	line	side	edge
9	luck	fate	chance	destination
10	groups	counts	numbers	volumes
11	more	many	some	such
12	natural	wild	savage	outside

Self help
- Underline and record those words and expressions from the text which describe an approximate rather than an exact number.

  Example:
  around 20 by 30 metres

- Can you add any further items to the list?

4 ⬭ Can you name any species currently threatened with extinction in your country?

What measures should be taken to safeguard these species?

5 Write four sentences, each including one of the wrong words from the text above. Leave a gap where the word should go, and give three options.

Example:

The new law _____ a significant change in the way animals were treated.
A *put out*   **B** *gave off*   **C** *brought about*

6 Ask your partner to complete the gaps in your sentences.

Reading:
CAE Part 3

Multiple choice

1 ◯ Do you enjoy watching wildlife documentaries on television? Why/Why not?

The photographs show Sir David Attenborough, the presenter of many such programmes. What do you think are the qualities of a good wildlife documentary presenter?

2 Read the following magazine article about Sir David Attenborough and for questions **1–7** on page 156, choose the correct answer, **A**, **B**, **C** or **D**.

DOING WHAT COMES NATURALLY

'This,' says a figure, dismounting from a single-seater ski-bike and addressing us from somewhere inside the world's thickest coat, 'is one of the coldest places. On earth.' The emphases are heavy and deliberate, but the voice is like a piano played gently. You feel at home with this voice, you know where you are with it, which, on this occasion, is in the High Arctic, on the trail of the Arctic fox, with the temperature hovering somewhere around 50 below. The voice is unmistakably that of Sir David Attenborough.

The words are those which open *The Life of Mammals*, Attenborough's new *magnum opus* for the BBC, the latest in an extraordinary line that passes back through *Life in the Freezer* and *The Life of Birds* to *Life on Earth*. We are familiar enough with his work now to know that a number of things can be guaranteed about *The Life of Mammals*. Attenborough will draw our attention to animals in places we didn't know existed. He will begin a sentence in, say, Australia and finish it in Brazil. We will marvel again at Attenborough, the great communicator, the peerless educator. (Oh for his insatiable curiosity and energy at 77! Oh for the civilizing effect of his knowledge!) And we will be variously appalled and intrigued by the ways in which mammals hunt, eat and form relationships. As Attenborough says in the introduction to the series, 'We will look at the lives of our closest relatives and they will lead us to ourselves.'

But will they lead us to David Attenborough? He recently wrote a 400-page account of his career in broadcasting, *Life on Air*. It is one of the few books ever published to contain tips on handling a Gaboon viper. ('Push a pole under one, about a third of its length from the back of its head, and it will be balanced so that you can gently lift it. Then dump it in a box and slam the lid down very quickly.') However, its author is far less forthcoming for anyone seeking to know the private man. The death in 1997 of his wife, Jane, which everyone close to Attenborough agrees devastated him, is approached in four sorrowful but guarded paragraphs. His brother Richard, who lives close to him and to whom he talks weekly, merits one mention in the book, and that in brackets. Attenborough, it seems, slams the lid down very quickly on his feelings.

Not surprisingly, perhaps, he keeps out of the limelight as much as possible, both on and off screen. His determination in this regard is founded in part on genuine anxieties he has about taking credit where it isn't due. Frequently, of course, Attenborough is present when the rare footage of, say, the naked mole rat is shot. But at other times he goes nowhere near the animal at all, adding his voice to the footage shot by a cameraman, who has been standing for months in a field in a pair of wet boots. Attenborough, too, has had his fair share of long nights spent on forest floors in damp sleeping bags, in disquieting proximity to leeches. Yet the elements of risk and discomfort in his work are things he would prefer to downplay. He considers himself the channel rather than the focus. If people discover afterwards what he's gone through to film a particular animal, then so be it, but he doesn't want it to be part of the programme.

Attenborough could have had a quieter life. He went to Cambridge in 1945 to read natural sciences and considered becoming an academic. But he eventually gave up on the idea. 'I know someone who went looking for an animal in Sumatra,' he recalls. 'He didn't even see it for the first three years. Went out and looked for it every day. Saw footprints, occasionally a hair. And after he'd found it, that was all he was allowed to look at for another eight years. Another chap I knew had to count the number of bees that went into a certain kind of orchid between certain hours of the day. He was stuck out in the middle of the Panama Canal counting bees. A caricature of the intellectual life, really.'

So, in the hope of finding something more stimulating, he joined the BBC. He rocketed up
85 through the ranks, lending the best of his energies to wildlife programming, which was then at an unpromisingly larval stage. In the Fifties the technology wasn't readily available to film in the field, so the natural world had to be borrowed from
90 London Zoo and brought to the studio in a sack. 'It gave you five minutes of very cheap programming, in which you showed a python.' In the classic tradition of these things, he only began to present programmes by chance, because the person who
95 was to have done it came down with something.

Ever since then, for over 50 years, he's been doing what comes naturally; entertaining and enlightening – and bringing comfort. For his programmes run reassuringly counter to the
100 reflex of our times, which is to mull fearfully over a depressing prospect for the world about us. Seen through Attenborough's eyes, the planet tends not to be scalded and smoking, breathing its last. It teems and thrives, blossoms and grows. The future
105 in Sir David Attenborough's world is big and bright.

1 The writer says that Sir David Attenborough's voice
   A is not immediately recognizable.
   B is comforting to the listener.
   C rises and falls frequently.
   D is not affected by extreme temperatures.

2 According to the writer, in his television programmes Attenborough
   A displays enviable qualities.
   B is rather too predictable.
   C does not look his age.
   D likes to shock the viewer.

3 What does Attenborough mean in line 30 when he says 'they will lead us to ourselves'?
   A The mammals will remind us of the value of cooperation in survival.
   B We will realize how far humans have evolved compared to other species.
   C The mammals will help us gain an understanding of our own behaviour.
   D We will learn more about ourselves than we will about the mammals.

4 In his book *Life on Air*, Attenborough
   A is anxious to respect the privacy of his family.
   B gives practical advice on taming animals.
   C expresses a lack of interest in his family.
   D reveals little about his emotions.

5 What do we learn about Attenborough's approach when making wildlife programmes?
   A He tries not to be the centre of attention.
   B He leaves more uncomfortable work to others.
   C He avoids dangerous situations when filming.
   D He prefers to keep his distance from animals.

6 Attenborough implies that academic work is
   A exhausting.
   B monotonous.
   C unappreciated.
   D pointless.

7 What does the writer say about Attenborough's early days at the BBC?
   A He never intended to present wildlife programmes.
   B He gained rapid promotion in the organization.
   C The BBC had little money to spend on wildlife programmes.
   D The technology for making wildlife documentaries had not been invented.

◯ **Reacting to the text**

Do you share Sir David Attenborough's view of the world, as expressed in the last paragraph? Why/Why not?

Language focus 1: Conjunctions and linking adverbials

The words in bold in the following extracts from the reading are all conjunctions; they connect two clauses in the same sentence.

*The emphases are heavy and deliberate, **but** the voice is like a piano played gently.*

*He went to Cambridge in 1945 to read natural sciences **and** considered becoming an academic.*

*The technology wasn't readily available to film in the field, **so** the natural world had to be borrowed from London Zoo…*

1   In sections **A** and **B**, complete each of the gaps with one of the conjunctions from the box.

A   Reason and result

in case   otherwise   so that

a   You'd better go now, _____ you'll miss your bus.
b   Leave early _____ you don't miss your bus.
c   Take some money for a taxi _____ you miss your bus.

B   Contrast and concession

however   even though   whereas

a   He went to see the match, _____ he doesn't like cricket.
b   He went to see the match, _____ I watched it on TV.
c   _____ you look at it, cricket is a boring game.

2   In less formal writing, conjunctions are sometimes used at the beginning of a sentence to connect it with the previous sentence, as in these extracts from the reading.

***And** we will be variously appalled and intrigued by the ways in which mammals hunt, eat and form relationships. **But** at other times he goes nowhere near the animal at all… **So**, in the hope of finding something more stimulating, he joined the BBC.*

However, linking adverbials are used to connect one sentence with another. They frequently appear at the beginning of a sentence, and are followed by a comma.

***However**, its author is far less forthcoming for anyone seeking to know the private man.*

***Ever since then**, for over 50 years, he's been doing what comes naturally…*

In sections **A** and **B** complete each of the gaps with one of the linking adverbials from the box.

A   Contrast and concession

Despite this   By contrast   On the contrary

a   He does not act hastily. _____ , he sometimes takes days to reach a decision.
b   The song of the blackbird is melodious, but limited in range. _____ , the starling mimics other birds and has an extremely varied repertoire.

c   The salary being offered was very low. _____ , there were over 650 applications for the job.

B   Time

By that time   From that time on   In the meantime

a   I hope to get a new computer next month. _____ , I'll use my husband's laptop.
b   We finally reached the campsite at sunset. _____ , I was exhausted and went straight to sleep in the tent.
c   The burglary affected us in other ways, too. _____ , we always made sure one of us was in the house.

In sections **C** and **D**, complete each gap in the linking adverbials with a word from the box. You will need to use one of the words more than once. All three adverbials in each section perform the same function.

as   for   from   in   of   on   to

C   Reason and result

Her health had deteriorated significantly.

a   ____ a result,
b   ____ account ____ this,   she decided it would be
c   ____ this reason,   best to retire.

D   Addition

The sharp spines of the saguaro cactus serve as a form of defence.

a   ____ addition ____ this,
b   ____ well ____ this,   they direct rainwater into
c   Apart ____ this,   the depressions of the plant.

🔍 Read more about conjunctions and linking adverbials in the Grammar reference on page 224.

3   Complete each of the sentences in an appropriate way. There is an example at the beginning (**0**).

0   You should start revising now,
    a   otherwise *you'll start to panic nearer the exam.*
    b   even though *the exam is in three months' time.*

1   It rained constantly during the first week of our holiday.
    a   As a result, _____ .
    b   What is more, _____ .
2   She sent him some flowers,
    a   so that _____ .
    b   whereas _____ .
3   He hadn't exactly had a stressful day.
    a   On the contrary, _____ .
    b   By contrast, _____ .
4   I wouldn't recommend it as a holiday destination,
    a   unless _____ .
    b   although _____ .

Listening 2:
CAE Part 4

Multiple matching

1 ⬤ What are the main issues involved in the following global concerns?

global warming   whale hunting   women's rights

child labour   human rights   GM foods

2 ⦿ 2.22–2.26 You will hear five short extracts in which different people are talking about action they have taken on global issues. **While you listen you must complete both tasks.**

TASK ONE
For questions 1–5, choose from the list **A–H** the speaker's motivation for taking the action.

A I hoped to change people's way of thinking.

B I was driven by feelings of guilt.

C I had always wanted to help others.

D A friend encouraged me.

E I wanted to prove a point to a friend.

F I had seen pictures of suffering.

G It would show me in a good light.

H I was impressed by other people's work.

	1
	2
	3
	4
	5

TASK TWO
For questions 6–10, choose from the list **A–H** the effect that the experience had on the speaker.

A I became disillusioned.

B It made me feel ashamed.

C It encouraged me to do more.

D It increased my self-respect.

E I suddenly became very popular.

F It made me regret what I had done.

G It helped me achieve an ambition.

H I felt I had not done enough.

	6
	7
	8
	9
	10

---

3 ⬤ Have you ever taken action similar to that of any of the speakers? If so, what was your motivation and how did you feel afterwards?

Should individuals take more action on global issues, or is this best left to governments? Why?

Language focus 2: Modal verbs 3

Must, need, should, ought to

1 Which of the speakers in the listening said each of these two groups of sentences?

A 1 *We **had to** do exactly the same work.*
   2 *There **must have** been about 500 of us altogether.*
   3 *We **should have** done it years before.*

B 1 *I thought at first they might not accept me because of my age and inexperience, but I **needn't have** worried.*
   2 *I **didn't need to** have any special skills.*

2 ⬭ For each group of sentences, explain the difference in meaning between the words in bold as they are used by the speaker.

3 ⬭ Which of the sentences in exercise 1 do **not** contain a modal verb? What are the main characteristics of a modal verb?
In which sentence could *ought to* be used instead of one of the words in bold, without changing the meaning?

4 ⬭ Explain the difference in meaning between the words in bold as they are used in the following sentences.

a I really **must** be going – my son **should** be home from school soon and I **have to** take him to his swimming class.
b I know you **shouldn't** tell lies, but you **don't have to** tell him the whole truth, either. You **mustn't** let him know you've been here.

5 Usually, there is no difference in meaning between *needn't* and *don't need to*. However, *needn't* tends to be used to give permission not to do something, and *don't need to* is used more often to talk about general necessity.

*You **needn't** do it now – we're in no hurry.*
*You **don't need to** be tall to be a good basketball player.*

Rewrite each of the two sentences so that the meaning is positive. Is the modal or non-modal form of *need* required?

🄶 Read more about the verbs in this section on pages 224 and 225 of the Grammar reference.

Practice

1 Underline the correct alternatives in the following sentences. Either one, two or all three alternatives may be possible.

1 I cleaned the flat specially for tonight, but I *mustn't/needn't/shouldn't* have bothered.
2 You really *must/need/should* do something about your handwriting.
3 What do you *have/ought/need* to do to become famous?
4 I'm meeting my partner's parents for the first time tomorrow. What *need/ought/should* I wear?
5 We're going into town, but you *needn't/don't need to/don't have to* come if you don't want to.
6 They *ought to/must/should* have got there by now. Why haven't they phoned?
7 I really *needed to study/must have studied/ought to have studied* hard at the weekend, but I did absolutely nothing.
8 If you *should/ought to/need to* happen to see my ex-boss there, can you give him my regards?

2 ⬭ Choose four of the sentences from exercise 1 and have four separate conversations with your partner, using a different sentence to start each conversation. Remember to say your first sentence with one of the correct alternatives.

Vocabulary 2: Attitude adverbials

The adverbs in the following extracts from the reading text on pages 155 and 156 express the writer's attitude or opinion.

The voice is **unmistakably** that of Sir David Attenborough.
Not surprisingly, perhaps, he keeps out the limelight as much as possible.
For his programmes run **reassuringly** counter to the reflex of our times.

In sentences **1–5** underline the best alternative.

1 Local residents have condemned the decision to build the factory, and *rightly/undoubtedly/clearly* so, in my opinion.
2 *Strangely/Apparently/Presumably* enough, I find myself agreeing with the Government on this issue.
3 *Fortunately/Disappointingly/Conveniently* for us, it was an unusually warm winter and we couldn't go skiing on the hills as we'd hoped.
4 They chopped down vast areas of woodland with *believably/predictably/miraculously* disastrous results for the local bird population.
5 After such a wonderful holiday I *understandably/astonishingly/curiously* felt rather sad when we had to come home.

Use of English 2: **Key word transformations**
CAE Part 5

For questions **1–8**, complete the second sentence so that it has a similar meaning to the first sentence, using the word given. **Do not change the word given.** Use between **three** and **six** words, including the word given. Here is an example (**0**).

0 The coral is going to die if we don't take immediate steps to protect it from pollution.

OTHERWISE

We must take immediate steps to protect the coral, _otherwise it will be killed_ off by pollution.

1 The government should have carefully considered the issue of global warming a long time ago.

ATTENTION

The government should _____ the issue of global warming a long time ago.

2 Except for John, who is still collecting data in Antarctica, we will all be able to attend the meeting.

TO

We will all be able to make _____ from John, who is still collecting data in Antarctica.

3 There's a chance that you might find some interesting wildlife, so take a camera with you.

HAPPEN

You should take a camera with you in _____ across some interesting wildlife.

4 It could be a long time before the dolphins swim past, so while we're waiting I suggest you relax.

MEANTIME

We could be waiting for a long time for the dolphins to swim past, so _____ to relax.

5 Because that store sells clothes made by child labour in foreign factories, he doesn't shop there any more.

ACCOUNT

He doesn't buy clothes from that store any more, _____ they sell clothes made by child labour in foreign factories.

6 The animal rights activist was so persuasive that I felt obliged to sign the petition.

ADD

I felt I had _____ to the petition because the animal rights activist was so persuasive.

7 I imagine it was tough for you to refuse every beggar that asked you for money.

TURN

It must _____ every beggar that asked you for money.

8 It was a waste of time attending the protest march this afternoon, as the council had already made its decision in the morning.

PART

We needn't _____ the protest march this afternoon, as the council had already made its decision in the morning.

Writing: CAE Part 2

Articles

1 Read the following Part 2 task. If you were to answer it, which problem would you write about?

You see the following announcement in *Global Concern*, an international magazine which looks at current issues affecting the world.

> # Youth Issues
>
> We are inviting you, the reader, to write an article on **one** of the problems facing young people in your country today. Tell us about the main aspects of the problem and suggest what should be done to overcome it.
>
> We will publish the best article from each country.

Write your **article**.

2 🔘 Read the following answer to the task in exercise 1. To what extent does this problem exist in your own country? Do you agree with the views expressed in the last paragraph?

Street Life

Imagine, if you can, a torrential downpour at the start of the rainy season suddenly turning your 'bed' into a muddy pool. You look around for a more sheltered sleeping spot, but of course, you come up against competition from others who are in the same situation, others who are bigger than you. So you keep searching until eventually you find a dry enough place to sleep. By this time, though, you are starting to fall ill.

Sadly, this is the plight of thousands of youngsters in my country; young children and teenagers who are forced by circumstances to live on the streets without regular support from family or relatives. They struggle to make ends meet, shining shoes, selling small items like chewing gum or, in some cases, resorting to petty theft.

Worryingly, the number of street children is growing steadily, as poverty increases and family structures continue to break down. In addition, more and more are moving into the cities from rural areas, sent by their parents to supplement the family income. But the street children barely earn enough to get by themselves.

So what can be done? Ideally, of course, our government should come up with the necessary money to put things right. Unfortunately, however, since severe poverty is the main cause of the problem, this seems very unlikely, at least in the short term. Our main hope is that relief organizations will continue to send support and that people in the developed world will keep up the pressure on their governments to take action. For who is more deserving of help than children?

---

3 Answer the following questions with reference to the model answer above. Give examples where appropriate.

   a Has the task been fully achieved?
   b Is the answer clearly organized?
   c Have linking devices been used effectively?
   d Has the writer used a wide range of language?
   e Is the register appropriate throughout?
   f What techniques are used to get the reader's attention and engage his or her interest?

4 Now write an answer to one of the tasks on page 208.

Open cloze

For questions **1–15**, read the text below and think of the word which best fits each gap. Use only one word in each gap. There is an example at the beginning (**0**).

CREATURE COMFORTS

Pampered piglets could soon be taking (**0**) _it_ easy, chilling out on furniture that's more (**1**) _____ home in a penthouse flat than a pigsty. Tests have shown that piglets nurtured on heated waterbeds stand (**2**) _____ greatly improved chance of surviving their first few weeks of life.

Piglets must (**3**) _____ kept warm in their first few days to discourage them from snuggling up to their mother. That's because 80 per cent (**4**) _____ so of piglet deaths occur during (**5**) _____ period, and most of them are due to the sow rolling over and crushing her young. (**6**) _____ an effort to tackle this, the trend in porcine interior design is away from unhygienic straw and (**7**) _____ underfloor heating or infrared lamps. But these approaches leave piglets (**8**) _____ only an uninviting concrete floor (**9**) _____ lie on. The hard surface also aggravates the injuries that piglets often suffer (**10**) _____ fighting for position at feeding time.

To find a solution, researchers studied the behaviour (**11**) _____ weight gain of almost 1,400 piglets held in pens with a variety of heating schemes. Very (**12**) _____ all of the piglets preferred the warm waterbeds to any of the alternatives, spending well (**13**) _____ half the day lying about on them and only getting up to play or feed. Interestingly (**14**) _____ farmers, the piglets on the waterbeds (**15**) _____ only developed fewer skin lesions, but also gained significantly more weight than those kept on concrete.

Modal verbs

Complete each gap in **1–8** with either the positive or negative form of one of the modal verbs in the box. In each section, the verb required for both gaps is the same. There is one verb you do not need to use. There is an example at the beginning (**0**).

shall	should	will	would	~~can~~
could	may	might	need	must

0 She seems very pleasant, but she _can_ be quite irritable at times.
I'm off to bed – I _can_ barely keep my eyes open.

1 We _____ have caught that train if you'd run a bit faster.
I wish I _____ remember where I put my glasses!

2 She _____ have to phone now, right in the middle of my favourite programme!
After he retired, he _____ often go back to visit his old workmates.

3 You _____ have phoned to say you'd be late! I've been so worried.
No one seems to want the last piece, so I _____ as well eat it.

4 You _____ explain – John's already told me what happened.
I know you were angry, but you _____ have shouted.

5 That's very kind of you, but you _____ have gone to all that trouble.
He's just popped out to the shops, so he _____ be long.

6 Just a moment, I'll put you through. Who _____ I say is calling?
Let's go out for lunch, _____ we?

7 If you _____ tell me, I'll have to tickle you until you do!
Phone her a bit later – she probably _____ have got up yet.

8 Why _____ you always interrupt me when I'm speaking?
It _____ have been a huge explosion – it was heard up to 30 miles away.

Collocation revision: Units 1–12

1 In each of the spaces below write one word which collocates with all three of the other words or expressions. The question numbers also refer to the relevant unit of the book where the collocations appeared.

1 face a
take up a   _____
rise to a

7 a dislocated
a sprained   _____
a bruised

2 significant
far-reaching   _____
sweeping

8 reach a
uphold a   _____
overrule a

3 a faint
a musty   _____
a strong

9 spectacular
breathtaking   _____
superb

4 kick-off
injury   _____
half

10 a squeaky
a booming   _____
a hushed

5 a close
a rocky   _____
a stable

11 a rare
a familiar   _____
a welcome

6 _____   soundly
rough
badly

12 _____   a challenge
with success
someone off the train

2 Use other collocations from the first twelve units of the book to help you create your own exercise. Write three words or expressions which can all be used with the same verb or noun, in the same way as in exercise 1. Write four examples like this for another student to complete.

Speaking

Introduction

Paper 5 consists of four parts and lasts fifteen minutes. You will probably take the test with another candidate, though it is possible to be part of a group of three. There are two examiners: the interlocutor, who conducts the test and asks the questions, and the assessor, who listens to the test and assesses your performance. The interlocutor also assesses and contributes to your final mark.

In the following advice to candidates, complete each gap with a word from the box. There is an example at the beginning (**0**).

> repetition   ideas   pictures   opinion   attention   opportunity
> ~~range~~   silences   element   vocabulary   discussion

Demonstrating your abilities

- Use a (**0**) _range_ of language and show your ability to link your (**1**) _____ .
- Avoid long (**2**) _____ and frequent pauses as you organize your thoughts.
- If you cannot remember or do not know a particular item of (**3**) _____ , use alternative words to paraphrase.

Following instructions

- Always pay close (**4**) _____ to the interlocutor's instructions. In Parts 2 and 3, questions are printed on the same page as the pictures to help you remember what you have to talk about.

- Don't be afraid to ask for (**5**) _____ if you have not heard, or clarification if you have not fully understood, what has been said.

- Don't just describe the (**6**) _____ you are given; tasks based on visual material also involve an (**7**) _____ of speculation, opinion-giving and/or evaluation.

Taking turns

- Don't attempt to dominate a (**8**) _____ , but rather give your partner the (**9**) _____ to speak, and respond appropriately to what he or she says.
- If your partner appears reticent, try to involve them by asking questions or inviting them to give their (**10**) _____ .

Part 1: Social interaction

In Part 1 the interlocutor will ask you questions about yourself.

1   Work in groups of three. One of you is the interlocutor and the other two are candidates. You have three minutes to do the following task.

Interlocutor
- Ask the candidates one or more questions from at least two of the categories below. You may ask each candidate the same or different questions.

Candidates
- Answer the questions from the interlocutor as fully as possible, giving reasons for your ideas and opinions.

What to expect in the exam

- Part 1 lasts approximately three minutes.
- Questions will be asked from a range of topics including, for example, interests, daily life, family and holidays.
- You may respond to the other candidate's comments, though you are not actively invited to do so by the interlocutor.

English
What are your main reasons for learning English?
Which aspect of learning English do you find hardest?
What do you need to do to help you pass the CAE exam?

Leisure time
What do you enjoy doing in your free time?
How important is sport and fitness in your life?
Do you like spending time alone?

Travel and holidays
What is one of the most interesting places you have visited?
Do you prefer going on holiday with your friends or your family?
Where would you most like to travel to?

House and home
What do you enjoy most about living where you do?
If you could afford your ideal home, what would it be like?
Would you ever consider living abroad?

The past
What were you doing this time yesterday?
What are some of your earliest childhood memories?
What have been some of the happiest moments in your life?

Future plans
What are you most looking forward to doing in the next few months?
What do you hope to achieve in the next three years?
Do you usually plan your weekends well in advance?

When you have finished, change roles and repeat the exercise with different questions.

2   👁   **2.27** Listen to two students, Janusz and Ana, doing the Part 1 task and comment on their performance. Consider the following:

- how well each student develops their responses
- the range and accuracy of their language

Part 2: Long turn

In Part 2 you are firstly given the opportunity to speak for one minute, without interruption, about some pictures. You then have 30 seconds to comment briefly on your partner's pictures by answering a question.

> **What to expect in the exam**
>
> - In Part 2, you have to compare two of the three photographs you are given, whilst at the same time speculating and giving your opinion about some aspect of their content.

Task One

1   Look at the following Part 2 task.

Work in pairs. Look at these pictures. They show people who are checking the time.

Student A:

Compare two of the pictures, and say why the people might be checking the time and how much influence time might have in their daily lives.

Student B:

When your partner has finished talking, answer the following question about all three pictures. For which person do you think time has the greatest influence in their daily life?

> - Why might the people be checking the time?
> - How much influence might time have in their daily lives?

Before you do the task, answer the question in exercise 2 on page 166.

2 How well does each candidate **a–c** approach the task in exercise 1? Comment on each extract, giving examples to justify your opinions.

a *This woman is in the kitchen or perhaps the dining room with her daughter. She's checking the time because maybe she's late. I think she's a businesswoman. This woman is an athlete in a race. She's checking the time because she wants to know how fast she's running. I think time has a big influence in her life because …*

b *I'm going to talk about this picture here which shows an athlete, then this one here which shows a woman and her daughter. If I have time, I'll speak about the one here with the little girl and her toy watch. Well, all three pictures show women, well, women and a girl, checking the time. This woman is an athlete and I think she is looking at her watch to …*

c *The pictures of the working mother and the athlete both convey the idea of racing against the clock, a need or desire to do something within a certain period of time. The mother looks rather stressed, suggesting something unexpected has happened. She might be phoning the office to let them know she'll be late because her car won't start, or her daughter's fallen ill. The athlete, on the other hand, is probably …*

3 Now you are ready to do the task.

Task Two

1 Change roles from task one. Turn to page 207.

2 👁 **2.28** Listen to Janusz and Ana doing the Part 2 tasks.

- How well do they each complete their main one-minute task?
- How varied is the language they use?

> **Don't forget!**
> - Avoid long silences and frequent pauses.
> - Paraphrase if you cannot remember a particular word.

Part 3: Collaborative task

In Part 3, the interlocutor does not take part, but listens while you and your partner perform a problem-solving task together for about three minutes. You are given a set of visual prompts, which form the basis for the task, and are asked to exchange ideas and opinions, make evaluations and/or speculate. You are expected to work towards a conclusion at the end of the task, although you will not be penalized if you fail to reach a decision.

1 On page 167 there are some pictures showing different jobs.

Talk to each other about the most and least satisfying aspects of these jobs, and then decide which two jobs are the most rewarding.

> **How to go about it**
>
> **Don't** merely describe each picture and what it shows.
> eg *This picture shows a tour guide talking to a group of tourists. He's probably explaining the history of the ruins behind him.*
>
> **Do** include the pictures naturally in your discussion, as you consider each job.
> eg *Probably the most fulfilling part of a tour guide's job is knowing that he or she is helping to make the tourist's visit to a particular place more interesting. It might be by explaining a little of the history of a building or ancient ruins, as in the picture, or it could be by showing …*
>
> **Don't** simply agree with your partner or repeat his or her ideas.
>
> **Do** express your own opinions or develop your partner's points by adding further comments of your own.
>
> **Don't** reach your conclusion too quickly, otherwise you will be left with nothing to talk about.
>
> **Do** take time to evaluate all the visuals: the conclusion should be a natural product of your discussion.
>
> **Do** make it clear in your discussion that you are working towards a conclusion.

- What are the most and least satisfying aspects of these jobs?
- Which two jobs are the most rewarding?

- Newspaper Journalist

- Dentist

- Tour Guide

- Cabinet Maker

- Pop/Rock Singer

- Politician

2 👁 **2.29** Listen to Janusz and Ana doing the Part 3 task and answer these questions.

- Which jobs do they choose?
- At what point in the discussion do they begin to make their choices?
- How well do Janusz and Ana interact with each other?

Part 4: Further discussion

In Part 4 the interlocutor asks further questions related to the issues raised in Part 3. As well as responding to these questions, you should also interact with your partner and comment on what he or she says.

1 Discuss the following questions with your partner.

- Which would you prefer to have: a job which is well paid but monotonous or one which is poorly paid but fulfilling? Why?
- Do you think that school prepares young people adequately for the world of work? Why/Why not?
- What difficulties do young people in your area face when searching for work?
- What do you think is the ideal age to retire? Why?
- How has computer technology affected the world of work?
- Do you think people who earn large amounts of money have a moral obligation to donate money to charity? Why/Why not?

2 👁 **2.30** Listen to Janusz and Ana doing the Part 4 task.

- How well do they each react to what each other says?

13 Food for thought

Vocabulary 1: Eating and drinking

1 All the verb phrases in each of the groups **1–8** below can be used in combination with one of the nouns in the box. Write an appropriate noun from the box in each of the spaces. There is an example at the beginning (**0**).

food	drink	hunger	thirst	
meal	~~dish~~	stomach	appetite	eater

0 prepare your favourite *dish*
   order a side

1 have a raging _____
   quench your

5 work up a big _____
   lose your

2 feel faint with _____
   satisfy your

6 be a fussy _____
   be a big

3 pick at _____
   gulp down

7 do something on a full _____
   do something on an empty

4 have a soft _____
   go out for a celebratory

8 heat up a ready _____
   have a square

2 Study the collocations in exercise 1 for two minutes. Then look at the nouns in the box and cover the exercise. How many collocations can you remember?

3 Use five of the collocations to write sentences about yourself and/or people you know.

Example:
Whenever I come home after a trip away, my mother prepares my favourite dish of lamb chops and fried potatoes.

4 ⬭ Compare and discuss your sentences with another student.

Speaking
CAE Part 2

Long turn

1 Look at these photos. They show people who are eating meals in different situations.

Student A:
Compare two of the pictures, and say what considerations might have been taken into account when planning for the meals and how much the people might be enjoying them.

Student B:
When your partner has finished talking, say which situation you would prefer to eat in.

- What considerations might have been taken into account when planning for the meals?
- How much might the people be enjoying them?

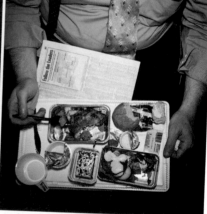

2 Now change roles. Follow the instructions again using the remaining pictures.

How to go about it

Student A
Some of the following considerations might be relevant to the photos you choose. Can you think of any more?

time	space	weight
cost	taste	quality	health

- Note the use of modal verbs in the instructions: *might have been taken into account* and *might be enjoying*. Use a range of language to speculate about the photographs.

Student B
Your comment should be brief, but you do have time to give reasons for your feelings or opinions.

Use of English:
CAE Part 3

Word formation

1 Use the word given in capitals at the end of some of the lines to form a word that fits in the gap **in the same line**. There is an example at the beginning (**0**).

EATING IN THE RIGHT PLACES

Food researchers have discovered that the (**0**) _appreciation_ of a meal	**APPRECIATE**
lies not so much in what you eat as where you eat it. They served up	
exactly the same chicken dish in ten different places and found that the	
better the (**1**) _____, the better people said the food tasted. A	**SET**
meal of *chicken à la king*, which got low marks from (**2**) _____	**DINE**
in a (**3**) _____ home for the elderly and a boarding school, was	**RESIDE**
given top marks when it was served up at a four-star restaurant, although	
it had been made from the same ingredients, cooked in the same kitchen,	
stored in the same plastic bag and accompanied by the same rice. The	
chickens even came from the same flock. These (**4**) _____ will	**REVEAL**
come as (**5**) _____ news to food snobs and celebrity chefs.	**WELCOME**
According to the researchers, the (**6**) _____ demonstrate that	**FIND**
food is (**7**) _____ and is actually often a great deal less important	**RATE**
than the environment in which it is eaten. 'Go out to a place where they	
serve pretty poor food, but where the atmosphere is pleasant, the company	
good and the waiter polite, and it is probably more (**8**) _____	**ENJOY**
than a stuffy place with excellent food,' said Professor John Edwards of	
Bournemouth University, who led the study. The meal, which was	
assessed on its (**9**) _____ , taste and texture, received the worst	**APPEAR**
overall marks when it was served at an army (**10**) _____ camp.	**TRAIN**

2 ⬭ Tell your partner about three very different places in which you have eaten meals.

What kind of food did you eat? To what extent was your enjoyment of the food influenced by the surroundings?

Writing 1:
CAE Part 2

Informal letters

1 ⬭ Read the following Part 2 task and the sample answer below it. Do you agree with the advice given? Is there anything else you would add?

An English-speaking friend of yours is in charge of organizing the food for a forthcoming event or activity and knows that you have some experience of a similar situation. The friend has written to you, expressing uncertainty and nervousness about the task which faces him/her and asking for your help. Write a **letter** giving advice on those aspects of the food arrangements which you consider to be most important and reassuring your friend of his/her ability to cope. You should write **220–260** words.

Dear Graham,

Great to hear from you! It's hard to believe that Luke's about to celebrate his fifth birthday. You're very brave to organize the party all by yourself and I'm not surprised you're a bit daunted by it all. Still, with Liz being away, I suppose you haven't got much
5   choice.

I can certainly pass on a few tips that I learnt from my own bitter experience in September. First of all, don't make the same mistake as I did and lay on a huge spread. Young children are fussy eaters and tend not to have big appetites, so there's no point preparing vast quantities of elaborate food, because they probably won't eat it. You'd
10 be much better off filling a few bowls with different flavoured crisps — they were the first things to disappear at Lara's party.

That's not to say you shouldn't put out other things for them to eat — some sweet, some savoury — but it's not worth going to a lot of trouble over it. And don't be surprised if they don't eat the birthday cake. Lara's friends hardly touched hers, so I
15 wouldn't spend hours making one if I were you — buy one from a shop and you won't be disappointed.

And finally, whatever you do, make sure you don't let them have the food until <u>after</u> the games. Children running around on full stomachs is not to be recommended!

Anyway, I'm sure Luke and his friends will have a great time, even if it leaves you utterly
20 exhausted. Let me know how it all goes, won't you?

All the best,

Elisa

2 Does the answer address all aspects of the task?

3 Underline those expressions in the answer which are used to introduce advice.

What other evidence of a wide range of language is there?

4 To make the answer seem more natural, the writer:
- shows interest in the forthcoming event
- refers to her own experience.

Find examples of these features in the letter.

5 Now write your own answer to the task in exercise 1.

How to go about it	**Don't forget!**

• Choose an event or activity and list the advice you might give. Here are six possible situations; can you think of any more?
camping holiday   hiking trip   barbecue   farewell party   picnic   family celebration
• Select four or five pieces of advice which you consider to be the most important and write a paragraph plan.
• Imagine yourself in the situation described in the task. This will help you write a more natural answer.
Remember to:
  • show interest in the forthcoming event or activity
  • make reference to your own experience
  • offer your friend some words of reassurance
	• Plan your answer carefully before you write. (See checklist on page 193.)
	• Include a wide range of language.
	• Write in a consistently informal register.

Reading:
CAE Part 1

Multiple choice

1 ⬭ Have you ever been ill as a result of something you have eaten? If so, what caused it?

Do you read the information on packets or tins of food? How useful do you think this is?

2 You are going to read three extracts which are all concerned in some way with food. For questions **1–6**, choose the answer (**A**, **B**, **C** or **D**) which you think best fits according to the text.

Yoghurts recalled after mould found

Almost half a million yoghurts are being recalled by Bewley Farms after the manufacturer discovered that part of the first batch of their newly launched product had been contaminated by mould. The Suffolk-based dairy recently extended its product range to include natural and fruit-flavoured yoghurts and yoghurt drinks.

The recall was ordered after a number of people had contacted consumer authorities or the company's own customer service department complaining of feeling sick after eating one of the yoghurts in the new range. A spokesman for Bewley Farms
18 said they had likened the flavour to that of blue cheese and had reported a pungent odour, like the smell of milk that has gone off, impregnating the contents of their fridges.

An advertisement announcing the recall appeared in all of the main national newspapers yesterday, as well as on the company's website. Consumers were informed that the mould did not represent a serious danger to health and that only a small proportion of the yoghurts were affected. The announcement said the entire batch was being withdrawn 'as a precautionary measure' and explained how compensation could be claimed. Consumers were told to dispose of the contents and forward the lid displaying the batch number and sell-by date in order to receive a voucher which could be exchanged for any Bewley Farm product.

The company has ceased production at its Ipswich factory while it investigates how the mould came to be in the yoghurts.

1 What does 'they' in line 18 refer to?
  A the yoghurts
  B Bewley Farms
  C affected consumers
  D consumer authorities

2 In their announcement, Bewley Farms
  A offered consumers a money refund.
  B attempted to reassure consumers.
  C asked consumers to return the product.
  D claimed to have identified the cause of the mould.

Extract from a novel

'How are you getting on?' she said.
Lying there with her eyes still closed, she hears her own voice boldly asking that because she couldn't think of anything else to say.
'OK' he said. 'Yourself, Felicia?'
'Out of work.'
'Weren't you in the meat place?'
'It closed down.'
He smiled again. He asked why Slieve Bloom Meats had closed down and she explained; again it was something to say. A woman failed to report a cut on her hand that went septic, and an outbreak of food-poisoning was afterwards traced back to a batch of tinned kidney and beef. No more than a scratch the little cut had seemed to Mrs Grennan, even though it wouldn't heal. Dr Mortell had seen it and given Mrs Grennan a note, but she had gone on working because when you went sick you sometimes found yourself laid off when you returned: since 1986, when there had been another food scare – one that was general in the processed-meat business then – the factory hadn't been doing well. There was an opinion in the neighbourhood that sooner or later it would have closed down anyway, and with some justification Mrs Grennan believed she was a scapegoat. 'Sure the work's gone and that's all there is to it,' Felicia heard another woman comforting her at the time. 'Does it matter whose fault it was?'

3 When Mrs Grennan cut herself,
   A she was initially very concerned.
   B her employers threatened to sack her.
   C she was advised to stay off work.
   D she kept it quiet from her workmates.

4 When the factory closed down, Mrs Grennan
   A was relieved not to have to work any more.
   B felt unfairly accused of being the cause.
   C was reluctant to say who was to blame.
   D greeted the news with surprise.

Appearances can be deceptive

Under cover as normal shoppers, Sue Davies, Principal Policy Adviser for Food Issues, and her team at the Consumers' Association, trawl the supermarkets and independent retailers, tracking down enticing packaging that is designed to mislead, and gathering samples that will provide evidence with which to name and shame the culprits.

There was the creamy chicken and sweetcorn pasta which contained only 2 per cent dried chicken and 1 per cent sweetcorn, or the maple syrup creams which contained no maple syrup. 'People now consume more processed food than ever before, so we have become more reliant on manufacturers to provide us with information about it. Yet this is frequently distorted, through the use of logos, pictures, claims and labelling, which suggest a product is something that it is not. Some companies will change their labels within a couple of hours of our writing to them, or publishing what we have found,' says Davies. 'Others don't acknowledge the problem at all, but in any case we are able to give ammunition to the Trading Standards officers who may be able to take action.'

Currently the team is homing in on misleading health claims such as 'good for the heart', 'can boost your immune system' or 'help support your body's natural defences'. These may be within the letter of the law, but flout its spirit. For example, the claim that a product is up to 90 per cent fat-free is misleading, given that strict guidelines state it should have no more than 3 per cent fat to qualify as a 'low-fat' product. These are the areas that make Davies' blood boil.

WARNING! MAY CONTAIN CHICKEN

5 Sue Davies says that food companies
   A can be reported to a higher authority.
   B generally ignore the findings of her team.
   C reveal little to consumers about their products.
   D are often unaware that they are breaking the law.

6 Sue Davies gets angry about labels which
   A exploit weaknesses in food legislation.
   B do not adhere to certain guidelines.
   C lie about the food's contents.
   D create a false impression.

⬤ Reacting to the text

'People now consume more processed food than ever before …'. Why is this?

How true is it   **a** in your country?   **b** in your family?

Language focus 1: Comparisons

A Comparisons

1 In these extracts from the Use of English text on page 170 and the reading texts on pages 172 and 173, complete each gap with one word.

a The appreciation of a meal lies **not so** _____ in what you eat _____ where you eat it.

b _____ **better** the setting, _____ **better** diners said the food tasted.

c They had _____ the flavour **to** that of blue cheese. (1)

d **No** _____ **than** a scratch the little cut had seemed to Mrs Grennan. (2)

e There was an opinion in the neighbourhood that **sooner or** _____ it would have closed down anyway. (2)

f People _____ consume more processed food **than ever** _____. (3)

2 Check your answers in the texts on pages 170, 172 and 173. The numbers in brackets refer to the relevant reading texts.

B Qualifying comparisons

Many words and phrases can be used to qualify comparisons.

Examples:
Peaches are <u>significantly/three times/slightly</u> more expensive than last year.
There isn't <u>nearly/half/quite</u> as much on the menu as there used to be.

Underline the correct alternative in the following sentences.

a Food is often a *great deal/a large amount/a high number* less important than the environment in which it is eaten.

b My brother eats *a lot of/by far/far* more chocolate than is good for him.

c It claims to be a health cereal but it contains *just/near/same* as much salt as ordinary cereals.

d I only weigh *slightly/little/bit* less than I did when I started this diet.

e It's *more/much/very* healthier to cook without salt.

C *Like* and *as*

Like is used with nouns, pronouns or gerunds to make comparisons.
As is used with nouns to indicate someone or something's job, role or function.

*I got a job **as** a waitress in a restaurant last summer. We worked **like** slaves.*
*He found a piece of wood shaped **like** a telephone and used it **as** a hammer.*

Both *as* and *like* can be used with clauses to make comparisons, although *like* is informal and considered incorrect by some.

*She walked down the aisle of St Anne's, just **as/like** her mother had done thirty years before.*

Complete each gap in these sentences from the reading texts with either *as* or *like*. Then check your answers in the texts.

a They …had reported a pungent odour, _____ the smell of milk that has gone off. (1)

b The announcement said the entire batch was being withdrawn '_____ a precautionary measure'. (1)

c Under cover _____ normal shoppers, Sue Davies … and her team … (3)

D *So* and *such*

1 Complete each gap with either *so* or *such*.

a It's not quite _____ a violent film as his last one.

b I'd never seen _____ tall a man before in my life.

c The bar wasn't _____ crowded as we thought it would be.

2 What do you notice about the types of words which follow *so* and *such*?

E Further expressions

Complete each gap with one of the words from the box.

long	near	close	better
as	like	much	

1 She enjoyed eating out every day, and **if** the restaurant overlooked the sea, then **so much the** _____ .

2 My host family was **nothing** _____ **as** reserved as I'd been expecting and the food **nowhere** _____ **as** bad.

3 I was rather disappointed by the size of the portions, _____ **were** my two fellow diners.

4 Prices varied greatly but the food was very _____ **the same** in each restaurant.

5 This is the best meal we've had all holiday, **by a** _____ **way**.

6 The lemon sorbet with white armagnac is delicious, but the chocolate mousse **comes a** _____ **second**.

Read more about comparisons on page 225 of the Grammar reference.

Practice

1 Select three of the following. Write three sentences for each pair, comparing and contrasting them. Use some of the language from sections **A–E** above.
   - two restaurants you have eaten in
   - two of your national or regional dishes
   - two places you have been to on holiday
   - two film actors or actresses
   - two jobs you have done
   - two pets you have had

2 Compare and discuss your sentences with your partner.

Vocabulary 2: Deception

1 Look at the following words in bold from extract 3 on page 173 and complete the table.

*Appearances can be **deceptive**
packaging that is designed to **mislead**
misleading health claims*

Noun	Verb	Adjective	Adverb
⎯⎯⎯⎯	mislead	misleading	_____
_____	_____	fraudulent	_____
deception	_____	deceptive	_____

2 Complete each of the gaps with the appropriate form of one of the words from the table in exercise 1. In each section **1–3**, the words required for both spaces **a** and **b** are different, but from the same word family. There is an example at the beginning (**0**).

0 He has been charged with _defrauding_ **the company of** £2 million.
Car insurance firms have expressed concern at the increase in the number of _fraudulent_ **claims**.

1 a With their pointed snouts, fruit bats are often _____ **referred to** as 'flying foxes'.
b The tobacco company was found guilty of publishing _____ **information** on the effects of passive smoking.

2 a The device, which is _____ **simple in appearance**, is capable of performing a number of extremely complex functions.
b You're _____ **yourself** if you think you can pass without studying.

3 a He is serving a six-year jail sentence for **tax** _____ .
b The court heard how Smith had _____ **obtained money** by posing as a charity worker.

3 Complete each of the gaps in the following newspaper article with one of the words from the box.

through	into	out	in	for	for

Retired widow loses life savings

A retired widow has been **tricked (1)** _____ of her life savings by a bogus financial adviser. 65-year-old Grace Smedley was completely **taken (2)** _____ by the smooth-talking confidence trickster, who **deceived** her **(3)** _____ handing over nearly £20,000. Mrs Smedley expressed her frustration at allowing herself to **fall (4)** _____ the conman's trickery

and failing to **see (5)** _____ his false promises of immediate high returns on her money. 'I've been **taken (6)** _____ **a ride**,' she complained. 'I feel a bit of a mug.'

The man, who is believed to be in his early thirties, claimed to have access to a high-yielding annuity scheme which would provide an

4 Underline and record any other words in the article which are related to deception.

5 ◯ Tell your partner about:
• a time in your life when you or someone else **told a lie**
• a television programme where **tricks are played on** people
• a **swindle** you heard about in the news or saw in a film
• someone you know who **cheated at** games as a child
• a time when appearances proved to be deceptive.

Listening:
CAE Part 1

Multiple choice

1 How much fruit do you eat each day? Which is your favourite? Which vegetables do you dislike?

How healthy are school meals in your country?

How many different types of diets have you heard about?

2 🔊 2.31–2.33 You will hear three different extracts. For questions **1–6**, choose the answer (**A**, **B** or **C**) which fits best according to what you hear. There are two questions for each extract.

Extract one

You hear part of an interview with a man that runs a stall at a farmers' market.

1 What is the man's opinion of produce sold at supermarkets?
   A It is not always clear where it came from.
   B The quality of the fruit and vegetables is poor.
   C Most items are more expensive than those sold at a farmers' market.

2 What do the man and the woman agree about?
   A the dangers of using chemicals in agriculture
   B the needless packaging used by supermarkets
   C the influence of appearance on consumer decision-making

Extract two

You hear part of a radio interview with Tricia Bryson, an official in the Department for Public Health.

3 What is the government's new policy concerning junk food in schools?
   A It should be inspected by teachers first.
   B It will not be available in the school canteen.
   C It may not be consumed on the school premises.

4 What does Tricia believe is the main cause of childhood obesity?
   A the availability of junk food
   B a lack of information about healthy diet
   C parents setting a bad example in eating habits

Extract three

You hear part of an interview with Shelley Matthews, winner of a weight-loss competition.

5 Shelley decided to enter the SlimRight weight-loss competition because
   A she wanted to prove to herself she could lose weight.
   B her children had put pressure on her to diet.
   C she wanted to regain her self-confidence.

6 Why does Shelley compare her nutritionist to a priest?
   A to suggest that he changed her attitude to life
   B to show that the diet he recommended was quite basic
   C to emphasize the amount of support she received from him

3 ⬤ How healthily do people generally eat in your country?

What changes have there been in eating habits in recent years?

Language focus 2: Adverbs of degree

1 Look at the following extracts from the recording.

    a You can see they're **a bit anxious**.
    b You look **absolutely marvellous**.
    c I suspect they were **very scared**.
    d It was all **fairly easy** to cook.

Absolutely is not normally used with the adjectives in **a**, **c** or **d**. Nor are *a bit, very, fairly* used with the adjective in **b**. Why is this?
What other adverbs of degree can be used with the adjectives in **a**, **c** and **d**?

2 Which of the following adjectives are gradable (used with *very, fairly,* etc) and which are non-gradable (used with *absolutely*)?

Example:
Gradable: <u>*tasty*</u>   Non-gradable: <u>*starving*</u>

tasty	starving	frightened	pleased
furious	dirty	ridiculous	tired
	huge	incredible	

3 What is the meaning of *quite* in these two sentences?

    a This fish is **quite** tasty.
    b This fish is **quite** delicious.

4 There are a number of other adverbs which can be used to intensify or emphasize adjectives, as in these examples.

The tap water here is **perfectly safe** to drink.
The water in this river is **highly toxic** to fish.
I am **fully conscious** of the risks involved in swimming here.

In **1–6**, cross out the adjective which does not normally collocate with the adverb at the beginning of the line. There is an example at the beginning (**0**).

0	**perfectly**	clear	normal
		~~dependent~~	capable
1	**highly**	gifted	promising
		talented	clever
2	**fully**	aware	worried
		booked	equipped
3	**wholly**	informed	inappropriate
		inadequate	unacceptable
4	**entirely**	free of charge	different
		old	wrong
5	**utterly**	ridiculous	opposed
		qualified	disgraceful
6	**totally**	unnecessary	unexpected
		independent	intelligent

5 Tell your partner about a time when you were:

- absolutely terrified
- completely lost
- utterly exhausted
- highly motivated
- totally wrong
- extremely embarrrassed

Writing 2:
CAE Part 2

Reports

You have been asked to write a report for an international survey about eating habits in your country. Your report should address these three questions:

- How have eating habits changed in your country in recent years?
- How positive are these changes?
- What developments may take place in the future?

Write your **report** in **220–260** words.

How to go about it

- Consider all three questions in the task and make notes under headings such as the following:
    Eating with family vs eating alone   *Health foods*
    Traditional food vs fast food   *Eating times*
    The headings you choose will depend on the situation in your country.
- Write a paragraph plan. Two possible alternatives are:

<u>A</u>
1 Introduction
2 Changes
3 How positive
4 Future developments

<u>B</u>
1 Introduction
2 Eating with family vs eating alone
    • changes, how positive, future developments
3 Traditional food vs fast food
    • changes, how positive, future developments
4 Eating times
    • changes, how positive, future developments

- For vocabulary of *Possibility*, see page 209 and of *Changes* see page 210.
- When you have finished the report, give it a title and add paragraph headings.

Vocabulary

Decide which answer (**A**, **B**, **C** or **D**) best fits each space. There is an example at the beginning (**0**).

0 Don't judge a book by its cover – appearances can often be very _____.
  A mistaking **B** fraudulent **C** <u>deceptive</u> **D** tricky

1 He went for a walk to work _____ an appetite for breakfast.
  A up **B** out **C** on **D** off

2 She had lost her appetite and could only _____ her meal, forcing down a mouthful or two.
  A gulp down **B** bite off **C** eat up **D** pick at

3 How could I have allowed myself to be _____ by his lies?
  A fallen for **B** taken in **C** tricked into **D** seen through

4 They eventually took the bronze medal, finishing a _____ third behind Poland.
  A tight **B** final **C** close **D** late

5 Some of the chocolate bars were found to contain glass and the whole batch had to be _____.
  A overdrawn **B** overthrown **C** recalled **D** retracted

6 His voice has been _____ to that of David Bowie.
  A equated **B** likened **C** equalled **D** associated

7 I ordered a _____ salad to have with my spaghetti dish.
  A side **B** spare **C** supplementary **D** part

8 She sat back in a _____ relaxed pose, her hands trembling slightly in her lap.
  A trickily **B** fraudulently **C** deceptively **D** deceitfully

9 She went under _____ as a waitress to write an article on tipping.
  A mask **B** act **C** pose **D** cover

10 _____ your child's hunger for knowledge with this CD-ROM version of our encyclopaedia.
  A Satisfy **B** Quench **C** Fulfil **D** Meet

11 A copy of the booklet can be obtained _____ free of charge from your nearest chemist's.
  A extremely **B** entirely **C** greatly **D** highly

12 The headteacher described his behaviour as '_____ unacceptable' and defended her decision to expel him.
  A wholly **B** fully **C** perfectly **D** deeply

Comparisons

Complete each of the gaps with **two words**. There is an example at the beginning (**0**).

0 She isn't anything _*like as*_ unpleasant as people say she is.

1 He was nowhere _____ tall as I thought he'd be.
2 It isn't so _____ restaurant as a bar that serves food.
3 The village looks very much the _____ it did 200 years ago.
4 The longer I live in this house, _____ I realize how badly built it is.
5 This is by _____ best curry I've ever eaten.
6 This isn't quite _____ nice hotel as the one we stayed in last year.
7 I'd like it by Friday, but if you can do it before, then so _____ better.
8 He went to Oxford University, as _____ father before him.

Use of English: CAE Part 5

Key word transformations

For questions **1–8** complete the second sentence so that it has a similar meaning to the first sentence, using the word given. **Do not change the word given**. Use between **three** and **six** words, including the word given. Here is an example (**0**).

0 The judge decided it was true that the four men had smuggled alcohol into the country.

GUILTY

The four men were _found guilty of smuggling_ alcohol into the country by the judge.

1 My brother and I have the same liking for junk food but he spends more time in the gym.

JUST

My brother _____ much as I do but he spends more time in the gym.

2 With only three buttons to push, this new food processor looks simple, but that's deceptive.

IN

With only three buttons to push, this new food processor _____ appearance.

3 The moment I saw the filthy state of the restaurant kitchen, I no longer felt hungry.

SOON

I lost _____ I saw the filthy state of the restaurant kitchen.

4 This recipe is really a lot more imaginative than the others in this book.

MOST

This recipe is by _____ in this book.

5 Since he was promoted to head chef, he has never been so stressed.

EVER

He has been suffering _____ since he was promoted to head chef.

6 I had expected the snake dish to be much worse than it actually was.

BAD

The snake dish was actually nowhere _____ I had expected.

7 This isn't nearly as good as the chicken soup you make.

SECOND

This chicken soup doesn't even come a _____ one you make.

8 You don't realize quite how much fat there is in that pizza.

DEAL

There's _____ fat in that pizza than you realize.

Collaborative task

Speaking:
CAE Part 3

The illustrations show some areas in which money plays a role. Talk to each other about how money, or the lack of it, affects these areas of our lives and then decide in which one money can have the most positive, and in which the most negative, effect.

How to go about it

- Look at the adjectives to describe *Effect* on page 213 and write down two words in each of the following categories. Use some of these words in your discussion.
  A negative effect   A positive effect
  A small effect   A big effect
- The illustrations will give you some initial ideas to talk about, but do consider other aspects of each area.

- How does money, or the lack of it, affect these areas of our lives?
- In which areas can money have the most positive and negative effect?

Sport

Education

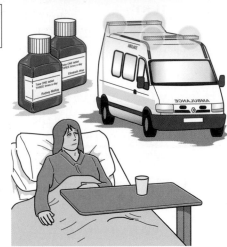

Health

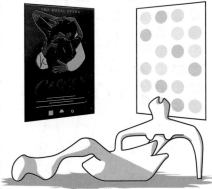

Culture

Relationships

Housing

Vocabulary 1: Money

1 In **1** and **2** below, match each phrase **a–d** with an appropriate sentence **1–4**. The first one has been done for you.

1 They paid…
  a in advance
  b in arrears
  c in instalments
  d in full

  1 They made regular payments over two years.
  2 They paid all the money that was owing.
  3 They paid for the hotel room before the holiday.
  4 They settled the bill after the work was finished.

2 She bought it…
  a on impulse
  b on hire purchase
  c at auction
  d in the sales

  1 Everything in the store was reduced by ten per cent.
  2 She offered the highest price for the painting.
  3 She saw the hat and immediately decided to buy it.
  4 She hasn't finished paying for her new fridge yet.

2 ⬭ Discuss the following with your partner.

In what situations do people or organizations usually pay
a in advance?   b in arrears?   b in instalments?

Do you ever buy things
a on impulse?   b in the sales?   c on credit?

Verb + adverb collocations

1 Complete each of the gaps with an appropriate adverb from the box.

hard   heavily   freely   generously

a 'Top sportspeople bring enjoyment to millions and deserve to be **paid** _____ .'
b 'There's no point being frugal when you're young – you should **spend** _____ and have fun.'
c '**Save** _____ , put down a deposit on a flat and leave home as soon as possible.'
d 'The government in my country needs to **invest** _____ in technology for schools.'

2 ⬭ Do you agree with each of the statements in exercise 1? Give reasons for your opinions.

Listening 1:
CAE Part 2

Sentence completion

1 ⬭ How careful are you with your money? Are you able to make it last?

2 ⦿ 2.34 You will hear John Lister, a counsellor at a university in Britain, giving advice on money matters to a new intake of university undergraduates. For questions 1–8 complete the sentences.

Students can borrow money for living expenses from the [1] .

Payments are usually made to students each [2] .

Students can obtain a personal [3] from the Internet.

He suggests choosing a bank with good [4] facilities.

John thinks that working [5] a week is enough.

Students are advised to talk to their [6] before buying books.

They should also consult the [7] in their department.

John tells students to make full use of their [8] card.

3 ⬭ What further advice might John Lister give to the undergraduates in order to help them make their money last? Imagine that the students are living away from home for the first time. Consider the following categories:

food   travel and transport   **other**

clothes   gas, electricity and phone bills

Writing 1:
CAE Part 2

Contributions: guidebook entry

1 Read the following Part 2 task and the advice which follows.

A guidebook is being produced in English aimed at young foreign visitors to your country. The book is entitled *On the cheap* and you have been asked to write the section for your area. Your entry should:

- give general information and advice on saving money during a short stay in your area
- suggest places to visit and things to do, which do not involve spending a great deal.

Write your **contribution to the guidebook** in **220–260** words.

How to go about it

- When giving general information and advice you might consider:
  Accommodation: inexpensive places to stay   *Shopping*: where to find reasonably priced souvenirs.
  Food: bars and restaurants with affordable   *Transport*: special tickets and discounts
- When suggesting places to visit and things to do, don't go into too much detail; the word limit is 220–260 words.

Useful language

Complete each of the following expressions with one of the words from the box.

discounts	costs	bargains
ticket	saving	money

a the chance to **make a considerable** _____
b food which is **excellent value for** _____
c restaurants which **offer special** _____
d the price of a **monthly season** _____
e the place to **pick up some good** _____
f a simple **way to cut** _____

2 Now write your answer to the task in exercise 1.

Don't forget!

- Plan your answer carefully before you write (see checklist on page 193).
- Use an appropriate and consistent register.
- Include a brief introduction and use paragraph headings.

Use of English: CAE Part 3

Word formation

1 ⬤ If you suddenly received or won a million pounds, how would you spend it? Would it make you happy?

2 Use the word given in capitals at the end of some of the lines to form a word that fits in the gap **in the same line**. There is an example at the beginning (**0**).

MONEY BUYS HAPPINESS

A recent study carried out by (**0**) _researchers_ at the University of Warwick **RESEARCH**

claims to show (**1**) _____ that money can buy you happiness. There **CONCLUDE**

has always been an (**2**) _____ that the more money you have, the **ASSUME**

happier you are, but until now it has been (**3**) _____ difficult to **SURPRISE**

prove. The study, which is based on the (**4**) _____ of 9,000 families **RESPOND**

in the 1990s, looked at the effects of windfalls – such as a lottery win or

the receipt of an (**5**) _____ – on people's wellbeing. It found that **INHERIT**

receiving just £1,000 is sufficient to change the average person's

(**6**) _____ on life, though it would take at least £1 million to jump **LOOK**

from being very unhappy and (**7**) _____ to being very happy and **SATISFY**

contented. And of course, a millionaire would require (**8**) _____ **CONSIDER**

more to make the same leap. However, it seems the happiness gained from

money does not last and the (**9**) _____ wears off as you get used to **PLEASE**

it. Professor Andrew Oswald, who led the research, also points out that

money is not the only source of (**10**) _____ , and other factors, such **CONTENT**

as a strong marriage, play an important role.

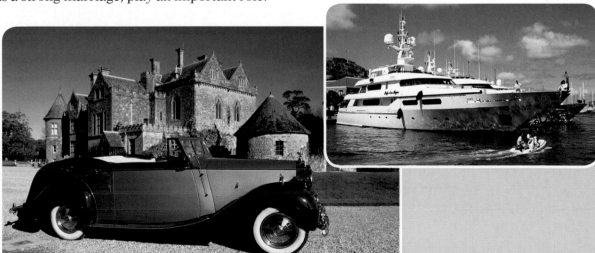

3 ⬤ Apart from money and a strong marriage, what 'other factors' might influence a person's happiness?

Multiple matching

1 ◯ How much importance do you attach to the type of clothes you wear? Do you buy a lot of clothes?

2 For questions **1–15** answer by choosing from the women, **A–D**. Some of the choices may be required more than once.

Which woman ...

mentions the usefulness of a skill she has?	1 ___
replaces clothes only when they are in very bad condition?	2 ___
has always been careful with money?	3 ___
mentions her work as a performer?	4 ___
had several clothes thrown away by mistake?	5 ___
used to spend money extravagantly on clothes?	6 ___
mentions the dangers of following fashion?	7 ___
criticizes people's motives for buying clothes?	8 ___
is concerned about the origin of the clothes she buys?	9 ___
mentions needing to wear particular clothes to be accepted socially?	10 ___
states that her way of doing things is different to the norm?	11 ___
does not have firm enough beliefs to take positive action over an issue?	12 ___
remarks that she no longer feels the urge to go into clothes shops?	13 ___
buys a lot of clothes?	14 ___
was influenced in a decision by local practices?	15 ___

WHAT DO YOU MEAN, YOU DON'T BUY CLOTHES?

Not everyone is a slave to the high street. Emily Davies meets four women who have rejected consumerism.

A Hilary

5 When I was a banker I would often go on huge shopping sprees all over London. But when I moved to Moscow five years ago I began to think differently about clothes, especially after I gave up my job and started 10 working for a charity. I came back to London a lot and, at first, I was still shopping and spending like a banker. One weekend I bought tons of clothes on the high street and took them all back to Russia. I was in 15 the middle of showing my boyfriend what I'd bought when I realized that I didn't actually need any of them. At that point I decided to stop shopping. The fact that I was living in a country where all of the clothes 20 are recycled and handed on to other people made me reconsider what I was doing. Now I wait until things are falling apart before I buy something new. I recently had a huge clear out and took heaps of clothes to charity 25 shops, but I still have enough to fill three wardrobes, including some items that have never been worn. I feel incredibly relieved to have got away from that feeling that what you buy will change your life. I simply don't 30 feel the pull of boutiques any more.

B Lucy

I'm a voracious clothes shopper – but almost exclusively in charity shops. If I'm tired of something, I never throw it away. My friends
35 and I have swap parties, when we throw bags of clothes into the middle of the floor and exchange things. I grew up this way; when I was little, frugality was a way of life, and my mother made all my clothes. I'd rather make
40 something out of stuff that has been thrown away; whether it's a cushion from a dress or a dress from some cushions, or a costume to wear when I'm on stage. A lot of my clothes and costumes come from the charity shop, Oxfam. I try not to buy anything which is, or
45 might have been, sourced from sweatshops, or from any company that I feel doesn't yet have an ethically sound code of practice.

C Karen

I buy most of my clothes second-hand – it's
50 a good way round the issue of excessive consumption and it saves money and resources. Knowing how to sew helps; it's invaluable in patching otherwise good things up, or sewing a fabric flower over a hole.
55 I buy only the odd new thing – socks, for instance, although I even try to buy those when they've been reduced in price. I'm aware that most people are not like me. It's partly due to time, which many people don't
60 have (or think they don't have), but people are often lazy and are embarrassed to try. People are being exploited because they are led to believe that they need new things all the time. There's a lot more now about 'must-
65 have' items. I've seen people driven to debt by their need for the latest Fendi bag, and I've been to parties where, if you don't have the right shoes, people won't talk to you. I got round that by wearing lots of vintage
70 clothes and seeming terribly creative, which confused them.

D Nicoletta

I hate shopping because I hate looking at
75 clothes. Even if there's something I need to buy, I detest it. I find it a waste of time and energy; there are so many other things that I could be doing. I can't even remember when I last bought something, or what it
80 was. It's not really about ethics, although I do think that there is too much importance placed on clothes and appearance. I don't feel strongly enough to object politically, it's simply that I don't consider it very
85 important. For lots of people I think that the clothes aren't even the point – it's more about the act of shopping. It's heavily linked to the fact that many people like being the centre of attention, and they like wearing
90 something that attracts attention. It makes them feel as if they have a strong identity or image. I've had to buy suits for work, which is tiresome, but at least it makes the decision for me about what to buy. Recently, a pile
95 of my clothes got chucked out because my flatmate thought they were rubbish. I was upset, but not because there was anything there that held any significance for me – I was just annoyed that it meant I'd have to go shopping all over again.

◯ Reacting to the text

How do you feel about wearing second-hand clothes or swapping clothes with others?

People are being exploited because they are led to believe that they need new things all the time.' Is this true in your country? If so, with which types of goods is it most noticeable? To what extent do you allow yourself to be 'exploited'?

Vocabulary 2: Quantifying nouns

1 Underline the following quantifying nouns in the text. Which noun is used after each one?

tons of   *heaps of*   *bags of*   *a pile of*

2 Complete each of the gaps with one of the words from the box.

> champagne   flames   salt   furniture
> youths   biscuits   homework   water

a Add just **a pinch of** _____ to the mixture.
b The tap had been dripping and there was **a pool of** _____ on the floor.
c The plane crashed in **a ball of** _____ .
d We've been given **masses of** _____ to do tonight.
e Her prize was **a crate of** _____ , donated by a local wine shop.
f Police are hunting **a gang of** _____ in connection with the crimes.
g No, Johnny, the sea bed is not **a piece of** _____ .
h It's not easy to speak with **a mouthful of** _____ .

3 For each of the following groups of words, cross out the one which is not normally used with the quantifying noun, for reasons of collocation or meaning.

Example:
0 a bunch of   flowers
               keys
               grapes
               ~~cheese~~

1	a set of	criteria children guidelines rules	**6**	a scrap of	paper evidence material furniture
2	a series of	events news experiments articles	**7**	a piece of	music work holiday advice
3	a pack of	cards lies words wolves	**8**	a lump of	milk sugar coal rock
4	a flock of	bees sheep birds geese	**9**	a grain of	truth wool salt rice
5	a handful of	occasions people progress coins	**10**	a ray of	hope light sunshine sadness

4 Write six sentences, each with a different quantifying noun from exercise 3. Leave gaps where the quantifying nouns should be and give the sentences to your partner to complete.

Example:
Business is bad – we never get more than a _____ of people in the shop at any one time.

Listening 2:
CAE Part 3

Multiple choice

1 ● 2.35 You will hear an anti-consumerist, Chris Dawson, being interviewed on a local radio station about Buy Nothing Day. For questions **1–6**, choose the answer (**A**, **B**, **C** or **D**) which fits best according to what you hear.

1 Chris explains that one of the aims of Buy Nothing Day is to
  A shock consumers into changing their ways.
  B encourage participation in alternative activities.
  C persuade shoppers to save more.
  D force shops to shut for the day.

2 What does Chris say about the effect of Buy Nothing Day?
  A For many people it has lasting consequences.
  B Certain products experience a fall in sales.
  C Some shops decide to offer less variety.
  D Some products are reduced in price.

3 What does Chris say about Christmas presents?
  A He buys them a long time in advance.
  B He argues with his family on the topic.
  C He never buys anything for his family.
  D He always feels obliged to buy them.

4 For this year's Buy Nothing Day, Chris
  A does not know yet what he will be doing.
  B wants to keep his plans a surprise.
  C will not be doing anything special.
  D will be playing some type of sport.

5 According to Chris, how did most shoppers feel about his stunt last year?
  A annoyed
  B amused
  C surprised
  D pleased

6 Chris says that the current success of Buy Nothing Day is mainly due to
  A good organization.
  B the official website.
  C television advertising.
  D people telling each other.

2 ◯ Would you ever consider taking part in a Buy Nothing Day in your country? In what other ways might people protest against consumerism?

Do you spend much money on presents for members of your family?
What type of presents do you usually buy?

Language focus: Noun phrases

1 Add each of the noun phrases from the recording to the appropriate column.

workers' rights	a threat to business
the January sales	the ethics of shopping
shopping malls	people's reactions
at the expense of the environment	

noun + noun
production methods

noun + 's/s' + noun
next week's Buy Nothing Day

noun + preposition + noun
a wealth of choice

2 In **1–10** below, decide which of the two underlined noun phrases is in the wrong form and correct it. There is an example at the beginning (**0**).

Example:
0 a   <u>The boss's leg</u> is still in plaster.
   b   He tripped over ~~the chair's leg~~. *the chair leg*

1 a   We drank quite a few <u>glasses of wine</u> at the party.
   b   We broke quite a few <u>glasses of wine</u> at the party.
2 a   Shall we have <u>chicken's soup</u> for lunch?
   b   This skirt is made of pure <u>lamb's wool</u>.
3 a   I caught my jumper on <u>the door handle</u>.
   b   They've kicked the ball onto <u>our house roof</u>.
4 a   I read it in <u>last Sunday's newspaper</u>.
   b   I always buy <u>a Sunday's newspaper</u>.
5 a   I get <u>four weeks' holiday</u> a year.
   b   I'm going on <u>a three days course</u> on marketing.
6 a   There's a lovely dress in <u>that window of shop</u>.
   b   I asked him what <u>his source of inspiration</u> had been.
7 a   The restaurant is perched high on <u>a mountain top</u>.
   b   Write your name at <u>the page top</u>.
8 a   Management has announced <u>a member of staff from the catering department's dismissal</u>.
   b   Management offered no explanation for <u>the employee's dismissal</u>.
9 a   The town hall is <u>a large brick construction</u> from the twenties.
   b   Police are looking for <u>an average height man</u> in his twenties.
10 a   Have you seen her <u>children's new clothes</u>? They won't thank her for buying those.
   b   We'll have some <u>children's new clothes</u> in stock after the January sales.

🔊 Check your ideas and read more about noun phrases in the Grammar reference on page 225.

3 🔊 Look back at each of the noun phrases in exercise 2 and discuss with your partner the rules governing the form of each one.

Example:
0   The 's genitive can be used to talk about parts of the body, so <u>The boss's leg</u> is correct. It isn't normally used for objects, so <u>the chair's leg</u> is not possible: you could say either <u>the chair leg</u> or <u>the leg of the chair</u>.

4 Match each of the sentence beginnings **1–8** with an appropriate ending, **a–h**. The items in bold are all common collocations.

Example:
1 d

1   Physical exhaustion gave way to an enormous **sense of**
2   After the lottery win money was no longer a **matter of**
3   A medical examination showed that his general **state of**
4   Market research surveys are still the principal **source of**
5   Regular reading of articles will increase your **chances of**
6   After the last place she had rented, this was the **height of**
7   The country was once again plunged into the **depths of**
8   He put his head round the door, but there was no **sign of**

a   **health** was good, and there was no sign of heart disease.
b   **luxury**, with its central heating and wall-to-wall carpet.
c   **information** about people's shopping habits.
d   **achievement** as she crossed the finishing line.
e   **concern** to him and he took pleasure in spending freely.
f   **life**, just the net curtain flapping in the open window.
g   **success** in the exam, and improve your general language level.
h   **recession** and many new businesses were forced to close.

5 You are going to write a similar exercise to the one in **4** above. Student A should turn to page 207, student B to page 208.

6 🔊 Discuss the following with your partner.

- The rich and famous receive a great deal of **media attention**. To what extent is this simply **the price of fame** and how much is it **an invasion of privacy**?

- We hear that money and power corrupt. Have there been any instances in your country recently of **an abuse of power** by someone in authority?

- How popular are **games of chance** with **money prizes** in your country? Give examples. Do you ever play?

Self help

Add the noun phrases from exercises 4, 5 and 6 to your vocabulary notebook.
Look back at the reading text on pages 184 and 185 and find more examples of noun phrases. Add these to your vocabulary notebook as well.

Writing 2:
CAE Part 2

Set books

1 Rank the following questions (**a–e**) from the one you would most like to answer about the set book you have read (1), to the one you would least like to answer (5).

   a A bookshop website you regularly order from invites customers to send in reviews of books for the benefit of other readers. Write a **review** for the website about the set book you have read, telling readers what you did and did not enjoy about the book and say whether you would recommend it.

   b Your teacher has asked you to write an essay, giving your opinions on the following statement:

   A good book both teaches you something and entertains you.

   Write your **essay**, explaining your views with reference to the set book you have read.

   c Your college magazine has asked readers to send in articles on the ingredients of a good book. Write an **article**, identifying two or three aspects of the set book you have read which helped to make it such a good, or a bad, read.

   d Your school intends to use the set book you have read in next year's advanced classes, where students are not preparing for an examination. The Head of Studies has asked you to write a **report** on the set book you have been reading. You should:
   - explain how the set book was used, both in lessons and for homework.
   - describe the reaction of your classmates to the book and the way it was used.
   - suggest improvements which could be made in the way the book is used next year.

   e Your teacher has asked you to write an **essay** comparing two of the characters in the set book you have read. You should describe the two characters and say which of them you prefer and why.

2 ⬭ Compare your list with your partner's, giving reasons for your choices.

3 Read the following example answer. Which of the above questions is it answering?

Paper Money

As Ken Follett tells us in the introduction to 'Paper Money', 'the book is supposed to show how crime, high finance and journalism are corruptly interconnected.' Certainly, we learn a great deal from the novel about corruption and the workings of business, through characters such as Laski, the crooked entrepreneur, and Derek Hamilton, the chairman of a company in difficulties. Of more interest, though, is the insight we gain into the life of a 1970s' London evening newspaper, the 'Evening Post'.

The 'Post' is the focal point of the action, providing us with information received from reporters, blackmailers, radio hams and politicians. The fact that the plot takes place in one single day makes for a fast-moving pace, ensuring the reader's enjoyment but also enabling us to follow the progress throughout the day of the newspaper. We read about some of the problems, attend an editorial meeting, learn some of the tricks of the trade and gradually see the first edition come together.

Similarly, the rich diversity of characters helps maintain our interest, but also exposes us to some of the personalities involved in the newspaper world, from the lowly messenger, George, who never stops complaining, right up to the editor, described as 'a poor boy made good'. In particular, the relationship between the disillusioned, middle-aged deputy news editor, Arthur Cole, and the young enthusiastic reporter, Kevin Hart, is both intriguing and extremely revealing.

Indeed, when Hart discovers he will not be able to print the truth about the corruption he has uncovered, Cole tells him, 'You've learned something today, haven't you?' So too, it has to be said, has the reader.

4 ⬭ How well has the writer answered the question? Comment on relevance, overall structure, use of sophisticated language, linking devices and quotations.

5 Choose one of the questions **a–e** in exercise 1 and write your answer in **220–260** words, with reference to the set book you have read.

Noun phrases

Complete the gaps using noun phrases formed from the words in brackets. There may be more than one answer and you may need to change some of the words from plural to singular. There is an example at the beginning (**0**).

0 It isn't from a _recipe book_ (book; recipes) – I got the idea for the dish from a _women's magazine_ (women; magazine).

1 We're all still in a _____ (shock; state) after _____ (his resignation; announcement).

2 I found the _____ (keys; car) at the _____ (back; drawer).

3 Every evening we had a _____ (cocoa; mug) made with fresh _____ (milk; cow) from the farm next to the _____ (site; caravans).

4 There was a _____ (delay; seven hours) on our flight, so we spent most of Friday in the _____ (airport; lounge; departures).

5 Police want to interview a 17-year-old _____ (youth; average build) in connection with _____ (robbery; yesterday).

6 He wears a thick _____ (chain; neck; gold) and a _____ (stud; nose; diamond). It's all a _____ (personal taste; matter), I suppose, but it's not my _____ (fashion; idea).

7 He was a real slavedriver; we did _____ (work; two months) for him and during that time we didn't have a _____ (rest; day).

8 She gave a _____ (talks; series) on a _____ (topics; number) relating to the _____ (environment; protection).

Vocabulary

Decide which answer (**A**, **B**, **C** or **D**) best fits each space.

1 There wasn't a _____ of truth in what he said.
  A ray   **B** lump   **C** grain   **D** pinch

2 Only a small _____ of volunteers turned up to help.
  A armful   **B** handful   **C** fistful   **D** earful

3 In order to cut _____, the company will no longer allow employees to claim for first-class travel on their expenses.
  A prices   **B** fees   **C** charges   **D** costs

4 There's a _____ of dirty washing in the kitchen and none of it's mine.
  A piece   **B** pool   **C** pack   **D** pile

5 He didn't have a _____ of evidence to support his claims.
  A sign   **B** scrap   **C** sense   **D** state

6 It's the _____ of stupidity to go walking in the mountains in this weather.
  A height   **B** depth   **C** source   **B** matter

7 We had to save _____ for our holiday in Australia.
  A long   **B** hard   **C** heavily   **D** strongly

8 The grant will be paid in three equal _____ over the course of the year.
  A occurrences   **B** episodes   **C** instalments   **D** inversions

9 Train travel works out considerably cheaper if you buy a monthly _____ ticket.
  A periodical   **B** overtime   **C** season   **D** prize

10 I bought the chocolates on _____: I saw them while I was queueing up to pay.
  A desire   **B** urge   **C** spontaneity   **D** impulse

Use of English:
CAE Part 4

Gapped sentences

For questions **1–5**, think of **one** word only which can be used appropriately in all three sentences. Here is an example (**0**).

0 He's going to buy a ___season___ ticket for United so he can go to all the home games without having to queue all night.

Add the vegetables to the frying pan and ___season___ well with pepper and salt.

It's the rainy _____ there between May and July, so book your holiday for later in the year.

1 The director of the play chose to keep the _____ simple so that the focus would be on the actors.

Taylor won the first _____, but the Belgian fought back to win the next two and claim her fourth championship in a row.

There's a _____ of instructions in the box that are written in German, but there's no English version.

2 There's no _____ in turning back now, as we've already walked over half way.

Ian is creative but he has no business _____ , which is why his restaurant went bankrupt.

Some young people become gang members in order to gain a _____ of identity.

3 Farmers are worried about the _____ winter that has been predicted for this year.

We need to think _____ about how we're going to compete with our rivals.

Tom finds it _____ to follow orders, so I don't think he's going to enjoy the army!

4 As a child I used to _____ apples and pears from the fruit trees in my neighbour's garden.

I suggest you go to a street market if you want to _____ up some really good bargains.

Be careful on the metro because that's where thieves go to _____ pockets.

5 It is said that everyone has their _____ but Senator Jacobson never accepted a bribe in his life.

Erica paid the _____ for her constant lateness when she was turned down for a promotion.

Most of the stock in that shop is being sold at half _____ today because it's closing down.

Writing

Introduction

In Paper 2 you have to complete two different writing tasks in 1 hour 30 minutes; the compulsory Part 1 task and another from a choice of five in Part 2. In Part 1 you are expected to write between 180 and 220 words, and in Part 2 between 220 and 260 words.

In Part 1 you will write either an article, a letter, a proposal or a report. You are given up to 150 words of input material, such as advertisements, extracts from letters, emails, postcards, diaries and articles. Read this material carefully, as you are required to use the information contained in it to complete the task.

In Part 2 you will write one of the following: an article, an essay, an information sheet, a contribution to a longer piece such as a guidebook or a brochure, a proposal, a report, a letter, a review, a character reference or a competition entry (for this task type, see Unit 1, pages 14 and 15). There are four questions to choose from in Part 2: the last of these, question 5, offers you the chance to write either an article, an essay, a report or a review on one of the two set reading texts. There are two options for this question, one for each set text.

Marking

The categories in the box are those used by examiners when marking Paper 2 answers. Match each category to the general advice in **a–i** below. The first one has been done for you.

Content	Target reader	Accuracy
~~Range~~	Organization and cohesion	

1 <u>Range</u>	**a** Use a variety of language appropriate to this level. **b** Avoid repetition of vocabulary wherever possible.
2 _____	**c** Ensure that your answer addresses all the points in the task. **d** In Part 1 you do not always need to use all the information you are given.
3 _____	**e** Write in clear paragraphs of a suitable length. **f** Points need to be appropriately ordered and connected.
4 _____	**g** Write your answer in a register which is appropriate to the task and the intended audience. **h** Adopt a suitable tone for your piece of writing to produce the desired effect.
5 _____	**i** Avoid making too many mistakes, particularly basic ones or ones which prevent understanding.

Planning and checking

The sentences below show the stages to follow when planning and checking your written work. Match each stage **1–9** to the piece of general advice in **a–i** above to which it corresponds.

Example: 1 c

1 Read the task at least twice, underlining key information and requirements.
2 Select appropriately from the information in the input material.
3 Decide whether you should use more formal or informal English.
4 Check whether the task requires you to achieve a specific aim such as persuading, reassuring, apologizing or justifying.
5 Make a list of ideas for your answer, then select the best ones and arrange them into logical groupings.
6 Note down words and expressions which might be suitable for linking your ideas.
7 Write down relevant words, collocations and structures which you might be able to include in your answer.
8 Think of synonyms for key words which are likely to occur more than once in your answer.
9 When you have written your answer, check spelling, punctuation and grammar.

Register

1 Below are two versions of the same letter, each one written in a different register. Use the information in the informal letter to complete the numbered gaps in the formal version. The words you need do not occur in the informal letter. Write **one word** in each gap. The exercise begins with an example (**0**).

INFORMAL LETTER

Dear Jilly
Thanks a lot for your letter – and congratulations on passing your exams! You did really well to get such a high grade.

You said you'd be interested in trying to get a job here with us in the family business. Believe me, we'd love to take you on. But because of the way the economy's been recently, I'm sorry to say we just can't offer you any work at the moment.

We'll certainly keep you in mind for when things get better – we'll be in touch as soon as they do. Until then, good luck with the job search!
All the best
Bob

FORMAL LETTER

Dear Ms Holden

I am writing with (0) _____reference_____ to your letter of April 18th. I would like to congratulate you on your recent (1) _____ in your examinations, and particularly on (2) _____ such a high grade.

In your letter you (3) _____ an interest in applying for a (4) _____ here at Graves, Snipe and Wesley. I assure you we would be delighted to offer you (5) _____ . However, (6) _____ to the current economic climate, we are unfortunately (7) _____ to make any new appointments at the present time.

We shall of course keep your letter on our files in anticipation of an (8) _____ in the situation. When this occurs, we shall (9) _____ you immediately.

In the (10) _____ , I would like to wish you luck in your attempts to find work.

Yours sincerely

Robert Snipe

2 Use the two letters to identify some of the differences between formal and informal language.

Example: The informal letter contains contractions such as 'you'd', 'I'm' and 'we'll' whereas the formal version does not.

Models and tasks

On the following pages you will find a model for each of the main task types, together with an additional task. You should answer the Part 1 task on page 195, and at least one of the Part 2 tasks. Read the relevant model, then follow stages **1–9** in the Planning and checking section on page 193. In order to help you demonstrate a good range of vocabulary you should select appropriately from the Useful Language section.

Part 1: Formal letter

> You are the social secretary at Lambert College. The local newspaper has commented negatively on relations between students at the college and local people. Read the extract from the article and your notes, and write a letter to the newspaper responding to the article **and** asking them to publish the school's version of the facts.

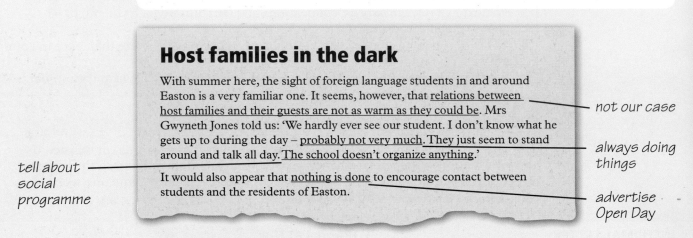

Host families in the dark

With summer here, the sight of foreign language students in and around Easton is a very familiar one. It seems, however, that relations between host families and their guests are not as warm as they could be. Mrs Gwyneth Jones told us: 'We hardly ever see our student. I don't know what he gets up to during the day – probably not very much. They just seem to stand around and talk all day. The school doesn't organize anything.'

It would also appear that nothing is done to encourage contact between students and the residents of Easton.

not our case

always doing things

tell about social programme

advertise Open Day

Write your **letter** in **180–220** words. You do not need to include postal addresses.

Model answer

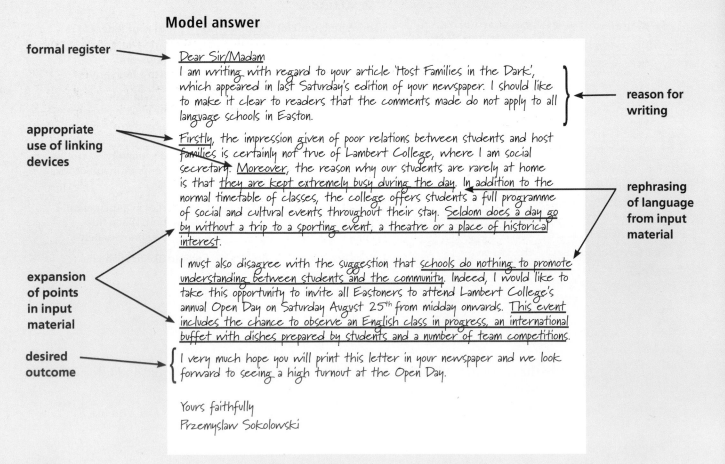

formal register

Dear Sir/Madam

I am writing with regard to your article 'Host Families in the Dark', which appeared in last Saturday's edition of your newspaper. I should like to make it clear to readers that the comments made do not apply to all language schools in Easton.

reason for writing

appropriate use of linking devices

Firstly, the impression given of poor relations between students and host families is certainly not true of Lambert College, where I am social secretary. Moreover, the reason why our students are rarely at home is that they are kept extremely busy during the day. In addition to the normal timetable of classes, the college offers students a full programme of social and cultural events throughout their stay. Seldom does a day go by without a trip to a sporting event, a theatre or a place of historical interest.

rephrasing of language from input material

expansion of points in input material

I must also disagree with the suggestion that schools do nothing to promote understanding between students and the community. Indeed, I would like to take this opportunity to invite all Eastoners to attend Lambert College's annual Open Day on Saturday August 25th from midday onwards. This event includes the chance to observe an English class in progress, an international buffet with dishes prepared by students and a number of team competitions.

desired outcome

I very much hope you will print this letter in your newspaper and we look forward to seeing a high turnout at the Open Day.

Yours faithfully
Przemyslaw Sokolowski

Task

You recently stayed at a hostel with a group of teenage students from the college where you work as Events Organizer. The hostel manager has written to you complaining about the students' behaviour. Read the extract from the manager's letter, on which you have made some notes, and write a letter to him explaining what happened and asking him to reconsider his decision.

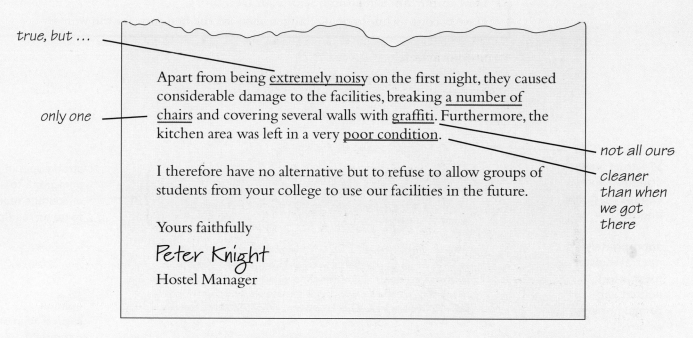

true, but …

only one

Apart from being <u>extremely noisy</u> on the first night, they caused considerable damage to the facilities, breaking <u>a number of chairs</u> and covering several walls with <u>graffiti</u>. Furthermore, the kitchen area was left in a very <u>poor condition</u>.

not all ours

cleaner than when we got there

I therefore have no alternative but to refuse to allow groups of students from your college to use our facilities in the future.

Yours faithfully

Peter Knight

Hostel Manager

Write your **letter** in **180–220** words. You do not need to include postal addresses.

Useful language for Part 1 formal letters

Reason for writing
I am writing with regard/reference to …
I am writing to express (my concern about/disappointment with/disapproval of/apologies for) …
I would like to draw your attention to/point out (certain inaccuracies) …

Introducing points
Firstly/To begin with/Moreover/Furthermore/In addition/Finally
(I feel) I must also (dis)agree with …
I should also like to point out that …
According to your (article)/Your (article) states that … However, …

Request for action
I would appreciate it/be grateful if you would …
It seems only fair that you should …
I look forward to receiving/seeing …
I trust/very much hope you will …

Part 2: Article

You see this announcement in an English language magazine.

Technological Revolution

We are planning to publish a series of articles on the effects of new technology on our lives today. We would like you, the readers, to write us an article, addressing the following questions:

- How important is technology in your own life?
- Have recent technological changes been for the better or for the worse?

Write your **article**.

Model answer

interesting title to attract reader's attention and engage his or her interest

appropriately neutral register for this task, neither very formal nor very informal

linking of points within the paragraph. Linkers more informal.

strong opening paragraph to encourage reader to go on reading

opinion expressed in each paragraph

linking between paragraphs

each paragraph devoted to different area of technology

leaving the reader something to think about

Technology – a curse in disguise

The technological revolution is full of paradox: it has enabled us to communicate more easily, yet it is killing conversation; it has supposedly freed up more time for leisure, yet it has made us slaves to our work.

Without a mobile phone, I would not be able to respond to the demands of my job. My clients would abandon me and my boss would sack me. So regrettably, and much to my family's annoyance, it is switched on 24 hours a day. I can spend whole weekends without saying a word to my husband or children, either because I am on the phone, or because they are too angry to want to speak to me.

My attitude to the computer is equally ambivalent. Thanks to my laptop I can reply to emails from almost anywhere as soon as I receive them. But the faster I work, the greater my clients' expectations become of me, and consequently the more pressures I create for myself.

Even in the home the computer seems to create more problems than it resolves. My husband and I are now in the habit of doing our supermarket shopping on the Internet. This means we have more time to watch a DVD or one of the 200 or so digital TV channels we have access to, but it also helps to cut us off from human contact and turn us into anti-social, overweight couch potatoes.

All of this leads me to the conclusion that mobile phones and computers should carry a government health warning: technology can seriously damage your health and your personality.

Task

You see this announcement in an English language magazine.

Sporting Life

We are planning to publish a series of articles on the importance of sport in people's lives. We would like you, the readers, to write us an article, addressing the following questions:

- How important is sport in your own life?
- Is too much emphasis placed on sport nowadays?

Write your **article** in **220–260** words.

Essay

Your class has recently been doing a project on people who are currently famous. Your teacher has asked you to write an essay, giving your opinion on the following statement.

Many young people wrongly believe that fame brings happiness.

Write your **essay**.

Model answer

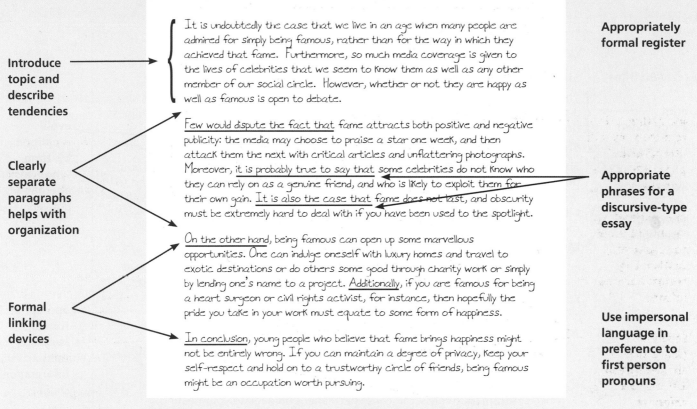

Introduce topic and describe tendencies

It is undoubtedly the case that we live in an age when many people are admired for simply being famous, rather than for the way in which they achieved that fame. Furthermore, so much media coverage is given to the lives of celebrities that we seem to know them as well as any other member of our social circle. However, whether or not they are happy as well as famous is open to debate.

Clearly separate paragraphs helps with organization

Few would dispute the fact that fame attracts both positive and negative publicity: the media may choose to praise a star one week, and then attack them the next with critical articles and unflattering photographs. Moreover, it is probably true to say that some celebrities do not know who they can rely on as a genuine friend, and who is likely to exploit them for their own gain. It is also the case that fame does not last, and obscurity must be extremely hard to deal with if you have been used to the spotlight.

On the other hand, being famous can open up some marvellous opportunities. One can indulge oneself with luxury homes and travel to exotic destinations or do others some good through charity work or simply by lending one's name to a project. Additionally, if you are famous for being a heart surgeon or civil rights activist, for instance, then hopefully the pride you take in your work must equate to some form of happiness.

Formal linking devices

In conclusion, young people who believe that fame brings happiness might not be entirely wrong. If you can maintain a degree of privacy, keep your self-respect and hold on to a trustworthy circle of friends, being famous might be an occupation worth pursuing.

Appropriately formal register

Appropriate phrases for a discursive-type essay

Use impersonal language in preference to first person pronouns

Task

You have recently had a class discussion on the role that money plays in people's lives. Your teacher has asked you to write an essay, giving your opinion on the following statement:

Making money has become too important to many people in our modern society.

Write your **essay** in **220–260** words.

Useful language for essays

Expressing an opinion
It is probably true to say that …
There can be no doubt that …
It is simply not the case that …
(see page 69 for further expressions)

Commonly held views
It is widely believed that …
No one would dispute the fact that …
Few people would contest/dispute (the fact) that …
It is generally agreed that …

Saying what other people think
There are those who argue that …
It has been suggested that …
It is often claimed that …
Opponents/Supporters/Proponents of (hunting) argue that …

Referring to sources
All the evidence suggests that …
A recent survey proved that …
Judging by the comments made by …
Interviews with (students) have revealed that …

Information sheet

> You have been asked by the manager at the music and DVD store where you work to produce an information sheet in English for foreign employees, explaining the company's policy on sickness and staff absence. You should:
> * explain how employees should go about informing the store when they are ill.
> * say what employees should do if they need to attend a medical appointment.
> * give general advice about preventing work-related health problems.
>
> Write your **information sheet**.

Model answer

relevant title →

brief introduction →

direct and informative paragraph headings →

avoid repetition by using synonyms or alternative phrases

appropriately formal language for this particular information sheet

appropriate use of bullet points →

polite ending →

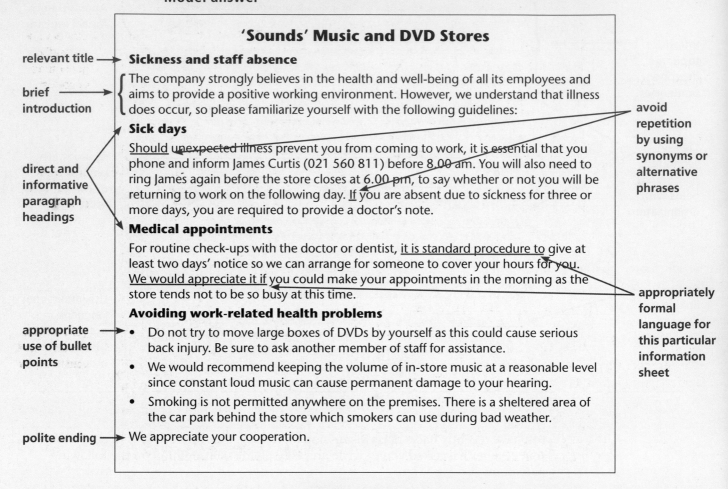

'Sounds' Music and DVD Stores

Sickness and staff absence

The company strongly believes in the health and well-being of all its employees and aims to provide a positive working environment. However, we understand that illness does occur, so please familiarize yourself with the following guidelines:

Sick days

Should unexpected illness prevent you from coming to work, it is essential that you phone and inform James Curtis (021 560 811) before 8.00 am. You will also need to ring James again before the store closes at 6.00 pm, to say whether or not you will be returning to work on the following day. If you are absent due to sickness for three or more days, you are required to provide a doctor's note.

Medical appointments

For routine check-ups with the doctor or dentist, it is standard procedure to give at least two days' notice so we can arrange for someone to cover your hours for you. We would appreciate it if you could make your appointments in the morning as the store tends not to be so busy at this time.

Avoiding work-related health problems

* Do not try to move large boxes of DVDs by yourself as this could cause serious back injury. Be sure to ask another member of staff for assistance.

* We would recommend keeping the volume of in-store music at a reasonable level since constant loud music can cause permanent damage to your hearing.

* Smoking is not permitted anywhere on the premises. There is a sheltered area of the car park behind the store which smokers can use during bad weather.

We appreciate your cooperation.

Task

The manager at the hotel where you work has asked you to write an information sheet in English for foreign kitchen staff about health and safety procedures. You should:

* suggest ways to prevent work-related accidents.

* provide information about what to do if an accident occurs.

* describe what to do in the event of a fire.

Write your **information sheet** in **220–260** words.

Useful language for information sheets

Saying what must be done
It is (absolutely) vital/essential/crucial that you + infinitive
You are required to …
It is standard policy/procedure to …
Your first step should be to..
(Do not) try to …

Advising
We would recommend/advise you (not) to + infinitive
We (would) recommend/

suggest/advise + gerund
It is well worthwhile + gerund *or* infinitive
Be sure to …
It is (not) advisable to …

Expressing conditions
In the (unlikely) event of an accident/fire/illness/injury …
Should an accident occur/fire break out, etc …
If an accident were to occur …
(See also pages 33 and 37 in Unit 3.)

Contributions: brochure and guidebook entries

An international guidebook is being produced for students wishing to study a foreign language in the country or countries where it is spoken. You have been asked to write the entry on your first language, giving advice to students on choosing a school in your country. You should include information on the types of schools where the language can be studied, and a general idea of prices and types of course.

Write your **contribution**.

Model answer

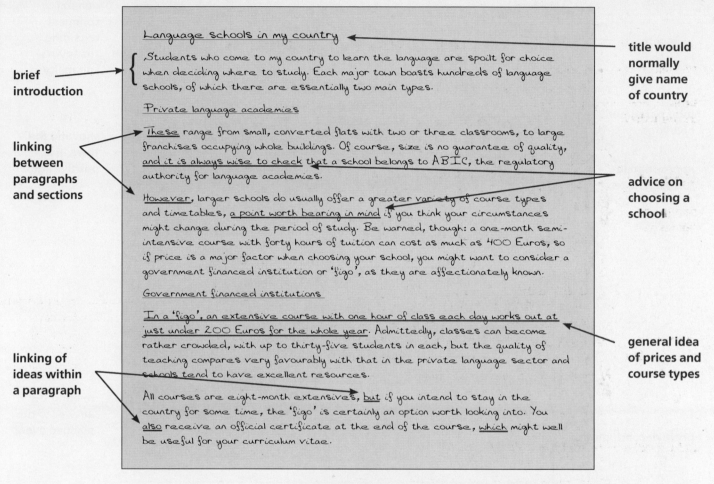

brief introduction

linking between paragraphs and sections

linking of ideas within a paragraph

title would normally give name of country

advice on choosing a school

general idea of prices and course types

Language schools in my country

Students who come to my country to learn the language are spoilt for choice when deciding where to study. Each major town boasts hundreds of language schools, of which there are essentially two main types.

Private language academies

These range from small, converted flats with two or three classrooms, to large franchises occupying whole buildings. Of course, size is no guarantee of quality, and it is always wise to check that a school belongs to ABIC, the regulatory authority for language academies.

However, larger schools do usually offer a greater variety of course types and timetables, a point worth bearing in mind if you think your circumstances might change during the period of study. Be warned, though: a one-month semi-intensive course with forty hours of tuition can cost as much as 400 Euros, so if price is a major factor when choosing your school, you might want to consider a government financed institution or 'figo', as they are affectionately known.

Government financed institutions

In a 'figo', an extensive course with one hour of class each day works out at just under 200 Euros for the whole year. Admittedly, classes can become rather crowded, with up to thirty-five students in each, but the quality of teaching compares very favourably with that in the private language sector and schools tend to have excellent resources.

All courses are eight-month extensives, but if you intend to stay in the country for some time, the 'figo' is certainly an option worth looking into. You also receive an official certificate at the end of the course, which might well be useful for your curriculum vitae.

Task

A guidebook aimed at readers aged between 18 and 25 is being produced for your town. You have been asked to write an entry on **one of the following categories**:

- museums
- restaurants
- parks

Your entry should include specific information on at least two examples of museums, restaurants or parks, giving advice to visitors on what to see, eat or do in each.

Write your **contribution to the guidebook** in **220–260** words.

Useful language for brochures and guidebook entries

Commenting on positive aspects
(The school/hotel/sports centre) boasts (a large indoor swimming pool/a wide range of facilities/five tennis courts).
No trip to (Paris) would be complete without (a visit to the Louvre).
(The restaurant) is noted for (its excellent cuisine).

Commenting on negative aspects
Admittedly, (this is a rather expensive option,) but …

(The quality of service) leaves a great deal to be desired.
Be warned, though: (delays are not uncommon).

Giving advice
It is always wise to check …
This is a point worth bearing in mind if …
If price/location/class size is a major factor when choosing (your school), you might want to consider …
… is certainly an option worth looking into.

Proposal

Your town has been short-listed to host a major international festival of folk music and dance next year. You have been asked to write a proposal for the festival organizers, stating why your town should be chosen from the list. You should include relevant information about accommodation, transport, concert venues and other leisure and entertainment possibilities.

Write your **proposal**.

Model answer

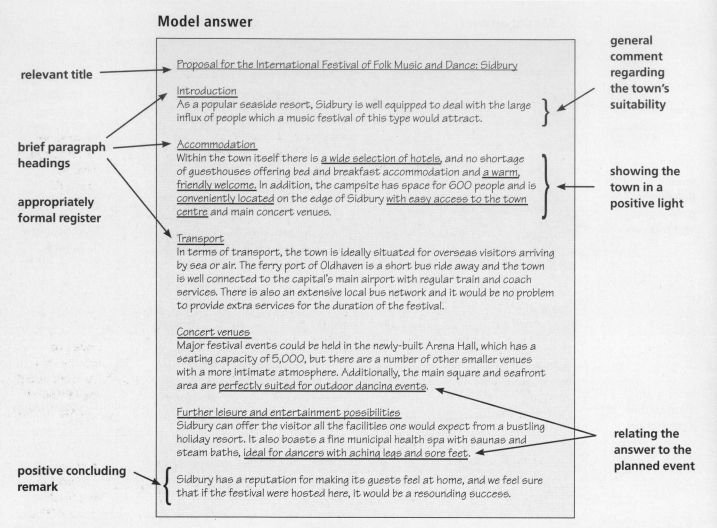

relevant title

brief paragraph headings

appropriately formal register

positive concluding remark

general comment regarding the town's suitability

showing the town in a positive light

relating the answer to the planned event

Proposal for the International Festival of Folk Music and Dance: Sidbury

Introduction
As a popular seaside resort, Sidbury is well equipped to deal with the large influx of people which a music festival of this type would attract.

Accommodation
Within the town itself there is a wide selection of hotels, and no shortage of guesthouses offering bed and breakfast accommodation and a warm, friendly welcome. In addition, the campsite has space for 600 people and is conveniently located on the edge of Sidbury with easy access to the town centre and main concert venues.

Transport
In terms of transport, the town is ideally situated for overseas visitors arriving by sea or air. The ferry port of Oldhaven is a short bus ride away and the town is well connected to the capital's main airport with regular train and coach services. There is also an extensive local bus network and it would be no problem to provide extra services for the duration of the festival.

Concert venues
Major festival events could be held in the newly-built Arena Hall, which has a seating capacity of 5,000, but there are a number of other smaller venues with a more intimate atmosphere. Additionally, the main square and seafront area are perfectly suited for outdoor dancing events.

Further leisure and entertainment possibilities
Sidbury can offer the visitor all the facilities one would expect from a bustling holiday resort. It also boasts a fine municipal health spa with saunas and steam baths, ideal for dancers with aching legs and sore feet.

Sidbury has a reputation for making its guests feel at home, and we feel sure that if the festival were hosted here, it would be a resounding success.

Task

Your town has been short-listed to host a two-day regional conference for students preparing for the CAE examination. You have been asked to write a proposal for the conference organizers, stating why your school should be chosen from the list. Your proposal should include relevant information about the facilities within your school, accommodation, transport and other leisure and entertainment possibilities.

Write your **proposal** in **220–260** words.

Useful language for proposals

Suitability
The (town/centre/stadium) is well equipped to deal with/perfectly suited for (such events).
It is conveniently located/ideally situated/well connected to (the capital).
There is little doubt that it would be a resounding success/of great benefit to the (town/company).

Amenities
There is no shortage/a wide selection of (hotels/cinemas) to choose from.

The (town/conference centre/school) boasts an impressive range of (amenities/facilities). Few (cities/schools) can offer such a large choice of …

Travel and transport
It is within easy reach/walking distance/driving distance of the (centre/hotel).
It is just a short walk/drive/bus ride/train ride from the (coast/station).
The (town) has easy access to (the motorway network).

Report

An international research group is carrying out an investigation into the housing situation for young people around the world. You have been asked by the group to write a report about your country, including the following points:

- the different housing options available in your country for young people in their early twenties
- the problems faced by young people with each option
- possible future changes in the housing situation for young people in your country

Write your **report**.

Model answer

relevant title and paragraph headings

opening paragraph outlining the purpose of the report

appropriately formal register

linking between paragraphs

rewording of language used in the task instructions

range of vocabulary items to avoid repetition of 'young people'

conclusion addressing the final point of the task

The housing situation for young people in my country

Introduction
The aim of this report is to examine the various housing options open to people in their early twenties in my country and the difficulties encountered with each one. It will also consider likely future developments in the housing situation for young people here.

Buying a property
Property speculation and soaring inflation have put house prices beyond the reach of the majority of first-time buyers. The few who do manage to raise the money for the deposit on a small flat, are likely to experience problems obtaining a mortgage. Banks are unwilling to lend money to anyone without a permanent contract, something which most young workers can only dream of.

Renting
An obvious alternative is to rent a property. However, rents, like house prices, have risen dramatically, forcing low-earners to share. For many twenty-somethings this can prove an enjoyable experience, but some soon discover that they are not suited to living with others. Local authorities provide some low-cost rented accommodation specifically for young single people, but this tends to be in very short supply.

Living with parents
It is hardly surprising, then, that a significant proportion of school and college leavers opt to continue living in the parental home until they have saved enough money to buy a place of their own. This may take some time, however, and friction between parents and children can result.

Future developments
As long as house prices continue to increase, the outlook for young people here will remain bleak. Only a substantial fall in property values will improve the situation and this seems unlikely in the near future.

Task

An international research group is carrying out an investigation into employment prospects for young people around the world. You have been asked by the group to write a report about your local area, including the following points:

- the types of employment available for young people in your area
- the difficulties faced by young people searching for work
- possible future developments in the employment situation for young people in your area

Write your **report** in **220–260** words.

Useful language for reports

Introducing the report
The aim/purpose of this report is to examine/ evaluate/describe/ outline …
It will also include/consider/ suggest/recommend …
The report is based on a survey conducted among (college students).

Predicting the future
The outlook for young people/ jobs/the country is (far from) bright/optimistic/ depressing.

The future looks bleak/remains uncertain/is promising.
This seems unlikely in the near/foreseeable future. (See also vocabulary of *Possibility* on page 209 of the Wordlist.)

Making recommendations
I would (strongly) recommend that (the school/company) should …
In the light of the results of the survey, I would (strongly) advise against …
I feel it would be to our advantage if …

Informal letter

You recently took part in an activity which you enjoyed very much. A friend of yours has written to you expressing an interest in the activity and asking how it went. Write a **letter** telling your friend about the positive and negative aspects of your experience, encouraging him/her to take part in a similar event.

Model answer

reference to a previous letter

relevant opening paragraph, providing lead-in to rest of letter

encouraging friend to take part throughout the letter

use of phrasal verbs

negative aspects offset by positive aspects

appropriate ending

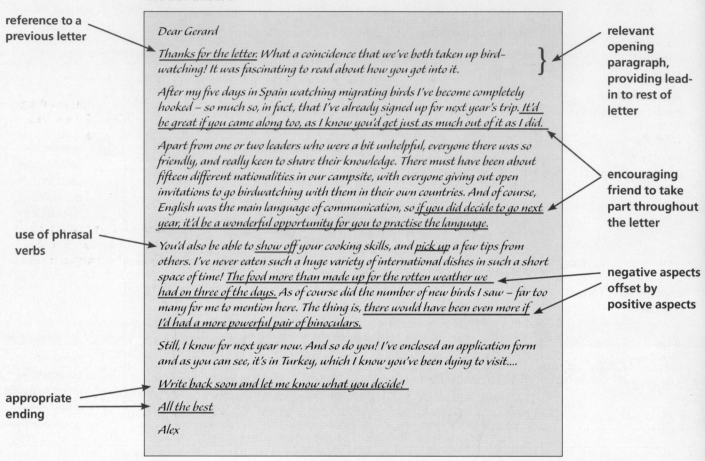

Dear Gerard

Thanks for the letter. What a coincidence that we've both taken up bird-watching! It was fascinating to read about how you got into it.

After my five days in Spain watching migrating birds I've become completely hooked – so much so, in fact, that I've already signed up for next year's trip. It'd be great if you came along too, as I know you'd get just as much out of it as I did.

Apart from one or two leaders who were a bit unhelpful, everyone there was so friendly, and really keen to share their knowledge. There must have been about fifteen different nationalities in our campsite, with everyone giving out open invitations to go birdwatching with them in their own countries. And of course, English was the main language of communication, so if you did decide to go next year, it'd be a wonderful opportunity for you to practise the language.

You'd also be able to show off your cooking skills, and pick up a few tips from others. I've never eaten such a huge variety of international dishes in such a short space of time! The food more than made up for the rotten weather we had on three of the days. As of course did the number of new birds I saw – far too many for me to mention here. The thing is, there would have been even more if I'd had a more powerful pair of binoculars.

Still, I know for next year now. And so do you! I've enclosed an application form and as you can see, it's in Turkey, which I know you've been dying to visit....

Write back soon and let me know what you decide!

All the best

Alex

Task

Either: **a** write your own answer to the task above;

or **b** answer the following question.

You recently went on holiday to a place which you enjoyed very much. A friend of yours has written to you expressing an interest in the place and asking what it was like there. Write a **letter** in **220–260** words, telling your friend about the positive and negative aspects of the place, encouraging him/her to go there next year.

Useful language for informal letters

Beginning the letter
Great/Lovely to hear from you (after so long).
Thanks (a lot) for the letter.
Sorry to hear about your …
Sorry I haven't written/been in touch for so long.

Persuading
You'd get so much out of it.
It'd be a wonderful/ marvellous opportunity for you to …
Just think of (all the people you'd meet).
Just imagine how it would (improve your cv), not to mention (the money you could earn).

Advising
Whatever you do, make sure you …
It's (not) worth/There's no/ little point + gerund
I'd/I wouldn't … if I were you.
You'd be much better off + gerund

Ending the letter
Write back soon and let me know how it goes.
Looking forward to hearing from you.
Can't wait to see you again.
(Give my) love/regards to …

Signing off
Friends: All the best/Best wishes/Bye for now
Close friends or relatives: Lots of Love/All my love/Love

Review

The magazine published by your school's English club is asking students to exchange information about non-fiction books they have enjoyed reading in English. Write a review of a non-fiction book you have read, saying what you learnt from it and encouraging others to read it.

Write your **review**.

Model answer

questions to engage the reader's interest

what the reader learnt from the book

final recommendation

brief summary of the book's content

encouraging others to read the book

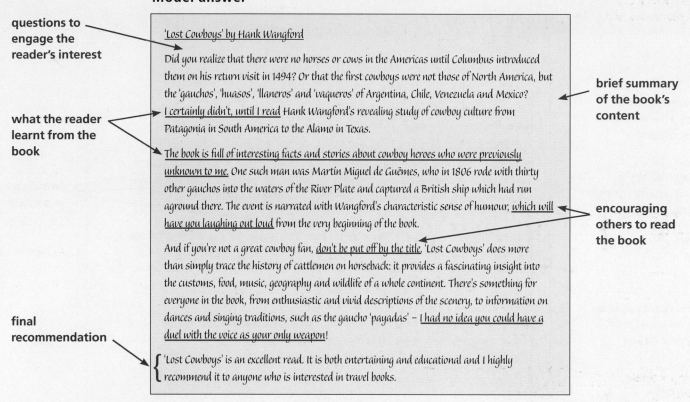

'Lost Cowboys' by Hank Wangford

Did you realize that there were no horses or cows in the Americas until Columbus introduced them on his return visit in 1494? Or that the first cowboys were not those of North America, but the 'gauchos', 'huasos', 'llaneros' and 'vaqueros' of Argentina, Chile, Venezuela and Mexico? I certainly didn't, until I read Hank Wangford's revealing study of cowboy culture from Patagonia in South America to the Alamo in Texas.

The book is full of interesting facts and stories about cowboy heroes who were previously unknown to me. One such man was Martín Miguel de Guëmes, who in 1806 rode with thirty other gauchos into the waters of the River Plate and captured a British ship which had run aground there. The event is narrated with Wangford's characteristic sense of humour, which will have you laughing out loud from the very beginning of the book.

And if you're not a great cowboy fan, don't be put off by the title. 'Lost Cowboys' does more than simply trace the history of cattlemen on horseback: it provides a fascinating insight into the customs, food, music, geography and wildlife of a whole continent. There's something for everyone in the book, from enthusiastic and vivid descriptions of the scenery, to information on dances and singing traditions, such as the gaucho 'payadas' – I had no idea you could have a duel with the voice as your only weapon!

'Lost Cowboys' is an excellent read. It is both entertaining and educational and I highly recommend it to anyone who is interested in travel books.

Task

Either: **a** write your own answer to the task above;

or **b** answer the following question.

The magazine published by your school's English club is asking students to give opinions on the coursebooks they have been using. Write a review of Ready for CAE, giving your views on the following points:
- its content
- its design
- how well it prepares students for the exam
- how much it has helped you improve your English

Write your **review** in **220–260** words.

Useful language for reviews

Commenting critically
… provides a fascinating/ valuable/revealing insight into …
I found the plot rather predictable/disappointing.
The acting is very impressive/ convincing.
She gives a compelling/ memorable performance as …
One particular strength/ weakness of the film/book/CD is …
The design/characterization/ production is second to none/ is not its best feature.

Encouraging others (not) to read/watch/listen
Don't be put off by the title/ critics/cover.
It will have you roaring with laughter/rushing out to buy the sequel.
It is a definite must-see.
I would definitely give it a miss.
I would highly recommend it to anyone interested in …
I would strongly advise you (not) to go out and buy/see it.

(For a list of adjectives used in reviews and the vocabulary of *Comparisons*, see page 212.)

Character reference

An English-speaking friend of yours has applied for a job as a guide in a history museum and you have been asked to provide a character reference for him/her.

The reference should indicate how long you have known the person. It must also include a description of the person's character and the reasons why he or she would be suitable for the job.

Write your **reference**.

Model answer

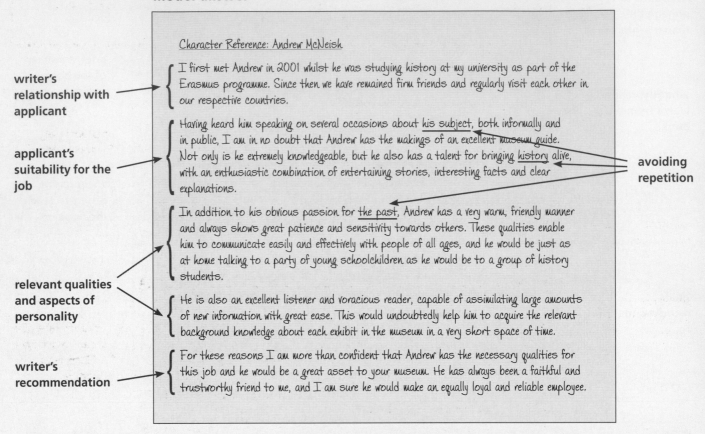

writer's relationship with applicant

applicant's suitability for the job

avoiding repetition

relevant qualities and aspects of personality

writer's recommendation

Character Reference: Andrew McNeish

I first met Andrew in 2001 whilst he was studying history at my university as part of the Erasmus programme. Since then we have remained firm friends and regularly visit each other in our respective countries.

Having heard him speaking on several occasions about his subject, both informally and in public, I am in no doubt that Andrew has the makings of an excellent museum guide. Not only is he extremely knowledgeable, but he also has a talent for bringing history alive, with an enthusiastic combination of entertaining stories, interesting facts and clear explanations.

In addition to his obvious passion for the past, Andrew has a very warm, friendly manner and always shows great patience and sensitivity towards others. These qualities enable him to communicate easily and effectively with people of all ages, and he would be just as at home talking to a party of young schoolchildren as he would be to a group of history students.

He is also an excellent listener and voracious reader, capable of assimilating large amounts of new information with great ease. This would undoubtedly help him to acquire the relevant background knowledge about each exhibit in the museum in a very short space of time.

For these reasons I am more than confident that Andrew has the necessary qualities for this job and he would be a great asset to your museum. He has always been a faithful and trustworthy friend to me, and I am sure he would make an equally loyal and reliable employee.

Task

A friend of yours has applied to work on an international summer camp for children aged six to sixteen, and you have been asked to provide a character reference for him/her. The job involves planning and running a variety of activities, including games, sports and other outdoor pursuits.

The reference should indicate how long you have known the person. It must also include a description of the person's character and the reasons why he or she would be suitable for the job.

Write your **reference** in **220–260** words.

Useful language for character references

Relationship
… and since then we have remained firm friends.
During the (five) years he has worked for me, (Peter) …
As a former colleague of (Susan's), I …

Overall suitability
She has the makings of an excellent (teacher).
He would be a great asset to your (company).
She would make a valuable contribution to your (school).

Abilities
Not only is she a highly talented (actress) but she is also an exceptionally gifted (musician).

He is a skilled craftsman/a proficient typist/an expert cook/a promising athlete/an accomplished singer.
He has a talent for bringing history alive/a flair for languages/a gift for music.

Qualities
(Paul) has a warm friendly manner/a determined nature/all the necessary personal qualities.
(Celia) shows great patience/sensitivity towards others/enthusiasm/potential.
These qualities enable (her) to …

(See also pages 56 and 57 in Unit 4.)

Letter of application

You have seen this advertisement in an international magazine.

WRITERS REQUIRED

We are looking for people to write for this magazine about environmental issues in their local area that would be of interest to readers in other countries. We would like to hear from anyone who has:
- an interest in environmental concerns
- an awareness of environmental issues affecting their local area
- some experience of writing.

Send us a letter of application, explaining why you think you are suitable and describing two environmental issues currently affecting your local area.

Write your **letter of application**.

Model answer

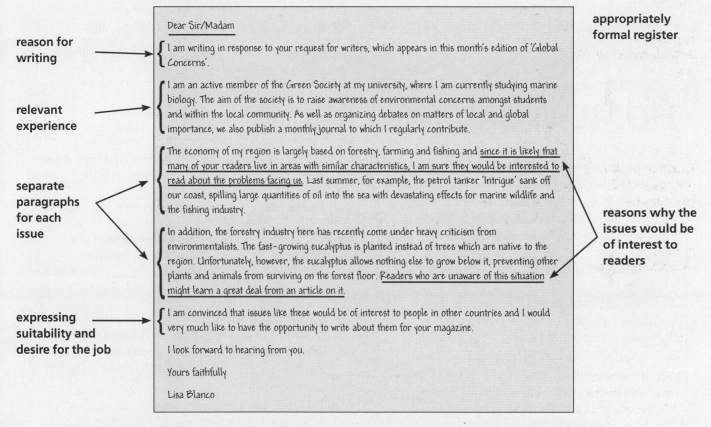

reason for writing →

relevant experience →

separate paragraphs for each issue →

expressing suitability and desire for the job →

appropriately formal register

reasons why the issues would be of interest to readers

Dear Sir/Madam

I am writing in response to your request for writers, which appears in this month's edition of 'Global Concerns'.

I am an active member of the Green Society at my university, where I am currently studying marine biology. The aim of the society is to raise awareness of environmental concerns amongst students and within the local community. As well as organizing debates on matters of local and global importance, we also publish a monthly journal to which I regularly contribute.

The economy of my region is largely based on forestry, farming and fishing and since it is likely that many of your readers live in areas with similar characteristics, I am sure they would be interested to read about the problems facing us. Last summer, for example, the petrol tanker 'Intrigue' sank off our coast, spilling large quantities of oil into the sea with devastating effects for marine wildlife and the fishing industry.

In addition, the forestry industry here has recently come under heavy criticism from environmentalists. The fast-growing eucalyptus is planted instead of trees which are native to the region. Unfortunately, however, the eucalyptus allows nothing else to grow below it, preventing other plants and animals from surviving on the forest floor. Readers who are unaware of this situation might learn a great deal from an article on it.

I am convinced that issues like these would be of interest to people in other countries and I would very much like to have the opportunity to write about them for your magazine.

I look forward to hearing from you.

Yours faithfully

Lisa Blanco

Task

Either: **a** write your own answer to the task above;
or   **b** answer the following question.

WRITERS REQUIRED

We are looking for people to write for this magazine about people in their local area whose work, achievements or lifestyle would be of interest to an international readership.

Send us a letter of application, explaining why you think you are suitable and giving examples of two local people, living or dead, that you would write about.

Write your **letter of application** in **220–260** words.

(For useful language, see page 49 in Unit 4.)

Additional material

Unit 3

Vocabulary: Smell (page 39)

4 ⬭ Use an appropriate adjective + noun collocation from the Vocabulary section on page 39 to describe these smells.

Example:

pipe tobacco: a delightful aroma or a stale smell.

> your classroom   a rose garden   disinfectant   old books
> freshly baked bread   your favourite cheese   decaying rubbish

Unit 4

Language focus 1: Punctuation (page 48)

3 *Suggested answer*

HOME-WORKING

If you had the choice, would you prefer to work from home or in an office? British workers seem to be in no doubt; one in four of them has given up commuting to the office in favour of a more domestic working environment – and the figure is growing.

"The number of home-workers is likely to increase by more than 50% over the next five years," claimed a spokesperson for Datamonitor, the London-based market research company. As a result of this trend, consumers will spend a great deal less on certain goods and services: transport, petrol, eating out and drinks. Moreover, because home-workers usually take fewer showers, the sale of personal care products such as deodorants and soap will also be affected.

The study, which shows that home-workers tend to be the more highly qualified professionals in a company, says that firms are in danger of losing their best employees if they do not allow home-working. Unfortunately, however, there are some who abuse the trust which has been placed in them. Datamonitor discovered that many like to watch television, listen to the radio and drink alcohol while they work.

Unit 6

Writing: CAE Part 2 Reviews (page 76)

Complete each of the spaces with one of the nouns from the box.

> lines   terms   similarities
> resemblance   difference   genre

1 Her latest novel, a tale of unrequited love, **bears little _____** to her earlier, more philosophical work.
2 **There is little to choose between** the two CDs **in _____ of** quality of production.
3 The plot of the novel **develops along very different _____ from** that of the film.
4 **There are** several **obvious _____ between** the two films, the first of course being that they are both set in Paris.
5 **There's a world of _____ between** the two records, despite their shared flamenco influences.
6 **What sets the film apart from others** of the same _____ is its ability to make us laugh.

Unit 8

Language focus 1: Determiners and pronouns

Practice (page 101)

3 Choose one of the following as the topic of your conversation:

Technology
Schooldays
Weekends
The world of work
The natural world
Health and fitness
The media
Relationships
Entertainment

Ready for Listening: Part 2 (page 125)

Match each answer on the answer sheet to one or more of the pieces of advice in the box.

Example 1 c

1 _____
2 *impressively titled Fine Arts Sculpture course*
3 *mesurements*
4 *person who gives the news on the television*
5 *metall*
6 *standing*
7 *oil paint*
8 _____

Advice for Part 2 Sentence completion tasks

a Check that your answer fits grammatically with the rest of the sentence.
b Check that your answer is spelt correctly.
c Do not leave any blank spaces on the answer sheet. If you are not sure of the answer, make a guess.
d Do not repeat information in your answer which is already contained in the question.
e Do not write long answers. You do not normally need to write more than three words.
f When you transfer your answers to the answer sheet, check that you have followed the numbering correctly.
g Try to write the words you actually hear on the recording.
h Beware of distractors.

Ready for Speaking: Part 2 Long turn Task Two (page 166)

The following pictures show people reading.

Student A:
Compare two of these pictures, and say what and why these people might be reading, and how they might be feeling.

- What might these people be reading and why?
- How might they be feeling?

Unit 1
Language Focus 2: Spelling (page 14)

1 **Student A**
1 Dictate the following ten items to your partner. When you have finished, your partner will check his/her spelling.

1 highly influential
2 desperately disappointed
3 utterly exhausted
4 comparatively unknown
5 fiercely independent
6 wholly unacceptable
7 academically successful
8 unnecessarily aggressive
9 extremely embarrassed
10 quite quiet

2 Now write down the ten items of vocabulary which your partner dictates to you. When you have finished writing, check your spelling on page 208.

Unit 14
Language focus: Noun phrases (page 188)

6 **Student A**
Choose six of the following phrases and write a similar exercise to that on page 188. Then give the exercise to your partner to complete.

sense of relief   chances of survival
matter of personal taste   height of summer
state of emergency   depths of despair
source of income   sign of respect

Student B:
When your partner has finished talking, answer the following question about all three pictures.

Which person is most interested in finding out what is written?

Unit 12

Writing: CAE Part 2 Articles (page 161)

4 Either:

Write an answer to one of the tasks in the announcements below
or:
Write your own answer to the task in exercise 1 on page 161.

You should write **220–260** words.

Include in your answer two or three attitude adverbials from the list on page 215.

> **Useful language**
> - For question 1 below, see the vocabulary of *Environment* on page 215.
> - For question 2 below, see the vocabulary of *Changes* on page 210.
> - For question 3 below, see the vocabulary of *Effect* on page 213.
> - For the task in exercise 1 on page 161, see the vocabulary of *Problems* on page 209.

'People have very little respect for the environment.'

Do you agree with this? What do you think?

Write us an article telling us what people in your country do and what they don't do to protect the environment.

'Women are still a long way from achieving equality with men.'

How true is this in your country?

Write us an article telling us about the extent to which the position of women has changed in recent years in your country, and how you would like to see it change in the future.

Taking Action

We would like you to write us an article, telling readers about action you have taken to help other people in some way. However great or small the action was, tell us what motivated you to take it and what effect you think it had.

Unit 1

Language Focus 2: Spelling (page 14)

1 Student B

1 Write down the ten items of vocabulary which your partner dictates to you. When you have finished writing, check your spelling on page 207.

2 Now dictate the following ten items to your partner. When you have finished, your partner will check his/her spelling.

1 mysterious disappearance
2 separate accommodation
3 eight-month guarantee
4 business arrangement
5 memorable occasion
6 unconscious decision
7 overall responsibility
8 frequent occurrence
9 guilty conscience
10 government committee

Unit 11

Vocabulary: *Read* and *write* (page 146)

3 Discuss the following with your partner. Give reasons in each case.

a Do you have **neat handwriting**, or do others find it hard to read?
b Are you **a fast** or **slow reader**?
c Are you **an avid reader** of any particular author, genre or magazine?
d Do you **read widely**?
e What was the last novel you read? Was it **a good read**?

Unit 14

Language focus: Noun phrases (page 188)

6 Student B
Choose six of the following phrases and write a similar exercise to that on page 188. Then give the exercise to your partner to complete.

sense of smell	chances of promotion
matter of life and death	height of fashion
state of shock	depths of winter
source of energy	sign of age

Wordlist

Unit 1

A Problems

combat		a common	
come up against		a major	
confront		a minor	
face		a potential	
face up to	a problem	a recurrent	problem
resolve		a serious	
rise above		a tough	
run into		a trivial	
sort out		an unexpected	
tackle		an urgent	

B Challenges and achievements

accept		high/strong		admit		a burning	
face		low/poor		be doomed to		my greatest	
pose	a challenge	personal	motivation	be resigned to		a lifelong	
present		political		end in	failure	my main	ambition
rise to		staff		meet with		a personal	
take up		student		result in		a secret	

a daunting		achieve		complete		a great	
an exciting		be assured of		continued		a major	
a formidable		deserve		dismal	failure	an outstanding	
a fresh		enjoy	success	inevitable		a remarkable	achievement
a major	challenge	guarantee		total		a scientific	
a new		meet with				a sporting	
a serious						a technological	

		be a/an	great	achieve		
improve			huge	fulfil		
increase			overnight	have	an ambition	
lack	motivation		resounding	success	pursue	
lose			roaring	realize		
strengthen						

C Possibility

There's every /little/no	possibility chance likelihood	of something (happening). that something will happen.

There's a (very)	real strong distinct good realistic faint slight remote	chance possibility	of something (happening). that something will happen.

They have/stand	every a good a fair a slim an outside little no	chance of doing something

She is bound/certain/sure to do it.
She is highly likely to do it.
She may/might/could well do it.
She could easily/conceivably do it.
She is hardly likely to do it.
She's highly unlikely to do it.
It is highly likely/probable/unlikely/improbable
  that she'll do it.

We are going to investigate/look into
One cannot ignore/rule out /exclude the
  possibility that…/of …
You should not overlook
In order to reduce

Wordlist

Unit 2

Changes
Verbs and nouns

bring about a / call for a / cope with / introduce a / lead to a / resist / welcome a / witness a	change

adapt to/ adjust to	change/college life/a new job
adjust	clothing/the volume/the height of
alter	plans/clothes/ your appearance
amend	a law/a document
change	places/the subject/your mind/your tune/ your ways
convert	a building/ money/to a religion

modify	your behaviour/ your language/a design
shift	the blame or responsibility for sthg onto sbdy
switch	sides/(over) to a new currency/TV channels
transfer	money to another account/to a team or department
transform	(the appearance or character of) a person/a place/a thing
vary	your diet/the menu/your routine/in price

Verbs and adverbs

| adapt/ adjust | automatically/ easily/effortlessly |
| alter | completely/ dramatically/ slightly |

change	drastically/ overnight/ significantly
modify	slightly/ substantially/ subtly
transform	completely/ instantly/ radically
vary	considerably/ greatly/widely

Adjectives and nouns

a dramatic economic / a far-reaching / a pleasant political / a refreshing / a significant social / a sudden / a sweeping / an unexpected / a welcome	change

Prepositions and nouns

a change in	attitude(s) government policy the law a patient's condition someone's fortunes the weather
a change of	address direction government heart luck mind mood pace plan scene

Unit 3

A Information

Verbs

access / broadcast / compile / find / gather / get / give / obtain / provide / publish	information

Adjectives

(in)accurate / (un)biased / comprehensive / confidential / limited / misleading / relevant / (un)reliable / up-to-date / useless	information

C Adjectives to describe methods and ways of doing things

controversial	novel
convenient	obsolete
(un)conventional	old-fashioned
costly	persuasive
cost-effective	(un)reliable
effective	subtle
efficient	traditional
familiar	tried and tested
ingenious	unique
innovative	(un)usual

B Smell

Verbs

detect / get rid of / give off / leave / notice / remember	a/the smell (of something)

smell good/bad

Adjectives

acrid	pungent
distinct	rancid
faint	sickly
foul	stale
fresh	strong
mouth-watering	sweet
musty	unmistakable
overpowering	
(un)pleasant	

Unit 4

A Time Verbs

allocate
be pressed for
devote
find
free up
invest
kill   } time
manage
run out of
set/put aside
take up
waste

Adjectives

free/leisure/spare
kick-off/injury/half
qualifying/winning/
    record-breaking
arrival/departure/flying   } time
peak viewing/off-peak
    viewing/prime
opening/closing/sale
sowing/milking/harvest

Other expressions

at a specific/set/predetermined time
in the time allocated/allowed/available
extend/(fail to) meet/miss/set/work to
    a deadline
take time off work
time is against you
a matter of time
make time for oneself

B Character and abilities
Adjectives of personality

approachable
arrogant
attentive
caring
clumsy
conceited
considerate
creative
dedicated
determined
disorganized
easy-going
flexible
impatient
indecisive
industrious
insensitive

knowledgeable
likeable
loyal
mature
moody
outgoing
patient
pompous
responsible
self-assured
self-centred
self-confident
sensible
single-minded
slapdash
stubborn
trustworthy
unreliable

Collocations

adopt an enthusiastic/a positive
    approach to one's work
show great potential/dedication/
    ability/patience
show/lack/develop/display/possess
    the right personal qualities
show/have strong leadership
    qualities
have a/an helpful/outgoing/
    sensitive nature
have a (strong) tendency to be
    domineering/take things to
    heart/worry over detail
have/acquire/develop advanced/
    outstanding/the necessary
    computer skills

Further skills

business
communication
interpersonal
language
management/
    managerial
organizational
personal   } skills
practical
problem-solving
secretarial
social
technical
technological
telephone

Unit 5

A Adjectives to describe relationships

business
close
difficult
family
formal
friendly
intimate
lasting
love-hate
personal
professional   } relationship
prickly
relaxed
rocky
solid
stable
strong
uneasy
working

B Adjective and noun collocations

heated/furious/fierce/pointless   argument
courting/elderly/married/young   couple
adoptive/extended/immediate/
    single-parent   family
inner/mixed/negative/strong   feelings
best/close/mutual/school   friend
brotherly/first/true/unrequited   love
family/heightened/rising/social   tension

C Further expressions

call someone names
call someone by their first name
fall for someone
fall out with someone
get on like a house on fire
get on someone's nerves
have it in for someone
keep oneself to oneself
keep in touch with someone
look up to someone
look down on someone
put a great strain on a relationship
put someone down
take an instant dislike/liking to someone
take after someone
take to someone
turn one's back on someone
turn to someone for help/advice
a relationship can turn sour

Wordlist

Unit 6

A Intelligence and ability
Adjectives and nouns

accomplished	dancer/pianist/singer
born	artist/teacher/writer
competent	driver/lawyer/skier
experienced	journalist/manager/professional
expert	cook/gardener/skier
gifted	musician/sportswoman/student
proficient	horsewoman/pilot/typist
promising	(young) athlete/player/student
skilled	craftsman/technician/worker
skilful	card player/diplomat/footballer
strong	swimmer
talented	actor/player/youngster

art/computer/wine expert

be brilliant/good/weak/terrible/hopeless at a subject,
   a sport or a skill

a brainy/brilliant/bright/gifted child
a whizzkid
a child prodigy

Expressions

be an ace at	solving puzzles/(playing) tennis
be good with your hands	
be a dab hand	at DIY/at painting/with a paintbrush
have a (natural) flair for	languages/design/improvisation
have a (natural) gift for	languages/music/writing
have an ear for	accents/language/music
have an eye for detail	
have a head for figures	
have a nose for a good news story	
have a good/poor memory	

Adverbs and adjectives

academically		enormously	
exceptionally		exceptionally	
highly	gifted	highly	talented
intellectually		hugely	
musically		outstandingly	
naturally			

highly		extremely	
incredibly	intelligent	highly	promising
remarkably		very	

B Adjectives for reviews

action-packed	exhilarating	overhyped
atmospheric	fast-moving	powerful
clichéd	gripping	predictable
compelling	implausible	sentimental
credible	impressive	stunning
disappointing	innovative	tedious
entertaining	memorable	unconvincing
excruciating	moving	

C Comparisons

a considerable/huge/marked/slight difference
a close/remarkable/striking similarity

be common to all/both
be (not) dissimilar from/to
be very much alike
be unlike another thing
bear a close/a striking/a strong/a slight/little/no
   resemblance to
differ from
one thing compares (un)favourably/well/badly with another
develop along different lines/in a different way from
have a great deal/little/nothing in common with
resemble each other
there is little to choose between them in terms of
there is a world of difference between
there are obvious/striking similarities between
what sets him/her/it apart from others is

D Sleep
Adverbs

sleep	badly/fitfully/heavily/lightly/peacefully/rough/ soundly/well

Verbs and expressions

be a heavy/light sleeper	lose sleep over something
be fast asleep	my arm/leg went to sleep
be/feel wide awake	send someone to sleep
doze off/drop off/nod off	sleep like a log
fall asleep	sleep on it
fall into a deep sleep	sleep through the night
get a good night's sleep	sleep through a storm
get to sleep	snooze
have/take a nap	stay up
have a sleepless night	suffer from insomnia
have an animal put to sleep	toss and turn
keep someone awake	wake up to the fact that
lie/stay awake	

Unit 7

A Health

Adjectives and nouns		Phrasal verbs			
aching	joints/limbs/muscles	break/come out in a rash		the effects of a drug wear off	
blocked	nose	a disease breaks out		wear sbdy out	
bruised	ribs/thigh	something brings on a heart attack			
chipped	bone/tooth	bring someone round		**B Effect**	
dislocated	hip/jaw/shoulder	an illness clears up			adverse
sprained	ankle/wrist	carry out tests			beneficial
swollen	glands/feet/lips	come down with an illness			catastrophic
torn	muscles/ligaments	come round			damaging
upset	stomach	come through a serious illness			dramatic
		come up with a cure/treatment			far-reaching
		pain eases off			good
acute/chronic	condition	get over an illness	have	harmful	effect (on
allergic	reaction	get round to (doing) sthg	a/an	immediate	sbdy/sthg)
blinding	headache	an illness or medical condition flares up		important	
high/low	blood pressure	pass on an illness		lasting	
high/low/mild	fever	pass out		limited	
(highly) infectious	disease	pick up an illness		long-/short-term	
medical	complaint	put one's back/shoulder out		minimal	
serious	illness	put sthg down to sthg		noticeable	
				side	
				significant	

Unit 8

A Computer technology

bookmark	laptop
bulletin board	mouse mat
chat room	search engine
disk drive	service provider
hardware	software
home page	webcam
keyboard	

B Verbs with *up, down, over, under*

downgrade	overrule	uproot
download	overthrow	upstage
downplay	update	undercut
downsize	upgrade	undergo
overhear	uphold	undertake

C Adjectives with *in, off, on, out, over*

inborn	oncoming	overcast
incoming	ongoing	overnight
inland	outdoor	overseas
off-duty	outgoing	
off-hand	outlying	

D Plans

Adjectives		Verbs	
audacious			abandon
bold			announce
brilliant			carry out
clever			conceive
controversial			devise
daring			draw up
detailed			jettison
devious			put forward
elaborate	plan		reject	a plan
emergency			reveal
impracticable			scrap
ingenious			shelve
intricate			unveil
(un)feasible			
(un)viable			
(un)workable			

Unit 9

A Doing things alone

Adjectives
independent
isolated
lonely
self-made (millionaire)
self-reliant
self-sufficient
single-handed
solitary
solo (album/flight/
   performance)
unaided
unaccompanied

Expressions
be by oneself
be on one's own
do one's own thing
do something single-
   handed
fend for oneself
go it alone
go solo
have a mind of one's
   own
have something (all) to
   yourself
keep oneself to oneself
leave someone to their
   own devices
prefer one's own
   company
think for oneself

B Anger

Adjectives and nouns
heated argument/debate/
   discussion
irate customer/letter/parent
sudden outburst of temper

Expressions
become irate
be cross/furious with sbdy
be seething with anger/
   indignation/rage
blow a fuse
blow one's top
calm down
fly into a rage
get worked up about sthg
go berserk/mad
let off steam
lose one's temper
maintain one's composure
make one's blood boil
scream blue murder
shake one's fist
stamp one's feet
throw a (temper) tantrum

C Criticism

Verbs	
arouse	
attract	
be impervious to	
be unmoved by	
be upset by	
come in for/under/up against	
draw	
express	criticism
give rise to	
meet with	
overcome	
respond to	
voice	

Adjectives	
considerable	
constructive	
fierce	
growing	
mounting	criticism
severe	
strong	
unjust	
valid	
widespread	

Wordlist

Unit 10

A Describing rooms and houses
Adjectives
bright and cheerful
cramped and cluttered
dark and dingy
light and airy
neat and tidy
spic(k) and span
warm and cosy

colourful
dull
elegant
gaudy
roomy
spacious
tasteful
tasteless
twee

Adverbs
badly/newly/poorly/
  solidly   built
lavishly/newly/richly/
  tastefully   decorated
comfortably/elegantly/
  simply/sparsely   furnished
brightly/dimly/poorly/
  softly   lit
centrally/conveniently/
  ideally/pleasantly   situated/
                                located

B Noise and sound
Voice, sound and noise

booming	
deep	
hesitant	
high-pitched	
hoarse	
hushed	voice
loud	
low	
monotonous	
rough	
shrill	
squeaky	

lose	
lower	your voice
raise	
shout at the top of	

buzzing	
crashing	
creaking	
distant	
distinctive	
faint	sound
muffled	
rumbling	
rustling	
unmistakable	

detect	
emit	
make	a sound
produce	
utter	

background	
banging	
constant	
continuous	
excessive	noise
incessant	
loud	
traffic	

	dies down
	fades away
noise	grows
	increases
	reverberates

Other noises

deafening	applause/cheer/explosion/music/roar/silence
piercing	cry/scream/shriek/whistle
rowdy	behaviour/crowd/fans/party
bells	chime/ring/tinkle
doors	slam shut/click shut/creak open
dogs	bark/growl/whimper/whine

music/a radio/a television blares out

Unit 11

Sight

give sbdy a/an angry/blank/cold/knowing	look
take a/an close/critical/fascinating/in-depth	look
a/an familiar/impressive/rare/welcome	sight
a breathtaking/spectacular/superb	view
have blurred/double/poor/twenty-twenty	vision
a/an clear/idealistic/realistic/terrifying	vision
high/good/reduced/low/poor	visibility

be hidden from view
be (in)visible to/with the naked eye
catch a glimpse of sbdy/sthg
catch one's eye
catch sight of sbdy/sthg
come into view
have/take a look at sthg
keep one's eye on sbdy/sthg
keep one's eyes open
keep out of sight
lose sight of sbdy/sthg

at first sight/glance
in full view of sbdy
in the public eye
in sight/view
on view/show/display

Read and write

a/an good/excellent/exciting	read
a/an avid/fast/slow/voracious	reader
a freelance/prolific/struggling/talented	writer
distinctive/familiar/legible/neat	handwriting

read	aloud/avidly/voraciously/widely
write	clearly/legibly/neatly/in rough/in plain language

put sthg (down) in writing
read sthg out
read too much into sthg
read up on sthg
write a debt off
write off to sbdy for sthg
write notes up
write out a cheque for (an amount)
write sthg into a contract or law

Unit 12

A Attitude adverbials

amazingly
apparently
astonishingly
(un)believably
clearly
conveniently
curiously
disappointingly
disturbingly
evidently
(un)fortunately
funnily
happily
indisputably
inevitably
interestingly
ironically
laughably
luckily
miraculously
naturally
obviously
personally
predictably
presumably
reassuringly
regrettably
rightly
sadly
sensibly
strangely
(not) surprisingly
understandably
undoubtedly
unexpectedly
unmistakably
(un)wisely
worryingly

B Environment

air/noise/river/sea/traffic
   pollution
bottle bank
cigarette butt
dog mess
dumping rubbish/waste
exhaust fumes
forest fire
global warming
litter/rubbish bin
NGO (non-governmental
   organization)
natural habitat
ozone layer
recycling facilities
traffic congestion
wildlife conservation

Unit 13

A Eating and drinking
Verbs
eat/drink up
finish off
gulp down
pick at
polish off

Adjectives and nouns
favourite/side dish
celebratory/soft drink
big/fussy eater
ready/square meal
raging thirst

Further expressions
be famished/peckish/full up
I could eat a horse
do something on a full/an empty
   stomach
eat into one's time/money
eat like a bird
eat one's words
eat sbdy out of house and home
feel faint with hunger
have sbdy eating out of your hand
lose one's appetite
quench one's thirst
satisfy one's hunger
work up an appetite

B Deception
Collocations
appearances can be deceptive
fraudulent claims/practices/trading
misleading impression/information/
   statement

deceptively easy/simple/straightforward
fraudulently obtain/use
misleadingly referred to a/termed/called

credit card/electoral/tax fraud

Verbs
be fooled/deceived/tricked by sbdy
cheat at sthg
deceive sbdy into doing sthg
fall for (a trick)
see through sbdy's lies/promises
swindle sbdy out of sthg
take sbdy for a ride
take sbdy in
tell a lie
trick sbdy into doing sthg
trick sbdy out of sthg

C Intensifiers

bitterly	cold/disappointing/ opposed/resentful
deeply	committed/concerned/ moving/suspicious
desperately	disappointed/keen/ lonely/ worried
entirely	different/free of charge/ new/wrong
fully	aware/booked/ clothed/ equipped/justified
highly	gifted/influential/ promising/talented
hugely	expensive/popular/ successful/talented
perfectly	acceptable/capable/ clear/ good/normal/safe
seriously	affected/ill/injured
totally	different/(in)dependent/ unexpected/unnecessary
utterly	disgraceful/exhausted/ opposed/ridiculous
wholly	inadequate/inappropriate/ unacceptable/unexpected

Unit 14

Money							
counterfeit			in advance	borrow	heavily	borrow	an idea/a phrase/a word
housekeeping		pay for sthg	in arrears	pay	generously/ handsomely	pay	attention/a compliment/ one's respects/tribute
pocket			in cash				
prize	money		in full	save	carefully/hard	save	effort/energy/time
ransom			in instalments	spend	extravagantly/ freely/wisely	lend	assistance/credibility/ support/weight
redundancy			on expenses				
sponsorship				invest	foolishly/heavily/ wisely	owe sbdy	an apology/an explanation/a favour
		buy sthg	on impulse on credit on hire purchase at auction in the sales				

Grammar reference

Unit 1

Modal verbs: *might, could, may, can*

1 *might, could* and *may* can be used to express present, future and past possibility:
*Try the shop on the corner – they **might have** what you're looking for.*
*Economists warn that house prices **could rise** even further next year.*
*She **may not have received** your letter yet.*

The addition of *well* after the modal verb expresses more probability.
*Take an umbrella – it **may/could/might well rain** later on.*

2 *might* and *could* can be used to express:
- past possibility which did not happen
*We **could have won** the game, but Joe missed a penalty.*
*It's a good thing I was wearing a crash helmet. **I might have been** seriously **injured.***
- annoyance
*You **could at least say** you're sorry!*
*He **might have told** me he was going to be late!*

3 *might* and *may* can be used to:
- express concession
*He **might have failed** his degree, but he's earning much more than me.*
(=Although he failed his degree, he's earning much more than me.)
*She **may be** very famous, but that doesn't give her the right to behave like that in public.*
- suggest what one should do when there is no better alternative
*I **might as well go** shopping with my parents – I've got nothing else to do.*
*You'll find out the truth sooner or later, so I **may as well tell** you now what happened.*

4 *can* and *may* (more formal) can be used to:
- give or refuse permission
*You **may/can borrow** up to three videos at any one time from the library.*
*You **can't/may not go** until you have finished.*
- make offers
***May I be** of assistance?*
***Can I carry** that for you?*

5 *can* and *could* can be used to:
- make requests
***Can/Could you give** me a hand, please?*
- ask for permission
***Can/Could I open** the window?*

The more formal *may* can also be used.
***May I ask** a personal question?*

6 *can* and *could*, in the negative form, can be used to express certainty:
*She **can't be** more than about 20 years old.*
*It **couldn't have been** a bear that we saw – it was far too small.*

7 *can* can be used to express
- theoretical possibility
*The new concert hall **can seat** over 3,000 people.*
- ability or inability
*I **can understand** some Italian, but I **can't speak** it very well.*
- criticism
*She **can say** some very hurtful things sometimes.*

8 *could* can be used to express:
- ability or inability in the past
*My late grandfather **could play** the banjo, but he **couldn't sing** very well.*

When we talk about ability to do something on one occasion in the past, *could* is not possible. Instead, *was/were able to, managed to* or *succeeded in* have to be used.
*I **managed to speak** to Frank last night, but I **couldn't persuade** him to come to the opera with us.*
- permission or prohibition in the past
*When I was at school the boys **couldn't wear** earrings, but the girls **could.***

When we talk about permission to do something on one occasion in the past, *be allowed to* has to be used.
*I **was allowed to leave** work early yesterday to go and meet my husband at the airport.*

Unit 2

Talking about the past

1 **Past simple**
The past simple can be used to refer to:
- completed actions, events or situations which happened at a specific time or over a specific period of time in the past
*I **sold** my car about three months ago.*
*When we **lived** in York, my father **ran** a small bakery.*
- habitual actions or behaviour in the past
***Did you bite** your nails when you were a child?*
*When I was a teenager, my mum **got** really angry if I **didn't tidy** my bedroom.*

Used to + infinitive can also be used to refer to past situations and habitual actions. *Would + infinitive* can be used to refer to past habitual actions, but not situations.
*Every summer we **used to/would go** to Scotland to visit my grandmother.*
*I **used to** (not would) **have** a parrot, but he escaped.*

2 **Past continuous**
The past continuous can be used to refer to:
- situations or actions in progress at a particular moment in the past
*This time last year I **was taking** the CAE exam.*
- a past situation or action which was in progress when another action occurred
*We **were** still **having** breakfast when Mark and Marian called round.*
- past actions or situations occurring at the same time
*She **was working** hard to earn some extra money and he **was spending** it all on drink.*
- repeated past actions, which the speaker finds annoying
*She **was** always **complaining** about something.*

3 **Present perfect**
The present perfect links past events and situations with the present.

A The present perfect simple can be used:
- to talk about recent past events which have some relevance to the present
*They can't afford to go on holiday – they**'ve just bought** a new car.*
- to describe situations which started in the past and continue to the present
*We**'ve had** these saucepans since we got married 43 years ago.*
- to talk about events which occurred at some time between the past and present. The exact time they

occurred is either unknown or unimportant.
*I've already **seen** United play three times this season.*
- after the expression *this/that/it is the first/second/third etc time…*
*This is the fourth time I've **seen** United play this season.*
- after the expression *it's (two/three etc) years/a long time since…* The past simple is also possible.
*It's years since I've **had**/I **had** bacon for breakfast.*
- with another present perfect to describe two states or actions which have existed or occurred together.
*We've **been burgled** twice since we've **lived** here.*

B The present perfect continuous is used with verbs which describe actions (eg *give, play, take*), but not with verbs which describe states (eg *be, know, like*). It can be used to:
- emphasize the duration of a situation or activity
*He's **been working** on his first novel for over ten years.*
- suggest that a situation or activity is temporary
*My kitchen's being redecorated so I've **been eating** at my mum's.*
- suggest that a situation or activity is incomplete
*I've **been reading** that book you lent me – I think I know how it's going to end.*
- focus on the repetition of a situation or activity. The number of times it is repeated can only be included with the simple, not the continuous form.
*Someone's **been phoning** you. She's **phoned** about six or seven times this morning.*

C Both simple and continuous forms of the present perfect can be used to talk about the present effects of a past event.
*I'm exhausted! I've **been cleaning** the house all morning.* (an activity)
*Sally can't drive for a while; she's **broken** her leg.* (a single action)

4 Past perfect

A The past perfect simple can be used:
- to show that a past event or situation occurred before another past event or situation
*As soon as the film started, I realized I **had seen** it before.*
- to describe situations which started in the past and continued to a later point in the past
*They **had known** each other for several years before they got married.*
- after *that/it was the first/second/third etc time…*
*We went to Switzerland last summer; it was only the second time we'd **been** abroad.*
- after *it was (two/three etc) years/a long time since…*
*It was a long time since she **had** last **seen** her old schoolfriend.*
- after certain time linkers eg *after, before, by the time, as soon as, once, when, until*
*It was dark by the time I **had finished** repairing the roof.*

The past simple can be used if the order of events is clear:
*I had a relaxing bath after I **got** home from work last night.*
or if the second event occurred as a result of the first.
*When the music **started**, everyone got up to dance.*

Participle clauses can sometimes be used in place of clauses with *when* or *after* and the past perfect.
***Having eaten** his sandwich, he put his coat on and left.*
(= *After he **had eaten** his sandwich, he put his coat on and left.*)
For more information on participle clauses, see Unit 10 below.

B The past perfect continuous can be used in similar ways to the present perfect continuous, but instead of linking past events and situations with the present, it links them with another point in the past. It is not used with stative verbs (eg *be, know, like*).
*I'd **been waiting** for over an hour when she finally arrived.* (duration)

*She found out that her son **had been using** her credit card to buy computer games.* (repetition)
*You only had to smell his breath to know he'd **been smoking**.* (effects of a past event)

5 Unfulfilled past events
The following structures can be used to talk about events which were intended to take place, but which did not happen.

*I **was going to send** you an email, but I had a few problems with my computer.*
*I **was about to call** the doctor, but then the pain suddenly disappeared.*
*She **had been/was thinking of going** to Iceland, but changed her mind and went to Norway, instead.*
*The meeting, which **was to have taken** place last weekend, was unexpectedly cancelled.*

6 Expressing preferences about the past
The following structures can be used to express how we would like the past to have been different.
- *would like/love/prefer to* + perfect infinitive, or *would have liked/loved/preferred to* + infinitive or perfect infinitive
*We **would like to have stayed** longer but we had to catch the train.*
*She **would have loved to tell/to have told** him what she thought of him.*

If the subject of *would like etc* is not the same as the subject of the verb which follows, an appropriate noun or object pronoun is inserted before the infinitive.
***She** would have preferred **him** to say it to her face, rather than put it in a letter.*
- *would rather/sooner* + perfect infinitive
*We stayed in a hotel but I'd **sooner have slept** in a tent.*

If the subject of *would rather/sooner* is not the same as the subject of the verb which follows, the past perfect is used.
***Would you** rather **I** hadn't said anything about it to Matt?*

For information on using *wish/if only* and conditional sentences to describe imaginary situations in the past, see section A in Unit 3 below.

Unit 3
Hypothetical situations and conditionals

Past tenses can be used to talk about unlikely, imaginary or impossible situations in the present, past or future.

A Past situations
- *wish/if only* + past perfect can be used to express wishes, regrets and criticisms about the past
*I **wish I hadn't eaten** my dinner so quickly. I've got indigestion now.*
*If only **you had listened** to my advice. You wouldn't be in this mess.*
- *should* + perfect infinitive can also be used to express regrets and criticisms about the past
*We **should have brought** an umbrella. We're going to get soaking wet now.*
*You **shouldn't have spoken** to him like that. I'm not surprised he's upset.*
- Third conditional sentences (*if* + past perfect, *would/might/could* + perfect infinitive) can be used to speculate about how things might have been different in the past
*If you **had been paying** attention, you **might have understood** what I was saying.*
(= You weren't paying attention, so you didn't understand.)
*If it **hadn't been for** that traffic jam on the motorway, we **would have got** here on time.*
(= Because of the traffic jam we arrived late.)

A more formal variation is to omit *if* and begin with *Had*:
Had she known about his criminal past, she **would never have employed** him.

- Mixed conditional sentences can be used to speculate about how a different situation in the past might have had different results in the present
  *If you **hadn't stayed** up to watch the film <u>last night</u>, you **wouldn't be** so tired <u>now</u>.*

or, alternatively, how changes to a present situation might have influenced the past
*If I **weren't** so broke at the moment, I **could have bought** you something decent for your birthday.*

The past simple is used in this last sentence to describe an unreal, or imaginary, situation in the present. The past simple can also be used in conditional sentences to describe real situations in the past:
*If I **arrived** late at the office, my boss used to get really angry. (If = Whenever)*

For information on *would like/love/prefer* and *would rather/sooner*, see section 6 in Unit 2 above.

B Present and future situations: conditionals

1 Zero conditional: *if* + present simple, present simple
   - We use the zero conditional to talk about situations which are always true
     *If I **eat** too much spicy food, I start to feel ill.*

2 First conditional: *if* + present simple, *will/going to/may/might/could* + infinitive
   - We use the first conditional to talk about possible future situations and their probable results
     *If you **don't water** that plant soon, it**'ll die**.*
   - *if* + *should/happen to/should happen to* makes the event seem more unlikely or more of a chance possibility
     *If I **happen to see** Mr Dee there, I**'ll ask** him for you.*
     *If you **should happen to miss** the train, I **could drive** you there myself.*
   - A more formal variation is to begin with *Should*
     Should you wish to change your holiday arrangements, we will do all we can to help.

3 Second conditional: *if* + past simple, *would/might/could* + infinitive
   - We use the second conditional to talk about imaginary, unlikely or impossible situations in the present and future
     *If I **had** an extra pair of hands, then I **could help** you!*
     *I **might work** harder if they **paid** me more.*
     *If it **weren't for** my savings, I **wouldn't be** able to survive. (= Thanks to my savings I can survive.)*
   - *if* + *were to* + infinitive makes the event seem more unlikely
     *If you **were to walk** in that direction for another thousand miles, you**'d** eventually **arrive** in Warsaw.*
   - A more formal variation is to begin with *Were*
     Were they to break the contract, we would of course take legal action.
   - *Suppose/Supposing/Imagine* can be used instead of *if*, particularly in speech
     Supposing you ran out of money, what would you do?
     Imagine you lost your job. Do you think you'd be able to find another?

4 *if* can sometimes be followed by *will*, *would* or *going to*, for example when making polite requests or describing the result of a course of action.
   *If you **would take** a seat for a moment, I**'ll tell** Mr Graydon you're here.*
   *If it **is going to be** more profitable for the company, then I think we should do it.*

Unit 4
Punctuation

1 **Commas**
   - Commas are normally used after subordinate clauses when these come first in a sentence.
     If I have any problems, I'll let you know.
     They are not normally used when the subordinate clause follows the main clause.
     We'll phone you as soon as we get there.
   - Commas are used after linking adverbials at the beginning of a sentence (see Unit 12).
     Meanwhile, darkness began to fall.
     For this reason, I have decided to resign.
     They are also used before adverbials if these are inserted in the sentence.
     The workers, however, have refused to accept the offer.
   - Commas are used to separate items in a list or series. They are not normally used between the last two items.
     She got up, had a shower, got dressed and went out.
   - Commas are used with non-identifying relative clauses but **not** with identifying relative clauses (see Unit 5).
     My father, who is a lawyer, advised me on the legal matters.
     The man who bought our house is a lawyer.
   - Commas are used to separate direct speech from the reporting verb.
     'Empty your bag,' he said. She replied, 'It's already empty.'
     They are not used before *that, if, where* etc in reported speech.
     She replied that it was already empty.

2 **Apostrophes**
   Apostrophes are used:
   - to indicate where letters have been omitted from contracted forms
     I don't think it's fair.
   - to indicate possession
     the **boss's** office   my **parents'** house
     the **children's** books

   Apostrophes are **not** used with possessive pronouns or adjectives.
   Yours is here.   **Its** tail is white.

3 **Semi colons**
   Semi-colons can be used:
   - in place of full stops where two sentences are closely related in meaning
     Some storks fly south in winter; others stay put, using local rubbish dumps as their food source.
   - to separate items in a list, particularly long or grammatically complex ones
     There were several reasons why Jeremy chose not to go abroad on holiday: he had an acute fear of flying (even though he had never flown before); long periods of exposure to the sun brought him out in a rash; he was suspicious of any food which was not 'good home cooking'; ...

4 **Colons**
   Colons can be used:
   - before explanations
     We moved to a different area: the noise from the traffic was becoming unbearable.
   - to introduce a list
     The park boasts several different species of trees: oak, ash, elm, beech, alder and a wide variety of conifers.

5 **Dashes**
   Dashes are used in informal writing:
   - in place of a colon
     We've bought a new car – the old one kept breaking down.
   - to create a pause in order to emphasize what follows
     I took my driving test yesterday – and I passed!

Gerunds and infinitives

A The infinitive with *to* is used:
- to express purpose
  I went out to get some fresh air.
- after some adjectives
  It's not easy to find work these days.
- after the verb *to be*, to give orders or to express an arrangement
  You're to stay here until I get back.
  The President is to visit Poland next month.
- after *would hate/like/love/prefer*, with or without an object
  Would you like me to do it now?
- after the following verbs
  agree, appear, arrange, ask, attempt, choose, decide, demand, deserve, expect, help, hesitate, hope, learn, manage, offer, prepare, pretend, refuse, seem, threaten

  If you need any help, don't hesitate to contact me.
- after the following verbs + object
  advise, allow, ask, challenge, enable, encourage, expect, force, get, help, intend, invite, order, persuade, recommend, remind, teach, tell, urge, warn

  My family encouraged me to go to university.

  If *advise* and *recommend* are used without an object, the gerund is used.
  I recommended her to apply to King's College.
  I recommended applying to King's College.
- after the following nouns
  ability, attempt, capacity, chance, decision, desire, determination, effort, failure, intention, need, opportunity, permission, plan, proposal, refusal, right, tendency, way, willingness

  It was the director's refusal to accept his proposals that led to his decision to resign.

B The bare infinitive (without *to*) is used:
- after modal verbs
  I shouldn't eat this really, but I can't resist it.
- after the following verbs
  help, had better, let, make, would rather/sooner

  We'd better go home now – it's very late.
  Can you help me tidy up, please?

  In the passive, *make* is followed by the infinitive with *to*.
  We were made to do all the dirty jobs.

C The gerund is used:
- as the subject, object or complement of a clause or sentence
  Playing golf helps me relax but I find watching it on television rather boring.
- after prepositions
  We thought about going to France this year.
- after the following expressions
  have difficulty/problems, there's no/little point, it's no good/use, it's (not) worth

  It's no use asking him – he won't know the answer.
- after the following verbs
  admit, adore, advise, appreciate, anticipate, avoid, can't help, can't stand, consider, delay, deny, detest, dislike, dread, enjoy, feel like, give up, imagine, involve, keep, (don't) mind, miss, postpone, put off, practise, prevent, propose, recommend, resent, resist, risk, suggest

  I resent having to do all the housework myself.
- after the following verbs + the preposition *to*
  adapt/adjust to, admit to, confess to, get round to, get used to, look forward to, object to

  She confessed to being surprised by her success.

Where the subjects of the main verb and the gerund are different, an object (pronoun) or possessive adjective is used.

I couldn't imagine him eating something like this.
We appreciate your coming to tell us so quickly.

D The following verbs can be followed by the gerund or the infinitive with *to* with no change in meaning:
begin, can't bear, continue, intend, start, hate, like, love, prefer

She suddenly started singing/to sing.

The infinitive is common for specific situations. Compare the following sentences:
I hate to say this, but your breath smells.
I hate getting up early every morning.

E The following verbs can be followed by the gerund or the infinitive with *to*, but with a change in meaning:
forget, mean, remember, regret, stop, try
- The infinitive is used with *remember, forget, regret* and *stop* when the act of *remembering*, etc comes first. The gerund is used when it comes second.
  I must remember to post this letter later.
  I distinctly remember posting the letter yesterday.
  Her car broke down and no one stopped to help her.
  I've stopped eating chocolate.

When *regret* is followed by the infinitive with *to*, it is normally used with verbs such as *say, tell* and *inform*. This use is formal.
We regret to inform you that your application has been unsuccessful.
- *try* + infinitive with *to* means *attempt. try* + gerund means *experiment with*.
  Please be quiet – I'm trying to sleep.
  If you can't sleep, try using earplugs.
- *mean* + infinitive with *to* means *intend. mean* + gerund means *involve*.
  I've been meaning to write to you for ages.
  Changing jobs also meant changing house.

Unit 5
Reference

1 *This, that, these* and *those* can be used to refer back to previously stated people, things, events or ideas. *This* and *these* are more common than *that* and *those*.

This and *that* can be used:
- before nouns or on their own
  … and he left school at 16. This (decision) did not please his parents.
  He hated school. That's why he left at 16.

These and *those* are more commonly used before nouns.
- *…the mobile phone and the computer. These two inventions have revolutionized communications…*
  … during the 1930s. In those days, of course, people didn't have computers.
  You've got so many toys. Let's get rid of those that you don't play with any more.

2 A number of other words can be used to substitute and avoid repetition of previously used words and phrases.
- *do/does/did* to replace a verb
  Paul didn't want to go, but I did. (= I wanted to go.)
- *do so* can also be used to replace a verb + object
  He told her to lock the door, but she had already done so.
- *so/nor/neither* + auxiliary verb + subject
  She likes dogs and so do I. (= I like dogs, too.)
  I've never been to Paris and nor/neither has he. (= he hasn't been to Paris either.)
- *so/not* to replace a *that*-clause after *expect, hope, seem, suppose, think*
  'Is he coming?' 'I think so.' (= I think that he's coming.)
  'Do you think it'll rain?' 'I hope not.' (= I hope that it won't rain.)

Note that *I don't think so* is more common than *I think not*.

- *if not/so* to replace whole clauses
  *Are you free on Friday? **If so**, do you fancy going to the cinema? **If not**, how about next week?*
- *one/ones* to replace countable nouns
  *What sort of **ice cream** would you like? **A plain one** or **one with chocolate sauce** on?*
  *Those red **apples** are much tastier than **these green ones**.*

Ellipsis

Ellipsis involves omitting words to avoid repetition.

1 It is common to omit words after *and* and *but*.
*I live and (**I**) work in Madrid.*
*John was impressed, but I wasn't (**impressed**).*
*We play tennis on Saturdays and (**we**) sometimes (**play**) on Sundays, too.*

2 The main verb can be omitted after an auxiliary verb.
*I'd do it myself if I **could**. (= if I could do it myself)*
*She said she would phone, but she **hasn't**.*
*He said he saw her there, but he **can't have**.*

Adverbs can be placed before the auxiliary.
*'Can you turn the heating on?' 'I **already have**.'*

be cannot be omitted after a modal verb.
*'Is the shop open yet?' 'It **might be**.'*

been can be omitted in a perfect passive, except after a modal verb.
*'Has she been promoted?' 'Yes, she **has**.'*
*He wasn't sent to prison but he **should have been**.*

3 Instead of repeating a full infinitive expression we can simply use *to*.
*I don't **eat much cheese** now, but I **used to**.*

Relative clauses

A Defining relative clauses

These contain essential information which identifies the person or thing being talked about. *Who* and *which* can be replaced by *that*, and the relative pronoun can be omitted if it is the object of the verb in the relative clause. No commas are required at the beginning or end of the relative clause.

*The woman **who/that** used to babysit for us has just got married.*
*It's not the kind of novel **which/that** appeals to me.*
*I know a boy **whose** father is a professional diver.*
*Just a quick note to thank you for the flowers **(which/that)** you sent me.*

When and *why* can also be omitted in defining relative clauses.
*I'll never forget the day **(when)** Geoff resigned.*
*The reason **(why)** he left is still unclear.*

Where cannot be omitted. Compare the following:
*That's the shop **where** we bought our bed.*
*That's the shop **(which/that)** we bought our bed in.*

In more formal English, prepositions can be placed before the relative pronouns *whom* and *which* (but not *that*).
*They returned to the shop **in which** the bed had been purchased.*

B Non-defining relative clauses

These contain non-essential information: we can identify which person or thing is being talked about without the information in the relative clause. *That* cannot be used and the relative pronoun cannot be omitted. Commas are required at the beginning and the end of the relative clause (except when the end of the relative clause is also the end of the sentence).

*Our former babysitter, **who** got married last year, has just had her first child.*
*His first novel, **which** was largely autobiographical, became an overnight success.*
*Alan Smith, **whose** father is a professional diver, is the only boy in our class who can't swim.*

Which is used in non-defining relative clauses to refer to a whole clause.
*He works twelve hours a day, **which** must be very tiring.*

What is **not** used to refer to a whole clause. It means 'the thing that'.
*Let me know **what** you decide to do.*
***What** I need right now is a cup of tea.* (see Unit 9)

Unit 6
Passives

A Form

The passive is formed with the appropriate tense or form of the verb *to be* and the past participle of the main verb:

*We should **have been told** earlier.*
*A full investigation **is** currently **being carried out**.*

The passive cannot be used with intransitive verbs.
The rabbit was disappeared by the magician. ✗

B Use

The passive is used to focus attention on the action or the person or thing affected by the action, rather than on the agent, the person or thing that performs the action.

Smith was jailed for three years.

If the agent is mentioned, the preposition *by* is used:

*The President was criticized **by members of his own party**.*

The choice between active and passive is often influenced by context. 'Given' or previously mentioned information usually comes at the beginning of a clause or sentence and new information towards the end. In the following example, *The letter* is 'given' information: it is referred to in the previous sentence (*Albert Einstein wrote to President Franklin Roosevelt*). Since it is not the agent of the verb *'compose'*, the passive form is necessarily used.

*In 1939 Albert Einstein wrote to President Franklin Roosevelt, urging the United States to develop an atomic bomb. **The letter was composed** by the Hungarian-born physicist and biophysicist Leo Szilard, a former colleague of Einstein, who felt it would have more influence if it were signed by his eminent friend.*

There is also a tendency to place long phrases towards the end of the clause. If, as in the above example, the agent is a long phrase (*the Hungarian-born physicist* etc) this appears at the end of the clause and the passive form is necessarily used. Also:

*The meeting was attended **by representatives of the five permanent members of the UN Security Council.***

C Not mentioning the agent

The agent is not usually mentioned in passive constructions:
- if the agent is unknown or unimportant
  *Lunch **will be served** from one o'clock in the canteen.*
- if it is obvious who the agent is
  *The musician **was arrested** at his home on Friday.*
- if the agent is 'people in general'
  *The passive **is not used** with intransitive verbs.*
- to avoid the use of 'you' in official notices
  *Unsold tickets **must be returned** by 16th August.*

D Further passive constructions

1 The infinitive or perfect infinitive with *to* can be used with

certain verbs to give generalized opinions or facts. Verbs used in this way include: *allege, believe, consider, estimate, expect, know, report, say, think, understand*, as well as *be rumoured* and *be reputed*.
She **is expected to make** a statement later today.
He **is rumoured to have sold** it for a six-figure sum.
A million people **were estimated to have taken** part in the demonstration.

2 *have* + object + past participle can be used to show that the subject arranges for the action to be done by someone else. *Get* is a more informal alternative to *have*. Compare:
I'm going to develop the photos myself.
I'm going to **have/get the photos developed** at the shop on the corner.

The same structure can be used for events which are outside the speaker's control.
I **had my passport stolen** on holiday.

3 *get* can also be used as an informal alternative to *be* in passive sentences.
We **got knocked out** of the Cup in the first round.

It is commonly used with the following past participles: *burned, caught, dressed, hurt, involved, left, lost, stuck*

She **got caught** shoplifting.
Do as I say and no one will **get hurt**.

Unit 7
Reported speech

A Changes
Some words and features of grammar used in direct speech may have to be changed in reported speech.

1 Tense changes
- Present tenses change to past; present perfect and past tenses change to past perfect.
'I'm having a great time,' said Paul.
Paul said he **was having** a great time.

'I've never ridden a horse,' said Clare.
Clare said she **had** never **ridden** a horse.

'We were trying to phone you,' she said.
She said they **had been trying** to phone us.

- The modal verbs *will, must, may* and *can* change to *would, had to, might* and *could*.
Would, might, could, should and *ought to* do not change, nor does *must* when it is used for deductions.

'It must be done by tomorrow,' she said.
She told me it **had to be done** by the following day.

'It must be raining,' she said.
She said it **must be raining**.

2 Other changes
Pronouns and certain words indicating time and place may have to change when we use reported speech.
'**I** saw **you here yesterday**,' said Alan.
Alan said **he** had seen **me there the day before**.

3 Tense changes are not necessary:
- if the statement being reported is still true
'I intend to retire next year,' he said.
He told me he intends to retire next year.
- if the reporting verb is in the present or present perfect
'We are going to get married.'
They have announced that they are going to get married.

'I never tell lies.'
She says she never tells lies.

4 When questions are reported:
- auxiliary verbs *do, does* and *did* are not used

- the word order is the same as for statements
- *yes/no* questions are reported with *if* or *whether*
- question marks are not used

'Where's Paul?'   He asked where Paul is/was.
'Did you enjoy it?' She asked if I (had) enjoyed it.

B Verb patterns
Several different verb patterns can be used in reported speech. Some reporting verbs can be used with more than one verb pattern. For example:

He **asked to leave**.
He **asked them to leave**.
He **asked that they should leave**. (Formal)

1 verb + *that* clause
eg *add, admit, announce, assure, claim, complain, concede, conclude, confirm, emphasize, estimate, explain, mention, point out, predict, remark, reassure, remind, repeat, say, state, stress, tell, warn*
Note that *assure, reassure, remind* and *tell* are followed by an object.

Critics **predicted that the film would be** a success.
My daughter **reminded me that I had promised** to take her to the zoo on her birthday.

2 verb + (that) sbdy (should) do sthg/sthg (should) happen
eg *advise, agree, ask, demand, insist, propose, recommend, request, suggest*

They **demanded that** he **should resign**.
We **suggested he apply** for the job.

3 verb + infinitive with *to*
eg *agree, ask, claim, demand, offer, promise, refuse, threaten*

He **claimed to be** an expert on ghosts.

4 verb + object + infinitive with *to*
eg *advise, ask, beg, convince, encourage, forbid, instruct, invite, order, persuade, recommend, remind, tell, urge, warn*

She **urged him not to** get involved.

5 verb + gerund
eg *admit, advise, deny, recommend, regret, suggest*

He **denied taking/having taken** the money.

6 verb + preposition + gerund
eg *advise, argue, protest, warn* **against**
apologize, blame, forgive, praise, tell off, thank **for**
discourage, dissuade **from**
accuse, speak **of**
congratulate, insist **on**
admit, confess, consent, object **to**

She **admitted to feeling** rather nervous.
He **told me off for singing**!
I **insisted on his/him wearing** a suit.

7 Some reporting verbs can be used in the passive after *it*. This structure can be used if the speaker does not wish to take responsibility for a statement or is reporting the views of others. Verbs include: *announce, believe, claim, confirm, estimate, rumour, suggest* and *think*.
It is thought that she may have left the country.
It has been suggested that the minister took bribes.

Unit 8
Determiners and pronouns

A Determiners

1 The following words are determiners: they come <u>before nouns</u> and can be used to indicate which thing(s) you are referring to, or to talk about quantities and amounts.

all, another, any, both, each, either, enough, every, (a) few, fewer, less, a lot of, (a) little, many, more, most, much, neither, no, one, other, several, some, this, that, these, those

2   Determiners can be used:
*   before singular countable nouns
    eg *another, any, each, either, every, neither, no, one, some, this, that*

Can I have **another** sandwich, please?

Either and *neither* are used to talk about two things. *Each* is used to talk about two or more things; *every* is only used to talk about more than two. All four determiners are followed by a singular verb.
*I've got two suits and **neither** fits me very well.*

Each/Every song sounds the same.
*   before plural nouns
    eg *all, any, both, enough, (a) few, fewer, a lot of, many, more, most, no, other, several, some, these, those*

We haven't got **enough** eggs to make an omelette.

Few means 'not many' or 'not as many as desired or expected'. *Very* can be used before *few* to emphasize it.
*There are **very few** apples left. We need to buy some.*

A few means 'some' or 'more than expected'.
*We've still got **a few** eggs – enough to make an omelette.*

Quite can be used with *a few* to mean *a fairly large number*.
*We've got **quite a few** kiwis – we need to eat them before they go rotten.*
*   before uncountable nouns
    eg *all, any, enough, less, (a) little, a lot of, more, most, much, no, some, this, that*

He's nearly bald – he's got **very little** hair left.

Some can be used to mean 'approximately' or 'a large amount':
*I was waiting for **some two hours** – that's quite **some time**.*

3   Sometimes more than one determiner can be used before a noun.
every few/five days   every other week   another few drinks
no other town/books   many more/other ways
these few examples

B   Pronouns

1   Most of the determiners above can also be used as pronouns. Pronouns are used <u>instead of nouns</u>. *Every, no* and *other* cannot be used as pronouns: *each* is used instead of *every, none* instead of *no*, and *others* instead of *other*. *A lot of* becomes *a lot* as a pronoun.

Bad reviews are better than **no** reviews. (Determiner)
Bad reviews are better than **none**. (Pronoun)

2   Pronouns can be used:
*   on their own
    'Would you like sugar on it?' 'Just **a little**.'
    'Do you prefer tea or coffee?' 'I don't like **either**.'

One another and *each other* are used as objects of verbs.
*Bob and Alice loved **one another/each other**.*
(Bob loved Alice and Alice loved Bob.)
*   with *of* + pronoun
    *They've got two boys – **both of them** are blond.*
*   with *of* + *the, this, that, these, those, my, your* etc + noun
    Try **some of my** wine.
    Neither of these books is mine.

of is optional with *all* and *both* before a noun
All (of) my clothes/Both (of) my socks are wet.
*   after a determiner
    There are no others. I've got a few more. Look at this one.
    Try each one. Would you like any more?

Modal verbs: *will, shall* and *would*

1   **Will** and **would** can be used to express:
*   present and past habits. This use is not possible with stative verbs (eg *be, know, like*).
    *She **will** often **fall** asleep in front of the television.*
    *He **would** always **read** us a story at bedtime.*
*   typical annoying behaviour. In speech, *will* and *would* are stressed.
    *He **will keep interrupting** when I'm talking.*
    *I **would get a cold** now, just as the holiday is starting!*
*   willingness to do something. This includes requests.
    *If you**'ll/would follow** me, Ms Ray will see you now.*
    ***Will/Would** you open the door a little, please?*
    *I wish he **would try** a bit harder.*
*   refusal to do something in the present and the past.
    *Mummy! Eva **won't let** me play with her dolls!*
    *I asked him, but he **wouldn't** tell me.*

2   **Will** can also be used to express assumptions about the present.
*'There's someone at the door.' 'That**'ll be** Lydia.'*

3   **Shall** can be used:
*   to make a request for advice or instructions
    *I'm very worried about Peter. What **shall we do?***
    *What time **shall we meet?***
*   to make an offer or a suggestion
    Shall I help** you carry that? **Shall we go?

Talking about the future

1   *will* and *going to* can be used to make predictions.
*I don't think **I'll be/I'm going to be** well enough to go to work tomorrow.*

2   *going to* also describes intentions or plans.
*I'm **going to work** really hard this year.*

3   The present continuous describes fixed arrangements.
*I'm **having** lunch with Brian tomorrow.*

4   Modal verbs express different degrees of uncertainty about the future.
*Dave **should be** here soon. (Probability)*
*We **might have** a party next week. (Possibility)*

may/might/could well + infinitive without *to* expresses probability.
*We **might well be moving** in the next few weeks.*

5   Verbs of thinking, such as *believe, doubt, expect* and *think*, are followed by *will* when referring to the future. *Hope* can also be followed by a present tense.
*I **expect I'll lose** again – I always do.*
*I **hope they (will) keep** in touch with us.*

6   *be (un)likely to* + infinitive expresses probability.
*The situation **is likely to get** worse.*

7   *be bound to* + infinitive expresses certainty.
*It's a ridiculous plan and it**'s bound to fail**.*

8   *be (just) about to* + infinitive/*be on the point of* + gerund can be used to talk about the immediate future.
*I'll call you back – I**'m just about to go** into a meeting.*

9   *be due to* + infinitive refers to scheduled times.
*The new supermarket **is due to open** in April.*

10   The present simple also refers to scheduled times.
*Hurry up! The bus **leaves** in ten minutes.*

11   *be + to* + infinitive can be used to talk about arrangements.
*Next year's tournament **is to be held** in Frankfurt.*
(See also Section A of Gerunds and Infinitives in Unit 4 on page 219.)

12 The future continuous is used:
  - to talk about actions or events which will be in progress at a certain time in the future.
    Don't call after eight – I'll be watching the match then.
  - to talk about a future action that will happen because it is regular or decided. It can be used to ask about someone's plans politely.
    I'll be seeing Joe later – I'll give this to him then.
    Will you be coming out with us tomorrow night?

13 The future perfect is used to talk about actions and events which will be completed by, or which continue until, a certain time in the future.
    I think we'll have finished the job by Friday.
    Next month I'll have been working here for 10 years.

Unit 9

Creating emphasis

If we want to give particular importance to a person, a thing or a clause in a sentence, we can use these structures: *It is/was … that …* or *What …is/was …*

It was <u>Norman's incredible sense of humour</u> **that** *first attracted me to him.*
What *I find strange* **is** <u>(the fact) that he never talks about his father</u>.

In each case, the underlined part of the sentence is being emphasized.

1 *It is/was … that …* can be used:
  - with *(only)* *when, while* or *not until* to emphasize a (period of) time
    It was while *he was in Spain* **that** *Lennon wrote 'Strawberry Fields Forever'.*
    It wasn't until *he took off his hat* **that** *I recognized him.*
  - with *because* to emphasize reasons
    Perhaps **it's because** *I'm a chef* **that** *people never invite me to their dinner parties.*
  - to emphasize prepositional phrases
    It was on the radio that *I first heard the news.*
  - to emphasize a thing or a person
    'who' can be used in place of 'that' if we are referring to a person.
    It was *Gary* **who** *broke the chair.*
    It's *his left arm* **that's** *broken, not his right one.*

Modal verbs can be used instead of *is* and *was*.
It can't be *my mobile phone* **that's** *ringing – it's switched off.*
It might have been *the fish* **that** *made me feel ill.*

3 *What …is/was …* can be used to emphasize:
  - a noun
    What *I most wanted to see in the Louvre* **was** *the Mona Lisa.*
  - an action or series of actions
    What *you do then* **is (to)** *add the flour and stir it in thoroughly.*
    What *happened* **was (that)** *I left my wallet in the café and had to go back.*

All can be used instead of *What* to mean 'the only thing that'.
All *he (ever) did during the school holiday* **was (to)** *play on his computer.*
All *I really want* **is** *a little house in the countryside.*

Unit 10

Participle clauses

Participle clauses are clauses which begin with a present or past participle. They help to express ideas concisely, and add variety to written English.

1 Participle clauses can be used:
  - instead of relative clauses

I recognize that man **standing** *over there.* (= who is standing)
Three of the people **injured** *in the crash are still in hospital.* (= who were injured)
  - instead of certain conjunctions

because/so
Not wishing *to offend my host, I ate everything on my plate.*

as/while
Looking *out of the window last night, I saw a shooting star.*

when/once/after
Having worked out *how much you can afford to pay for your computer, you need to decide on the model.*

and
He fell off the ladder, **breaking** *a leg and three ribs.*

if
Cooked *in their skins, potatoes retain most of their nutrients.*
  - after the objects of the following verbs: *see, hear, watch, notice, feel* and *find*

Police **found him lying** *unconscious on the kitchen floor.*
I could **hear something moving** *in the bushes.*

2 Note that:
  - Stative verbs (eg *be, want, know*) are not normally used in continuous tenses, but the *-ing* form can be used in participle clauses.
    I am being a very shy person, so I never enjoy going to parties. ✗
    Being *a very shy person, I never enjoy going to parties.* ✔
  - The subject of a participle clause is usually the same as the subject of the main clause.
    Working *as a waitress,* **I** *have all my meals in the restaurant.*

However, it is possible to have a participle clause with a different subject. Instead of:
Having been damaged *by vandals,* **Helen** *had to walk rather than go on her bicycle.* ✗
we can say:
Her bicycle having been damaged by vandals, Helen had to walk. ✔
  - *with* is sometimes used to introduce a different subject.
    With both my parents working *all day,* **I** *have to cook my own lunch.*

Unit 11

Inversion

Certain adverbs and adverbial phrases with a negative or restrictive meaning can be placed at the beginning of a sentence for emphasis. In this case, the position of the subject and verb is reversed, as in question forms. This occurs mainly in written English or more formal speech.

1 Where the main verb is used with an auxiliary verb, the position of the subject and auxiliary verb is reversed.
    I will never lend money to Richard again. (Normal word order)
    Never again will I *lend money to Richard.* (Inversion)

Where no auxiliary verb is present, either *do, does* or *did* is inserted.
    Steve hardly ever turned up on time for his lectures.
    Hardly ever did Steve *turn up on time for his lectures.*

2 Inversion is used:
  - after certain phrases with *not*
    Not since *I was little* **have I** *enjoyed myself so much.*
    Not until *we got to my parents' house* **did we** *realize we'd left all the Christmas presents at home.*
    Not only did he *leave dirty footprints all over our carpet,* **but** *he* **also** *sat on my glasses.*

223

- after certain phrases with *only*
  Only when I tell you **can you** put your books away.
  Only then was I made aware of the potential dangers.
  Further examples: *only recently, only later, only in the last few weeks, only at the end of the lesson*
- after certain phrases with *no*
  On no account must you speak to other candidates.
  Under no circumstances should the door be left open.
  In no way will we give in to their demands.
  At no time were you in any danger.
- after certain frequency adverbs
  Never have I seen such an ugly building.
  Rarely/Seldom does one find antique furniture of this kind in such perfect condition.
  Hardly ever is he in his office when I phone.
- with *No sooner … than…* and *Hardly/Barely/Scarcely … when …*
  No sooner had I got into the shower **than** the phone rang. (= As soon as I got into the shower …)
  Hardly had we finished breakfast **when** we were told it would soon be time for lunch.
- after *Little*, meaning *not at all*
  Little did they realize that their conversation was being recorded. (= They had no idea …)

Unit 12
Conjunctions

Conjunctions connect two clauses in the same sentence.

Reason, result and purpose
eg *as, because, in case, in order (not) to, otherwise, so, so as (not) to, so that*

in case and *so that* can be followed by the present simple to refer to the future.
*Take an umbrella **in case it rains** later on.*
*I'll lend you some gloves **so that you don't get** your hands dirty.*

Contrast and concession
eg *although, but, however, (even) though, whereas, while/whilst*

As a conjunction, *however* means 'no matter how'.
*You can decorate your room **however** you want.*

in spite of the fact that and *despite the fact that* can also connect two clauses
*She continued to support him, **despite the fact that** he had treated her so badly.*

Time
eg *after, as, as soon as, before, by the time, hardly, no sooner, once, since, then, until, when, whenever, while*

Many of these conjunctions are followed by a present tense or present perfect to refer to the future.
***Once** it **stops/has stopped** raining, we'll go out.*

For information on *hardly* and *no sooner*, see Inversion in Unit 11 above.

Linking adverbials

Linking adverbials connect one sentence with another. They frequently appear at the beginning of a sentence, and are followed by a comma.

Reason and result
eg *As a result, Because of this, Consequently, For this reason, On account of this, Therefore*

*There was a power cut this morning. **Consequently,** I couldn't do any work on the computer.*

Contrast and concession
eg *All the same, At the same time, By/In comparison, By/In contrast, Even so, However, In spite of/Despite this, Likewise, Nevertheless, On the contrary, On the other hand, Similarly*

On the contrary is used to introduce a positive statement which confirms a negative one.
On the other hand introduces a point which contrasts with a previous one.
*The lottery win did not bring happiness. **On the contrary,** it caused the breakup of his marriage.*
*It's a rather ugly city to live in. **On the other hand,** house prices here are very low.*

Time
eg *After that/Afterwards, Before that/Beforehand, By that time, Eventually, Ever since then, Finally, From that time on, Initially, In the end, In the meantime/Meanwhile, Until then*

*The bed's being delivered next week. **In the meantime,** I'm sleeping on the sofa.*

Addition
eg *Additionally, Besides (this), Apart from this, As well as this, In addition to this, First of all, Secondly, Finally, Furthermore, Moreover, What is more*

*… and the campsite shop rarely opened on time. **Furthermore,** the staff there were rude to me on a number of occasions.*

Modal verbs: *must, need, should, ought to*

A Must

1 *must* and *have to*
must + infinitive is used to give orders or strong advice, or to tell oneself what is necessary. The authority comes from the speaker.
*All questions **must be answered**.*
*You really **must see** Russell Crowe's new film.*
*I **must remember** to get some bread.*

Although not a modal verb, *have to* + infinitive is also used to talk about obligations. The authority comes from someone other than the speaker.
*We **have to wear** a swimming cap in the indoor pool.*

2 *mustn't* and *don't have to*
mustn't expresses prohibition; *don't have to* expresses lack of obligation or necessity.
*You **mustn't touch** this, darling – it's very hot.*
*You **don't have to come** if you don't want to.*

3 *must have done* and *had to do*
must have + past participle is used to speculate about past situations; *had to* + infinitive expresses past obligation or necessity.
*Sean's late – he **must have got** stuck in a traffic jam.*
*The bus broke down so I **had to walk**.*

B Should/Ought to

1 *should* and *ought to* + infinitive are used to give advice or express opinions about what is right and wrong. *should have* and *ought to have* + past participle can be used to criticize past actions, express regret or talk about things which were supposed to happen but didn't.
*You **shouldn't play** with matches – it's dangerous.*
*You really **shouldn't have shouted** at him like that.*
*We **ought to have asked** Jill if she wanted to come.*
*Where's Bob? He **should have been** here ages ago.*

2 *should* and *ought* can also be used to talk about probability.
*If you leave now, you **should be/ought to be** there by midday.*

C Need

1 *need* and *need to*
need + infinitive is not used in ordinary statements and is very rare in questions; *need to* + infinitive is much more common for expressing necessity.
*I **need to get** some new shoes. (not: I **need get** …✗)*
*What **do we need to take** with us?*
*My brother-in-law and his family stayed with us at Christmas. **Need I say** more?*

2 *needn't* and *don't need to*

Usually, there is no difference in meaning between *needn't* + infinitive and *don't need to* + infinitive: they both indicate a lack of obligation to do something.

However, *needn't* usually refers to immediate necessity and tends to be used to give permission not to do something; the authority comes from the speaker.
You **needn't come** tomorrow if you don't want to.

don't need to tends to indicate general necessity; the authority does not come from the speaker. *don't have to* can be used in the same way.
You **don't need to/don't have to spend** a fortune to keep fit.

3 *needn't have done* and *didn't need to do*

needn't have + past participle is used to talk about an action which was performed but which was unnecessary.
You **needn't have bought** those batteries – we've got plenty in the drawer.

didn't need to + infinitive is used to talk about an action which was unnecessary. It usually indicates that the subject did not perform the action.
I **didn't need to spend** very long on my homework last night – it was quite easy.

Unit 13
Comparisons

A The following structures and expressions can be used to talk about similarities and differences.

1 Comparing past with present
Where once he was at the top of his profession, he **now** struggles to find work.
We **now** depend on technology **more than ever before**.

2 *The* + comparative, *the* + comparative is used when one thing is the result of another.
The more he laughed, **the angrier** she became.
The easier I find a subject, **the less** I enjoy it.

3 *as* + auxiliary + subject
He **lived** to a ripe old age, **as did** his wife and children.

4 *Like* is used with nouns, pronouns or gerunds to make comparisons.
She ran **like the wind** back to her flat.
Getting him to talk is **like getting** blood out of a stone.

As is used with nouns to describe someone or something's job, role or function.
She used her scarf **as a bandage**.
He's just started work **as a postman**.

As is used with a verb phrase to make comparisons. *Like* is used informally, and is considered incorrect by some.
She believes, **as I do**, that the President is wrong.

5 *as* + adjective/adverb + *as* can be used to show similarities. *so* can be used instead of the first *as* in negative sentences.
You're **as stubborn as** your father.
He's **not so silly as** he looks.

so can be used in following structures.
He is known **not so much** for his singing **as/but** for his charity work.
If you can park close to the station, then **so much the better**.

Note the position of the article when *so* and *such* are used before nouns.
Nothing gives **so bad an impression as** arriving late for your interview.
It isn't quite **such a cold winter as** last year.

B The following words and expressions can be used to modify comparisons.

1 With comparatives
a bit, a little, slightly, much, (quite) a lot, far, significantly, considerably, three times etc, a great deal
I'm feeling **considerably better than** I did yesterday.

2 With superlatives
by far, easily, by a long way
China is the company's **largest** market, **by a long way**.
She is **by far the most gifted** musician in the band.

3 With *as … as…*
not quite, (not) nearly, almost, just, half, twice, three times etc, nothing like, nowhere near
She earns **twice as much as** me and works **half as many** hours.

4 With *the same … as …*
not quite, (not) nearly, almost, just, (very) much
I have **much the same** opinion **as** my colleague.

Unit 14
Noun phrases

A **Noun + noun** is used when referring to:
- what things are made of
  a silver spoon   a metal door   a stone wall
- products from dead animals
  a lamb chop   a leopard skin   a chicken sandwich
- things that occur or appear regularly
  the evening shift   a Saturday job   daytime television
- duration. The first noun is hyphenated and in the singular.
  *a five-hour delay   a twenty-minute speech
  a two-week holiday*
- containers
  a beer bottle   a tea cup   a biscuit tin

Noun + noun is also used in a large number of commonly accepted compound nouns. The two nouns describe a single idea.
a shop window   a door handle   a fire engine

B **Noun + 's/s' + noun** is used when referring to:
- possession by a particular person or animal
  Sally's bicycle   the dog's bone   my children's toys
  An adjective can be placed between the two nouns.
  my children's new toys
- something that is used by people or animals in general
  children's shoes   women's clothes   an ants' nest
  Adjectives are placed before the two nouns.
  a monthly women's magazine
- an action done to or by a particular person
  *Mr Smith's resignation   her husband's murder
  the Labour Party's defeat*
  The 'noun *of* noun' structure is preferred if the modifying noun is a long phrase.
  the resignation of several members of the committee
- products from living animals
  goat's milk   a hen's egg   sheep's wool
- things that occurred at a specific time
  *this evening's newspaper   yesterday's storm
  last Saturday's programme*
- parts of people's and animals' bodies
  the boy's foot   a sheep's head   the dog's tail
- duration, as an alternative to the noun + noun structure
  two years' absence   a day's work   an hour's delay

C **Noun + preposition + noun** is used:
- for containers and their contents
  a bottle of beer   a cup of tea   a tin of biscuits
- with words like *top, bottom, side, edge, back, front, beginning, middle* and *end* to indicate a part of something
  *the top of the picture   the back of the book
  the middle of the week*
  There are a number of common exceptions: eg *a mountain top, the day's end, the water's edge*
- to describe the characteristics of a person or thing
  *a man of average build   a place of great beauty
  a ring of little value*
- where no commonly accepted compound noun exists
  *a book about parks   the roof of the house
  a woman on the radio*
- in a large number of collocations
  a source of inspiration   an invasion of privacy

Listening scripts

1 Aiming high

 1.1–1.3

Extract one
(I = Interviewer; S = Steve)

I: Thanks for being here, Steve, especially when you've got the pressure of a European tour. Now you know what I'm going to ask. You won 'Best New Artist' yesterday, and you didn't turn up to collect the award. Why?

S: You know, when we heard we'd been nominated – and we knew who the other nominees were – well, just for a brief moment I guess we got a bit of a kick out of it. I mean the other bands are guys we really respect, but we've always used our music to attack capitalism. It would be incredibly hypocritical to accept an award from the corporate world.

I: OK. I get that, but even if you have no respect for the music industry, it was your fans that voted for you.

S: I don't know if that's true. Look, we've been together for four years now, and the people who liked our music from the start, the ones who keep coming to the gigs, they know what we're about, our politics, our principles. And they wouldn't go in for that kind of thing. But, you know, you get your first number one single and the mainstream music listeners think you're a new band and they go out and vote for you. For a moment in time you're on everyone's iPod, and then, then you're deleted.

Extract two
(I = Interviewer; R = Richard)

I: Twenty years in the game, Richard, and no one has yet come close to breaking the records you set. What do you put your success down to?

R: Well, I've had a lot of experience after all that time, endless hours of practice. But for me it's more to do with the psychological approach: maintaining discipline and focus, setting an aim and not getting distracted, no matter whether the game is going well or against us. I reckon for some sports it's about a physical advantage you're born with, but with cricket, it's applying your mind in the right way.

I: Is there any advice you'd give to up-and-coming young players?

R: Not advice as such. Whether a match has been a resounding success or its ended in failure, we each have to analyse our strengths and weaknesses, and use that to get the best out of our next team performance. Something I find to be a negative development, though, I'm afraid, is the rather aggressive manner in which certain young players celebrate their performance, I mean the way they now punch the air, and those other gestures of victory. Cricket is supposed to be a dignified game; there's no place for showing off.

Extract three
(I = Interviewer; L = Lily)

I: Lily, for listeners who have maybe never heard of *40-hour Famine*, can you tell us a little bit about it?

L: Yeah, sure. Well, it's about young people, students mainly, not eating food for 40 hours, although water is allowed. The idea is to promote a bit more awareness of what it's like for poor people who are starving because of famine. Many students are too young to volunteer to go overseas and help out directly and they haven't got the cash to make monthly donations to charity, but taking part in *40-hour Famine* is something they can do, to show they care. And of course, the sponsorship they get does go to excellent charities.

I: And this is the second year you've taken part?

L: Yes, last year I only made it to 35. I felt really dizzy and had to give up. But no-one made me feel like I'd let them down, they were simply concerned with my health. I thought 'Oh well, I'll just have to have another go. I've got a year to prepare and next time round nothing will stop me.' And look … in another four hours I will have fulfilled that promise to myself.

2 Times change

 1.4

Hello, good evening. Well, as you know I'm here to talk about my great passion in life – time capsules. Now if you're not sure, a time capsule is a container filled with typical objects from a particular time and in most cases buried underground for safekeeping. The idea behind this, of course, is that future generations will be able to learn about life in the past when they open up the capsule and study the objects.

So, when did all this burying business begin? Well, the idea of storing objects for posterity in this way goes back over a century to the nineteen hundreds. The problem was, and indeed still is to some extent, that most of these have been lost to history. 'Why is this?' you might ask. Well, it's either because of thieves and the fact that the capsules weren't sufficiently well protected, or – and this is the most usual explanation – because no one bothered to keep proper records and we don't know for sure where the capsules are.

To give you just one example, they buried seventeen of them back in the Thirties in California in a place called Corona – and not one of them has ever been found. Amazing, isn't it? And do you remember the popular television programme M*A*S*H? Well, in 1983, some of the cast put costumes and props from the show in a capsule and buried it in a secret ceremony, refusing to tell anyone not connected with the show where exactly they'd put it. All they'd say was that it was somewhere in the 20th Century Film Studios' car park in Hollywood. Now, of course, they've built a huge hotel on the site and no one knows where on earth to look for it.

But the, er, the modern-day passion for time capsules really began in the late nineteen thirties, when a man called Dr Thornwell Jacobs, the President of Oglethorpe University in Atlanta, was doing some research into ancient civilizations. Well, he was so frustrated by the lack of accurate information that he came up with a plan to ensure that the same thing wouldn't happen to future generations. He built the 'Crypt of Civilization' – that's what he called his time capsule – in an area the size of a swimming pool, in the basement of one of the university buildings, Hearst Hall. You can still see it today, in fact. But you can't see any of the contents – the crypt won't be opened for another 6,000 years!

It's got all sorts of things – newsreels, important radio speeches, er, scientific instruments and – wait for it – over 640,000 pages of material on microfilm, including the Bible, the Koran, the Iliad and Dante's Inferno. But it's not all serious stuff. There's also a Donald Duck doll, and literally thousands of everyday objects like cooking utensils, ornaments and tools. Very sensibly, Dr Jacobs didn't put in any real items of jewellery, because he thought that might attract robbers. But he did include models of necklaces and earrings, as well as papier maché fruit and vegetables, and even a small capsule of beer.

Since then, of course, all sorts of people have put all sorts of objects into time capsules. Now, if you're interested in burying your own time capsule, I can…

 1.5–1.9

1

I'd given up just about everything – the job, the house, the car – and gone to Spain to be with my husband. And six months later it was all over. Both of us believed we'd rushed into marriage too soon and there was little that made us compatible as spouses. At the same time, we felt the friendship that had drawn us together in the first place was just too valuable to throw away and the only way to save it was by splitting up. The thing is, I remember hugging Alfonso at the airport, boarding the flight to Manchester and waiting to feel some kind of relief. It didn't come. By the time we landed, I had this awful sense that we'd rushed just as fast into a divorce. A year has passed and I still can't help wishing we'd put a bit more effort into staying together.

2

I was a no-hoper at school, see. No one had heard of dyslexia in those days, so my teachers just classed me as an 'idiot'. I might have behaved myself later if I'd been given a bit more attention then but I was told time and time again that I was going to be a failure. It surprised no one, including myself, that I ended up in prison, but all that time on my hands gave me the chance to think. I realized I'd turned out just how they said and I wanted to prove it could be different. I did a law degree while I was inside, and it was tough, I tell you, but since I got out, I've never looked back. I'm about to become a partner in a law firm and that's an achievement that gives me immense satisfaction.

3

I'd always wanted to do voluntary work, ever since I qualified as a nurse. Marriage and children always got in the way of my plans, though, but now that the kids were older, there didn't seem any reason to put it off, even though I was coming up to my fiftieth birthday. And once I'd got their backing, there was no stopping me, really. Of course, I missed them all when I was there, but I just threw myself into my work. I had to really. It was a very isolated rural area – there was no running water, no medicines and so much poverty. But I can't tell you how much I appreciate the fact that I was given the chance to go – it was real eye-opener and I learnt so much about their culture and about myself – for that I'll always be thankful.

4

I'd worked my way up to supervisor and got just about as far as I could go in the company. It was a responsible position and gave us a certain amount of security and I suppose that's why I stuck it for so long. Inevitably though, it got to the point where the routine just got too much. I wasn't developing professionally and nothing about the job pushed me to better myself. So when Sue suggested taking over a café franchise, I jumped at the chance. Neither of us had a background in catering but we refused to be daunted. We had to learn all aspects of the business in a very short time but I found it all very thrilling, and still do. Even now I wake up every day really looking forward to going in to work – being in a new environment and dealing with the fast pace.

5

I'd been biting my nails since I was a three-year-old, apparently. It had never really bothered me before, despite my parents' constant moaning. They made me put this liquid on them called 'No-bite'. Tasted horrible, it did – until I got used to it, that was. When I started work, though, I began noticing the looks of mild horror on the customers' faces. Every time I was wrapping up a present or was just resting my hands on the counter, I could sense them staring and it made me incredibly self-conscious. So I had these plastic tips put on and that gave my nails the chance to grow. No one notices them anymore so the problem is essentially solved but it has nothing to do with my will power. It's actually humiliating for a 23-year-old to be wearing plastic tips. It's a secret I would hate my boyfriend to find out.

3 Gathering information

 1.10

(P = Presenter; H = Helena)
P: With me today on *Infospeak* is journalist and writer, Helena Drysdale. Hello, Helena, and welcome to the programme.
H: Thank you. Good morning.
P: Helena, you spent the last two years travelling round Europe doing research for a forthcoming book. What were you trying to find out?
H: Yes, we went in search of Europe's minority languages to determine exactly what state they're all in, particularly given today's climate of mass culture and so on. We travelled right up to northern Scandinavia and the Arctic circle, where the Sami reindeer herders live, and we got down as far as Corsica and Sardinia in the sunny Mediterranean. Then there were the mountains of northern Italy where Ladin is spoken, and we had a rather wet and rainy time in Brittany in the west of France with its Celtic Breton. Thirteen countries and fifteen minor languages in all.
P: By 'us' and 'we', you're referring to your family, of course.
H: Yes, my husband Richard, and our two young children, Tallulah and Xanthe – not forgetting the Mob, of course, our trusty mobile home.
P: What was that like? Two years together in a mobile home can't have been easy.
H: It got a little cramped at times, particularly when the weather kept us in. The kids couldn't run around, they'd start playing up, tempers would overheat, and everyone fell out. But apart from that, fine.
P: Yes, I can see. And how did you go about gathering your information? What were your sources?
H: I did some research in the library and on the Internet after we came back, but the only real way to get the kind of information I was looking

for was by actually talking to people. We met writers, teachers and artists, who generally gave a more intellectual analysis of the situation, and we were able to balance that with the more down-to-earth, personalized accounts of people in the rural areas. That's where many of these languages are most frequently spoken and also where people, particularly the older generation, seemed less reluctant to open up and give us their honest opinion.
P: And I imagine they had some very interesting stories to tell about the past.
H: Yes, indeed. For example, we often heard stories of punishments that people received for speaking their own language at school. One old lady in the south of France told us how she used to have to wear a stone or a stick round her neck if she was caught speaking Provençal. She had to keep it on until someone else committed the same offence and then they'd have to wear it. And whoever had it at the end of the day was made to pay a fine, or sometimes even beaten.
P: Hard to believe, really.
H: Mm. She's able to laugh about it now, but at the time it was considered deeply shaming to have to wear *le symbole*, as she called it. Sometimes it could be a wooden shoe or a pottery cow, which represented the country bumpkin, someone to be despised.
P: And were these punishments effective? Did they contribute to the decline of some of these languages?
H: Yes, they lowered the status of a language. But sometimes they helped to keep a language going – at least in the short term, anyway. They caused resentment and made people more defiant towards the authorities. You know, it can be a bit like pruning a tree – if you cut it back, it grows much stronger. But there were and still are other more powerful forces which represent a much bigger threat to the survival of Europe's minority languages.
P: By that you mean globalization, I presume.
H: That's right. And tourism. Now although tourism can give a language status by attracting outside interest in it, it can also have a negative effect on local cultures. You know, in one place we visited, the natives moan about the influx of outsiders and how they buy up land at giveaway prices to build holiday cottages, and how it's destroying their culture, and so on. But then the very same people are selling up their farms so they can run hotels or open souvenir shops. Understandable, perhaps, but they're encouraging the very thing they're complaining about.
P: Are languages like Sami and Provençal endangered species, then?
H: Well, I think it's true to say that if no

227

positive action is taken, they'll simply die out. The problem is that some people are indifferent, and even hostile to their own language. They think it's of no use in the modern world, which they so desperately want to be part of. Fortunately, though, there are enough people around who realize that to lose your mother tongue is like losing a part of yourself. Your language makes you who you are. And if you spoke a different language, you'd be a different person. But people on their own can only do so much. It really is up to the European Union to legislate to ensure the survival of minority languages.

P: And how exactly do you legislate to save a language?

H: Well, I think there are several things you can do. Firstly, of course, the EU would have to bring in…

4 Work time

 1.11–1.15

1
I was told the best way to prepare for an interview is by going to the company's website and finding out everything you can about them. The idea, of course, is that it creates a good impression and proves that you are keen on working for them because they can see you've done your homework. The trouble was that they hadn't done theirs – the webpage hadn't been updated for over a year, so I asked all these questions about products they didn't produce and subsidiaries that no longer existed. They must have thought I wasn't very well prepared. It wasn't my fault, though, and I kind of lost enthusiasm for the job once I found out what had happened. I mean, it's a bit slack, isn't it?

2
So there I was the night before, in the living room talking to the dog. A bit strange, you might think, and you'd probably be right. But I was getting ready for the next day, you see. The dog was the interviewer, and I was trying out all my questions and answers on him. I'm not sure that's what the writer of the article had in mind when she said, 'Rehearse the situation with a friend', but it seemed like a good idea to me. Anyway, it was all a bit of a waste of time really. I overslept the next morning and by the time I got there they'd already taken somebody on.

3
'Now you're not to get all uptight and on edge, like you normally do,' was what my mum said. And that's more or less what the careers teacher told us at school: 'Projecting self-confidence at an interview is vital for success'. Those were his exact words. So I put on my best suit to give me that confidence, cleaned my shoes and off I went. Well, my hands were shaking so much, you wouldn't

believe it. I nearly spilt my coffee down my trousers. I think I managed to hide it, though. Course, what I couldn't hide was the fact that I'd failed my maths GCSE. They wouldn't take me on without it. Shame, really – the money wasn't too bad.

4
'Don't lean back in your chair', he says. 'If you do that, it might look as though you're trying just a bit too hard to cover up your nerves. Either that or you're not interested in the job.' So according to this Dr Benson, it's advisable to lean forward, keep your legs uncrossed and smile confidently. Well, I did all that. In fact, I smiled so much my face began to ache. But they somehow seemed to realize that I don't normally walk around with a permanent grin from ear to ear – they said they were looking for lively, bubbly people for their sales team, and they weren't convinced that I fitted the bill.

5
I saw this video in the university careers office where they recommended imagining the interviewer in the bath, playing with a plastic duck, of all things. The idea is that they're only human, so there's nothing to be frightened of. So, anyway, I thought about the type of questions they might ask me and I got to the interview about half an hour early so I could go over the answers I was going to give. But, bath or no bath, the interviewer turned out to be not so human after all. It was like an interrogation, and the things he asked were really tricky – nothing like what I'd prepared for. I just didn't know what to say. I felt pretty sick about the whole thing afterwards, I can tell you.

 1.16

Time, ladies and gentlemen, is one of our greatest assets, and in this fast-moving competitive world, poor management of our time is a major cause of stress both in the workplace and at home. The first and most essential element of effective time management is forward planning. If you start the morning by mapping out what you hope to achieve during the day, you can go a long way to avoiding unnecessary frustration and wasted effort. Be realistic, though, in terms of what you hope to achieve in the time available, and think through carefully how and when you will achieve it. Unmet expectations will only serve to put you under more pressure, to create more stress – and you'll only have yourself to blame if that happens.

Of course, tiredness – rather than any lack of ability – can often present a major obstacle to our obtaining the goals we've set ourselves, or indeed to meeting the deadlines that others have set for us. If that's the case, stop, turn your computer off, take a break. If you feel you can't go on, or you're just too

snowed under, don't make yourself ill. Work should always take second place to your health. It can be counterproductive to carry on regardless, particularly if the next day you have to phone in sick and take time off work.

And also, if time is against you, if you're pressed for time, be prepared to adapt to the circumstances – don't worry if what you produce is less than wonderful. We cannot, we should not always aim to achieve perfection. It slows us down, it reduces productivity and means we have no time for other tasks. Good enough is still good, and in all probability no one will notice the difference. And the same principles apply in the home as they do at work. A similar dose of self-discipline is needed when we take on the household chores. Limit the amount of housework you try to do in a day, lower your expectations and relax if the shirts you've just ironed still have creases. It doesn't matter.

Because ultimately, let's face it, what we all work for is to make time for ourselves, to free up time for the things we really want to do outside of work. It's essential to set aside enough time to pursue your interests, to do the things which are most fulfilling for you in life. Many people fail to achieve the right balance between work and relaxation and once again, stress is the outcome. And just a word of warning here – if by relaxation you understand slumping in front of the television, think again. It is a poor use of time, and it usually ends up making you feel more tired, and time-pressured than before.

Now, technology has done a great deal to …

5 Getting on

 1.17

(P = Presenter; J = Julie; B = Bryan)

P: Now in this special programme on the state of marriage in Britain today, we ask two people about their experiences and views on the topic, Julie Sanders and Bryan Simpson. Now, you're both married – not to each other, I hasten to add! – so perhaps I should start by asking you both 'Why?', given that in this country over one in three marriages end in divorce. Julie?

J: Well, I'd been living with Peter for just over a year – in fact, we'd recently celebrated our first anniversary in the flat – when suddenly, one evening, he got down on one knee and asked me to marry him. It was so romantic – I didn't have the heart to turn him down! No, but of course, we'd spoken about it before and we both agreed it was the right thing to do – a natural stage in our relationship and a way of making it official. And of course, our parents were delighted!

P: Was it a church wedding?

J: Oh yes, the whole works. I'd always dreamed of having a wedding dress and walking down the aisle. We had nearly 300 guests – it was all very lavish. Peter didn't share my enthusiasm at first – particularly when he thought of the cost of it all – but as the big day got nearer he worried less about the money and more about making sure it'd be the best day of our lives.

P: And you, Bryan? You've done it twice, haven't you? Did you know that you are twice as likely to get divorced if you and your partner have done so already?

B: It doesn't sound too good, does it? But anyway, Chrissie – my current wife – and I got married more for the tax advantages than any need to make a public statement or keep our parents happy. At the time there were a whole load of benefits and allowances for married couples which we wouldn't have had access to if we'd just lived together. So it was just a quick registry-office job for us – much cheaper and less fuss.

P: What about love? Didn't that come into it at all?

B: Oh yes, of course, but only in the sense that Chrissie was the sort of person I knew I could grow to love more, rather than someone I was besotted with and who'd end up disappointing me. And that's the way she saw things as well. There wasn't a great deal of passion in our romance but we do have a good marriage based on mutual respect and we still enjoy each other's company.

P: That's good to hear. Julie, you've been married for just six months now. How is your marriage working out? Has it changed your relationship?

J: Well, it's a little early to say, yet. We're still very much in the honeymoon period, I suppose. But it's not all domestic bliss – I notice that we do argue more than before, but it's usually about trivial things, so it's over and done with in about half an hour. So far we haven't had any fights over major issues – we haven't been throwing plates at each other, or anything like that!

P: Have you ever reached that stage in your marriage, Bryan?

B: Well I haven't, but I'm not sure how close Chrissie's come to it… No, but there have been some difficult times. Having my own business put a tremendous strain on my first marriage – having to work twelve hours a day, six days a week doesn't do much for a relationship. So I sold the business soon after I married Chrissie. Now our 'major issue', as Julie describes it, has been the children. With two it was fine, but three proved to be something of a crowd – at least until we got over the nappies and bottle stage. Now we don't feel quite so restricted by it all – we're not tired and irritable all the time.

P: And how do you both see the future? The average marriage lasts just over ten years. Will you both last that long?

J: I sincerely hope so – we've just taken out a 25-year mortgage! No, I do feel very positive about the future. I can see the two of us being retired together. There'll be bad times, I know, but you've just got to work at it and be truthful with each other. Getting divorced is the easy way out – the hard bit is to stick at it and work through the problems.

P: Bryan?

B: Ask me in three years' time. There's just nothing certain about the future – least of all in this marriage business.

P: Julie, Bryan, thank you for coming in. After the break we'll hear from Marriage Guidance Counsellor, Margie Freeburn, who'll…

 1.18–1.20

Extract one
(I = interviewer; M = Miriam)

I: Miriam – the curtain goes up on your new play next week – are you at all anxious or is opening night an occasion which no longer bothers you?

M: Well it depends on the production but in this case, I've been privileged again to have Malcolm Rush as a director. He doesn't care whether you're exhausted, mentally, physically, emotionally – it's immaterial, he'll just continue pushing until every scene is simply perfect. You don't just learn the part – you live it, which takes away any fears you might have of not being able to persuade an audience you're real.

I: Malcolm does have a reputation of being quite the dictator. No one dares voice their opinion, I hear.

M: Well I do! Malcolm is entirely willing to listen to your point of view once you gain his respect. When we're working on a play, it's a two-way process in which one person comes up with an idea – we see how it works out – and then we don't hold back on any constructive criticism. If you're relatively new to the stage, he's going to be tough with you – but once you've proved yourself, it's all about co-operation and being open to changes.

Extract Two
(A = Anya; S = Stephen)

A: I have to say, Stephen, I was expecting more from this director. The whole thing seemed terribly formulaic to me – we have two mismatched cops, one of whom plays by the rules and the other is a rebel. Isn't this the kind of scenario we've seen too many times already?

S: The tense relationship between the detectives is definitely a cliché, I admit, but I think the quality of the acting makes this work far superior to others in the genre. And the plot, which is actually quite sophisticated, keeps you guessing all the way through. It's not just relying on stunts and explosions to fill up time.

A: Well, the female characters – the wife and the girlfriend – have more to say than usual. They do seem to be there for valid reasons, rather than decoration.

S: And unusually for a commercial film, the two heroes, or anti-heroes if you like, do not suddenly develop great affection for one another. There's a level of respect – a recognition that the other man is a professional, someone you can depend upon to do the job and who will never be corrupted. But when it's all finally over, they want nothing more to do with one another. They just both find one another offensive in some way.

Extract three
(I = Interviewer; D = David)

I: So David, with the next rally less than twelve hours away, how confident are you of holding your position in front?

D: Well – the team has done an incredible job sorting out all the problems with the car – it's running at peak performance now. The big issue, as you may know, is that my co-driver, Scott King, broke his leg last week and so that's it – he's out for the foreseeable future. Fortunately for us Eddy Houseman stepped in at the last minute, though of course, he's never partnered me before, which is a bit of a concern. At least the conditions are favourable, the worst of the ice has cleared, just a few patches left we can deal with.

I: Scott's been with you from the start, hasn't he?

D: Yes, people often underrate the co-driver's role, the glory always goes to the driver. But it's Scott who has the map and the notes, without him I'd be truly driving blind. You have to have complete faith that what he says is right, I have to know exactly how fast I can take a corner, and be sure that we don't end up rolling into a ditch. That's not to say that he's always to blame for every crash! And I don't know how Eddy's going to deal with my temper, Scott's got used to it after all this time …

6 All in the mind?

1.21–1.25

1

I went to, if you like, 'normal' school Monday to Thursday, and I didn't particularly excel in anything, and if that'd been my sole form of learning experience, I probably wouldn't be where I am today, I mean playing in front of huge European audiences. You see, on Fridays I went to an independent school, where they set up a project for the day, say something on volcanoes. You learnt the usual stuff but then they encouraged you to respond in your own way. So for example, the arty kids would make a sculpture, the practical-minded kids built models, and I used to get the instruments out and compose something, just in the corner by myself at first, but then I gained confidence. For me, that's what education should be about, getting kids to express themselves, to use their imagination as a means of developing their abilities.

2

I think I got into this profession partly as a reaction to my own teachers, I wanted to show them how teaching should be done. You know, there's nothing worse than when a teenager has a go at something and then they're criticized for getting it wrong. It humiliates them, makes them reluctant to speak out in front of who they see as the brainy kids. My colleagues and I all have the attitude that participation should be rewarded. See – rather than just telling them, 'You're wrong' it's better to help them out with a few more leading questions that'll direct them to the right answer. In that way you're sending the message that it's better to have a go even if their answer isn't quite right than sit there in silence and be excluded.

3

There was never any doubt that we were going to send Andrew to boarding school – it's a tradition that goes back four generations in our family – although Andrew is back with us at weekends and I only ever returned for the holidays. The academic advantage is clear – with far smaller classes you get greater individual attention. That allows you to really master a subject. But also, the reason why this kind of private education system works is that the whole ethos is about becoming self-sufficient – it is up to the individual student to ensure they spend a good amount of time on their homework or studying in the library. It is up to them to be in class on time and keep their rooms in order. That kind of discipline is invaluable when it comes to the real world.

4

For the last thirty years or so, the majority of schools have allowed boys and girls to study side by side. Whereas their integration within the classroom may benefit them in terms of their social development, the studies we have carried out show that boys consistently underperform when learning alongside girls. Our investigations were based on observations within classrooms that we visited as well as the examination results from a hundred schools over the last three years. Many parents find the notion of educating their son or daughter separately from members of the opposite sex rather old-fashioned, but I believe that school should provide the opportunity for a learner to do as

well as they possibly can. While not every child may be naturally gifted, it is possible to develop their intelligence to a far greater extent in the right learning environment.

5

My father was rather unconventional and he took it upon himself to educate me at home. This often involved visiting castles, art galleries, and of course, the wonderful Science Museum. And that's where it all began for me: I was fascinated by the models of atoms and by the early microscopes. I would read up about the stuff I'd seen at home and my father would always say 'When you're ready, we'll have a little test and see what you can remember,' but there was no strict schedule. He knew that it takes time to absorb information. In my laboratory I have to do everything with extreme care and it is vital you do not rush things, but the end result makes it all worthwhile. The same approach should be applied to education.

 1.26

We've all seen images of the TV hypnotist who manages to get members of the audience doing outrageous things in front of the cameras – shy accountants doing Elvis impersonations or reserved librarians declaring their love for items of furniture. But there is a serious side to hypnotism – and a history.

Born in 1733, the Austrian physician Dr Anton Mesmer moved to the French capital in 1778 at the age of 45, taking with him a revolutionary new healing method. 'Mesmerism' was based on the idea that each living body contains a potent therapeutic force which he called 'animal magnetism'. Mesmer claimed that he – or any other trained individual – could control this force to cure a range of conditions including deafness, rheumatism and even paralysis. His success had members of high society flocking to his dimly-lit rooms for treatment. Surrounded by astrological symbols decorating the walls, patients were told to sit in tubs of water, while Mesmer used iron bars and other gadgets to harness their magnetic force and effect a cure. At a time when anaesthetics were unknown to medicine, mesmerism was used by some early nineteenth century practitioners to relieve pain during operations. The word 'hypnotism' was first used in 1841 by the surgeon James Braid, who defined mesmerism as 'neurohypnology', or the science of sleep. In fact, it was the Englishman Braid who first used the familiar swinging watch to hypnotize his patients. The watch may seem something of a cliché, but it does serve a practical purpose. Imitating what happens when we dream, hypnosis causes the left brain, the side associated with logic and reason, to switch off, allowing the right brain, the side of fantasies and imagery, to take over. To

achieve this, hypnotists get the left brain to focus on something monotonous such as the swinging watch, often accompanying this with a low droning voice – the typical 'Your eyes are getting heavy, you are falling into a deep sleep, a very deep sleep.' Many other aids have been used to hypnotize people, though, including chloroform, magnets applied to the head or magical symbols painted on card.

Once the right side of the brain is in control, it will respond to the hypnotist's suggestions in a dream-like way, treating everything he or she says as if it were true. Hypnotherapists claim that by making suggestions in this way they can do such things as cure insomnia or encourage patients to lose weight. Apparently, people can be made to believe that chocolate tastes of petrol or that beer smells of rotting food. Of course, this type of treatment has its detractors, sceptics who say it is the person's existing decision to change and not hypnotism that has the effect. However, it is now widely believed that hypnotism does have its place in medicine, and is especially effective with illnesses that have a psychological basis – stomach problems, skin disorders and chronic headaches, to name but a few.

Some of these problems may have their origins in childhood, and age regression, when the patient relives their childhood, is another area of hypnotism…

7 Feeling good
 1.27

(P = Presenter; DE = Dr Evans; L = Lynnie)

P: In search of a more youthful appearance, many people nowadays are turning to Botox, the botulism toxin which is purified and used in small doses to remove unwanted wrinkles. With me is Dr Duncan Evans, who regularly turns up at parties to inject the guests with the toxin, and Lynnie Highfield, one of Dr Evans' patients and a regular Botox party-goer. Dr Evans, perhaps I should begin by asking why this treatment takes place at parties, and not in a surgery?

DE: That's very simple, really. It's easier, and more convenient, for people to go to a social gathering at a friend's house, than to give up their valuable time getting into central London. When I first started out in this business, I'd often be asked to go to the homes of the rich and famous, the type of people who didn't want to get caught by the press going into a clinic. Now, though, it's mainly people who've simply got too much going on in their lives to justify making the journey in.

P: Is that your case, Lynnie?

L: Yes, it is. Plus of course we have a good time. I've been to several parties in the last couple of years and you tend to meet up with the same people. That's largely because the benefits of the injection tend to wear off after three or four months so we all keep going back for more.

P: Is it painful?

L: Nowhere near as painful as having your legs waxed, I can tell you! Just a slight discomfort as the needle goes in, that's all. And there are no serious side-effects – or so Dr Evans tells us – just some minor bruising and an outside chance of getting some fluey, cold-like symptoms.

P: So, Dr Evans, how does it work? Why would anyone want to have a poison injected into their body?

DE: Well, yes, poison it most certainly is, and a deadly one at that. But injected in small quantities into the forehead it does nothing more than paralyse the muscles that cause frown lines and wrinkles. Different people use it for different reasons – to make them feel better, to look younger, to enable them to get work on television – whatever. Of course, I need to set a good example if I want to convince people of the benefits of the treatment, so I regularly hand over the needle to my wife, who does it for me. She's a qualified nurse, so I have every confidence in her.

P: Does it work for you?

DE: Well, I make a living, if that's what you mean, but perhaps I should have started younger – as you can see, I've still got one or two faint lines there.

P: And how about you, Lynnie? Why do you have the injections?

L: For me it's a way of growing old gracefully. I mean, we all use moisturizer, we all take care of ourselves. I think it's just an extension of that. Many people might baulk at the price, but I think it's fairly affordable. It's certainly worth doing, anyway. I look upon it now as normal maintenance – something that needs doing on a regular basis. I also like doing meditation, as well. I want to feel beautiful on the inside as well as on the outside.

P: And have other people noticed the effects?

L: Yes, they have. And they've grown used to my new look now, of course, but when I first went for treatment, they didn't say, 'Oh, you do look younger', which is of course why I had it done. It was more of a 'you look less stressed' or 'you don't look so depressed'. Before the treatment, you see, I had these terrible hereditary lines, a kind of constant frown, which made it look as though I was permanently unhappy. I was always saying, 'I'm fine. Really. It's just the way I look'. Now I don't have to make excuses for my appearance any more.

P: You must be very proud of your work, Dr Evans, knowing the effect it can have on people's lives. And it's fun too, I imagine.

DE: It's certainly a wonderful feeling seeing people grow in confidence and self-esteem. I'm not a great one for being charming and chatty when I'm working, though – that would just be too draining. Dealing with twenty-odd patients in one evening is not normal, by any stretch of the imagination, and it takes a lot out of you. But no one seems to notice that. I'm obviously so fresh-faced and young-looking…

P: Now it's funny you should mention that, because I've been dying to ask you about your age…

 1.28–1.29

Male doctor
We know that non-smokers living with smokers inhale small amounts of nicotine. This poses a risk to their health, as they are probably taking in a proportionate amount of the life-threatening components, too. It's difficult to predict exactly how great the danger is for passive smokers, as that depends on the exposure, but studies have shown that passive smokers have a 20 per cent increased risk of heart disease.

The fact is that half of all active smokers will die of an illness related to their smoking and that tobacco will most certainly be one of the biggest causes of death in the world's population this century. It is nonsense to suggest that passive smoking has zero risk.

Female doctor
Passive smoking poses no risk at all. Researchers have been into homes and recorded nicotine levels in the blood of passive smokers. The figure is too small to be of any real danger and it cannot possibly cause a 20 per cent increased risk of heart disease.

Research has also shown that smokers do not include fresh fruit and vegetables in their diet and have a high intake of saturated fats. This in itself can lead to a higher risk of getting lung cancer. Obviously, people living with smokers will share their lifestyle and diet. That's what causes them to fall ill, not the passive smoking.

8 This is the modern world

1.30

Fashion accessory, work tool or just in case of emergencies? Mobile phones mean different things to different people, and information about who uses them and why is of great interest to the companies that produce them. One leading manufacturer has divided customers into four main types.

First, there are the 'rational' buyers, those who use their phones for email and Internet access, as well as making calls. This kind of buyer puts performance and extra features above style and appearance. That's more the priority of the second category, the so-called 'style bandits', who look upon the mobile phone more as an art object than a communication device. These people are willing to pay whatever it takes to ensure their phone projects the right image.

The final two categories, the 'hedonists' and the 'resisters', are similar in one respect, but very different in another. Both want easy-to-use phones at low cost, but the 'hedonists' are young, fun-loving people whose phone seems permanently attached to their ear, while the 'resisters' are against mobile phones but feel they have to own one. Whatever type of user you are, you can guarantee the manufacturers have designed a mobile phone to suit your needs.

They'll also have produced a handset or a replacement cover in a colour to suit your personality. According to psychologists, the colour of a mobile phone speaks volumes about its user. Yellow, for example, is a bold, bright colour which appeals to the lively, energetic type, whereas someone who is calmer and more reflective may choose green or brown. Many people are attracted by food colours, like honey, apple or marshmallow, which, it seems, can stir up memories of our childhood and all the good things associated with it.

Colour, of course, is not the only feature we have a choice in – ring tones can also be personalized. You can download them from the Web, buy them on a scratch card or order them over the phone. Incredibly, over fifty per cent of teenagers in the UK have paid for a ring tone at some point. It's a lucrative business – in Europe alone it is worth hundreds of millions of pounds each year.

Ring tones cover every musical genre including themes from the Bond movies, classical music, country dancing and, for the teenage market, whatever happens to be in the charts. And because that changes every week, it's hardly surprising that teenagers are spending more on ring tones than anyone else.

At the top end of the market there's another type of personalization available to users. Companies are paying huge sums for mobile phone numbers that are easy to remember. Numbers with a repeated pattern, such as 450 450 will cost around three hundred pounds, but a string of the same digits like 555 555 or a run of consecutive numbers – 123 456 – can fetch upwards of twenty thousand pounds. In China, eight is a lucky number, and Chinese businessmen are apparently offering incredible amounts of money for any number with a series of eights …

Listening scripts

 1.31–1.35

1

I think a lot of the science fiction scenarios of miniature computers the size of a matchbox and phones you can wear like a button on your jacket are going to be too impractical to be put to general use. You only have to look at a wide-screen TV to realize there's little chance of that happening. My own belief is that electronic gadgetry will actually take over our living space – you won't be able to move in your own home for fear of knocking into some device or other. That's a big shame, really – life was so much simpler before, so much more free of clutter. And I'm not talking about the dim and distant past here, but a relatively recent one.

2

There's little doubt that the average lifespan will be greater, but I can't help feeling more than a little concerned about the quality of life we'll be leading when we reach the end of our days. I'm not sure, for example, that we'll have achieved what we need to in terms of finding cures for certain degenerative diseases such as Alzheimer's or Parkinson's. There's a great deal of enthusiastic talk about genetics and how absolutely marvellous it is that we've mapped the human genome. Now that's all very well, but I'm afraid I just can't see myself, or anyone else for that matter, playing tennis at the age of 120.

3

It always irritates me when people go on about population growth and how it's getting out of control and so on. If you look at the figures, you'll see that predictions of exploding populations made twenty or thirty years ago are simply not coming true. It's probably the same people that worry about the number of vehicles on the roads, as well. Let's face it though, fifteen years from now most of us will be working from home on a computer, which means fewer people getting stuck in jams on their way to work, and a consequent reduction in pollution. Now that's definitely something worth looking forward to, isn't it?

4

They sent me on a computer training course last month – at my age! We had a right laugh about it in the office, I can tell you. Still, you've got to keep up with it all, else they won't keep you on, will they? There seems to be more and more technology every day – it's going to change the way they do things here completely, you know. In fifteen years from now you won't recognize the place at all. Of course, I'll have left long before then, and I'll probably be enjoying a long and healthy retirement somewhere. But it does make you wonder whether they're up to something – you know, Big Brother and all that. I've always been suspicious of change, me. Can't help it.

5

Where I live, you'd be forgiven for thinking the size of the population is mushrooming. Every weekend there are more and more houses going up, and you see more and more traffic on the roads. But what's happening, of course, is that the existing population is financially healthier than it used to be, so more and more people can afford to buy themselves a second home in the country – which is where they're all driving out to on a Friday evening. And because the price of land is so expensive, these places are gradually shrinking in size – so much so that by the time I've raised enough money to buy my own place, I won't be able to swing a cat in it. Sounds funny, but it's a real nuisance, I can tell you.

9 Going places

 1.36

Presenter
Now on *The Travel Guide*, we go back in time to trace the origins of the good old package tour. Roger, you've been doing some research on a Mr Cook…

Roger
That's right Debbie, Thomas Cook, the man who founded the global travel agency with the same name. Now Thomas Cook actually had quite a few jobs before he hit on the idea of organizing package tours. He started out as a market gardener, then he handed in his notice and became a wood turner, and he also tried his hand at printing. What many people don't know about Thomas Cook, though, is that he was a very religious man and in 1828, when he was just twenty, he started working as a Bible-reader and village missionary in the Leicester area. And it was this religious streak that led him to become a member of the Temperance Society. In case you don't know, the Temperance Society was an organization whose members were against drinking alcohol in any shape or form – no beer, no wine, no spirits.

'But what's all this got to do with the tourist industry?' you might ask. Well, one day he said to himself 'wouldn't it be great if we could use the newly invented train to help us in our mission to get across the idea of temperance?' and in 1841 he got together about six hundred temperance supporters in Leicester and packed them off on the 8.15 to a temperance meeting fifteen miles away in Loughborough – all for the modest price of one shilling. And it was such a popular idea that he did it again the year after, and the next two years after that, too. But it wasn't until 1845 that he actually thought about making a profit from his idea. That's when he organized a pleasure trip to Liverpool, with the option of going on to Dublin, the Welsh coast or the Isle of Man. And that was the first ever package tour.

After that excursion, the world was his oyster. By the early 1860s he'd moved upmarket and from his travel firm in London was arranging tours for the English middle classes to different parts of Europe – especially Italy – Tuscany mainly, famed for its beautiful scenery, its history and its artistic heritage. He booked them into the best hotels, gave them a guidebook for the trip, and issued them with 'circular notes' – what we know today as traveller's cheques. They could cash these in at any hotel and bank which Cook had made arrangements with – well over a thousand different places in the 1880s. By then he'd already organized his first world tour – that was in 1872 – and he was now taking on responsibility for postal services and military transport for England and Egypt.

Thomas Cook died in 1892 at the age of eighty-three, leaving behind him the beginnings of a major global industry – oh, and a pub in Leicester, which is named after him. Cheers, Mr Cook!

 1.37

See page 115 Language Focus: Creating emphasis

 1.38

(P=Presenter; J=James)

P: It started with road rage in the nineties, then we had air rage, and now it's trolley rage, surf rage, movie rage and even dot.com rage. Anger, it seems, is all the rage these days. But why? With us is James Frith, head of road safety at the British Automobile Club. James, what makes people so aggressive on the roads?

J: Well, it's all about control, really. Once people get in their car, they feel a false, a dangerous sense of security and control. They're in their own little world, their own safe environment where they can deceive themselves into thinking they're better drivers than they really are. But this of course contrasts with events that happen outside the car, events over which they have absolutely no control whatsoever.

P: And when they lose control, they lose their temper, right?

J: That's right. For instance, most people set deadlines for their road journeys, and if someone threatens to prevent them from meeting that deadline, from not getting where they want to, when they want to, they blow a fuse. And that's when we get road rage, or in many cases now, revenge rage.

P: Another rage! What's revenge rage, James?

J: Well, it's similar to road rage, but less active. People get worked up inside, but just think nasty thoughts about other road users, without actually doing anything. They imagine, for example, going after someone who's cut them up and forcing them off the road. The problem is they get so caught up in their angry dreams of revenge that they fail to concentrate on the essential task of driving safely. And there's more of a risk of them causing an accident themselves than there is for the driver who has offended them.

P: And who are these angry people, these so-called 'road' and 'revenge ragers'?

J: We carried out a study recently and we found it was mainly 18- to 25-year-old men who committed acts of road rage, and these people often had criminal records, histories of violence or drug or alcohol problems. In the case of 'revenge ragers', people who merely fantasize about violent acts, they are more evenly spread across the age groups and between the sexes. The majority, though, are low-mileage motorists, those who only average between thirty and sixty miles a week. And the people who are most likely to trigger revenge rage, the ones who cause these people to lose their temper, are inexperienced youngsters who drive quickly, elderly drivers, and drivers of big articulated lorries or vans.

P: Makes you wonder why people don't just get the bus! Surely that's a calmer, more comfortable way to travel? Or is there bus rage, too?

J: Not exactly. But people do get fed up, don't they, when the bus just crawls its way along the route because the driver's busy taking people's money, giving them change or answering questions. And other road users don't respect the bus lanes, so you can end up in the same congestion, the same anger-inducing situations that you tried to avoid by leaving the car at home.

P: So what is the solution? How can drivers keep their calm on the roads?

J: I'm not sure there are any easy answers. But in one experiment, Dr David Lewis, the man who coined the term 'road rage', gave twenty-five stressed-out city drivers a kit containing real grass and a spray of grass scent. He told them to park their cars, take off their shoes and socks, and enjoy the sensation of grass beneath their bare feet.

P: The point being… ?

J: Well, changes in their heart rate and blood pressure were measured and they were clearly more relaxed with the smell and sensation of grass around them. Now, you'd expect a higher proportion of calm drivers on country roads, because there is considerably less traffic, but it's the combination of silence in the car, the smell of our immediate environment, and what we can feel that can really help calm us down and have a positive influence on our driving habits.

P: So can we expect grass kits to be on the market soon?

J: Possibly. I'm sure the research will be put to some use. What we do have already, though, is a kind of back-seat computer. Engineers have developed a hi-tech car which criticizes drivers when they are behaving rashly or have poor control of the car. A message comes up on the control panel. It also praises them for good road manners when they are driving considerately. If the driving becomes too erratic, the car stops.

P: Sounds like a good idea.

J: As long as drivers don't rely on it. We're always interested in technology that helps drivers' control, but not technology that takes it away from them. Certainly, though, we've all been in that situation with someone in the passenger seat telling us to calm down – it can be annoying, but very effective. And if this works in much the same way, then fine – though I can see stressed-out drivers becoming even more irate when their car suddenly stops!

P: Yes, indeed! Now, James, some of our listeners have written in with their own suggestions as to how we can maintain our composure in the car. Alan Hammans writes in from Tooting telling us how he uses spoken-word tapes…

Ready for listening
Part 1

 2.1–2.3

Extract 1
(I = Interviewer; D = Donald)

I: Donald – TV 1's programme on global warming has stirred up a lot of debate in this country. Do you think it is in any way irresponsible to present the views of a minority of scientists who say that global warming doesn't exist?

D: Well, the first thing any journalist learns is that you must have a balanced approach to reporting. That means allowing the public to hear both sides of an argument. At the same time, we know that a real balance does not exist. You wouldn't for example, give as many column inches to the enemy opinion in a war. The same goes for the global warming debate. Realistically, far more attention is given to the scientific view that climate change *is* happening – and not to the few voices that deny it.

I: But don't you think that people watching the programme may now decide it's pointless taking steps to save the environment?

D: If the media really had that much influence, people would already be behaving in a far more environmentally friendly way. At the end of the day, people are slow to change their habits if there's no immediate effect. Only government regulations will stop people using cars so much, or make them recycle.

Extract 2
(I = Interviewer; A = Andy)

I: Andy, your company, Kiss Chocolates was established a good twenty years before you took over. What made you suddenly decide to take a leap into chocolate-making?

A: Actually a combination of random events. I was made redundant in 2002, and although I absolutely loved advertising, it was a relief to leave because it meant that all the uncertainty about whether the job would last was gone. At the same time, my wife had just happened to come across the chocolate shop and was buying a gift box, when she overheard the owner mention her desire to retire. We both thought the product was excellent – and we both knew there would always be a demand for chocolate.

I: Yes, indeed! And there are probably a lot of people listening who are very envious of you. What's the best part of the job for you, Andy?

A: Well the product is certainly hard to resist! But because people come in to buy the chocolate as a gift, as a token of love or of appreciation for another person, you never have to face anyone in a bad mood. That's what makes it all so rewarding for me, even more than the prospect of long-term financial security.

Extract 3
(J = Jennifer; A = Andrew)

J: I have to say that I found *The Children of Hurin* completely absorbing, far more so than I expected. But it's hardly uplifting, is it?

A: No. Even from the early pages, one has a great sense that all is not going to end well for the central character, Turin. He *is* a hero in the sense that he is a brave, honourable man on a mission, but fate delivers him one cruel blow after another. As events unfold, you can see how tragedy is inescapable.

J: Now the book is based on various manuscripts that JRR Tolkien never completed before he died. And it's taken his son Christopher thirty years to put them together as a single cohesive story.

A: That's right – and overall, he really has produced a thing of beauty. Readers will notice, however, that one passage may be written in some kind of ancient English and then the next in a more contemporary manner – as you'd expect in a book pieced together from manuscripts written over a fifty-year period, and that can be a little distracting. Tolkien's characterization is sometimes underdeveloped but not so this time, as Christopher has given us a hero who we can identify …

Part 2

 2.4

Well, hello everyone. My name's Amanda Tyler and I've come to tell you something about my work as a waxwork sculptor. Um… I spend nearly all of my time hidden away with my colleagues in the studio of the wax museum. It's a rather sad room with no windows down in the basement, so it makes a really nice change to be here with so many people and so much natural light!

I suppose I became interested in sculpting at school, where I was doing an A Level in art and design. My teacher was very encouraging and she advised me to go on and specialize at Loughborough University on their impressively titled Fine Arts Sculpture course. Um… I have to say I never imagined that once I'd graduated, I'd be working in a museum with the likes of Eminem, Bill Clinton and Ronaldo!

Well, firstly, I'd like to tell you a little bit about the process that goes into making a waxwork figure. Um… The first and perhaps most enjoyable stage is when we take measurements of our subject – that's the person we want to make a model of. This is a real highlight of the job, as you get to travel and meet celebrities. It's not easy though, getting them to sit still for two hours or more while you struggle to get the information you need!

Now, as you can't have failed to notice, I have on the table the head of the well-known TV newsreader, David Wainright. He's not looking too good, is he? But that's because we're still in the early stages. At the moment he's made of clay which I've moulded onto an 'armature'. That's this thing here, which is basically a frame built out of wire netting. Back in the studio I have an armature for his whole body – that's got metal rods as well, which I've cut to size for his arms and legs.

It's important to show each individual in a pose which is normally associated with that person. So a politician, for example, might be in a standing position, giving a speech; when I've finished him, dear old David here will be seen sitting behind a huge desk; and in the museum we've got the athlete Carl Lewis running across the finishing line.

The whole thing is a very slow process. It can take me about three or four weeks just to get the clay model stage we have here, and I may need as much as five months to make one figure – from the time I start to the time it's ready to go on display.

So what's next? Well, from this clay model I'll make a plaster mould and fill that with hot liquid wax. And when it's cooled, hey presto, we have our wax head. Um… Then it's time for the eyes. What we do is select two acrylic eyeballs that are roughly the same as the subject's. Then we touch them up by hand with watercolours to get a more exact copy. That's usually my job. Then I hand it over to our make-up artist, who uses oil paint together with more conventional cosmetics for the rest of the head.

The hair is probably the most laborious part and can take weeks. This is the tool we use – unfortunately, it can only insert two hairs at a time, so you can imagine…

Part 3

 2.5

(I=Interviewer; S=Sandra; D=David)

I: On this week's *In Partnership* programme we talk to Sandra Peyton and David Sadler, who together run the successful media company, Advert Eyes, specializing in the making of TV commercials. Sandra, if I could start with you. What were you doing before you set up in partnership with David and what made you change?

S: Well, I was directing – er, drama mostly – for a small satellite TV company. It was an interesting, experimental time for me – they were a young, dynamic group and seemed to be going places. But these were troubled times for the business in general and they just weren't making enough money. Anyway, things weren't looking too good for me; as I'd been the last to arrive, I reckoned I'd probably be the first to have to leave.

I: So you jumped before you were pushed, so to speak.

S: That's right, and that was a great shame, because I'd never felt so comfortable working in a team as I did with that group of people.

I: David, you had a similar background, didn't you?

D: Yes, I'd also made a name for myself directing TV drama, but with the much larger Trenton TV. I left them because they were moving in a different direction to where I wanted to go. But the experience proved invaluable for the future – I can see that now.

I: In what way?

D: Working in close collaboration with others is an integral part of this business – that's always been clear to me – but I came to realize that you can't rely on other people to make things work. It's a tough old world

and ultimately it's down to you – it's a question of attitude. Things only happen if you let them – and if you only see grey skies and gloomy days ahead, that's what you'll get.

I: So the whole thing focused you for your future with Advert Eyes.

D: That's right, I did a lot of growing up with Trenton.

I: Well, tell us how you met each other, Sandra.

S: We were introduced at a party by a mutual friend. I remember I was very wary of David at first. He already had quite a reputation in the business – his past work spoke for itself. And he looked so serious, so apparently indifferent to everything. He mentioned some vague idea he had for setting up a business, something to do with advertising – but that wasn't what struck me most. I just couldn't get over how animated, how passionate he became when he talked about – well, everything really. It was difficult not to be carried along by his words.

I: So when he asked you to join him, you had no hesitation in accepting?

D: Well, it was actually Sandra who asked me. And I was the one who had no hesitation. My colleagues at Trenton had warned me against going into business with a complete unknown – they said it was too much of a gamble. But when I met Sandra, it was like looking into a mirror. Here at last was someone on my wavelength, someone who looked at life through the same camera lens. And anyway, I felt it was time to do something different, to live a little dangerously.

I: And has it been? Dangerous, I mean.

D: Anything but. Funnily enough, though, it's turned out that we do have quite a lot of differences, but these have all been to our advantage. Sandra, for example, has much more of a business brain than I do.

I: Is that right, Sandra?

S: Well, yes, it seems to be a hidden talent of mine. But I've had to learn the hard way. Raising money, for example, was an absolute nightmare – we just couldn't seem to get the finance.

I: That must have been quite disheartening.

S: Well, no, you can't afford to let things like that get you down. It was no good getting upset about it; throwing a tantrum in a bank manager's office is never a good idea – you might need to go back there one day. No, I just couldn't work out what the problem was, given our experience and the way the advertising market was shaping up at the time. We were just a small concern, asking for a small amount of money.

I: But you obviously got the money.

S: Yes, I met an investor who understood what we were about – and then, once we'd made a couple of ads, money was easier to come by.

I: David, how does, er, advertising work compare with TV drama? Is it very different?

D: Well, for a start there's more money around than for normal TV work, and that can be very liberating. But the market's understanding of quality may not be the same as yours and you find your creativity stifled. Yes, it's our own company, and it may seem a creative business to an outsider. But an advert is not your own baby in the same way that a TV drama might be. There are too many people who have a say in what you do and what goes into the advert.

S: Yes, I'd go along with that, although for me, running a business can be incredibly creative.

I: So what does the future hold for Advert Eyes? What are your plans for the company?

S: Well, we can't really say too much at the moment. It's not that we're not willing to, it's just that we're not entirely certain how things will work out ourselves.

D: That's right. The normal thing might be to look at some type of long-term growth for the business, but at the moment we're concentrating on consolidating our position, rather than branching out. Who knows what the future will bring?

I: Sandra, David, the very best of luck for the future. There we must leave it. Thank you.

S&D: Thank you.

Part 4

 2.6–2.10

1

I could barely string two sentences together when I first arrived, and now I'm reasonably fluent. In that sense, then, I've achieved what I set out to do – just by being here and mixing with the locals. I've met some great people since I got here, especially the family I'm living with. But there's a big downside to all this. I decided to come here on my year out because it's so different to all the other places I could have gone to. Plus it seemed so exciting when I came here two years ago. However, that was on holiday and I realize now that living here is actually rather dull. I really wish I'd gone somewhere on the mainland now – my girlfriend's having a great time there.

2

My father studied here as a young man, so I knew quite a lot about the country before I came. And when the head of my company's overseas operations told me our branch here wasn't doing too well, and would I please go and sort things out, I was very happy to accept. My husband came out shortly after I did and like me, immediately fell in love with the place. The pace of life suits us to a tee and the food is just out of this world. Ultimately, though, we're home birds and

when this posting's over we'll want to go back to be nearer our grandchildren – if we ever have any, that is!

3

I was working in the dullest job you can imagine – nine to five every day on the computer, answering customers' email queries. But it was thanks to that job that I got to know Patti, who was over on a work exchange programme in another department. She only stayed for three months, though, so after that nearly all our contact was by email. Of course, you can't keep something going like that indefinitely, so I took the plunge and moved out here. Life is fine – despite the overcast skies and regular downpours! I have to admit, though, it does get me down sometimes. I'd like to get back home more often, but it's just too far.

4

I only wish I'd made the break earlier. It's so vibrant in this part of the world – there's so much more going on. I think if I was still back home, I'd be so depressed, what with the current climate there and so on. The fact is I was in a bit of a rut. I was sick of the same old thing, day in, day out and I thought, 'There's got to be more to life than this'. So I looked into the price of property in different parts of southern Europe, and this area was one of the cheapest. It didn't take me long to settle in – the language isn't much of a problem and I've even got myself a little part-time job. Keeps me out of trouble!

5

A few years ago I set up in business with a friend of mine. Then I decided to go it alone and bought out my partner's share. Unfortunately, before long, things started to go wrong and I was up to my eyes in debt. Call it cowardice, but I just couldn't deal with it and I moved out here. It got me out of a mess, but I can't say I'm having the time of my life. I know a lot of different people here, but I just don't seem to fit in with them. We share the same language – more or less – but we're worlds apart in most other respects. One thing's for sure – if ever I do go back to face the music, it'll be for good.

10 House and home

 2.11–2.15

1

We used to live above a gym. I say 'used to' cause they had to close it down and go somewhere else. Some of the neighbours got together, see, and got someone from the Council to come round. It wasn't so much the music because the place was pretty well sound-proofed. It was more all the coming and going – especially at night, around 10ish, when it shut and the people would all leave at the same time and then one engine after another would start up. In the winter they'd leave them running

for a bit – time to defrost the windows I suppose – and the neighbours said it made too much of a racket. I can't say I noticed it much, though – live and let live, I say. We've all got to make a living somehow.

2

Well, one day I was upstairs in my office and was just about to start on a new chapter when I heard this – noise. At first I thought someone was actually in pain and I leapt up to the window – but then I saw my neighbour Sheila and I guess a couple of her friends in her back room. What they were doing, you see, was practising for the local amateur operatic group. The din was unbearable and it completely put me off my writing. And I've got deadlines to meet that I cannot put off and I was getting nowhere! It went on every morning for a fortnight and then just suddenly stopped. Perhaps they went to practise elsewhere. I live in dread that it'll start up again.

3

Nothing but trouble, that man. Fancy bringing a cockerel to live in a residential area! That sort of thing you'd expect in the countryside, but not here. Being a cockerel, it would start at five – this awful racket and it'd wake up the baby and she'd start wailing so there was no way we could ignore it. We tried to reason with him but he said we were making a fuss over nothing. Then that afternoon there were a whole bunch of hens clucking around his back garden too. It got so bad that we realized the only course of action was to take him to court. Which we did and we won. It was expensive but worth it. He was ordered to have the cockerel destroyed or sell it. Whatever he did – we can now sleep peacefully.

4

One of the benefits of working as a builder – all that physical activity knocks you out for the night. But since I did my back in and had to take a desk job, it's harder for me to get off to sleep. This woman down the road has a teenage son, and every Friday and Saturday night their house seems to be the meeting point for all their mates. They hang around in the road and maybe they don't realize how far their voices carry – or maybe they just don't care. Why can't they have a conversation indoors? I used to be a laid-back kind of guy but now I feel angry a lot of the time. That's not how I want to be – and I resent the effect it's had on me.

5

Night after night he'd have it blaring out at full volume – news programmes and reality shows mostly – and all we could do is sit there, seething. He said he couldn't hear it if he had it on any lower. Deaf as a post, he was. It really brings out the worst in you, something like that, and it put a tremendous strain on our marriage. We were so stressed out by it all and we rowed like we'd never rowed before, often about the silliest of things. Anyway, we got so sick of it all, we sold up and bought a place in the country. Shame really, 'cause I like having people around me and there are days here when all I have for company are the pigeons and other birds we have nesting up in the trees across the road.

 2.16

1 door creaks open
2 door slams shut
3 'Keep quiet' – hushed voice
4 dog growls
5 'Oh dear' – squeaky/high-pitched voice
6 'Shh – listen!' – hushed voice
7 distant/constant sound of machinery
8 bell rings
9 noise of machinery fades away
10 muffled sound of angry voices (in other room)
11 unmistakable sound of gunshot
12 high-pitched scream
13 deafening silence
14 dog whines
15 people bursting into room, shouts and fight scene – terrible racket
16 booming voice –'Get back'

11 A cultural education
 2.17–2.19

Extract one
(I = Interviewer; D = Diane)

I: Diane. It's quite traditional for American children to go to camp every summer, isn't it? But what makes non-Americans – I mean young people from other countries – want to work there?

D: Well I think a big draw is the chance to see America – the camps are situated in beautiful locations, and the chance to go travelling after camp's over is also very appealing to applicants. But once our foreign staff actually arrive at camp – they're often surprised at how multi-cultural it is. You could be working alongside someone from Denmark, Australia, Ireland… It may be the first time you've met someone from these places and you can find out how much in common you really have. It's a real education.

I: And if someone listening to this programme wants to apply to work for Summer Camps USA, how can they go about it?

D: They should look out for our advertisements in *The Globe*, the international student magazine, or they can apply online. But I must advise people that working at camp is not the equivalent of a luxury holiday in a hotel. While it is a very satisfying experience – it may feel a little like military camp at times. That's not to say that you're taking orders and have no say – it's all very much about team work. It's more to do with the hours – you're often on duty for long periods – including night supervision of the children.

Extract two
(I = Interviewer; J = James)

I: James – I believe we both had great-great-grandparents who came to Australia as gold miners in the mid-nineteen hundreds. But did you know much about that era before you did the documentary?

J: I'm ashamed to say not much. You know, I've always seen myself as a Chinese Australian – but that was more to do with family values and the traditions of our culture. And we grew up relatively wealthy – and with a good education and I've achieved a good level of success, thanks to that. But I know now that I took it for granted. Making the film showed me just what hardships our ancestors went through, and the sacrifices they made, so we could be where we are today. I learnt an awful lot.

I: From your own experience – and going by the interviews you carried out for the programme – do you believe that Chinese Australians are now seen as 'genuine' Australians?

J: I think we've come a long way. Our communities used to be hidden from view but now they're much more integrated. We're not hidden away in cafes and market gardens anymore! And it's no longer the case that Chinese parents are insisting their kids become doctors or lawyers. You've now also got Chinese Australians performing as musicians, artists, writers – that was a rare sight not so long ago. But it still occasionally happens that when I'm introduced to a European Australian, they like to compliment me on my good English. It doesn't occur to them that my family may have been here longer than theirs.

Extract three
(I = Interviewer; J = Jeremy)

I: Jeremy, an exhibition on tattooing – it's not really regarded as mainstream art, is it?

J: Well, not in the West, no. But one of the reasons for putting the exhibition together is to break down people's preconceptions about this art form. There's this stereotype of tattoos being worn by sailors or people trying to show they're non-conformist in some way – but certain cultures have long been wearing tattoos to show exactly where they *do* fit in society – and they're seen as sacred, rather than merely fashionable. The exhibition really does provide a fascinating look at the history of tattooing.

I: A large part of the exhibition is dedicated to the Maori people of New Zealand. Were their tattoos purely decorative?

J: Well, as with other Polynesian cultures, tattoos for the Maori people were actually an indication of a man's rank in society – his degree of authority within a tribe. But unique to the Maori was how facial tattooing indicated a man's ancestry:

the design on the left side of his face showed his father's side, and the right, his mother's. Such markings would also make a warrior more attractive to women. That isn't to say that women weren't also tattooed – but it tended to be a design on the chin or just an outline around the lips. There's also a collection of tools on view – the bone chisels they used and …

 2.20

Presenter
Now, in our regular *Confessions* spot, we listen to award-winning writer Gaby Longfellow, who was recently described as 'the most versatile and prolific writer of her generation'. So what is Gaby's confession?

Gaby
People assume that because I'm a writer, because I come from Oxford, and because I spend hours poring over books in university libraries doing research for my work, then I must have gone to university myself. And the plain truth of the matter is, of course, that I didn't. I don't have a degree.

During my school years I had a very full social life: I was in a theatre group, I sang in a choir, I had a boyfriend, I went rock climbing. Right through my teens, concentration was never my specialist subject at school. I'd always be looking out of the window, thinking of the hundred and one other things I could be doing.

And so it was with my A levels. Which I failed, quite spectacularly. I could have retaken them of course, but I was too worried the same thing might happen again. Failing once wasn't too bad – nearly everyone put it down to bad luck, as opposed to any lack of effort on my part. But if I'd failed again, I would have been officially declared stupid. Or at least, that's how I saw it then.

But it never occurred to me that I was any less intelligent than my friends who did go to university. In fact, at the time I thought *I* was the clever one for not going, and I probably came across as being rather arrogant as a result. I went to live in London and had a wonderfully exciting time, experiencing many things that my undergraduate friends could not. It was a period that gave me ideas and inspiration for my writing. I also read voraciously and *always* seemed to have a book in my hand. My reading gave me a passion for language and all its various features; an aptly chosen word, a well-crafted phrase, a striking metaphor – these are all things I try to emulate in my own writing.

Do I have any regrets? No, none at all. Indeed, many of my friends agree that university was rather a waste of time. And some of them feel bitter because their degrees pushed them into the types of professions that are detrimental to family life, ones that keep them away from home. They always seem to be worried about losing their well-paid jobs and they have little time or energy to devote to the things, or rather the people, that really matter. I even detect a certain amount of envy from some quarters. A lawyer friend of mine is always asking if he can swap lives with me. I have a great deal of admiration and respect for lawyers, but not, I have to say, enough to want to become one.

But I wouldn't try to discourage young people today from going to university. It has its advantages as well as its drawbacks and people have to make up their own minds. But it doesn't help now that when graduates start work in their chosen profession, many of them are hopelessly in debt, simply because they have had to borrow huge sums in order to pay their way through university. The idea is that those with degrees will have well-paid jobs and can easily pay off loans in the future. There's no guarantee of that, of course, and besides, it tends to convert money and the prospect of higher earnings into the main incentive for university education. And that, I confess, is not something I agree with.

12 The world about us

 2.21

Deserts cover about one seventh of the earth's land area. Rainfall is scarce and temperatures as high as 58 degrees celsius have been recorded there. Nevertheless, deserts are home to a rich variety of plants and animals, all of which have their own strategies for coping with the harsh conditions.

The desert holly, for example, draws up salt from the ground and releases it onto its leaves. The white mineral covers the leaves entirely and helps to reflect some of the daytime heat, in much the same way that white clothes do for humans.

The huge saguaro cactus, which grows in the Sonoran Desert of Arizona and Mexico, can live for more than 200 years. This is partly due to its ability to expand and store water. The cactus has ribs running along its length, which open out like an accordion, enabling the rain which falls in the short wet season to be kept in its trunk. This allows the saguaro to flower every year, regardless of rainfall. A giant of the cactus world, the saguaro is a slow grower but it can reach heights of up to fifty feet and weigh as much as eight tons.

Like the plants, desert birds are also well equipped to deal with the conditions. The road runner, for example, uses its long tail as a parasol, bringing it forward over its head to create shade, thus enabling the bird to keep cool – a simple, yet effective strategy in an environment which offers little protection from the sun's rays. Birds, of course, also have their feathers to help them. In other, cooler parts of the world, these serve to keep body heat in. In the desert, though, their main function is to keep external heat out, and as a result many birds can spend long periods unharmed in the hot desert sun.

Mammals tend to avoid the sun, usually coming out only after night has fallen. The jack rabbit in America and the fennec fox in the Sahara, however, do venture out during the daytime. Their protection against the heat is a pair of extremely large ears. As well as enabling the animals to hear better, these contain blood vessels which are so close to the surface of the skin that any air blowing across them cools the blood that runs through them.

Those most archetypal of desert animals, camels, have a number of useful techniques and devices. Their nose is equipped with muscles, which enable them to close one or both of their nostrils and keep the sand out during sandstorms. Their feet have only two toes which are connected by skin. This spreads out as they walk on soft sand and keeps them from sinking into it. They can also retain vast quantities of water in their stomachs – not their humps as many people think. As a result, they can go without drinking anything for four times longer than a donkey and ten times as long as a man.

So if it's not used for storing water, what purpose does the hump on a camel serve? Well, it may surprise you to hear that it's actually used by the camel to…

 2.22–2.26

1
So there I was, the rich tourist in a developing country. Of course, you get people begging at home, but there it was on every street corner. The poverty is so evident, so widespread, and I couldn't help feeling, as a wealthy Westerner, that I was in some way to blame. So I decided to do something to help, despite the attempts of my friend and travelling companion to persuade me otherwise. Every day we were there I put aside a certain amount of money to give to beggars. My friend told me I was being overgenerous, but when I got back home I couldn't help thinking I should have given more.

2
A mate of mine often complained about all the suffering in the world – but he never did anything about it. He said it was difficult for individuals to change things. Well, I just couldn't accept that. I took it as a kind of challenge and applied for voluntary work overseas in a school for street children. I thought at first they might not accept me because of my age and inexperience, but I needn't have worried – I didn't need to have any special skills or anything. In fact, that was part of the trouble. Most people were as green as me, so there was no real organization to talk of. Plus, I felt the government there could have done a lot more to help. A shame really, because I was so enthusiastic when I went out there.

3
I did a concert last year to raise money for an international relief organization. My manager said it'd be good for my image – you know, to be seen to be caring about other people's suffering and so on. I'd love to be able to say that I did it because I admired the work they were doing, and I was concerned about the issues they were fighting for. But that was more of an afterthought, really. I'm embarrassed to admit that my first instinct was to consider what was in it for me, what I stood to gain from it all. Sure, I did the concert for free and helped to raise lots of money for charity, but it's not something I boast about. I'm not at all proud of myself.

4
I saw this photograph of activists in a small rubber dinghy moving up alongside one of those huge whaling boats. It was a striking image, and it made me think that if they can risk their lives in this way to stop the suffering of an animal, then I can surely risk some of my money to help them. The trouble was, though, I chose the wrong moment to be generous – I didn't realize just how little money there was in my account when I sent off the cheque. It left me with next to nothing, and I couldn't afford to go away on the weekend trip I'd planned with my friends. I wished afterwards that I hadn't been quite so willing to help out.

5
Back in the Sixties, of course, women's rights still wasn't much of an issue. People just seemed to accept that we got paid a lot less than men, even though we had to do exactly the same work. Amazing, really. I mean, if I'd been a man, I'd have felt so guilty about it all. I wanted to help put that right, to challenge existing perceptions. So I got all the girls on the shop floor to go on a protest march through the town – there must have been about 500 of us altogether. We should have done it years before. They couldn't sack us, of course – there were too many of us – and when I realized that, it spurred me on. In fact, that's what made me go into politics, so I could continue the struggle.

Ready for Speaking

 2.27–2.30

Listening scripts in Teacher's Book.

Listening scripts

13 Food for thought

 2.31–2.33

Extract one

(I = Interviewer; MSH = Market Stall Holder)

I: Good morning sir. Jane Marsh from Devonport Community Radio. Is all your produce organic?

MSH: Yes, from the carrots to the cauliflower. And what you get here actually tastes of something, I mean the flavour is really superb. Here, and see, the carrots crunch the way they're supposed to. Not like those bland, cardboard things you find in the supermarket. The fruit and vegetables there may have come all the way from some exotic place but they're all dried up by the time they get here. We're charging a little bit more for our stuff, but when you try it, you'll see why.

I: And I suppose you're also having to persuade people that a few marks on an apple or a cucumber that's a bit bent, well that's how they're supposed to look. People can be a bit fussy like that, can't they?

MSH: Well, the first thing to say of course is that we don't use pesticides or anything that isn't natural. That explains why the fruit and veg looks the way it does and what attracts regular customers to the market. They also know it's extremely fresh. Straight from the field to here. But yes, you're right, first-time customers – you can see they're a bit anxious because a pear or a potato isn't perfect on the outside. But as I say, once they've tried it, they keep coming back for more. And it makes me laugh how they bring along their old plastic bags from the supermarket. It's good to see some recycling – although I'd prefer my name on the bag!

Extract two

(P = Radio Presenter; T = Tricia)

P: Good morning Tricia. We've had a lot of messages from listeners this morning about the government's new policy about the kind of food eaten in schools. There seems to be some misunderstanding about what the policy actually means.

T: Yes, some people have missed the point. We're not saying what pupils can and can't bring to school. If they want to eat a chocolate bar at break time, or have a fizzy drink before class, we won't be asking teachers to go out there and confiscate them. But we do say that schools must now be responsible for what they provide. So rather than having pies and chips on the menu five days a week, well, they'll be serving up things like pasta, wholegrain sandwiches, fresh fruit and so on.

P: I see. But isn't the childhood obesity problem in this country more the responsibility of the parents? Shouldn't they be keeping an eye on their kids' consumption?

T: I believe that most do. At least when they can, but there's all that time when their children are out of their sight. Even though we've had a great many campaigns on the obesity issue – I mean, today's children do know about what's good for them and what's not – it's hard to say no when temptation is right in front of you. Junk food at school is just part of a wider junk food culture. It's in the corner shop, in the petrol station – not to mention all the fast food outlets. We just want to exclude school as an outlet.

Extract three

(I = Interviewer; S = Shelley)

I: Shelley – you've just been voted SlimRight Winner of the Year. You look absolutely marvellous but how do you feel about winning?

S: Oh, thrilled, and so are my kids. I mean, they never said anything about my weight but I suspect they were very scared. They probably knew more about the health risks than I did. I suppose that's why I never made an effort before – I didn't feel particularly ill, and my appearance had never really bothered me. It's never stopped me socializing. But one day I overheard someone say that once you get to my size, my old size, there's nothing you can do. And I thought that's ridiculous, and it sort of motivated me to set myself a challenge. Being a SlimRight winner is a bonus, but it was more about my own goal.

I: And how did you actually go about losing the weight? I'm sure many people would love to know your secret.

S: Well, you need a nutritionist. Mine put together a whole series of menus that were balanced and healthy. Some things were new to me like lentils and beans, nuts – that kind of thing – but it was all pretty tasty and fairly easy to cook. Having someone really take a personal interest in your well-being – it reminded me of the lovely priest in the church I used to go to as a child. Even when I admitted one time that I'd given in and pigged out on chocolate, he just gave me a recipe for home-made muesli bars and said 'Here, try these instead.' I had that kind of patient encouragement all the way, I couldn't have done it without him.

14 Money matters

 2.34

Hello, I'm John Lister from the Student Financial Advice Centre here on the university campus. My main aim today is to give you one or two bits of advice on money matters before you get down to the main task of studying next week.

As you may know, not so long ago you might have received a student maintenance grant from the Local Education Authority to pay for all your living expenses. Now, of course, these grants don't exist and you have to borrow that money from the Student Loans Company. If you haven't applied for your loan already, make sure you do it soon, otherwise you may have to wait several months for your first payment. If you have, then you can expect to receive the money once a term; in other words, in three equal instalments over the course of the year.

And that's the first problem, really. Many students find that their money disappears almost as soon as they get it – and it's often because they fail to plan their finances carefully. To prevent the same thing happening to you, you can download your very own budget planner from the university website. It'll help you record your expected income and expenses for the year and then calculate how much you've got left over for yourself each month. It's worth having a look.

Even then, you may still find that you need a bit of extra financial help, particularly in the first term when your outgoings will probably be quite high. So if you haven't already opened a bank account, bear in mind that some banks offer better overdraft facilities than others. Shop around a bit – find out how much you can go overdrawn without asking for permission from the bank, and without paying any extra interest.

You can, of course, supplement your income by working part time, but you have to make sure you strike a balance between work and study. Some students here work over twenty hours a week in part-time jobs, but I personally wouldn't recommend any more than two evenings a week. That's for you to decide, of course, but I'd certainly wait a few days before applying for jobs, at least until you've got your timetable.

Now it's clear that a major expense each year is going to be books. For that reason, it's well worth having a word with your course tutor before you rush out and buy everything on your reading list. He or she can advise you on which books are the most important to have. You might also find that you can buy some secondhand from students in higher years who don't need them any more. Keep an eye on the noticeboard in your faculty building for that.

And when you pay for things, always make a point of asking for student discounts. Don't just assume the shop assistant knows you're a student – not even in the university bookshop. Get the most out of your student travel card and be very careful how you use your credit card. Every year dozens of students come to us at the Advice Centre with huge debts they can't pay off – and in most cases, it's all down to their credit card.

👁 2.35

(I=Interviewer; C=Chris)

I: When was the last time you spent the whole day without buying anything? With us today on *Local Lookout* is Chris Dawson, a committed anti-consumerist who will be taking an active part in next week's Buy Nothing Day. Chris, apart from buying nothing, what exactly is the aim of Buy Nothing Day?

C: Firstly, let me say that it is anything but a day of militant action with angry anti-government slogans and boarded-up shops closed for business. We're much more into persuasion than provocation as a means of bringing about change. We want to make shoppers question the need to consume and get them doing other things, like spending time with people, as opposed to spending money on them.

I: The obvious question here is 'Why?' What's wrong with shopping?

C: We're not saying people are bad because they go shopping. But they do need to think more about the products they buy. Whether, for example, their new trainers were produced using cheap labour in countries where workers' rights are virtually non-existent. What materials and production methods went into producing them, and the effect this might have on the planet. It's all very well for shopping malls to offer a wealth of choice, but this should not be at the expense of the environment or developing countries.

I: Indeed. But if people buy nothing on just one day, is it really going to change all that?

C: Well, for quite a few, Buy Nothing Day will indeed be a life-changing experience, not just a one-off thing. In previous years a lot of people have made long-term commitments to consuming less and recycling more. And that can only be a good thing.

I: So it's an annual event, then?

C: Yes, it is. In Europe it's always the last Saturday in November, while in the States they always have theirs on the day after Thanksgiving, at the start of the Christmas shopping season.

I: Presumably then, Chris, you're against Christmas shopping, too?

C: Good question! I'm afraid to say my family would never forgive me if I didn't get them anything, though they know how I feel about the whole thing. I just get so annoyed at the whole run-up to Christmas – already in October the shops have got their Christmas stock in, and the January sales start before you've even had a chance to finish your turkey. So it's handkerchiefs and socks if they're lucky, and maybe something special for my girlfriend.

I: Let's come back in time if we may, Chris, to next Saturday. What exactly will you be doing then, apart from not buying anything, that is?

C: Ah well, er, I'm not so sure I can tell you that, I'm afraid. Don't want to give the game away. Of course, there'll be the usual handing out of leaflets and putting up of posters and so on. But as for the rest, I can't say. You'll have to wait and see.

I: Last year, then. Tell us about that.

C: Last year was all a bit surreal, really. A group of us – fifteen altogether – all dressed up as sheep and went from shop to shop making loud sheep noises. And behind us we had a shepherd with a sign saying 'Don't follow them, follow your conscience'.

I: And what were people's reactions to it all?

C: Well, the shopkeepers were generally quite hostile, though we were expecting that. I suppose they saw us as a threat to business, and most of them moved us on. Quite a few of the customers saw the funny side of things and had a little chuckle – one or two even joined in – but on the whole they couldn't quite believe that someone was questioning the ethics of shopping. It certainly made them think – which is what we wanted, of course.

I: Is interest in Buy Nothing Day growing? How do you advertise yourselves?

C: It's getting bigger every year. Yes, we have our leaflets and posters – which you can download from the Internet, by the way – but up until now, at least, it's mostly been down to word of mouth. That may change, of course, as we get bigger and better organized. At the moment it's celebrated by about a million people in nearly fifty countries – and that's without the support of TV. In the US, for example, none of the major channels wanted to run the Buy Nothing Day commercial, because they said it went against the country's economic policy.

I: Yes, indeed. So, Chris, if we want to get involved in all this, how do we go about it? Who organizes it all?

C: That's the beauty of it all, really – you do. You just go to the Buy Nothing Day website – buynothingday dot co dot uk – and they give you ideas for what to do. You might want to dress up as something, set up a swap shop…

Answer Key

Unit 1 Aiming high

Speaking: Long turn Page 6

Useful language

very happy delighted, elated, thrilled, overjoyed
sad or *wanting to cry* tearful, miserable, close to tears, weepy
nervous or *worried* anxious, apprehensive, tense, on edge

Reading: Multiple choice Page 7

1

1 – the type of person who would take up such a challenge
The last paragraph talks about 'the simple Derbyshire girl' and mentions a change to 'a heroine and an inspiration to others of her generation'.
– their reasons for doing so
The beginning of paragraph 3 talks about how her passion for sailing started.
– the preparation required
In paragraph 3 we read about the 2,000 letters she wrote to get sponsorship and the 60,000 miles she sailed in preparation.
– their feelings during and after the event
During: From her comments at the end of paragraph 6 we understand that she was very determined, but we learn little, if anything about her feelings
After: In paragraph 5 we are told that 'she looked remarkably composed and seemed to take the change from solitude to public adulation very much in her stride'. We also read about her disappointment at not winning.
– the conditions they experience at sea
The harsh conditions are mentioned in paragraph 4.

How to go about it

'fêted': admired, honoured and entertained
'runners-up': a person or team that does not finish first in a competition or race, but that wins a prize
'landlocked': surrounded by land
'tenuous': weak, easily proved false
'spark off': cause something to start, especially suddenly

2

1C Lines 11–14 the winner ... were reversed
2B Lines 35–41 Antie Thea ... lifelong passion.
3D Lines 61–62 She wrote ... sponsorship + lines 66–74
　　And in terms ... 60,000 miles.
4C Lines 83–86 She endured ... windless Doldrums.
5C Lines 112–117 Her thoughts ... or five years.
6B Lines 123–134 But despite ... into victory.
7A Lines 150–end she is a heroine ... .

Language focus 1: Modal verbs 1

Page 10

1
1　Annoyance
2　Past possibility which did not happen
3　Past possibility
4　Future possibility
5　Present possibility
6　Lack of enthusiasm – 'might/may as well' is a fixed phrase.
7　Concession

2

Possible answers
1　I'm so angry with him. I do think he might have phoned to say he couldn't come.
2　We've missed the beginning, so we may as well go home and watch a video.
3　It was rather dangerous. Someone could have fallen over it and broken their leg.
4　I can't find it anywhere. I think I may have left it on the bus on my way home.
5　She might have a university degree, but she has no idea how to talk to the public.
6　Cheer up! It might stop raining later and then we can go out.
　　('Cheer up! It might never happen' is often said to someone who looks sad.)
3
1 theoretical possibility **2** criticism **3** request **4** inability
5 deduction **6** prohibition

4

Suggested/possible answers
2　This could be a girl telling off her boyfriend. It could be that he played a practical joke on her, but she didn't see the funny side of it.
3　This might be a magician, asking someone in the audience for help.
4　This could be a younger brother. He could be trying to retrieve a football from a tree.
5　This might be a parent trying to dissuade a teenager from eating a bar of chocolate.
6　This could be a parent refusing to allow their young child to stay up beyond their bedtime to watch something on TV.

Extension

1
a　'faint' suggests that it is not very possible. The other adjectives express the opposite.
b　'fair' express a reasonable degree of possibility. The others suggest it is not very possible. Note that *could, might* and *will* can all be used with these two

sentences. *may* is less frequent.

c 'good' is not correct. ('a good' would be correct)

d 'Predictably' is not possible here. It is an attitude marker meaning 'as is to be expected', often found at the beginning of a sentence and usually with past reference:
Predictably, house sales rose as a result of the cut in the interest rate.
He was predictably turned down for the job because of his poor health.
It is also often used to qualify adjectives. *He is predictably upset at what happened.*

e 'highly likely' means 'very probable'

f 'hardly likely' means 'not very probable'

2

Possible sentences

1 I think I stand a good chance of passing the CAE exam.
2 To improve my chances of doing so, I need to read a lot outside of the class.
3 In the world today we face the very real possibility that computers will one day replace books in schools.
4 There's an outside chance that I could be going to the States on holiday next year.
5 It seems highly unlikely that I will get a decent pay rise this year.

Vocabulary: Collocations Page 11

1–5

1 a success **b** ambition **c** motivation **d** failure **e** challenge
Note that 'an overnight success' means it is sudden and unexpected.
4 fulfil/realize *an ambition*
achieve/enjoy *success*
take up/rise to *a challenge*
end in/result in *failure*
improve/lack *motivation*
5 a challenge **b** ambition **c** failure **d** success **e** motivation

Listening: Multiple choice Page 12

1 A 2 B 3 C 4 A 5 C 6 B

Word formation: Nouns Page 13

1

1 achieve-ment motiv-ation fail-ure

2

1 refreshments **2** disapproval **3** eagerness **4** procedures
5 insignificance **6** simplicity **7** secrecy **8** membership
9 breakage(s) **10** likelihood **11** independence **12** anxiety

3

1 pleasure exposure closure
2 appearance annoyance reliance
3 storage shortage package
4 rehearsal renewal proposal
5 efficiency intimacy vacancy
6 enjoyment requirement commitment

7 prosperity originality familiarity
8 leadership companionship partnership
9 neighbourhood fatherhood adulthood
10 absence persistence evidence
11 selfishness tiredness carelessness
12 explanation interpretation application

4

2 endurance, reluctance
4 survival
6 disappointment
8 sponsorship
11 thoroughness
12 imagination, information, preparation, realization, inspiration
Also: heroine, spectator, winner, competitor, desalinator, success, thoughts, runners, achievers, savings, favourites, heat, solitude, conference
The following have typical noun endings but are not formed from a commonly used verb, adjective or noun: emotion, conditions, adulation, ambition, celebrity

Language focus 2: Spelling Page 14

2

referring limiting setting upsetting targeting (*targetting* is also used. This is true also of *focusing/focussing* and *benefiting/benefitting*) forbidding writing waiting travelling (*traveling* in American English) panicking

3

1 pleasent – pleasant
Note the differences between the noun *appearance* (see example 0) and the adjective *apparent*.
2 neccessary – necessary
3 publically – publicly
4 definate – definite
5 irresponsable – irresponsible
6 leafs – leaves
Other examples with this spelling change are *calf – calves; half – halves; life – lives; loaf – loaves; self – selves; shelf – shelves; wife – wives*
7 preceeding – preceding (from the verb *precede*)
Note the spelling difference between *exceed/proceed/succeed* and *precede/recede/concede*.
8 bussiness – business
9 dissappointed – disappointed
disappear is also commonly misspelt by students.
10 recieve – receive
Seize and *weird* are correct, exposing the often quoted spelling 'rule' of 'i before e, except after c'. This only seems to be true (and worth learning) for words such as *believe, relieve, achieve* and *conceive, receive, deceive*.
11 influencial – influential
12 factery – factory

Writing: Competition entries Page 14

1

The answer addresses all aspects of the task and would

have a positive effect on the competition judges.

2B

3

The writer uses a variety of language throughout the entry.

Sophisticated language
the likelihood that I will ever fulfil my ambition …
doesn't seem very high
my lifelong passion
achieving fame and fortune
be put off by dull statistics
research their genre thoroughly
My bookshelves … are stacked with the novels …
despite knowing all the time 'whodunnit'.
I've turned out dozens of short crime stories
possess enormous self discipline
devote the necessary time and effort to producing
that has meant burning the midnight oil
in anywhere near publishable form
no easy task
who could possibly fail to

Requirements (avoiding repetition)
Reading is important
all writers need to research their genre thoroughly
being a writer requires imagination
You have to develop your own personal style
successful writers possess enormous self-discipline

4

Register
Elements of Informal language
Contractions: I'll, doesn't, I've, We've
Linkers: And, But, So (at the beginning of the sentence), Last but not least
Punctuation: dash: 'important – all writers need to' and 'magazine – some have been published'
Phrasal verbs: put off by dull statistics, turned out dozens of short stories
Use of 'get': only one gets published, we've all got a novel inside us, getting it out
Use of *you/your*: eg 'You have to develop your own personal style'

6

Engaging the reader
The title and opening paragraph are crucial in this respect. The title should grab the reader's attention and the opening paragraph should make him or her want to carry on reading. The writer here uses a statistic in the form of a question to interest and involve the reader from the very first sentence.

The choice of idiomatic language adds colour to the piece and also suggests informality: ('put off by dull statistics', 'burning the midnight oil', 'my bookshelves are stacked

with the novels …'). The final paragraph rounds off with a summarizing and thought-provoking statement, 'We've all got a novel inside us' and a question to make people think: this could apply to anyone and their secret ambition. The writer begins and ends with a rhetorical question – it is a nice stylistic device if the end can mirror the beginning in some way, so that there is a sense of 'full circle' or completion.

Sample answer

<u>A professional golden boot?</u>

My secret ambition has always been to become a professional football player. That's what I'd really like to do in my life, just playing football every day so I can delight all the items relationed with the job, as money, cars, fame … Time is getting on and I am not getting younger, so now is the time to act.

First of course you need be good at football. In my local amateur league I was principal goal scorer last season and I think I have every chance of winning the 'golden boot' trophy again this season. Friends say I have the necessary skills, but you also need have a stroke of luck and perhaps can seen by a scout from a big team. 'Masterclass' could be the opportunity I am waiting for.

Then of course to improve your chances of becoming a professional, you need train a lot and be fit. There is no one day when I do not kick a ball, or I am in a gym doing exercise. For me it is like drug: I am addicted to training and I think I am in good condition for being professional.

Finally, however, you also need be a bit special if you want that other people consider you as good player. By this I don't mean you cause problems for trainers or other players, but you need have a creative character, if you want to be star player. My teammates call me 'crazy horse' which I think is a compliment.

So, I think I have the ingredients to be a professional player. Now all I need is a stroke of luck and if I have an appearance on your programme.

Examiner's comment
Content: The content of the task is covered.
Organization and cohesion: Clearly organized and paragraphed. The penultimate paragraph is a little confused and there are problems with coherence in some sentences eg *'so I can delight all the items relationed with the job, as money, cars, fame …'*.
Accuracy: Reasonably accurate, though there are some errors in the use of articles, *need* is consistently used with the bare infinitive and some grammar is rather awkward, eg *'you also need be a bit special if you want that other people consider you as good player'*.
Range: There is evidence of a good range of structures

and vocabulary eg *'I have every chance of winning the 'golden boot' trophy', 'a stroke of luck'* and *'to improve your chances of becoming a professional'.*

Register: The register is consistently neutral and appropriate.

Target Reader: The target reader would be reasonably informed, though might be slightly confused by the penultimate paragraph.

Mark: Band 3

Review 1 Pages 16 and 17

Modal verbs

1 can, have **2** may/might **3** to, well
4 unlikely/improbable, may/might/could **5** at, no **6** in, to

Spelling

1 important **2** generally **3** objective **4** identifies
5 successful **6** themselves **7** of **8** to **9** confident
10 factors **11** were **12** interest **13** their
14 improvement **15** perceive

Use of English: Word formation

1 expectations
2 payment(s)
3 performance(s)
4 recognition
5 ability
6 academically
7 difficulties
8 financial
9 failure
10 judgement/judgment

Word combinations

1 strong **2** slightest **3** every **4** stand **5** tears **6** delighted
7 enjoyed **8** rose **9** lifelong **10** light

Unit 2 Times change

Listening 1: Sentence completion

Page 18

4

Possible answers

2 probably a time expression (for ages? for x years? etc.)
3 probably something which people making time capsules sometimes forget to do
4 two nouns which are things related to TV programmes
5 a place/room
6 something the doctor was researching
7 a room/part of the grounds
8 something valuable/worth stealing

1 buried (underground)
2 more than/over a century
3 keep (proper) records
4 costumes and props

5 (film studio) car park
6 ancient civilizations
7 basement
8 (real) (items of) jewellery

Speaking: Collaborative task Page 19

Useful language

1 would not be complete without
2 is a part of everyday life
3 be intrigued to see
4 would demonstrate very clearly
5 might conceivably be obsolete
6 are unlikely to be using

Use of English: Open cloze Page 20

2

1 since **2** by **3** as **4** that **5** with **6** At **7** down
8 however/though **9** into **10** as **11** did **12** such **13** whose
14 not **15** an

Language focus 1: Talking about the past Page 20

A Review

1 (had) never kissed/met *The past perfect of 'kiss' is optional since the sequence of events is made clear by 'until'.*
2 have had
3 has been crying
4 was always losing *(indicating irritation)*
5 ate *(first she ate the chocolate, then she started to feel sick)*/was eating *(she started to feel sick while she was eating it)*/had eaten *(focus on the completed action: she had finished eating it before she started to feel sick)*/had been eating *(focus on the activity rather than the completed action)*
6 Marjorie left when Paul arrived: *She left after Paul arrived, possibly as a consequence of his arrival.* Marjorie had left when Paul arrived: *She left before Paul arrived.* Marjorie was leaving when Paul arrived/was arriving: *Both events occurred simultaneously.*
7 told/were telling *(no difference in meaning)* bought/have bought *The speaker may be situating in his/her mind the action of buying at some specific past time (eg last week), hence the possible use of past simple. The present perfect can be used to indicate a recent past event with a present result (the book he/she is holding now).*
8 didn't do/hadn't done did (do)/had done *The past tenses in both these sentences are used to refer to past time. The past simple indicates a regular action. The past perfect can be used to emphasize the sequence of events.*

B Further ways of talking about the past

1 used to know/knew. *would* cannot be used with a verb which is used statively.
2 I've ridden/I rode

3 All three are possible.

4 I'd seen

5 hadn't made

6 going to work/to have worked (*thinking of/about working*)

7 After he'd done/Having done.

8 All three are possible.

Writing: Formal letter Page 21

3

Content: Has the writer answered the questions fully?

No, she has failed to mention the fact that there was not enough room for all the demonstrations.

Has she expanded on any of the points in the input material?

No, she has limited herself to writing the bare minimum, adding no relevant information of her own.

Organization: Is the letter organized into suitable paragraphs?

Yes, each point is dealt with in a separate paragraph.

Vocabulary/Structures:

The language in the letter is mostly accurate but there is no evidence of a wide range of language; what the writer has not copied from the input material is expressed in very simple, conversational language.

Register: Is the register consistently appropriate?

No, it is mostly informal – contractions, informal punctuation, phrasal verb (turn up), linking and other informal language. The opening paragraph is too blunt and aggressive and the closing paragraph too threatening. The last paragraph is an example of inconsistent register.

4

Possible answers

1 There was a (complete/total) lack of parking facilities/space.

2 It was a huge/resounding/great/real success.

3 You suggested that attendance was poor/low.

4 Many commented on the high standard of (the) dancing.

Sample answer

Dear Editor,

I am writing on the part of the Black Knight Medieval Society to express our dissatisfaction with the report published on November the sixth about Brampton's fifth annual Fair. Our performance has been missinterpreted and we feel that we deserve at least, public excuses.

To begin with the entertainment value, we must expose that the consideration of dull event according to the low attendance might be easily explained if the lack of parking facilities are taken into account. Our sources testify severe difficulties in arriving to the venue with their own vehicle. In the same time, our demonstrations were unfortunately limited to the availability of the space.

As for the criticism of our show, we can assure that our high standards of dancing, music, superb cookery and overall costume ambience have been always praised.

The captivating archery is one of the children's favourite activities, as well as a pleasure for everyone with feeling for this skillfully sport decorated for the occasion with medieval attire.

To sum up, our jugement of the event results very positive and without doubt it has been a resounding success. Consequently, we request a professional report based on analysis rather than superficial impressions as a signal of respect for the readers and the quality of the newspaper.

We are looking forward to reading a decent article.

Yours sincerely
Cécile Dupont

Examiner's comment

Content: The writing attempts to cover the highlighted points indicated in the task. However, successful communication is not always fully achieved. '*The captivating archery is one of the childrens's favourite activities, as well as a pleasure for everyone with feeling for this skillfully sport …*'.

Organization and cohesion: The introductory paragraph introduces the purpose of the letter well and subsequent paragraphs are reasonably well organized. There are problems with coherence at sentence level eg '*To sum up, our jugement of the event results very positive … *'.

Accuracy: The grammar is sometimes awkward. In addition, there are a number of spelling errors ('*missinterpreted*', '*skillfully sport*') and cases of inappropriate word choice ('*public excuses*', '*costume ambience*').

Range: The writer attempts to display a range of vocabulary and tenses but this results in frequent error and evidence of translation from L1.

Register: The register is generally appropriately formal.

Target reader: The target reader would be informed in the main but confused in patches. The tone of the writing is also somewhat aggressive and might have a negative effect on the reader. The criticism of the newspaper is rather too strong given that the task is to persuade them to publish a correction.
Mark: Band 2

Reading: Multiple matching Page 24

1 From left to right: The Berlin Wall, York City Wall, Hadrian's Wall, The Great Wall of China

2

1 B **2** C **3** A **4** D **5** B **6** A **7** B **8** D **9** B **10** C **11** A **12** D **13** B **14** A **15** C

Language focus 2: Nouns in formal English Page 25

1
1 The main difference is the greater number of nouns in the second sentences from the text and the higher frequency of verbs in the first, alternative sentences. For instance, in **3**, there are five verbs and one noun in the first sentence, compared with one verb and three nouns in the second.

2
1 disappointment; application
2 disapproval; suggestion/proposal/request; reduction
3 dissatisfaction; delay(s); claim/assertion/guarantee/ assurances
4 failure/inability; importance; result/consequence; awareness/knowledge; education/teaching

3
The following features appear in **a** and are more characteristic of an informal style.
● contractions
● phrasal verbs *turned down*
● informal language such as *get* (3a), *a bit* (1a), *just* (2a)
Note also there are more words in **a** than in **b** eg (2a) 33 words (2b) 17 words

Listening 2: Multiple matching Page 26

1

1 C **2** E **3** F **4** D **5** A **6** B **7** F **8** E **9** A **10** C

Vocabulary: Changes Page 27

A Verb + noun collocations
Possible answers
your name you don't like it/you become a performer/you get married (some women in some countries)
your mind someone persuades you or you realize you're wrong/your opinion simply changes
your tune (= to express a different opinion or behave differently) when your situation changes and it no longer interests you to express a certain opinion
gear (on a bike or in a car) you want to increase or decrease your speed/you go up or down a hill
the subject (= to start talking about a different thing) what you are talking about is embarrassing or causing people to get upset or angry
sides you no longer share the opinions of the people or group (eg political party) you have previously supported
places to see a film, play etc better/you want to sit next to someone else/you want to move to a non-smoking section
a tyre when you have a puncture or when the tyre is bald (= worn down)
your ways (= behave much better) after a period of time in prison or bad behaviour at school

B Adjective + noun collocations
1 c **2** d **3** a **4** b
C Other verbs of change
1 D **2** C **3** C **4** A **5** B

Review 2 Pages 28 and 29
Language focus: Talking about the past
1 had been/gone/travelled/worked …
2 Having achieved/fulfilled/realized **3** has worn
4 have played **5** was taken **6** would read/tell
7 been given/granted **8** did let

Vocabulary: Changes

1
1 Same: both mean 'to get used to a new situation by changing your behaviour and/or the way you think'.
2 Different: if you adjust a piece of clothing, you move it slightly and correct its position so that it is in the right place or more comfortable. eg *He looked in the mirror and adjusted his tie*. If you alter a piece of clothing, you make changes to it so that it fits better. eg *The jeans I bought are a bit too long, so I've asked my mum to alter them slightly*.
3 More or less the same: both mean to change a building in order to use it for a different purpose. ['Transform' perhaps emphasizes the fact that there has been a complete change.]
4 More or less the same: both express the idea of changing the negative aspects of your behaviour in order to make it more acceptable. 'Modify' usually suggests that these changes have been small.
5 Different: if you change your tune, you behave differently or express different opinions when your situation changes. eg *He always used to be criticizing management, but he soon changed his tune when he got promotion*. (See **4** for 'change your ways'.)
6 Different: if a restaurant varies the menu, it changes it regularly. If a restaurant adapts the menu, it makes changes to it to suit a particular situation or group of people eg vegetarians, children, a wedding party.
7 Same: both can have the meaning of no longer sharing the opinions of the people or group you previously supported.
8 Different: if a country switches to the euro, the euro

is adopted as the official currency of that country, replacing the previous one. If someone converts money into euros, they change a certain amount of the money of their own country, in order to use it, for example, on holiday or on a business trip.

2

2 convert **3** adjust **4** switch **5** modify

Use of English: Multiple-choice cloze

1

In the second paragraph, the writer is negative. In the final paragraph, the writer is positive.

2

1 B **2** A **3** D **4** C **5** C **6** D **7** A **8** A **9** C **10** B **11** C **12** A

Unit 3 Gathering information

Speaking: Collaborative task Page 30

Useful language
1 Positive: efficient/convenient/cost-effective
Negative: costly/unreliable/frustrating
2 Positive: accurate/up to date/comprehensive/reliable
Negative: biased/misleading/useless/limited

Reading 1: Multiple choice Page 31

1 B **2** D **3** A **4** C **5** D **6** B

Language focus 1: Hypothetical past situations Page 33

A *Wish/If only* **and alternatives**

1

a Yes
b The speaker is very unhappy about this.

2

The sentences will refer to the present or future if the present infinitive is used.

Practice

1 have gone to France (instead)
2 you'd/you had phoned earlier
3 you hadn't done that
4 you'd/you had gone to university
5 have mentioned it before
6 to have stayed longer

B Past conditionals

2

1 c **2** f **3** a **4** e **5** b **6** d

3

1 Sentences 1, 2, 3 **2** Sentences 4, 5 **3** Sentence 6

Practice
Possible answers
1 He wishes he'd revised for his exams.
2 If I'd taken a few books with me on holiday, I might not have got bored.
3 If it hadn't been for Steve, we couldn't have got the car started.
4 I'd rather my parents had bought me a DVD player (than a video recorder).
5 I'd really like to have seen the film on telly last night.
6 I might have got the job if my French wasn't so bad/ was better.
7 I'd rather have watched the football than looked at all their holiday snaps.

Word formation: Adjectives and adverbs Page 34

1

1 countless/heartless/pointless
Note that the suffix *-ful* cannot be added to these three nouns.

2

1 approachable applicable believable
2 argumentative administrative provocative
3 introductory contradictory preparatory
4 chatty muddy rocky
5 luxurious mysterious monstrous
6 endless priceless sleepless
7 persistent apparent obedient
8 managerial secretarial territorial

3

1 imagin**ative 2** **un**satisfact**ory 3** increas**ingly 4** **dis**courte**ous**
5 knowledge**able 6** hope**lessly 7** substant**ial 8** strateg**ically**

Writing: Reports Page 34

1

A is the better answer. The register is appropriately formal and shows a wider range of language.

3
How to go about it
How else could you structure your report?
Students could reverse the order of paragraphs 4 and 5. They might also have two recommendations paragraphs – one for each advertising medium.

Introduction

The aim of this report is to describe the situation of two of the most important ways of advertising in Spain: TV and the sponsorship of sports.

TV

Undoubtedly, TV is the most important mass media. An advertisement broadcasted at prime time can grab the people's attention in a way absolutely unthinkable for any other form of publicity.

Nevertheless, the high price of this kind of advertising is an inconvenience that prevents companies from offering their products through TV. Moreover, the interruption of the programs with the best audience rating by an advertisement usually annoyes the viewers who, frequently, switch channel until the end of the break.

Sport

Nowadays, sport is one of the preferred pastimes of people. Consequently, the sponsorship of sports events or even the existence of teams with commercial names, like it happens in cycling, is a very profitable way of advertising.

However, something to take into account is the great rivality and hatred around the world of sport; the presence of a brand's name in a football team shirt may be free advertising for the competitors among the rival team supporters.

Recommendations

Since the high cost of a TV commercial is a considerable problem, a good solution could be the making of shorter adverts. The saving would be significant without affecting the effectiveness. In fact, the most resounding successes in the last years have been achieved by marketing campaigns whose adverts lasted few seconds.

As far as the sporting world is concerned, the key point is probably the carefulness at the time of choosing the event or team to sponsor. This decision can led either to a huge success or to a total failure.

By José Vicente Acín Barea

Examiner's comment

Content: The task has been completed reasonably well. It is informative and deals with each of the bulleted items. The introduction could be rather longer. More references could be made to the situation in Spain – this is, after all, the point of the report. In a few places the report reads a little like a discursive composition.

Organization and coherence: Report features are included and the writing is appropriately paragraphed. However, sentences are sometimes too long and slightly difficult to follow eg '*Moreover, the interruption of the programs with the best audience rating by an advertisement usually annoyes the viewers who, frequently, switch channel until the end of the break.*' It is not clear what is meant by the references to advertising for competitors.

Accuracy: The writing is generally accurate despite a few errors of word choice and spelling eg '*annoyes', 'rivality'.*

Range: There is evidence of a range of vocabulary and tenses in use, with some good collocations in the final section.

Register: The register is appropriately formal

Target reader: Would be fairly well informed (but see comments in *Content* section).

Mark: Band 3

Listening: Multiple choice Page 36

1

Sami northern Norway, Finland, Sweden and part of Russia
Breton Brittany, north-west France
Ladin South Tyrol, northern Italy
Provençal Provence, south of France
Frisian coastal area – northern Netherlands, north-west Germany, west of Denmark
Galego Galicia, north-west Spain

2

1 D 2 A 3 B 4 C 5 D 6 B

Language focus 2: Present and future conditionals Page 37

1

Zero conditional: c Second conditional: a First conditional: b

2

B The first sentence refers to the present. The second one refers to the past.

3

1 broken 2 happen 3 would 4 if 5 have 6 to

If + will/would/going to

1

1 Insistence (stress 'will' very strongly when saying this)
2 Refusal 3 Result 4 Intention 5 Willingness

Reading 2: Gapped text Page 38

How to go about it

Smell is part of the body's reaction system to danger. (paragraph after gap 2).

If we have no sense of smell we may not be able fully to appreciate food (paragraph after gap 3).

Smells are often the trigger that give us 'flashbacks' of memory. These things can be very powerful and make our lives richer. (paragraph after gap 4).

2

1 E 2 A 3 G 4 B 5 F 6 C D not used

Vocabulary: Smell Page 39

Adjective + noun collocations

1a

1 smoke, bodies 2 coffee, bacon 3 rubber, fumes
4 milk, date 5 spices, fruit

b Possible answers
2 a kitchen or a café **3** an airport runway or a car racing track **4 a** fridge in an abandoned house **5 a** market

2

Positive	Negative	Neutral
mouth-watering	stale	pungent (often negative)
	acrid	
	rancid	

3

fresh	musty	unmistakable
sweet	overpowering	faint
	sickly	strong (often negative)

4 Possible answers

your classroom	an unmistakable odour
a rose garden	a pungent aroma
disinfectant	an overpowering smell
old books	a musty smell
freshly baked bread	a mouth-watering aroma
your favourite cheese	a strong smell
decaying rubbish	a sickly odour

Review 3 Pages 40 and 41

Use of English: Word formation
1 global **2** suspicion **3** factual **4** editorial/editing
5 objective **6** reliable **7** inaccuracy/inaccuracies
8 controversial **9** expertise **10** trustworthy

Use of English: Open cloze
1 was **2** more **3** by **4** which **5** then/and **6** more/longer
7 in/with **8** A **9** had **10** not/hardly/barely **11** way **12** off
13 to **14** can/may **15** its

Use of English: Key word transformations
1 we had never gone
2 you had kept my news secret
3 would prefer to have given/would have preferred to give
4 not for his strange sense of
5 should/if you happen to come, if you should happen to come
6 he does/will keep (on) turning/showing
7 would probably not have/probably would not have come/jumped
8 have given Tom a second chance/opportunity

Ready for Reading

Parts 1 and 3: Multiple choice Page 42

3
1 C *that would make the world reappraise their idea of Chris Rea.*
2 A *I began to wonder if my throwaway comment had*

proved to be the final straw in the mind of some EastWest executive that a double was out of the question.
3 D *A man who … saw a career for himself along the lines of guitarist Ry Cooder found himself instead bracketed for his vocals alongside Dire Straits and Phil Collins.*
4 D *he blames himself for being too compliant.* (and following quote)
5 C *I don't know how many copies the new album will sell.*
6 C *This is real pain he's talking about.* (and following quote)
7 A *is surprisingly radio-friendly … catchy tunes*

What to expect in the exam
These are the distractors which refer to the remaining highlighted sections of the text.

2 B **3** B **4** A **5** A **6** B **7** D

Part 2: Gapped text Page 44

2
making a pizza: shape balls of dough into a perfect circle using your hands only. This involves covering it with flour, pressing out the dough from the centre, twirling it to shake off the flour and stretching it over the edge of the table. Then it is covered in tomato sauce and mozzarella cheese and put into a hot oven.

going wrong: He had problems shaping the dough to make a circle. The wet dough got stuck to his fingers. Then he overdid the stretching and pressing with the result that his pizza was all thick edges and had a hole in the thin centre.

5
1 F **2** A **3** D **4** G **5** C **6** B

Part 4: Multiple matching Page 46

2
Possible answer
They are clearly enthusiasts with a lot of technical knowledge.

3
1 C **2** A **3** E **4** B **5** D **6** E **7** A **8** C **9** B **10** E **11** A
12 C or D **13** D or C **14** B **15** A

Unit 4 Work Time

Language focus 1: Punctuation Page 48

2
1 avoided." **2** chance?" **3** People who **4** me. I **5** don't
6 It's **7** offers

Writing 1: Formal letters: application
Page 49

1
Suggested answers
possess good communication skills, be well-organized, have relevant experience, an eye for detail, an ability to work well under pressure, an ability to work to deadlines, an ability to use your initiative, be dynamic, of smart appearance, versatile etc.

2
The following are incorrect:
1 apply 2 must 3 enveloped 4 destined 5 place
6 number 7 chores 8 conduct 9 sorting 10 learned
11 rise for 12 own 13 complete 14 welcome 15 actual

3
How to go about it
Paragraph organization in Lara Goodrich's letter
1   Reasons for writing
2   Relevant experience
3   Reasons for applying. Suitability for job
4   Availability
5   Closing comment

Listening 1: Multiple matching Page 50

2
1 D 2 F 3 H 4 A 5 G 6 B 7 D 8 F 9 C 10 G

Language focus 2: Gerunds and infinitives Page 51

A Review
2   Modal verbs (*can, should, must* etc) are followed by the infinitive without 'to'
3   Here, the verb 'to be' + infinitive is used to give a kind of order.
4   If the verb is the subject of the sentence, the gerund is usually used.
5   The infinitive of purpose (to = in order to), giving the reason why he put on his best suit.
6   'manage' is followed by the infinitive of the verb.
7   'to be' + adjective + infinitive
8   'recommend' is followed by the gerund (or object + infinitive – see 7 in section B Common problems)

B Common problems
1 a *let me leave/allow me to leave* 'let' is followed by an object and the infinitive without 'to'. 'allow' is also followed by an object, but is used with the full infinitive.
2 b *get used to sharing* 'to' is a preposition in both sentences and is therefore followed by the gerund
3 a *It's not worth making* 'It's not worth' and 'There's no point' (and 'It's no use') are all followed by the gerund
4 b *would like you to be* 'would like' (+ object) + infinitive. The use of the possessive adjective 'your' before a gerund [appreciate your agreeing] is typical of more formal English. The object pronoun 'you' would also be possible.
5 b *stop ringing* 'stop + gerund'; 'stop' can be used with

the infinitive of purpose, meaning 'you stop doing one thing in order to do another' eg 'He stopped eating (in order) to have another cigarette'. This is not the case here in sentence b). ['Start' can be used with the infinitive or the gerund, with no difference in meaning.]
6 a *mind going* 'mind' + gerund
7 b *recommended him to have/recommended having/ recommended (that) he (should) have*
the infinitive is only used with 'recommend' if 'recommend' is followed by an object.
8 b *breaking/having broken* 'admit to doing something'. In this case, 'breaking' would be a more elegant answer, avoiding the repetition of 'have' and 'having'.

C Nouns followed by the infinitive
1 determination, effort 2 tendency, attempts
3 opportunity, refusal 4 capacity, decision
5 willingness, ability

Reading: Multiple matching Page 52

2
1 C 2 A 3 D 4 B
5 A I got sucked in too at first – you'd make sure other people knew what designer labels you were wearing, that they could see your cell phone was top of the range
6 C She accepted the one that was offering perks such as free tickets to major sporting events and a flash company car.
7 B The whole experience was quite traumatizing and I was too emotionally immature to deal with it..
8 C But, exceptionally, in her case, she had already been looking for an escape route
9 D "My colleagues seemed utterly mystified and tried to talk me out of it."
10 A "We weren't poor but I don't think my parents ever bought anything that wasn't secondhand. That definitely played a role in my motivation.
11 C "but there were plenty of workmates perfectly able to step into my shoes," she admits
12 A Tanya Burrows bears no grudge towards the corporation that rewarded her with five promotions within the same number of years. "At twenty-seven, I was able to buy my own luxury apartment," she says. "For that reason I'll always be grateful to them."
13 B after receiving news of the promotion she was elated. "I rang round just about everyone I could think of," she laughs. "But the next day I felt nothing. I had no inclination to get out of bed and face the constant pressure."
14 D She admits to being a perfectionist, an attribute which saw her rise through the ranks in no time. "It's a weakness, too," she says. "It can mean that you're reluctant to delegate and end up with the pressure of doing it all yourself."
15 C I felt I should have been carefree at that age but the burden of responsibility was enormous. I felt trapped."

Use of English: Gapped sentences
Page 54

1

1 grudge 2 role 3 position/role 4 pressure 5 favour
6 contract 7 ranks 8 notice

2

1 to continue to dislike someone because they once treated you badly or unfairly
2 to be an influence in a particular situation
3 to gain a (better) job in the same company
4 to have to deal with difficult or stressful situations
5 to support or agree with something
6 to be given the chance to work for a company
7 to be given a series of promotions
8 to inform your boss (usually in writing) that you intend to leave your job

3

1 position 2 bear 3 face 4 favour 5 rise

Listening 2: Sentence completion
Page 55

1 (forward) planning
2 realistic
3 tiredness
4 (our) health
5 achieve perfection
6 self-discipline
7 (most) fulfilling
8 television

Vocabulary: Time Page 55

1

1 in 2 off 3 against, for 4 for, up 5 aside

2

a half: *football*
b record-breaking: *athletics*
c flying: *aeroplanes*
d prime: *television*
e sale: *shops*
f harvest: *farming*

Writing: 2 Character reference Page 56

1

1 a very positive way of saying something potentially negative – he's shy.
2 rather negative – she seems very lacking in self-confidence, though the writer is defending the nature of the applicant's work.
3 wholly positive
4 wholly negative
5 wholly positive

2

The character reference is, on the whole, extremely positive. She clearly has relevant experience of 'correspondence and diary management', as 'she is familiar with all aspects of office work'. She has experience of booking travel. As an 'office manager' she seems fully qualified to take on the role of PA. 'Contact with business people at a high level' is not specifically demonstrated in the character reference, but this is compensated for by other qualities. All in all, it would seem Lara has a good chance of being selected for interview.

3a

Paragraph 1: writer's relationship with the applicant and time he/she has known her
Paragraph 2: applicant's personal qualities and attitude to work
Paragraph 3: applicant's personal qualities and relationships with other people
Paragraph 4: applicant's relevant skills
Paragraph 5: writer's recommendation

3b
Suggested answers

I have known and worked with … for … years
… has shown great enthusiasm for her work
… has always managed to combine a … nature with a … approach
… has been a major asset to the company
have a tendency to … + negative quality
this is a mark of her …
… is one of her greatest strengths
… has excellent … skills (see Wordlist for possibilities)
The whole of the last paragraph

3c

She can be sensitive to criticism and does have a tendency to take things to heart. However, this is a mark of her perfectionism, which generally manifests itself as a positive attribute.

4a

2 reluctance: the only negative word
3 lack: the only one meaning 'not having'
4 become ill: this relates to health; the others relate to personality
5 poor: the only negative word
  parenting: the others usually relate to the world of work
6 slapdash: the only negative word

4b
Some adjectives are open to interpretation.
Positive

approachable	easy-going	outgoing
attentive	flexible	patient
responsible	caring	industrious
self-assured	considerate	knowledgeable
self-confident	creative	likeable
sensible	dedicated	loyal
single-minded	determined	mature
trustworthy		

Negative

arrogant	indecisive	slapdash
clumsy	insensitive	stubborn
conceited	moody	unreliable
disorganized	pompous	
impatient	self-centred	

Sample answer

To: Whom it may concern,

AR MUSTAFA

I have known Mr. Mustafa for a very long period of time. He was working with me over six years. His ability reflects in his promotion from a customer service assistant to a sales floor manager within a short period of time.

His keenness to learn and dedication to work is one of the main characteristics which paved the way to success. Although he is one of the hardest working people in the company, it never banned him from being kind and considerate to his colleagues. He was very friendly and helpful to customers as well as to colleagues.

He is an excellent communicator in his mother tongue as well as in English. With his great sense of humour he always keeps the atmosphere light. Sometimes it may be unsuitable for the situation, but never the less it acquired him affection of his collegues and customers.

He is very keen on travelling. He has done a degree in leisure and tourism while working in the company. His familarity with the Bangladeshi tourist attraction lead to his additional responsibilitie of organizing company's anual tour to the countryside.

In all those tours, he has proven himself as an excellent tour organiser.

In light of my personal experience with him, I am confident that he is well suited for the post in your company. I am happy to give this personal reference.

By Nariya Wareham

Examiner's comment

Content: Personal qualities are well described and this a satisfactory character reference. There is adequate, though not very detailed, information about Mr Mustafa's previous experience and relevant knowledge. There is clever mention of a negative point about Mr Mustafa's character, which is then turned to his advantage.

Organization and cohesion: The letter is well organized and paragraphed, although the short single sentence should not be a paragraph of its own. The letter would benefit from more overt linking devices.

Accuracy: There are some errors – in the use of verbs (*was working, keenness … and dedication is*), in structure (*it acquired him*) and in the use of vocabulary (*banned*), but these do not impede communication.

Range: There is a satisfactory range of structure and vocabulary, and some evidence of ambition, especially in the second and third paragraphs.
Register: The register is appropriate and consistent: fairly formal, serious and respectful.
Target reader: The target reader would be reasonably well informed about Mr Mustafa's suitability for the post.
Mark: Band 3

Review 4 Pages 58 and 59

Word combinations
1 handed in 2 bear 3 pressed 4 viewing 5 set 6 available
7 way 8 hate 9 great 10 every

Gerunds and infinitives
1 going, trying, to get, to go
2 smoking, eating/to eat
3 noticing, asking
4 not to keep, to think
5 giving, to come, talk
6 agreeing, to help, to set, to do
7 to enter, cutting
8 to claim, seeking

Use of English: Key word transformations
1 makes no difference to my boss
2 was the brains behind
3 admit/confess to being
4 handed in/gave in my notice
5 had/felt no inclination to get
6 to step into his shoes
7 (to be) in favour of
8 is no such thing

Unit 5 Getting on

Listening 1: Multiple choice Page 61

1
1 C 2 C 3 D 4 A 5 D 6 B

Reading: Gapped text Page 62

2
1 F 2 A 3 C 4 G 5 B 6 E **D** not used

Vocabulary 1: Verb + Noun collocations Page 63

1
express their feelings
take pains (to do something)
show physical affection
show their emotions

2

drift off to sleep: gradually fall asleep

broken up with his girlfriend: ended the relationship with his girlfriend

let down their defences: lower their (emotional) defences and open up

go through many career highs and lows: experience good and bad moments in their career

see through the mask: understand the truth behind the appearance

Language focus 1: Reference and ellipsis Page 64

A Reference

1

a   in my own student years

b   sons leaving home at 18 to move into jobs for life.

c   ways of putting up new defences

d   encouraging boys to show their emotions

e   the fact that boys call their mothers on mobile phones more than anyone else

f   confide in their mothers

2

1 so 2 not 3 do 4 ones 5 those, one 6 This

B Ellipsis

1

a midnight b stumbled on motherhood's best-kept secret c he, prevail

2

1 A Do you think you'll be home before midnight?
B I should be ~~home before midnight~~.
2 I asked him to play a tune on the piano and he said he didn't want to ~~play a tune on the piano~~.
3 She always comes to class on Tuesdays but ~~she~~ hardly ever ~~comes to class~~ on Thursdays.
4 He left without saying goodbye. I have no idea why ~~he left without saying goodbye~~.
5 A I have a feeling he was sacked from his last job.
B Yes, he might well have been ~~sacked from his last job~~.
6 He told me to apologize to her but ~~I'd already apologized to her~~ I already had (*or* I'd already done so).

3

Possible answer

For most of **her** working life my mother taught chemistry in a secondary school. She always said the reason she had entered the teaching profession was because her father had virtually forced her **to (do so.) Her parents were both teachers**, though she herself had no intention of becoming **one**. However, whereas my grandmother felt that my mother should only follow in their footsteps **if she wanted to (do so)**, my grandfather was determined that she should teach for a living – **so she did**.

She'd actually like to have become a pharmacist and run her own business, but she wasn't sufficiently qualified **(to do so)**. Apart from **this**, she might well have had problems raising the necessary capital, and if she'd asked her father to lend **it to her**, he probably wouldn't have **(done so)**. I think my mother resented my grandfather for the pressure **he** had put on her, and **she** always encouraged me to make my own decisions. **I did (so)** – and now I work as a teacher, and my son **does too**!

Vocabulary 2: Relationships Page 65

1

1 **a/b** get 2 **a/b** put 3 **a/b** had 4 **a** turned 4 **b** turn
5 **a/b** took 6 **a/b** look 7 **a** kept 7 **b** keep

2

1 **a** positive **b** negative
2 **a** negative **b** negative
3 **a** negative **b** negative
4 **a** negative **b** negative
5 **a** positive **b** negative
6 **a** positive **b** negative
7 **a** usually negative **b** positive

Listening 2: Multiple choice Page 67

1 B 2 C 3 C 4 A 5 A 6 B

Language focus 2: Relative clauses Page 68

1

1   **a**   Scott
    b   an occasion
    c   all that precedes it, ie the fact that you don't just learn the part, you live it.
    d   two mismatched cops
    e   the plot

2 c, **d** and **e** contain non-defining relative clauses, but **a** and **b** contain defining clauses.
3 *who* and *which* in **a** and **b** respectively
4 *which* or *that* – In a defining relative clause such as this, if the relative pronoun (here: *which* or *that*) refers to the object (*scenario*) of the verb in the relative clause (*we've seen*), the pronoun can be omitted.

2

1   I went walking with my husband at the weekend, **which** is something **which/that**/*omit* we haven't done for a long time.
2   The novel is set in Kaunas, **which** at that time was the capital of Lithuania. The initial chapters focus on Vitas's father, **whose** fiery temperament had a lasting effect on the boy.
3   **What** I'd like to know is what happened to that boxer **who/that**/*omit* she was seeing. Are they still going out together?

4 He left all his money to a woman **who/that** had never shown him any affection. The reason **why/that**/*omit* he did this has never been fully understood.

5 Her mother, **who** hated city life, longed to return to the village **which/that**/*omit* she grew up in and **where** she still owned a small plot of land.

6 Is there anyone **who's/that's** got a car or **whose** mum or dad could give us a lift?

Writing: Essays Pages 68 and 69

1 C

2

a *words and expressions which introduce a contrast*

Despite this, however

by contrast

on the other hand

(This is not) however (the case)

whilst

nevertheless

b *words and expressions which introduce the writer's main points*

The first point to bear in mind is that

A further point is that

Finally

c *other useful words and expressions for writing essays*

evidence seems to suggest that

a recent survey found that

in addition

it would be wrong to argue that

it is generally agreed … that

this is not the case with

to conclude

some argue that

3

Agreeing with a statement	Disagreeing with a statement
It cannot be denied that There can be no doubt that It is my firm belief that It is true to some extent that	It is simply not the case that I would dispute the claim that It is difficult to accept the idea that

Examiner's comment

Content: The content of the task is covered.

Organization and cohesion: The answer is well organized and there is evidence of use of a range of cohesive devices (*'The first point to bear in mind…'*, *'A further point is…'*).

Accuracy: Reasonably accurate with some grammatical errors (*'despite of the fact'*, *'always your meals are cooked for you'*) or incorrect choice of vocabulary (*'rising greatly'*, *'breaking up with'*).

Range: There is evidence of a good range of vocabulary and tense usage. (*'you may pay some rent to your parents but…'*, *'…put a great strain on your relationship'*).

Register: The register is appropriately formal.

Target Reader: Would be clear about the writer's opinion and their reasons.

Mark: Band 4

Review 5 Pages 70 and 71

Vocabulary

1 down **2** on **3** on **4** to **5** on **6** in for **7** to **8** down on **9** up with **10** through

Reference and ellipsis

1 old one keeps **2** I hope not **3** and neither/nor is
4 but I do. **5** If so **6** It should be **7** I have already! *or*
I already have! *or* I've already done so! **8** love to.
9 should have been. **10** he hasn't

Use of English: Open cloze

1 were **2** would **3** them **4** when **5** Despite **6** which
7 without **8** it/this/that **9** What **10** over **11** have
12 their **13** to **14** out **15** such

Unit 6 All in the mind?

Speaking and reading Page 72

2
Gardner would rank them all the same.

Listening 1: Multiple matching Page 73

1 D **2** C **3** H **4** A **5** G **6** G **7** H **8** D **9** E **10** B

Language focus 1: Passives 1 Page 74

1
a J.K.Rowling **b** Claude Monet **c** Marie Curie
d Charles Darwin **e** Meryl Streep

2
a She is of course famous for <u>writing/having written</u> a series of books about
The stories, which have <u>been</u> translated into
b These masterpieces of Impressionism <u>were all</u> painted at the end of the nineteenth century by the man who <u>is/was</u> generally regarded as the leader of the movement.
c He was <u>introduced</u> to her by a Polish acquaintance
the study she had been <u>commissioned</u> to do by the Society for the Encouragement of National Industry.
d <u>He arrived</u> at Salvador, Brazil, aboard the HMS Beagle ['arrive' here is an intransitive verb. Only transitive verbs can be used in the passive.]
and he was plagued/he was to be plagued by fatigue and intestinal sickness
e she should <u>have</u> been awarded an Oscar for her part in *Silkwood*
complaints about radiation sickness are ignored <u>by</u> the management

3
1 c (teachers) **2** d **3** b **4** a

4b
b These masterpieces of Impressionism: passive
c Hc: passive
d During his travels there he: active (*contracted*) then passive (*was plagued*)
e This dramatic film/whose: passive

5b
b the man who is generally regarded as the leader of the movement
c Polish acquaintance … Encouragement of National Industry.
d fatigue and intestinal sickness
e the management of the plutonium factory where she works

Practice
1 Change to passive; agent required.
The item was written by Steven Ward, former Olympic athlete and manager of the Crowfield sports centre, which sponsored the event.
2 No change. The second sentence begins with given information: 'This development'
3 Change to passive; no agent required.
The event could be held in the 2,000-seater Mulberry Hall Function Room in Scarcroft Road.
4 Change to passive; agent required.
The survey was carried out during the busy pre-Christmas period by first-year students at Holmbush Business College, who designed their own questionnaire as part of their course work.
5 Change to passive; no agent required.
I have recently been promoted to the post of Chief Accounts Clerk, in charge of a staff of five.

Vocabulary 1: Intelligence and ability Page 75

1
a a whizzkid **b** brainy **c** I'm a dab hand at painting.
d I'm (an) ace at tennis. **e** I'm hopeless at cooking.

4
a practically **b** largely **c** absolutely

Writing: Reviews Page 76

3
Paragraph 1:
Basic information on content of two films, including overall opinion and comment on acting performances.
Paragraph 2:
Similarities between two films, including further comment on plot and opinion on Russell Crowe's appearance.
Paragraph 3:
Differences between two films, including further opinion on Kate Winslet's acting and use of flashback technique.
Paragraph 4:
Overall strengths of films with personal recommendation.

All paragraphs include the writer's opinion.

4

Adjectives in text
entertaining afternoon's viewing
moving portrayal
remarkably convincing
very credible (Kate Winslet)
to good effect (adverbial phrase)
powerful acting
visually appealing
plausible
a definite must-see (noun)

Adjectives in Wordlist
Some adjectives are open to interpretation
Positive
action-packed, atmospheric, compelling, credible,
entertaining, exhilarating, fast-moving, gripping,
impressive, innovative, memorable, moving, powerful,
stunning
Negative
clichéd, disappointing, excruciating, implausible,
overhyped, predictable, sentimental, tedious,
unconvincing

5
Both focus on
common to both films is the fact that
'Iris' differs from 'A Beautiful Mind' in this respect,
relying instead on
unlike the more linear American film
more visually appealing but no less plausible

Vocabulary Page 206
1 resemblance **2** terms **3** lines **4** similarities **5** difference
6 genre

Sample answer

The exciting world of spies is beautifully reppresented
by James Bond films. In Sean Connery's 'Dr No', James
Bond fights against a scientist who utilises atomic
energy for the motive of diverting rockets and missiles.
In Pierce Brosnan's last edition 'Die another day', the
enemy holds a powerfull weapon, a satellite with a
diamond crown that functionates as an enormous laser.

Common to both films is the way James Bond saves
the world from terrible disasters. Another similarity is
the exotic and atractive settings. 'Dr No' takes place in
appealling crystal water beaches of Jamaica and 'Die
another day' moves from picturesque 'La Habana' to
the very impresive views of Iceland. But the more great
similarity of all, made in propurse of course, is that
in both films there is a comparable scene of Ursula
Andress in the first one and Halle Berry in the second
one, which coming out of the water dressed in exactly
the same bikini.

What sets one film apart from the other is the gap
of time between both of them. Old James Bond
was sciovinist and even a bit racist instead Pierce
Brosnan's Bond treats Halle Berri as an equal and as
well behaves it could be said as a perfect gentleman.
It is also noticeable in respect of the gadgets they use,
there is no comparasion between the Giger Counter (to
measure radioactivity) used by Sean Connery and the
invisible car of Pierce.

Both films are action-packed and compelling, which
makes the perfect choice for a diverting evening's
viewing, however, if you prefer a visually appealling
experience, but I have to say maybe less plausible also,
then 'Die another day' is the film for you.

By Donatella Fiore

Examiner's comment
Content: The writing successfully addresses the different
parts of the question. The task is well fulfilled and
certainly analytical rather than merely descriptive.
Organization and cohesion: The writing is well
organized and introduces similarities and differences in
an appropriate and logical manner. There is clever use
of paragraphing, each paragraph being clearly about
something different.
Accuracy: There are a number of mistakes which suggest
a lack of control: *'which coming'* and *'more great'*.
Range: There is a range of tense and vocabulary usage,
including some impressive language such as *'Common
to both films is…'*. However, this ambition is not always
successful *'a diamond crown that functionates as an
enormous laser.'*
Register: The register is appropriately semi-formal,
as befits an arts review in a newspaper. It correctly
addresses the reader directly and gives the personal
opinions of the reviewer.
Target reader: Would be informed and would consider
using the piece in the magazine.
Mark: Band 3

Use of English: Gapped sentences
Page 77

1 mind 2 bright 3 slow 4 head 5 thought

Reading: Multiple choice Page 78

3
1 C 2 A 3 B 4 D 5 C 6 C 7 B

Vocabulary 2: Sleep Page 79

1
a snooze
b nod off, fall asleep, doze off

2
A
1 good 2 soundly 3 deep 4 fast
B
1 rough 2 wide 3 sleepless 4 light

Language focus 2: Passives 2 Page 80

A Reporting verbs

2
a The Prime Minister is expected to announce his resignation later today.
b The 22-year-old striker is understood to be considering a move to a Spanish club.
c The band are rumoured to have sacked their (*or* is rumoured to have sacked its) lead guitarist.
d He was alleged to have been selling stolen goods.
e She is reported to have been paid over £2 million for her part in the film.

B *Have/Get something done*

1
a We're painting the house at the weekend.
We're doing it ourselves.
b We're having the house painted at the weekend.
We're paying someone to do it for us.
c We're getting the house painted at the weekend.
We're paying someone to do it for us. (slightly more informal than b)

2
a I had my watch repaired last week.
Someone repaired my watch because I asked/paid them to.
b I had my watch stolen last week.
Someone stole my watch. I did not ask them to! This use of the structure is for unpleasant events (usually) over which the subject has no control.

C Other passives with *get*
Practice

1
Possible answers
c have had/got this dress/suit
d to get lost/to have got lost
e would have/get your eyes
f of having/getting my nose
g got caught
h to get/have the car
i had/got our house/flat
j should/ought to/'d better get/have your hair

Listening 2: Sentence completion
Page 81

2
1 1778 2 deafness 3 tubs of water 4 surgeon 5 switch off
6 magical symbols 7 lose weight 8 psychological

Review 6 Pages 82 and 83

Use of English: Word formation
1 infections 2 unfortunately 3 participants 4 analysis
5 spatial 6 visualizing 7 disorganized 8 comparison
9 fictional 10 systematically

Vocabulary
1 poor 2 strong 3 gift 4 bright 5 promising 6 get
7 badly 8 fast 9 sets 10 choose

Use of English: Key word transformations
1 to be fully assessed
2 taken aback when he was/at being/by being
3 thought to have made
4 house done up
5 being taken for granted
6 has been put off
7 fewer/ less than six people are required
8 be weak at speaking

Ready for Use of English

Part 3: Word formation Pages 84 and 85

1
1 definition 2 emotional 3 variety 4 psychological
5 beliefs 6 theoretically 7 tolerance 8 unbearable
9 length 10 accompanies

2
1 *definition* is a noun.
2 *emotional* is an adjective.
3 *variety* is a noun. There is a spelling change: *-y* at the end of *vary* becomes an *i*.
4 *psychological* is an adjective.

5 *beliefs* is a noun in the plural form.
6 *theoretically* is an adverb.
7 *tolerance* is a noun.
8 *unbearable* is an adjective. The prefix *un-* makes it negative.
9 *length* is a noun. There is a spelling change: *o* in *long* becomes an *e* in *length*.
10 *accompanies* is a verb. It has the prefix *ac-*.

4
1 entitled **2** halved **3** finding **4** enthusiasts
5 expertise **6** threatens **7** perception **8** diversity
9 establishment/establishing **10** unavoidable

Part 4: Gapped sentences Pages 85 and 86
1 ahead **2** aim **3** figure **4** open **5** will

Part 5: Key word transformations
Page 87

Help questions
1 speak / gerund / in
2 gerund / do
3 it's not a surprise / noun
4 past / take
5 speech / on – of
6 stop + *gerund* / make
7 wish + *had* + past participle / pay / to
8 today's / adverb / comparative forms of adjectives and adverbs, *more* and *less,* verbs

1 speaking/talking about herself in
2 losing (some/a little) weight would/will do
3 as no surprise
4 have taken more care in/while/when
5 a speech on behalf of
6 until it stops/has stopped making
7 I had paid more/greater attention to
8 considerably better in today's test than

Unit 7 Feeling good
Reading: Multiple choice Page 88
2
Text A matches with picture 3
Text B with picture 1
Text C with picture 2

3
1 A **2** B **3** C **4** C **5** B **6** D

Vocabulary: Health Page 90
A Health problems

1a
1 chronic **2** pressure **3** allergic **4** blinding **5** infections

2a
1   tooth, bone

2   ankle, wrist
3   nose
4   shoulder, hip, jaw
5   ribs, thigh
6   glands, lips, feet

B Phrasal verbs
1 carrying out **2** set up **3** got round **4** taken back
5 ease off **6** put down

Use of English: Multiple-choice cloze
Page 91

2
1 A **2** C **3** C **4** A **5** D **6** D **7** A **8** A **9** C **10** B **11** C **12** C

Self help box
0   fall ill
1   come out in a painful rash
2   a mild fever
be diagnosed as having + illness (eg shingles)
3   the doctor prescribed + medicine etc
4   relieve the pain
5   medical consultation
8   medical complaint
10 contract + disease (eg malaria)
basic medical facilities
12 serious illness

Speaking 1: Collaborative task Page 92
Useful language

1
a utterly **b** elementary

2
a *significant* implies a much greater effect than in the case of the other three. Preposition: *on*
b *reasonably* suggests that it is less effective than in the case of the other three. Preposition: *in*

3
a *pay, to* **b** *take, of*

Listening: Multiple choice Page 93

2
1 C **2** A **3** A **4** D **5** B **6** D

Language focus: Reported speech
Page 94

A Direct and reported speech

1
Tense changes: present perfect in direct speech changes to past perfect in reported speech.
Other changes: use of 'if' when reporting yes/no question; changes to pronouns and possessive adjectives (*my* to *her*); changes to time adverbials (*now* disappears in the reported speech version).

2
1 admitted, had sold, pointed out, had given
2 predicted, would be, warned, might be
3 concluded, had to, reminded, didn't/did not, would go
4 announced, intends, stressed, has not/had not

Note

This 'back tense' effect is standard and common, but native speakers sometimes mix past reporting verbs with present following verbs.

In 1 *has sold* and *has given* are also possible – present perfect would suggest this is either recent or new information.

In 2 *will be* is also possible if the protest has not yet taken place.

In 3 *must/have, don't, will go to* are also possible if the speaker is thinking of the future.

B Alternative verb patterns

2
1 C 2 B 3 A 4 D

3
threaten: B   recommend: A, C, D   persuade: A
ask: A, B, D   encourage: A   demand: B, D   offer: B

C Verbs and dependent prepositions
1 for 2 on 3 of 4 against 5 to

Practice

3
Possible answers
Answers may include the following main ideas:
The man claimed that 50% of smokers would die of a smoking-related illness.
The woman claimed that passive smoking was not a risk.
The woman pointed out that smokers tended not to eat a lot of fresh fruit and vegetables, and that this could also cause lung cancer.

Word formation: Verbs Page 95

1
1 classify exemplify simplify identify <u>generalize/ise</u>
2 differentiate <u>qualify</u> captivate evaluate assassinate
3 characterize stabilize familiarize <u>dominate</u> computerize
4 strengthen sadden <u>enrich</u> deafen heighten
5 enlarge <u>widen</u> ensure endanger encourage

2
reappear, disappear
reread, misread
renumber, outnumber
reload, overload, unload
rehear, overhear, mishear
reuse, overuse, misuse (disused and unused – both adjectives)

3
1 evaluated 2 deafening 3 disqualified 4 outnumbering

5 familiarizing/ising 6 outlived 7 validated 8 ensures

Writing: Letter Page 96

2
A member of the health club is writing to the General Manager, so one would expect the register to be more formal than informal. However, you should not go too far: the Manager's letter is semi-formal, with its use of bullet points and 'Kind regards'. The most important thing is that the register should be consistent throughout the letter.

3
appreciative, friendly, polite and constructive.

4
purchase of equipment for the gym → take on extra instructors for classes
building of a second sauna → extend changing room

Useful language

1
demand, insist and *warn* would not be in keeping with a polite, friendly, constructive and appreciative tone; *reckon* would be too informal for this task.

2
1 suited (*suitable* would be possible)
2 short
3 complete

> **Sample answer**
> ....
> Dear Mr Roberts,
>
> The reason of this letter is to present my opinions about the changes to the club that the management proposed and also to propose additional changes.
>
> To begin with, if you purchase some extra equipment for the Gym, it is not essential and would take up more space than the one currently available. So I suggest hiring more instructors so a greater variety of classes can be offered to the members.
>
> It could be nice to have a second sauna. However, I should point out that this improvement is not what the club is in the greatest need of. More useful maybe to extend the area dedicated to changing facilities, provided they are big enough to fit everyone in.
>
> Finally, for improving the snack bar, I believe that buying a second microwave and some other cooking facilities would allow people to enjoy a wide range of dishes. The acquisition of a wide screen TV makes for a cost I feel to be not afordable.
>
> I expect the proposals to be useful for you when you make the final desicion and look forward to know what do you think for them.
>
> Yours sincerely,
> Olaf Johansson

Examiner's comment
Content: The writing addresses the main points successfully.
Organization and cohesion: At paragraph level the letter is well organized and coherent – the various pieces of information from the different input texts have been cleverly combined. Some sentences and phrases, however, read somewhat awkwardly eg *a cost I feel to be not affordable'*.
Accuracy: There are minor problems in accuracy eg *The reason of this letter, look forward to know.*
Range: There is evidence of a good range of vocabulary and tense usage (*'The acquisition of a wide screen TV…'*, *'…is not what the club is in the greatest need of'*).
Register: The register is generally appropriately formal.
Target reader: Would be well informed and clear about what is expected.
Mark: Band 4

Review 7 Pages 98 and 99

Use of English: Word formation
1 tiredness 2 combinations 3 noticeably 4 unwanted
5 purifies 6 sharpens 7 moisturizing/moisturising
8 growth 9 immunity 10 memorize/memorise

Health crossword
Across: 2 complaint **6** foot **7** ankle **9** headache **11** rash
12 thigh **13** nose
Down: 1 stomach **3** pain **4** tooth **5** ill **6** fever **8** muscle
10 drug

Reported speech

1
1 having 2 about 3 need 4 them 5 of

2

Possible answers
1 She insisted we go and visit them some time and assured us we would love it there.
2 He apologised/apologized for not phoning earlier and explained that he had been very busy.
3 He warned her that it was a very dangerous part of town and urged her not to go there on her own.
4 She recommended he wear gloves on the run the next day, and reminded him to do some warm-up exercises beforehand.
5 He predicted it might rain at the weekend, but promised to take them all to the funfair if it didn't.

Unit 8 This is the modern world

Listening 1: Sentence completion
Page 100

1 rational/ (a) rational buyer
2 art object
3 low cost
4 personality
5 childhood

6 50%/fifty per cent/half
7 in the charts
8 easy to remember/memorable

Language focus 1: Determiners and pronouns Page 101

1
1 <u>one</u> respect 2 in <u>another</u> 3 <u>Both</u> want 4 own <u>one</u>
5 <u>Many</u> people 6 <u>every</u> musical genre 7 <u>another</u> type

2
1 determiner 2 pronoun 3 pronoun 4 pronoun
5 determiner 6 determiner 7 determiner

3
a
1 All 2 every 3 Several

4
a
1 every many 2 another one month 3 no many

Practice

1
1 Every other year *or* Every two years, each other *or* one another
2 most of them play, none is very welcoming
3 there's every likelihood, no intention
4 on the other hand, as much/many as twenty hours

2
1 lot, little
2 none
3 every .
4 Either
5 All, any
6 few, most
7 one
8 each

Vocabulary 1: Amount Page 102

1
1 no limit 2 full refund 3 great deal 4 small discount
5 high cost 6 large/high number

2

Possible answers
1 The details of a competition.
2 A mail order company explaining the rights of customers who are not satisfied with a product they have ordered.
3 A newspaper article about a forthcoming event such as a concert or sporting contest.
4 A shop offering discount to customers who pay in cash rather than by credit card.
5 A company explaining to retailers the reasons for a recent price increase.
6 A warning letter to an employee whose work or behaviour has been the subject of complaint

Use of English: Gapped sentences
Page 103

1

1 full **2** deal **3** cost **4** high **5** limit

Reading: Gapped text Page 104

2

1 C **2** G **3** B **4** F **5** E **6** A **D** not used

Vocabulary 2 Page 106
Verbs formed with *up, down, over* and *under*

1 *overthrown* This is the only use of the word – a government/dictator etc. being overthrown. The meaning is something like 'remove from power'.

2 *downsizing* Again, this is the only use of the word – when a company reduces the size of its operation, in the interests of cost and efficiency.

3 *overrule* This means something like 'use your superior authority to change a decision' – could be anyone in a position of higher authority eg a police inspector, a Head Teacher etc.
upheld When a decision that has been questioned is confirmed as correct.

4 *undertook* In this context could mean 'promise', but also has the sense of 'made themselves responsible for'

5 *undergone* In this context could mean 'had' but generally means something like 'go through an unpleasant process'.
downplaying Could also be 'playing down', meaning something like 'make it appear less important than it is'.

6 *uprooted* This means 'leave a place where you have settled down'.

Language focus 2: Modal verbs *will, shall* and *would* Page 106

2

1 Refusal You could say 'It refuses to start' or 'he refused to move it'. Here *wouldn't* is simply the past of *won't*, so we have present and past refusal.

2 Willingness An unusual use of *will* which may surprise students – in this case you can use *will* with 'if'.

3 Habit This use of *would*, meaning 'used to', is well known, but *will* can be used in the same way.

4 Assumption This is assumption, because the phone rings and the speaker assumes the caller is Mike.

5 Annoying behaviour *Would* is used when there is a sense of frustration from the speaker and a feeling of 'How typical!'.

6 Request for advice/instructions Note that *will* is <u>not</u> normally used in this case.

3

1 car **2** television **3** Nintendo GameBoy
4 telephone (receiver) **5** oven **6** fridge/freezer

Listening 2: Multiple matching Page 109

2

1 D **2** A **3** H **4** C **5** B **6** D **7** C **8** F **9** G **10** B

Language focus 3: Talking about the future Page 109

1

a I'll probably be enjoying

b I'll have left

2

1 D *I hope she passes* means 'I want her to pass'. *I expect she'll pass* means 'I think she'll pass'.

2 S No difference

3 D *Will you come* is a request or invitation. *Will you be coming* is a polite way of asking about someone's plans. The speaker is suggesting that the other person, the 'you', will already have decided whether to come or not.

4 D *The parcel should arrive* means it is expected to arrive.
The parcel might arrive is simply suggesting a possibility.

5 S No difference, although whereas *due to* refers to only one train, the present simple can be used to refer to the regular daily/weekly service.

6 S No difference. Note that these two structures are more common in the past: *I was about to/on the point of.*

7 D *She's bound to get the job* means 'she's certain to get the job'.
She's likely to get the job means 'she'll probably get the job'.

8 D *He's confident of success* means 'He thinks he will succeed' ie it is his opinion.
He's assured of success means 'He is certain to succeed' ie it is the speaker's/other people's opinion.

9 D *They're planning on getting married* suggests they are more decided than in the other sentence.

10 D *The Government is to spend* means 'The Government will spend'.
The Government is expected to spend is less certain.

Review 8 Pages 110 and 111
Determiners and pronouns

1 another **2** other **3** others **4** few **5** little **6** every **7** each **8** all **9** much **10** either

Use of English: Key word transformations

1 made the most of

2 are second to none

3 be driven/used every other

4 of every single one of/made by every single one of

5 would not/wouldn't keep changing

6 would often compete with one

7 probably have been/got held/caught

8 has no intention of making/has no wish/desire to make

1 B 2 C 3 B 4 B 5 A 6 D 7 B 8 C 9 C 10 D 11 C 12 B

Unit 9 Going places

Reading: Multiple matching Page 112

2

1, 2 A & D in any order 3 C 4 E 5 A 6 B 7 C
8, 9 B & E in any order 10 D 11 A 12 C 13 A
14 B 15 E

Vocabulary 1: Doing things alone
Page 114

1

1 self-made 2 single-handed 3 self-reliant 4 solitary

2

The following words to be crossed out:
1 with, with, at 2 by, on 3 with, by

Listening 1: Sentence completion
Page 114

2

1 wood turner
2 (village) missionary
3 (newly invented) train
4 (society) meeting
5 (ever) package tour
6 middle classes
7 traveller's cheques
8 postal services

Language focus: Creating emphasis
Page 115

1

a he was a very religious man
b this religious streak
c wasn't until 1845

2

b This religious streak led him to become a member of the Temperance Society.
c He didn't actually think about making a profit from his idea until 1845.

3

a an action or series of actions; a noun
b the only thing that
c a prepositional phrase; a moment in time

4

1 I'd like to know is how old she is.
2 did was (to) start up his own business.
3 was the music (that) I enjoyed most about the film.
4 was in June (that) they got married, not July.

5 when he took his hat off that I recognized him.
6 until I spoke to Jerry that I found out she'd moved.
7 I did was (to) switch it on.
8 he (ever) thinks about is his precious car.

Writing: Contributions to brochures
Page 116

3

1 destination 2 walkway 3 picnic 4 views 5 past 6 sands
7 air 8 distance 9 life 10 countryside

Listening 2: Multiple choice Page 118

2

1 A 2 B 3 D 4 A 5 C 6 C

Vocabulary 2: Anger Page 119

1

more informal: blow a fuse, get worked up

2

1 heated 2 irate 3 cross 4 seething 5 berserk

3

1 top (note that this is particularly informal) 2 rage
3 outburst 4 steam 5 tantrum

Speaking: Long turn Page 120
Useful language

2

1 might have 2 may well 3 looks as 4 fair chance
5 very likely 6 looks like

Word formation: Alternatives from the same prompt word Page 121

1

composition, composer

2

1 a timeless (an untimely death/end)
2 adopted (adoptive is not common in English – it is mainly used in 'adoptive parents')
3 deceptive (deceitful is used when talking about people wilfully deceiving others: eg deceitful person, his deceitful attempt to persuade her … deceptive seems to be used with 'things' or rather abstract concepts eg deceptive appearance, deceptive pace)
4 supporting (a supportive friend/colleague/boss)
5 appreciable (an appreciative audience)
6 identity (identity is about 'who you are' and identification is about papers. You show identification to prove your identity)
7 consulting (a consultative committee/role)
8 entries (entrance = a door or the act of coming in – make a spectacular entrance)
9 hardship (hardness is a neutral word – the hardness of a metal)

10 advisory (It is advisable to = a good idea to)
11 imaginable (an imaginary game/situation)
   (an imaginative child)
12 respective (a respectable person is considered by
   society to be good and proper, a respectful person is
   one who feels or shows respect)

Review 9 Pages 122 and 123

Use of English: Word formation

1 destructive 2 regardless 3 residential 4 composure
5 respectful 6 easily 7 inconvenience 8 relating
9 irritable 10 background

Vocabulary

1

A Anger

2 e fly into a rage 3 a let off steam 4 b throw a tantrum
5 f blow a fuse 6 d go berserk

B Doing things alone

2 f fend for yourself 3 e leave you to your own devices
4 c keep yourself to yourself 5 d have a mind of your own
6 a go it alone

2

1 let off steam 2 fend for herself 3 went, berserk
4 keeps himself to himself 5 throws a tantrum

Use of English: Gapped sentences

1 spots 2 entry 3 worked 4 view 5 cross

Ready for Listening

Part 1: Multiple choice Page 124

2

1 A 2 C 3 C 4 B 5 B 6 A

3

Listening script 2.1–2.3
(I = Interviewer, L = Lecturer, A = Andrew, J = Jennifer) **Extract 1** **I:** Donald – TV 1's programme on global warming has stirred up a lot of debate in this country. Do you think it is in any way irresponsible to present the views of a minority of scientists who say that global warming doesn't exist? **L:** Well, the first thing any journalist learns is that you must have a balanced approach to reporting. That means allowing the public to hear both sides of an argument. <u>At the same time, we know that a real balance does not exist. You wouldn't for example, give as many column inches to the enemy opinion in a war.</u> The same goes for the global warming debate. Realistically – far more attention is given to the scientific view that climate

change *is* happening – and not to the few voices that deny it.

I: But don't you think that people watching the programme may now decide it's pointless taking steps to save the environment?

L: If the media really had that much influence – people would already be behaving in a far more environmentally friendly way. At the end of the day, people are slow to change their habits if there's no immediate effect. <u>Only government regulations will stop people using cars so much, or make them recycle</u> ...

Extract 2

I: Andy, your company Kiss Chocolates was established a good twenty years before you took over. What made you suddenly decide to make a leap into chocolate-making?

Andy: Actually a combination of random events. I was made redundant in 2002, and although I absolutely loved advertising, it was a relief to leave because it meant that all the uncertainty about whether the job would last was gone. At the same time, my wife had just happened to come across the chocolate shop and was buying a gift box when she overheard the owner mention her desire to retire. We both thought the product was excellent – <u>and we both knew there would always be a demand for chocolate.</u>

I: Yes, indeed! And there are probably a lot of people listening who are very envious of you. What's the best part of the job for you, Andy?

Andy: Well the product is certainly hard to resist! But because people come in to buy the chocolate as a gift – as a token of love or of appreciation for another person – <u>you never have to face anyone in a bad mood. That's what makes it all so rewarding for me</u> – even more than the prospect of long-term financial security.

Extract 3

J: I have to say that I found *The Children of Hurin* completely absorbing, far more so than I expected. <u>But it's hardly uplifting, is it?</u>

A: No. Even from the early pages, <u>one has a great sense that all is not going to end well for the central character,</u> Turin. He *is* a hero in the sense that he is a brave, honourable man on a mission, but <u>fate delivers him one cruel blow after another. As events unfold, you can see how tragedy is inescapable.</u>

J: Now the book is based on various manuscripts that JRR Tolkien never completed before he died. And it's taken his son Christopher thirty years to put them together as a single cohesive story.

A: That's right – and overall, he really has produced a thing of beauty. <u>Readers will notice, however, that one passage may be written in some kind of ancient English and then the next in a more contemporary manner</u> – as you'd expect in a book pieced together from manuscripts written over a fifty-year period, <u>and that can be a little distracting.</u> Tolkien's characterization is sometimes underdeveloped but not so this time, as Christopher has given us a hero who we can identify with ...

Part 2: Sentence completion Page 125

2

1 basement 2 Fine Arts Sculpture 3 take measurements
4 newsreader 5 metal 6 sitting/seated 7 five months
8 oil paint

3

2 a, d, e 3 a, b 4 e, g 5 b 6 h 7, 8 The answer to 7 has
been omitted (c). The answer to 8 has been recorded as
the answer to 7 (f).

Part 3: Multiple choice Page 126

3

0 C Sandra: *I reckoned I'd probably be the first to have
to leave.*

4

Suggested answers

A *We are only told by Sandra that the company 'weren't
making enough money'; she does not comment on her
salary.*
B *Sandra says 'they were a young, dynamic group' but she
does not say she was too old.*
D *She says 'I'd never felt so comfortable working in a
team as I did with that group of people'; she does **not**
say 'I never felt comfortable working in a team'.*

5

1 B 2 D 3 B 4 A 5 B 6 C

Listening script 2.5

(I = Interviewer; S = Sandra; D = David)

I: On this week's *In Partnership* programme we talk to
Sandra Peyton and David Sadler, who together run the
successful media company Advert Eyes, specializing in
the making of TV commercials. Sandra, if I could start
with you. What were you doing before you set up in
partnership with David and what made you change?

S: Well, I was directing – er, drama mostly – for a small
satellite TV company. It was an interesting, experimental
time for me – they were a young, dynamic group and
seemed to be going places. But these were troubled times
for the business in general and they just weren't making
enough money. Anyway, things weren't looking too good
for me; as I'd been the last to arrive, I reckoned I'd
probably be the first to have to leave.

I: So you jumped before you were pushed, so to speak.

S: That's right, and that was a great shame, because I'd
never felt so comfortable working in a team as I did with
that group of people.

I: David, you had a similar background, didn't you?

D: Yes, I'd also made a name for myself directing TV
drama, but with the much larger Trenton TV. I left
them because they were moving in a different direction
to where I wanted to go. But the experience proved
invaluable for the future – I can see that now.

I: In what way?

D: Working in close collaboration with others is an
integral part of this business – that's always been clear
to me – but I came to realize that you can't rely on other
people to make things work. It's a tough old world and
ultimately it's down to you – it's a question of attitude.
Things only happen if you let them – and if you only see
grey skies and gloomy days ahead, that's what you'll get.

I: So the whole thing focused you for your future with
Advert Eyes.

D: That's right, I did a lot of growing up with Trenton.

I: Well, tell us how you met each other, Sandra.

S: We were introduced at a party by a mutual friend. I
remember I was very wary of David at first. He already
had quite a reputation in the business – his past work
spoke for itself. And he looked so serious, so apparently
indifferent to everything. He mentioned some vague idea
he had for setting up a business, something to do with
advertising – but that wasn't what struck me most. I
just couldn't get over how animated, how passionate he
became when he talked about – well, everything really. It
was difficult not to be carried along by his words.

I: So when he asked you to join him, you had no
hesitation in accepting?

D: Well, it was actually Sandra who asked me. And I
was the one who had no hesitation. My colleagues at
Trenton had warned me against going into business with
a complete unknown – they said it was too much of a
gamble. But when I met Sandra, it was like looking into
a mirror. Here at last was someone on my wavelength,
someone who looked at life through the same camera
lens. And anyway, I felt it was time to do something
different, to live a little dangerously.

I: And has it been? Dangerous, I mean.

D: Anything but. Funnily enough, though, it's turned
out that we do have quite a lot of differences, but these
have all been to our advantage. Sandra, for example, has
much more of a business brain than I do.

I: Is that right, Sandra?

S: Well, yes, it seems to be a hidden talent of mine.
But I've had to learn the hard way. Raising money, for
example, was an absolute nightmare – we just couldn't
seem to get the finance.

I: That must have been quite disheartening.

S: Well, no, you can't afford to let things like that get
you down. It was no good getting upset about it;
throwing a tantrum in a bank manager's office is never
a good idea – you might need to go back there one day.
No, I just couldn't work out what the problem was, given
our experience and the way the advertising market was
shaping up at the time. We were just a small concern,
asking for a small amount of money.

I: But you obviously got the money.

S: Yes, I met an investor who understood what we were
about – and then, once we'd made a couple of ads,
money was easier to come by.

I: David, how does, er advertising work compare with TV drama? Is it very different.

D: Well, for a start there's more money around than for normal TV work, and that can be very liberating. But the market's understanding of quality may not be the same as yours and you find your creativity stifled.

Yes, it's our own company, and it may seem a creative business to an outsider. But an advert is not your own baby in the same way that a TV drama might be. There are too many people who have a say in what you do and what goes into the advert.

S: Yes, I'd go along with that, although for me, running a business can be incredibly creative.

I: So what does the future hold for Advert Eyes. What are your plans for the company?

S: Well, we can't really say too much at the moment. It's not that we're not willing to, it's just that we're not entirely certain how things will work out ourselves.

D: That's right. The normal thing might be to look at some type of long-term growth for the business, but at the moment we're concentrating on consolidating our position, rather than branching out. Who knows what the future will bring?

I: Sandra, David, the very best of luck for the future. There we must leave it. Thank you.

S and D: Thank you.

6

1

A *This idea comes up but is denied in 'but I came to realize that you can't rely on other people to make things work'.*

C *This is a misinterpretation of 'It's a tough old world'. This is not the point being made.*

D *The opposite is true – 'Working in close collaboration with others ...'.*

2

A *David's 'reputation in the business' was undoubted, but it was not that which impressed her.*

B *Definitely not – he looked serious and indifferent.*

C *No, these were vague and didn't strike her.*

3

A *His colleagues warned him that it would be a risk, but there's no reference to him enjoying risks.*

C *We don't know this; we are only told she was a complete unknown.*

D *Again we don't know this; we are only told she has a good business brain.*

4

B *The idea of being depressed is there, but what Sandra is saying is that there's no point in getting depressed.*

C *She then goes on to make the same point about being angry.*

D *Sandra says 'We were just a small concern ...'. Concern here is nothing to do with worrying; it's a noun meaning 'enterprise' or 'business'.*

5

A *This is a likely idea given the context, but is not present in the text.*

C *The opposite is true. He finds the large amounts of money available a positive point.*

D *The point made about the clients is that they get too involved and stifle his creativity, not that they have unrealistic expectations.*

6

A *This idea is suggested but then contradicted by 'It's not that we're not willing to ...'.*

B & D *For both of these, the opposite is true – 'the normal thing might be to look at some type of long-term growth for the business, but at the moment we're concentrating on consolidating our position, rather than branching out.'*

Part 4: Multiple matching Page 127

2

1 C 2 D 3 A 4 G 5 F 6 E 7 H 8 B 9 D 10 G

3

Listening script 2.6–2.10

Speaker 1

I could barely string two sentences together when I first arrived, and now I'm reasonably fluent. In that sense, then, I've achieved what I set out to do – just by being here and mixing with the locals. I've met some great people since I got here, especially the family I'm living with. But there's a big downside to all this. I decided to come here on my year out because it's so different to all the other places I could have gone to. Plus it seemed so exciting when I came here two years ago. However, that was on holiday and I realize now that living here is actually rather dull. I really wish I'd gone somewhere on the mainland now – my girlfriend's having a great time there.

Speaker 2

My father studied here as a young man, so I knew quite a lot about the country before I came. And when the head of my company's overseas operations told me our branch here wasn't doing too well, and would I please go and sort things out, I was very happy to accept. My husband came out shortly after I did and like me, immediately fell in love with the place. The pace of life suits us to a tee and the food is just out of this world. Ultimately, though, we're home birds and when this posting's over we'll want to go back to be nearer our grandchildren – if we ever have any, that is!

Speaker 3

I was working in the dullest job you can imagine – nine to five every day on the computer, answering customers' email queries. But it was thanks to that job that I got to know Patti, who was over on a work exchange programme in another department. She only stayed for three months, though, so after that nearly all our contact was by email. Of course, you can't keep something going like that indefinitely, so I took the plunge and moved out here. Life is fine – despite the overcast skies and regular downpours! I have to admit, though, it does get me down sometimes. I'd like to get back home more often, but it's just too far.

Speaker 4

I only wish I'd made the break earlier. It's so vibrant in this part of the world – there's so much more going on. I think if I was still back home, I'd be so depressed, what with the current climate there and so on. The fact is I was in a bit of a rut. I was sick of the same old thing, day in, day out and I thought, 'There's got to be more to life than this'. So I looked into the price of property in different parts of southern Europe, and this area was one of the cheapest. It didn't take me long to settle in – the language isn't much of a problem and I've even got myself a little part-time job. Keeps me out of trouble!

Speaker 5

A few years ago I set up in business with a friend of mine. Then I decided to go it alone and bought out my partner's share. Unfortunately, before long, things started to go wrong and I was up to my eyes in debt. Call it cowardice, but I just couldn't deal with it and I moved out here. It got me out of a mess, but I can't say I'm having the time of my life. I know a lot of different people here, but I just don't seem to fit in with them. We share the same language – more or less – but we're worlds apart in most other respects. One thing's for sure – if ever I do go back to face the music, it'll be for good.

4

7 Speaker 2: *we'll want to be nearer our grandchildren*
8 Speaker 3: *I'd like to get back home more often*
9 Speaker 4: *I'd be so depressed, what with the current climate there*
10 Speaker 5: *If ever I do go back to face the music, it'll be for good*

Unit 10 House and home

Vocabulary 1: Describing rooms and houses Page 128

1

1 c cheerful **2** e airy **3** a tidy **4** b dingy **5** d cosy
6 f cluttered

2

a lit **b** furnished **c** decorated **d** built **e** situated

Use of English: 1: Open Cloze Page 129

2

Housework is strenuous, boring, repetitive and never-ending. It is also unpaid and women, who still do most of it, often go out to work, which means they

cannot do it as thoroughly as they might like.

3

1 to (The verb 'suggest' would need to be in the third person singular form for a relative pronoun to be possible.)
2 are
3 is
4 without
5 how
6 for
7 no
8 out
9 from
10 some (Only a determiner is possible here as there is no definite or indefinite article.)
11 lot
12 too
13 may/might/could/can
14 we
15 under

Reading: Multiple choice Page 130

3

1 C **2** A **3** C **4** D **5** C **6** B **7** D

Vocabulary 2: Metaphorical meanings Page 132

2

Land that *rolls out* or is *rolling* (adj) has gentle slopes, continuing for some distance. There is of course no real movement, as in the literal sense.

A view or landscape that *sweeps* over an area, stretches over or covers that area in a long, wide curve. The movement of a broom as it *sweeps* the floor can also be in a long wide curve.

If you *choke*, you are unable to breathe because your throat is blocked. If a ditch, pond, river etc is *choked with weeds*, water cannot flow easily because the weeds are blocking it.

Literally, *fringed* means 'containing fringes', threads that hang from a piece of cloth or clothing to decorate it. Hills, lakes or coastlines that are *fringed with trees* have a strip of trees running around them or along their edge.

A *sea of mud* is a large area of mud.

The *heart of the countryside* is the central part of it, furthest away from large towns.

3

A Verbs

1 thunders **2** towers **3** sits **4** hugs **5** nestles **6** stretches

B Nouns
1 tide 2 roar 3 stream 4 nightmare 5 eyesore
6 patchwork

Language focus: Participle clauses
Page 133

1

So this man, (who was) living on a labourer's wage, clearly believed he was just locked out of the lifestyle.

2

a Having become rather frail and vulnerable in recent years, he and his wife were heavily reliant on the good nature of one neighbour … (line 32)

b Fleeing from Estonia in 1946, he came to Britain … (line 53)

c Shocked beyond belief by what they saw when they visited the house, these people began to put pressure on the council … (line 74)

d 'That's the good thing about the country,' he says, looking out over the familiar prospect. (line 88)

3

As the Grammar reference explains, the subject of a participle clause is usually the same as the subject of the main clause in a sentence. Sentence 2 (a) shows that a participle clause can be given its own subject to avoid ambiguity.

1 Sentence (a) suggests that the police were driving home from the pub when they stopped him.
Sentence (b) means that the police stopped him as he was driving home from the pub.
Sentence (b) is more likely.
2 Sentence (a) means that Elisa took over all the manager's responsibilities because the manager was ill.
Sentence (b) suggests that because she was ill, Elisa took over all the manager's responsibilities.
Sentence (a) is more likely.

Practice
Possible answers

1

1 *After* he won the silver medal in the 100 metres, he went on to take gold in the 200 metres and long jump.
2 Don't look now, but the woman *who* is sitting next to you is wearing shoes *which* are made of crocodile skin.
3 *If* it is drunk in moderation, red wine is thought to protect against coronary disease.
4 Mr Brown, *who* was wrapped in a blanket and looked tired after his ordeal, was full of praise for the rescue services.
5 *When* he reached for the sugar, he knocked over his glass *and* spilt wine over her new dress.
6 *Because* he had never been abroad before, Brian was feeling a little on edge.

2–3

1 Living within walking distance of the centre, I rarely use the car. *City*
2 Cycling in to work the other day, I saw a deer. *Rural area*
3 Having never had so much peace and quiet before, we found living here a little strange at first. *Rural area*
4 Situated at the back of the building, our bedroom has some superb views over the rooftops towards the docks. *City*
5 Played at full volume, it really annoys the neighbours. *Either*
6 Being a little off the beaten track, our house is not that easy to find. *Rural area*
7 The children having all left home, we decided to move away from the hustle and bustle. *Rural area*
8 Although not known for its tourist attractions, our neighbourhood does have one or two treasures waiting to be discovered. *City*

Use of English 1: Multiple-choice cloze Page 134

Don't forget!
What has caused the decline in communication between neighbours in Britain?
longer hours spent working at the office, together with the Internet and satellite television
What has been one of the effects of this decline?
a rise in burglaries and vandalism

2

1 B 2 A 3 D 4 A 5 C 6 B 7 C 8 D 9 C 10 A 11 B 12 B

Listening: Multiple matching Page 135

1 F 2 H 3 A 4 B 5 D 6 F 7 G 8 H 9 A 10 D

Vocabulary 3: Noise and sound Page 135

1

a loud unpleasant noise that lasts for a long time

2

1 *hushed*: very quiet; the other two describe a loud voice.
2 *unmistakable*: very easy to recognize; the others describe a sound which is/appears quiet.
3 *excessive*: too loud; the others describe noise which continues for a long time.

3

1 *goes off* (a gun, bomb or alarm *goes off*)
2 *rustle open* (leaves or paper *rustle*)
3 *hoot* (car horns *hoot*)
4 *engine* (*rowdy* describes people and their behaviour)
5 *groan* (*piercing* describes high-pitched sounds)
6 *ear* (ears can be *deafened* but not *deafening*: *deafening silence* is used when it is very noticeable that nothing was said or done)

4

1 hushed voice **2** distant sound/constant noise
3 noise dies down **4** rowdy fans **5** deafening silence
6 door slammed shut

6

Possible answer

Detectives enter a building where a gang of counterfeiters are making money. The criminals argue amongst themselves, one shoots another, the detectives rush in, fight, and leader of gang warns detectives to get back.

Writing: Information sheets Page 136

1

Yes. The three headings cover the three content points, but, cleverly, different words are used.

2

The student's ability to use a wide range of vocabulary and structures is demonstrated in all but the section entitled 'Where do I look?'.

Examples of complex language in the other sections include:
no easy task
hard to come by
to help you on your way
outside their price range
a matter of personal choice
the vast majority of students
within easy walking distance of the school
*Flats here **may** be slightly more expensive, **but** you save on ....*
be sure to ask for a receipt
things might not work out as planned
the flat may not live up to your expectations

3

The answer contains many examples of more informal language, including contractions, informal punctuation (dashes and exclamation marks), phrasal verbs and direct address (the use of *you* and *your*). This is entirely appropriate for the task, helping to create the impression of a friendly school which welcomes its new teachers.

4

As one would expect from a piece of more informal writing, linking expressions are short, individual words (or dashes). Note the absence of linking words in the section entitled <u>Where do I look?</u> (see 4 above)
<u>What's available?</u>
as, and, also, further, dash, *though, but*
<u>What happens next?</u>
Before, this, also, since, and, Finally, dash

Examiner's comment
Content: The writing addresses the main points successfully.
Organization and cohesion: Clearly organized and paragraphed, with attention paid to use of cohesive devices.
Accuracy: The writing is quite accurate, with a few slips such as the use of '*for*' as infinitive of purpose, '*free from charge*', '*and so (on)*'.
Range: The range of vocabulary is quite impressive ('*break down some cultural barriers*', '*suit everyone's tastes*') and there are some fairly complex, well constructed sentences, showing a range of grammar.
Register: The register is appropriate for the context and the student audience: the use of direct address ('*you will find*', '*This will give you the opportunity*') ensures a more friendly, personal tone.
Target Reader: Would be informed about the events of Welcome Week and what to do in order to meet people throughout the year.
Mark: Band 4

Review 10 Pages 138 and 139

Vocabulary

1 c 2 f 3 b 4 g 5 d 6 a 7 h 8 e

Participle clauses

Looking through a newspaper one day, he saw a cottage for sale in a picturesque rural area. Situated in a small village near the church, it had a conservatory and a large garden containing fruit trees; it seemed perfect. Not known for his decisiveness, Charlie surprised everyone by putting down a deposit on it the very next day. Having seen it once, he immediately made up his mind to buy it.

Having moved into the cottage, he soon realized it was not the peaceful rural idyll he had expected. Chiming every hour on the hour, the church bells kept him awake at night. Also, the village being in an area of outstanding beauty, coachloads of tourists arrived every weekend disturbing the peace and quiet. Worst of all, objecting to the presence of outsiders in the village, the locals were very unfriendly towards him. Having lived there for six months, Charlie decided to move back to the city.

Use of English: Word formation

1 disagreeable 2 privacy 3 satisfying 4 ensure 5 freely
6 safety 7 curiosity 8 procedure(s) 9 setting(s)
10 ineffective

Unit 11 A cultural education

Listening 1: Multiple choice Page 140

1 B 2 C 3 C 4 A 5 A 6 B

Vocabulary 1: Sight Page 141

1

a look b view c sight d look e view

2

1 sight 2 eye 3 view 4 look 5 vision

Reading: Gapped text Page 142

2

1 E 2 G 3 A 4 F 5 C 6 B D not used

Language focus: Inversion Page 144

1

The order of subject and auxiliary verb is reversed. Where there is no auxiliary verb, as in a and d, *do, does* or *did* is inserted before the subject.
The writer is adding emphasis to these words by placing them at the beginning of the sentence.

2

b We have no sooner settled …/As soon as we have settled …

c You should on no account kiss …/You should not kiss your children on any account …

d I do not whistle along to the music at weddings either.

Practice

1

1 do we go to the cinema these days
2 have I seen such a terrible performance of Hamlet
3 must bags be left unattended
4 the very last page is the identity of the murderer revealed
5 someone complained at reception did they realize the painting had been hung upside down

2

1 Never again would he play in front of a live audience.
2 Hardly had she sat down to watch her favourite programme when the phone rang.
3 Under no circumstances will you be allowed to enter the auditorium once the play has started.
4 Not only did we go to the National Gallery, but we also saw a West End musical.
5 Not since Amy went to the circus as a child had she enjoyed herself so much.

Word formation: Nouns formed with *in, out, up, down, back* Page 144

1

a drawbacks b background c outburst

2

1 downpour 2 upturn 3 income(s) 4 outbreak 5 insight
6 outcome 7 setback/upset 8 output 9 upbringing
10 breakdown

Listening 2: Sentence completion Page 145

1

1 university libraries 2 concentration 3 bad luck
4 arrogant 5 language 6 family life 7 envy 8 debt

Vocabulary 2: Read and write Page 146

1

A 'prolific writer' is one who writes a lot.
To 'read profusely' is to read a lot.

2

1 aloud 2 avid 3 good 4 widely 5 well 6 rough, neatly
7 plain

Writing: Proposals Page 148

3
- the overall length of the answer
  The answer contains nearly 400 words and is far too long. In the exam, over-length answers are penalized if they include irrelevance and/or have a negative effect on the reader.
- the writer's selection and use of the input material
  The writer has included all the input information rather than selecting what is relevant. As a result, the answer exceeds the word limit. It is not necessary to use all the input information for this task. In addition, he/she has lifted large sections of the input material instead of reworking it into original language. The writer has made only minimal attempts to expand on the input material and add his/her own ideas:
  eg *a good friend of mine* and *Why don't we include a review too?*
- the appropriacy and consistency of the register
  Given the target reader – the secretary of the Arts club – any register would be appropriate as long as it is consistent. In this answer, the writer switches freely between formal and informal language: compare *an excess of art is not desirable.*
  with
  some stuff about local events and loads of different people
- the quality and range of the language
  Rather simplistic throughout.
- the organization of ideas and use of linking devices
  The proposal is organized into logical paragraphs with relevant headings. However, the answer is often rambling, and there is unnecessary repetition of the free tickets as prizes. The bracketed comments *(see below)* and *(I shall say more about that later)* are unnecessary. Linking is in evidence but limited to *and, so, but, also, too, because,* most of which are used more than once.

4
I suggest (that) you/we (should) include *or* I suggest including
I recommend you to inform *or* I recommend informing

Review 11 Pages 150 and 151

Use of English: Word formation
1 eventful 2 childhood 3 freshness 4 literary
5 considerable 6 inspiration 7 socially 8 minorities
9 output 10 unequalled

Vocabulary
1 read 2 taking 3 write 4 Look 5 suffered 6 catch
7 came 8 kept 9 turned/came 10 broke

Use of English: Open cloze
1 behind 2 of 3 be 4 both 5 that 6 like 7 which
8 much 9 would 10 until 11 by 12 is 13 what
14 instead 15 while/although/though/whilst

Unit 12 The world about us

Listening 1: Sentence completion
Page 152

2
1 (white) salt 2 store/keep (rain) water 3 fifty/50
4 (long) tail 5 (their) feathers 6 large ears 7 skin
8 donkey

3
The camel's hump is used for storing food reserves in the form of fat. Part of this can be converted into liquid if necessary.

Vocabulary 1: Verbs with more than one use Page 153

1
it – the road runner's tail
their – feathers of desert birds
This – the skin which connects the camel's two toes

2
stay cool
make external heat stay out
prevents them from sinking into it

3
1 know
2 welcome
3 pay
4 meet
5 wish

4
Possible answers
1
a inform/tell her
b become familiar with
c be familiar with the names of/be able to name
2
a be happy to receive/grateful for your ideas/ recommendations
b very pleased to greet/have with us
c something you are happy to see
3
a it is not to your advantage if you
b say something nice to me
c take much notice of
4
a be waiting for you on the station platform
b be at all successful
c do what is necessary to deal with the problem
5
a intend to be impolite
b hope she does well
c given the possibility to make something happen (by magic)

Use of English 1: Multiple-choice cloze Page 154

2

Andy Johnson set up the farm to commercialize crocodile meat. His idea was to sell the meat more cheaply than illegal meat and so protect crocodiles from poaching. Dr Clifford Warwick says that crocodiles are stressed in a captive environment.

3

1 A **2** A **3** D **4** C **5** B **6** C **7** A **8** D **9** B **10** C **11** A **12** B

5 The answer to the example is C.

Self help
Some 300,000 Australian saltwater crocodiles
has roughly tripled
a million or more animals
upwards of 90,000

Reading: Multiple choice Page 155

2

1 B **2** A **3** C **4** D **5** A **6** B **7** B

Language focus 1: Conjunctions and linking adverbials Page 157

1

A a otherwise **b** so that **c** in case
B a even though **b** whereas **c** However

2

A a On the contrary **b** By contrast **c** Despite this
B a In the meantime **b** By that time **c** From that time on
C a As **b** On, of **c** For
D a In, to **b** As, as **c** from

3

Possible answers
1   **a** we came home early.
    b the rainwater leaked in through a hole in the tent.
2   **a** he would receive at least one present on his birthday.
    b he gave her absolutely nothing.
3   **a** he'd had time to write emails to eight of his friends.
    b she'd had to stay at work until 9.30 so as to get everything finished.
4   **a** you particularly enjoy sharing a beach with 3,000 other bathers.
    b it's certainly worth spending a day there.

Listening 2: Multiple matching Page 158

1
Possible answers
Child labour: In many developing countries, children are forced to work in poorly paid jobs, sometimes in subhuman conditions. This is usually as a result of poverty, and in some cases because they have been orphaned by Aids. Some work in sweat shops, producing goods for Western markets. This leads to children missing out on an education and the perpetuation of poverty in the country.

The World Day against Child Labour is celebrated every year on June 12th.

Global warming: The build-up of carbon dioxide in the atmosphere, caused for example by high energy consumption, leads to a rise in the earth's temperature. This in turn can lead to a melting of glaciers and the polar ice caps, and a consequent rise in sea levels, flooding and destruction to coastal areas.

Whale hunting: This is still authorized by a small number of countries, despite an international moratorium and protests from environmentalists. It is justified either on scientific grounds or for commercial purposes and to prevent the whale population from growing too large and consuming huge stocks of fish.

Human rights: On December 10, 1948 the United Nations proclaimed the Universal Declaration of Human Rights. It included the following:
- All human beings are born free and equal in dignity and rights.
- No one shall be held in slavery or servitude.
- No one shall be subjected to torture or degrading treatment.

Violations of human rights occur throughout the World.

Women's rights: According to the Universal Declaration of Human Rights, women are entitled to the enjoyment of all human rights and to be treated equally to men in both economic and social life.

GM foods: Genetically modified foods, or GM foods, are grown from crops which have been altered through biotechnology to make them more resistant to insects and disease. The most common GM crops are soybeans, corn, cotton and sugar beet and are mainly used in processed foods or in animal feed.

Supporters of genetic modification say that it makes crops more productive and can also increase their nutritional value. Opponents point to the dangers of cross-pollination, whereby GM crops can spread their genes to other plants growing nearby. While producers say there are no health concerns associated with GM foods, opponents maintain that insufficient tests have been carried out and the long-term effects on health are unknown.

Since April 2004 strict regulations have been in force in the European Union concerning the labelling of foods which contain genetically modified produce.

2

1 B 2 E 3 G 4 H 5 A 6 H 7 A 8 B 9 F 10 C

Language focus 2: Modal verbs 3
Page 159

1

A Speaker 5 (women's rights)
B Speaker 2 (voluntary work abroad)

2

A

past obligation: we were obliged to
speculation about the past: there were probably
past regret: it would have been better if we'd done

B

I worried but it wasn't necessary
It wasn't necessary to have any special skills and I didn't have any.

3

had to and *didn't need to* are not modal verbs.
Modal verbs go with a main verb (*I can go*; can = modal, go = main)
Modal verbs express the mood or attitude of the speaker and are followed by the infinitive without *to* (with the exception of *ought to*). In addition, an auxiliary verb is not used to form the negative of a modal verb (*I must not, I shouldn't* etc.)
'We should have done it years before' could also be written as *'We ought to have done it years before'*.

4

a must – internal obligation: I think it is necessary to go
should – expectation: my son is expected to be home
have to – external obligation: I am required to take him

b shouldn't – recommendation: it is not good/advisable to tell lies
don't have to – no obligation: it is not necessary to tell him the whole truth
mustn't – prohibition: I don't want you to let him know

5

The modal form of *need* is not used in positive sentences, so the non-modal form is required in both cases.
You need to do it now – we're in a hurry.
You need to be tall to be a good basketball player.

Practice

1

1 needn't/shouldn't 2 must/should 3 have/need 4 should
5 needn't/don't need to/don't have to 6 ought to/must/

should 7 needed to study/ought to have studied 8 should

Vocabulary 2: Attitude adverbials
Page 159

1 rightly 2 Strangely 3 Disappointingly 4 predictably
5 understandably

Use of English: 2: Key word transformations Page 160

1 have paid/given careful attention to
2 it to the meeting apart
3 case you happen to come
4 in the meantime try/I advise you/I recommend you/ you ought
5 on account of the fact (that)
6 (an obligation) to add my name/signature
7 have been tough/difficult/hard to turn down
8 have taken part in

Writing: Articles Page 161

3

a Yes

b Yes. There are four paragraphs of similar length, each performing a separate function:
Paragraph 1: Example situation
Paragraph 2: Explanation of problem and further examples
Paragraph 3: Current trends and main causes of problem
Paragraph 4: Suggested action
The article has also been given a relevant heading.

c Yes. A range of linking devices has been used, including several attitude adverbials.
Attitude Adverbials: *Sadly, Worryingly, Ideally, Unfortunately*

d Yes. There are numerous examples, including:
a torrential downpour, a more sheltered sleeping spot, they struggle to make ends meet.
Several phrasal verbs are used.

e Yes. There is a slight mix of registers, but this is entirely appropriate, given the aim of the first paragraph, to engage the reader and provide an illustration of life on the streets. Paragraphs 2 to 4 are a little more formal and appropriate to the aim of explanation and giving an opinion on a serious issue.

f The first paragraph involves readers and engages their interest by asking them to imagine themselves in the situation of a street child. Note the direct address and repeated use of *you*. The finally paragraph includes rhetorical questions, the second of which gives the reader food for thought.

Review 12 Pages 162 and 163
Use of English: Open cloze

1 at 2 a 3 be 4 or 5 this/that 6 In 7 towards/*toward

8 with 9 to 10 while/whilst/when 11 and 12 nearly
13 over 14 for 15 not
* more common in American English

Modal verbs
1 could 2 would 3 might 4 needn't 5 shouldn't 6 shall
7 won't 8 must

Collocation revision: Units 1–12
1 challenge 2 changes 3 smell 4 time 5 relationship
6 sleep 7 ankle/wrist 8 decision 9 views 10 voice
11 sight 12 meet

Ready for Speaking

Introduction Page 164

1 ideas 2 silences 3 vocabulary 4 attention 5 repetition
6 pictures 7 element 8 discussion 9 opportunity
10 opinion

Part 1: Social interaction Page 164

2
Comments
Ana's contributions are of reasonable length, though
they could certainly be developed more. She is clearly
hindered by the level of her language: she uses a limited
range of vocabulary and her responses are rather
inaccurate.

Janusz is clearly a stronger student. He develops his
responses well, uses a much wider range of language, and
in this part of the test at least, there are no inaccuracies.

Part 2: Long turn Page 165

Task One

2
Comments
a   No attempt is made to compare the pictures. The
    contribution is limited to a description of the two
    pictures with a single, short comment on why they
    might be checking the time. This candidate will
    probably find it difficult to continue talking for one
    minute, as he/she is likely to run out of things to say.
    Linking of ideas is limited to the use of 'because'.

b   Candidates often waste time identifying the pictures
    they are going to talk about, rather than getting on with
    the task. Students should be made aware that they will
    only ever have to compare two of the three pictures.
    They should not, as this candidate seems to want to
    do, attempt to talk about all three. Candidates should
    also avoid merely repeating information given in the
    instructions ('all three pictures show women checking the
    time') or stating the obvious ('This woman is an athlete').

c   This candidate begins comparing the pictures
    immediately, rather than merely describing them.
    Ideas are linked well ('both convey', 'the athlete, on the
    other hand', and 'suggesting something unexpected has
    happened') and there is an attempt to use a range of
    grammar and vocabulary.

Task Two

2
Comments
Janusz's language is very varied, particularly when
speculating. He uses a range of modal verbs and other
structures for this purpose:
*She might have realized, she may be phoning, she could
also be phoning, she's most probably learning, she doesn't
seem to be, the little girl looks as if she's watching.*
However, he fails to address the part of the task which
asks him to say 'how much influence time might have in
their daily lives'. He seems to have forgotten this and the
fact that the questions are printed on the visuals page,
and he struggles to find more things to say.

Ana, on the other hand, completes her task satisfactorily,
though once more her language is not very varied. She
opens with *in this picture* each time and her language of
speculation is limited to the use of *I think* and *maybe/
perhaps* with present simple or present continuous, or
else *seem(s) to be*. She searches for words, repeats *or
something (like that)* and uses language incorrectly (eg
*it's probable this is the mother, put her a new washing
machine, he seems to be concentrated*).

Part 3: Collaborative task Page 166

2
Comments
Ana chooses the musician and the cabinet maker; Janusz
chooses the musician and the politician or journalist.
Note that students do not have to agree in their
conclusions.

They tentatively make their first choice after discussion of
the third photo, and move towards making their second
choice near the end of the three minutes. This is good
technique: students who decide too soon often struggle to
talk for the full three minutes. In addressing the second
part of the task 'as they go', they are making it clear to the
examiners that they are working towards a conclusion.

Interaction in this part of the test is very good. They
respond to what each other says, sometimes inviting their
partner to comment with a question: *Don't you agree?
What do you think? Really?*

Part 4: Further discussion Page 167

2

Comments

In contrast to Part 3, in this part Janusz and Ana have not understood that they can and should interact with each other. The interlocutor continually has to prompt them to respond to each other's comments, sometimes leaving a pause, which they fail to pick up on. At one point, Ana tentatively asks, *Can I say something more?*, showing that she is unaware that this is a discussion rather than a simple question and answer session. In her last turn, she does respond to a point made by Janusz (*I agree with you*) but then limits herself to repeating the same ideas that he has just expressed.

Unit 13 Food for thought

Vocabulary 1: Eating and drinking
Page 168

1

1 thirst **2** hunger **3** food **4** drink **5** appetite **6** eater
7 stomach **8** meal

Use of English: Word formation
Page 170

1 setting **2** diners **3** residential **4** revelations
5 unwelcome **6** findings **7** overrated **8** enjoyable
9 appearance **10** training

Writing 1: Informal letters Page 170

2

No. The writer has not made any attempt to reassure her friend. On the contrary, comments such as *'I'm not surprised you're a bit daunted by it all'*, *'my own bitter experience'* and *'even if it leaves you utterly exhausted'* will only serve to make him more nervous.

3

The following expressions introduce advice:
don't make the same mistake as I did and lay on
there's no point preparing
You'd be much better off filling
That's not to say you shouldn't put out
it's not worth going
I wouldn't spend hours making one if I were you
whatever you do, make sure you don't let
… is not to be recommended
Other evidence of a wide range of language includes:
you're a bit daunted by it all
pass on a few tips
my own bitter experience
lay on a huge spread

4

Showing interest in the event
It's hard to believe that Luke's about to celebrate his fifth birthday.
I'm sure Luke and his friends will have a great time
Let me know how it all goes, won't you?

Referring to her own experience
a few tips that I learnt from my own bitter experience in September
don't make the same mistake as I did
they were the first things to disappear at Lara's party
Lara's friends hardly touched hers

Sample answer

Hi Berti

Yes I can certainly give you some advises about preparing a barbecue for your football club's dinner. I've gone to lots of these parties for end of season.

The first thing to think is when you want to serve the food. Obviously is the barbecue difficult to take to the venue, and it takes time to set up all the tables etc and take all the food from your car. If you serve the food too early some people may not arrive yet. If too late and the children may get so hungry, they start getting tired and silly. So I would recommend to tell people you will serve the food at, for example, 8 o'clock.

Of course, for a barbecue, even in summer, you'll need a plan for if it rains. When I prepared it we hired a small tent. In the end we needn't have it, but better safe than sorry.

Third thing, you need to know how many people are coming and if there are vegetarians. You can get 'veggie burgers' for them. But don't go crazy with the salads – it always seems the salad that gets thrown away. It's so difficult to eat lettuce from a paper plate with a plastic fork – most people don't bother.

Anyway, that's all I can think of now, but give me a ring if you need anything. Just relax yourself and prepare it in detail – then you'll be absolutely fine and it will too!

Dietmar

Examiner's comment
Content: The writing is slightly under length although the letter adequately covers the first two points (detailing your previous experience and giving advice), more attention to the reassurance section would enhance the completion of the task. Simply to say *'relax yourself and prepare it in detail … .'* is not very reassuring.
Organization and cohesion: The organization is appropriate and logical for an informal letter. The paragraphing nicely reflects three different points the writer considers important (timing of food, a bad weather plan, preparing salad). However, a number of sentences are confusing or difficult to follow eg *'If you serve the food too early some people may not arrive yet.'*, *'In the end*

we needn't have it … .'
Accuracy: The writing is mostly accurate despite some confusing sentences. The use of language is sometimes rather vague (*'When I prepared it …' 'and it will too!'*) and the use of the word *'advises'* in the second line.
Range: The range of language used is sufficient yet unambitious (*'you'll need a plan for if it rains', 'Third thing you need to know…'*).
Register: The register is appropriate for an informal letter.
Target reader: The reader would be partially informed, if not very reassured.
Mark: Band 3

Reading: Multiple choice Page 172

2
1 C 2 B 3 C 4 B 5 A 6 D

Language focus 1: Comparisons
Page 174

A Comparisons
Where alternative answers are given, the first answer is that which appears in the text.
1a much, as **b** The, the **c** likened/compared **d** more **e** later **f** now/currently/nowadays, before

B Qualifying comparisons
a a great deal **b** far **c** just **d** slightly **e** much

C *Like* **and** *as*
a like **b** as **c** as

D *So* **and** *such*
1 a such **b** so **c** so
2 *so* is followed by adjectives and *such* is followed by an indefinite article in the examples given in the Coursebook.

E Further expressions
1 better **2** like, near **3** as **4** much **5** long **6** close

Vocabulary 2: Deception Page 175

1

Noun	Verb	Adjective	Adverb
——	mislead	misleading	misleadingly
fraud	defraud	fraudulent	fraudulently
deception	deceive	deceptive	deceptively

2
1 a misleadingly **b** misleading
2 a deceptively **b** deceiving
3 a fraud **b** fraudulently

3
1 out **2** in **3** into **4** for **5** through **6** for

4
a bogus financial adviser
the smooth-talking confidence trickster
the conman's trickery

his false promises
I feel a bit of a mug (informal)

Listening: Multiple choice Page 176

2
1 B 2 C 3 B 4 A 5 A 6 C

Language focus 2: Adverbs of degree
Page 177

1
Absolutely is used with non-gradable adjectives such as *marvellous, fascinating* or *freezing*. *Very, fairly* and *a bit* are used with gradable adjectives such as those in a, c and d. We do not normally say *very marvellous, fairly fascinating* or *a bit freezing*. Nor so we say *absolutely anxious* or *absolutely easy*.

Examples of other modifiers which can be used with gradable adjectives are:
a little, slightly, rather, quite, somewhat, relatively, moderately, reasonably, pretty, extremely, really

2
Gradable: *frightened, pleased, dirty, tired*
Non-gradable: *furious, ridiculous, huge, marvellous*

3
a fairly **b** absolutely

4
1 clever **2** worried **3** informed **4** old **5** qualified **6** intelligent

Review 13 Pages 178 and 179
Vocabulary
1 A 2 D 3 B 4 C 5 C 6 B 7 A 8 C 9 D 10 A 11 B 12 A

Comparisons
1 near as **2** much a **3** same as **4** the more **5** far the **6** such a **7** much the **8** did his

Use of English: Key word transformations
1 likes junk food just as
2 is deceptively simple in (its)
3 interest in eating/my appetite as soon as
4 far the most imaginative (recipe/one)
5 from more stress/stress more than ever (before), *or* more than ever (before) from stress/from more stress ever
6 near as bad as
7 close second to the
8 a great deal more

Unit 14 Money matters

Vocabulary 1: Money Page 180

1
1 a 3, b 4, c 1, d 2
2 a 3, b 4, c 2, d 1

Verb + adverb collocations

1
a generously b freely c hard d heavily

Listening 1: Sentence completion
Page 181

2
1 Student Loans Company 2 term 3 budget planner
4 overdraft 5 two evenings 6 (course) tutor
7 (faculty) noticeboard(s) 8 (student) travel

Writing 1: Contributions: guidebook entry
Page 182
Useful language
a saving b money c discounts d ticket e bargains f costs

Examiner's comment
Content: The content is appropriate and each point is adequately developed.
Organization and cohesion: The contribution for the brochure is well organized, and good use is made of headings. It would have been improved by the inclusion of a concluding paragraph. The sentences are often too short and would benefit from linking.
Accuracy: There are many errors, though these do not impede communication – ('*not stay only in big cities …*', '*even they can not speak any of your language!*', '*when you arrived at station*'). Punctuation and spelling are sometimes also at fault.
Range: The range of structures used is too limited for CAE level, but the vocabulary is adequate and there is some good phrasing – ('*traditional Japanese style B&B*', '*good handmade souvenirs*', '*share the taste with your friends*').
Register: The register is consistent and wholly appropriate.
Target reader: The target reader would be informed, but distracted by the errors.
Mark: Band 2

Use of English: Word formation
Page 183

2
1 conclusively 2 assumption 3 surprisingly 4 responses
5 inheritance 6 outlook 7 dissatisfied 8 considerably
9 pleasure 10 contentment/contentedness

Reading: Multiple matching Page 184

2
1 C Knowing how to sew helps
2 A I wait until things are falling apart before I buy
   something new
3 B I grew up this way; when I was little, frugality was
   a way of life
4 B a costume to wear when I'm on stage
5 D a pile of my clothes got chucked out because my
   flatmate thought they were rubbish
6 A I would often go on huge shopping sprees
7 C I've seen people driven to debt by their need for the
   latest Fendi bag
8 D there is too much importance placed on clothes and
   appearance ... attracts attention.
9 B I try not to buy anything ... code of practice.
10 C I've been to parties where ... confused them.
11 C I'm aware that most people are not like me.
12 D I don't feel strongly enough to object politically
13 A I simply don't feel the pull of boutiques any more
14 B I'm a voracious clothes shopper
15 A The fact that I was living ... I was doing

Vocabulary 2: Quantifying nouns
Page 186

1
Clothes is used after all of them.
tons of clothes (line 13)
heaps of clothes (line 24)
bags of clothes (line 35)
a pile of my clothes (line 94)

2
a salt b water c flames d homework e champagne
f youths g furniture h biscuits

3
1 children 2 news 3 words 4 bees 5 progress
6 furniture 7 holiday 8 milk 9 wool 10 sadness

Listening 2: Multiple choice Page 187

1
1 B 2 A 3 D 4 B 5 C 6 D

Language focus: Noun phrases Page 188

1
noun + noun: production methods, the January sales,
shopping malls
noun 's/s'+ noun: next week's Buy Nothing Day, workers'
rights, people's reactions
noun + preposition + noun:
a wealth of choice, a threat to business, the ethics of
shopping, at the expense of the environment

2
1 **b** wine glasses
2 **a** chicken soup
3 **b** the roof of our house
4 **b** a Sunday newspaper
5 **b** a three-day course
6 **a** that shop window/the window of that shop
7 **b** top of the page
8 **a** the dismissal of a member of staff from the catering
   department
9 **b** a man of average height
10 **b** new children's clothes

3
1 'Noun of noun' (*glasses of wine*) is used to refer to the
   drink.
   'Noun + noun' (*wine glasses*) is used to refer to the
   container.

2 The 's genitive (*lamb's wool*) is used for products from
   living animals.
   'Noun + noun' (*chicken soup*) is used for products
   from dead animals.

3 *door handle* is an accepted compound noun: *house
   roof* is not, so an *of* structure is required. The 's
   genitive (*house's roof*) is not likely since house is an
   inanimate object.

4 The 's genitive (*last Sunday's newspaper*) with a time
   expression is used to refer to specific moments or events.
   'Noun + noun' (*a Sunday newspaper*) is used to refer
   to things that occur or appear regularly.

5 The 's genitive is used with time expressions to refer
   to duration (*four weeks' holiday*).
   When the head noun (*course*) is countable, the
   modifying noun (*three-day*) is normally in the singular
   and hyphenated. Since the modifying noun functions
   as an adjective, no plural s is added.

6 *Shop window* is a recognized compound noun and
   normally found in that form. Note the position of the
   demonstrative in the *of* structure.
   Whilst the *source of his inspiration* is also correct,
   source of inspiration is a collocation and generally
   found in that form.

7 Nouns such as *top, bottom, middle, side, edge, back,
   front, beginning* and *end*, which refer to a part of

something, are normally used in an *of* structure. Mountain top, roadside, seaside are exceptions.

8   When the head noun (*dismissal*) is modified by a long and/or complex phrase (*a member of staff from the catering department*) the *of* structure is preferred. Note that the 's genitive can be used for an action done by or to a person.
eg *Mr Smith's resignation, the President's murder*

9   'Noun + noun' (*brick construction*) can be used when talking about what something is made of. In other cases, when describing the characteristics of a person or thing, the 'Noun of noun' structure is used.

10 **a** (*children's new clothes*) is a 'specifying genitive' here: it refers to specific clothes worn by specific children. In this case the adjective describing the clothes can be placed between the two nouns.
b (*new children's clothes*) is a 'classifying genitive' here: it refers to clothes worn by children in general. In this case the two nouns cannot be separated.

4
2 e   3 a   4 c   5 g   6 b   7 h   8 f

Self help
Noun + noun: go on huge shopping sprees (A), charity shops (A and B), a voracious clothes shopper (B), swap parties (B), a fabric flower (C), the latest Fendi bag (C)
Noun of noun: (this list does not include those quantifying nouns which have been focused on in the Vocabulary section) a way of life (B), an ethically sound code of practice (B), the issue of excessive consumption (C), the centre of attention (D), the act of shopping (D), a waste of time and energy (D)
Other *of* structures: the pull of boutiques (A), the middle of the floor (B)

Writing 2: Set books Page 189

3   b
4
Relevance: The writer explains how the structure of the novel and the diversity of characters both teach and entertain the reader.
Overall structure: The writer has structured the answer well, with an introduction, clear development and an appropriate conclusion.
Sophisticated language: The answer contains many instances of advanced level vocabulary including *gain an insight into, makes for a fast-moving pace, learn the tricks of the trade, maintain our interest, print the truth*
Linking devices: Cohesive devices are used appropriately throughout, both within (eg *Certainly* and *Of more interest, though*) and between paragraphs (*Similarly* and *Indeed*).
Quotations: These are used appropriately in paragraphs 1, 3 and 4.

Review 14 Pages 190 and 191
Noun phrases
1   state of shock, the announcement of his resignation/ his resignation announcement
2   car keys/keys to the car, back of the drawer
3   mug of cocoa, cow's milk, caravan site
4   seven-hour delay/delay of seven hours, airport departure lounge/departure lounge of the airport
5   youth of average build, yesterday's robbery
6   gold neck chain/gold chain around his neck, diamond nose stud/diamond stud in his nose, matter of personal taste, idea of fashion
7   two months' work, day's rest
8   series of talks, number of topics, protection of the environment

Vocabulary
1 C   2 B   3 D   4 D   5 B   6 A   7 B   8 C   9 C   10 D

Use of English: Gapped sentences Page 191
1 set   2 sense   3 hard   4 pick   5 price

Ready for Writing

Marking Page 192
2 Content   3 Organization and cohesion   4 Target reader   5 Accuracy

Planning and checking Page 193
2 d   3 g   4 h   5 e   6 f   7 a   8 b   9 i

Register Page 193

1
1 success   2 obtaining/achieving/attaining
3 expressed/showed/[*or in present tense* express/show]
4 position/post   5 employment   6 owing/due   7 unable
8 improvement   9 contact   10 meantime

2
Suggested answers

Informal letter	Formal letter
● the use of *get* in informal register	
get a grade	*obtain/achieve a grade*
try to get a job	*apply for position/post*
get better	*an improvement*
● use of phrasal verbs in informal register	
take you on	*offer you employment*
● greater use of nouns in formal register	
passing your exams	*your recent success in your examinations*
you said you'd be interested	*you expressed an interest*
the way the economy's been recently	*the current economic climate*

- use of abbreviations in informal register
  exams   *examinations*

- linking words
  But   *However*

- informal punctuation
  dashes and exclamation marks

- other differences
  Believe me   *I assure you*
  we'll be in touch   *we shall contact you*
  as soon as they do   *When this occurs*
  Dear Jilly/All the best *Dear Ms Holden/Yours sincerely*

Macmillan Education
Between Towns Road, Oxford OX4 3PP
A division of Macmillan Publishers Limited
Companies and representatives throughout the world

ISBN 978-0-2300-2886-9 (+key edition)
ISBN 978-0-2300-2887-6 (-key edition)

Text © Roy Norris with Amanda French 2008
Design and illustration © Macmillan Publishers Limited 2008

First published 2008

Original design by Andrew Jones
Page makeup by eMC Design Ltd. www.emcdesign.org.uk
Illustrated by Phillip Burrows, Richard Duszczak, Jim Eldridge, Roger Fereday,
Tim Kahane, Julian Mosedale, Gary Rees, Peters & Zabransky
Cover design by Barbara Mercer
Cover photograph © Aflo Foto Agency / Alamy

Authors' acknowledgements
Roy Norris would like to thank his wife, Azucena, and daughters, Lara and
Elisa, for all their support and understanding. Amanda French would like to
thank Liam Keane for his help and encouragement. We would also like to thank
all the teachers and students at International House, Madrid, who helped with
piloting, especially Christina Anastasiadis, José Vicente Acín Barea, Wilson
Berrueta García, Patricia Bezunartea Barrio, Ana Folguera de la Cámara,
Lynne-Felicity Highfield, Marina Díez Jiménez, Marta García Tomás, David
González Pardo, José Ramón Martínez Villalaín, Steven McGuire, Luis Olmos
Camacho, Kate Pickering, Mónica Posada Sánchez, Carmen Rey Mamolar,
Fernando Sánchez-Tembleque Cameselle and Alistair Wood. We are also very
grateful to Peter Sunderland for his invaluable comments. Thank you, too, to
everyone at Macmillan who had a hand in the project, but in particular the
editorial team of Amanda Anderson, Helen Holwill, Vivienne Richardson and
Sarah Curtis.

The publishers would like to thank all those who participated in the
development of the project, with special thanks to Agata Adamska; British
Council, Warsaw and Kraków; Paulette Dooler; George Drivas; Xenia
Exindavelloni; Soren Gauger; Robin Gill; International House, Warsaw; Edwina
Johnson; Kanakari School, Athens; Linguaphone Institute, Athens; Mr English
Club, Moscow; Małgorzata Osiejuk; Irini Papageorgiou; Pappas School,
Athens; Marcin Smolik; Vafopoulou School of English, Thessaloniki.

The authors and publishers are grateful for permission to reprint the following
copyright material: Extract from 'Creator of Barbie' by David Usborne
copyright © The Independent 2002, first published in The Independent
29.04.02, reprinted by permission of the publisher.
Extract from Stark by Ben Elton (Sphere Books Limited, 1989), copyright © Ben
Elton 1989, reprinted by permission of McIntyre Management.
Extract from 'Scents and sensitivity' by Lucy Mangan copyright © Lucy
Mangan 2004, first published in The Guardian 20.07.04, reprinted by
permission of the author.
Made up interview with Helena Drysdale using extracts from 'Mother Tongue'
reprinted by permission of the A P Watt Ltd on behalf of the author.
Extract from 'Felicia's Journey' by William Trevor copyright © William Trevor
1994, 1995, reprinted by permission of Penguin Group.
Extract from 'The new generation' by Lesley Garner first published in Saga
Magazine December 2002, reprinted by permission of the publisher.
Extract from 'Listening to Vegetables' first published in Fortean Times
September 2002, reprinted by permission of the publisher.
Adapted extract from 'Smart Shoes decide on television time' by Will Knight
copyright © New Scientist Magazine 18.5.05, reprinted by permission of the
publisher.
Adapted extract from 'Amnesiacs struggle to imagine future events' by
Roxanne Khamsi copyright © New Scientist Magazine 15.01.07, reprinted by
permission of the publisher.
Extract from 'What does David Beckham have in common with Albert
Einstein' by Steve Keenan copyright © N I Syndication, London 1999,
first published in The Times 23.11.99, reprinted by permission of the N I
Syndication Ltd.
Extract from 'My constant fight to stay awake' by Bryony Gordon, first
published in The Telegraph 01.10.02, reprinted by permission of the publisher.
Extract from 'Captain Corelli's Mandolin' by Louis de Bernières, published by
Vintage, reprinted by permission of Random House Group Limited.

Extract from 'Singular pleasures' by Mark Hodson copyright © Sunday Times/
Mark Hodson 2003, first published in The Sunday Times 23.02.03, reprinted by
permission of NI Syndication Ltd.
Extract from 'The joy of plumbing' by Natasha Walter copyright © The
Independent 1999, first published in The Independent 16.03.99, reprinted by
permission of the publisher.
Extract from 'Working Britons don't even know their neighbours' by Senay
Boztas copyright © Senay Boztas 2000, first published in The Sunday Times
05.03.00, reprinted by permission of the author.
Extract from 'Modern audiences do anything but listen' by Stephen Pollard
copyright © The Independent 2002, first published in The Independent
04.12.02, reprinted by permission of the publisher.
Extract from 'What Comes Naturally' by Giles Smith copyright © The
Telegraph/Giles Smith, first published in The Sunday Telegraph 26.10.02,
reprinted by permission of the publisher.
Extract from 'Happy as a pig … in a waterbed' by Michelle Knott, first
published in New Scientist Magazine 23.11.02, reprinted by permission of the
publisher.
Extract from 'Taste test reveal unpalatable truth' by Roger Dodson copyright ©
The Independent 2003, first published in The Independent 20.04.03, reprinted
by permission of the publisher.
Extract from 'The case of the adulterated chicken breast' by Sheila Keating
copyright © The Times/Sheila Keating 2003, first published in The Times
Magazine 28.06.03, reprinted by permission of N I Syndication Ltd.
Extract from 'The perils of pizza making' by Chandos Elletson copyright © The
Times 1999, first published in The Times 16.10.99, reprinted by permission of N
I Syndication Ltd.
Extract from 'Fool if you think it's over' by Mark Edwards copyright © The
Times 2002, first published in The Times 01.09.02, reprinted by permission of N
I Syndication Ltd.
Extract from 'The last unwired man on earth' by Martin Newell copyright ©
The Independent 1999, first published in The Independent 17.12.99, reprinted
by permission of the publisher.
Extract from ''Britain's maligned moths suffer drastic decline' by Terri Judd
copyright © The Independent 2007, first published in The Independent 20.7.07,
reprinted by permission of the publisher.
Extract from 'Designer's' gadgets for the future' by Chris Millar, first published
in The Evening Standard 21.6.02, reprinted by permission of Solo Syndication,
London.
Extract from 'Slopes at the top of the world' by Sean Newsom copyright ©
the Times 2001, first published in The Sunday Times 4.11.01, reprinted by N I
Syndication Ltd.

These materials may contain links for third party websites. We have no control
over, and are not responsible for, the contents of such third party websites.
Please use care when accessing them.

Although every effort has been made to contact copyright holders before
publication, this has not always been possible. If notified, the publisher
undertakes to rectify any errors or omissions at the earliest opportunity.

The authors and publishers would like to thank the following for permission
to reproduce their photographs:
Advertising Archive p167 (br);
Alamy: pp6 (mcb, mct), 30(br), 23(l), 60(tl, tr),100(l), 112,(m),167(tl, bl, bm),
169(b), Cre8tive Studios; 31 Powered by Light/Alan Spencer; 38 (t) Stock
Connection, (bl) Michael Dzaman; 67(r) Chris Knapton; 151 Profimedia Int.;
176(m) Jeff Morgan; 183(l) Motoring Picture Library, (r)Travelshots.com, 207(l)
Bob Purdue, (m) Stock Connection Blue;
Aquarius Collection p66 (br);
Bananastock pp12 (b), 46/7; 56, 98, 108;
Corbis pp7, 18(l), 23(mr); 52; 72(tr, br, m), 73; 88(m); 100(c, cm), 103, 112(l),
116(t,b),139, 140(r); 141, 147(tr, bl, mr); 158(tl, r),168, 202(r).;
Getty Images pp6 (t, b), 18(r), 23(ml), 42, 72(tl, c, l), 76, 88, 100(tr, cr), 103, 16(c),
125, 140(t), 147(tl), 152(m), 154(b), 155, 167(tr, tm), 169(t, m), 185, 207(r);
Image Source pp6(c), 34(m), 96(l), 100(lb), 132, 139, 152(t, b), 165, 184, 187,
207(m);
Kobal Collection p.70;
PA Photos pp12 (m); 67(l); 176(b);
Panasonic p30 (mr);
Photofusion Picture Library pp63; 66(tl);
Photolibrary Group pp18(c), 21, 23(r), 30(mr,l), 34(b), 36, 55, 56, 60(bl, br),
72(mcr); 73, 78, 85, 88(c, r), 96(t, br), 105, 112(r), 128, 130, 140(b), 141,145,
147(m, b), 153, 154(t), 156, 158(bl);
Rex Features pp12 (t), 42, 66(m), 70, 167(bm);
Science Photo Library pp66 (tr) Steve Percival; 81 Oscar Burriel; 82 Mehau
Kulyk; 85 M.H. Sharp; 88(r) Adam Gault; 167(m) BSIP/Mendil;
Still Images p169 (l);
Roger Scruton pp: 30(tr); 38 (br); 39; 176(t).

Printed in Thailand

7 DAY
BOOK